UNIVERSITY OF ST. THOMAS LIBRARIES

Jonathan Edwards
at Home and Abroad

Jonathan Edwards
at Home and Abroad

Historical Memories, Cultural Movements, Global Horizons

EDITED BY
David W. Kling AND
Douglas A. Sweeney

University of South Carolina Press

© 2003 University of South Carolina

Published in Columbia, South Carolina, by the
University of South Carolina Press

Manufactured in the United States of America

07 06 05 04 03   5 4 3 2 1

Library of Congress Cataloging-in-Publication Data

Jonathan Edwards at home and abroad : historical memories, cultural movements, global horizons / edited by David W. Kling and Douglas A. Sweeney.
   p. cm.
Includes bibliographical references and index.
  ISBN 1-57003-519-9 (cloth : alk. paper)
  1. Edwards, Jonathan, 1703–1758—Congresses. I. Kling, David William, 1950– II. Sweeney, Douglas A.
BX7260.E3 J655 2003
285.8'092—dc22
                                              2003016599

To Dr. Thomas A. Schafer, pioneer and patriarch of critical scholarship on Jonathan Edwards, with profound gratitude and affection.

Contents

Acknowledgments ⹋ ix
Introduction ⹋ xi
  David W. Kling and Douglas A. Sweeney

Part One
Remembering Edwards's Ministry

The Quest for the Historical Edwards: The Challenge of Biography ⹋ 3
  George M. Marsden

A Different Legacy? The Cultural Turn in Edwards's Later Notebooks and the Unwritten *History of the Work of Redemption* ⹋ 16
  Michael J. McClymond

Remembering Jonathan Edwards's Ministry to Children ⹋ 40
  Catherine A. Brekus

Bad Books and Bad Boys: The Transformation of Gender in Eighteenth-Century Northampton, Massachusetts ⹋ 61
  Ava Chamberlain

Part Two
Edwards and American Culture

Jonathan Edwards, the Edwardsians, and the Sacred Cause of Free Trade ⹋ 85
  Mark Valeri

The Political Economy of Depravity: The Irrelevance (and Relevance) of Jonathan Edwards ⹋ 101
  James D. German

All Things Were New and Astonishing: Edwardsian Piety, the New Divinity, and Race ⹋ 121
  Charles E. Hambrick-Stowe

Beyond the Men in Black: Jonathan Edwards and Nineteenth-Century Woman's Fiction ❧ 137
   Sharon Y. Kim

Gary Marshall's *Runaway Bride* in Light of *The Religious Affections* and *The Nature of True Virtue*: Reflections on Popular American Culture ❧ 154
   Amanda Porterfield

PART THREE
Edwards around the World

Remembered around the World: The International Scope of Edwards's Legacy ❧ 177
   David W. Bebbington

The Reception of Jonathan Edwards by Early Evangelicals in England ❧ 201
   D. Bruce Hindmarsh

Jonathan Edwards's Scottish Connection ❧ 222
   Christopher W. Mitchell

Missions and Historical Memory: Jonathan Edwards and David Brainerd ❧ 248
   Andrew F. Walls

The Expanding Knowledge of God: Jonathan Edwards's Influence on Missionary Thinking and Promotion ❧ 266
   Stuart Piggin

An Honor Too Great: Jonathan Edwards in Print Abroad ❧ 297
   M. X. Lesser

Contributors ❧ 321
Index ❧ 325

Acknowledgments

Several organizations have provided financial support for this volume and the conference at which earlier versions of its essays were presented. The most significant funding has come through *The Works of Jonathan Edwards* (Yale University Press) and from the Pew Charitable Trusts, the Lilly Foundation, and the Henry Luce Foundation. We are especially grateful to General Editor Harry S. Stout and Executive Editor Kenneth P. Minkema for their generous assistance. Additional funding has come from the Pew-funded Institute for the Advanced Study of Religion at Yale University, the College of Arts and Sciences at the University of Miami, and Trinity Evangelical Divinity School, Deerfield, Illinois.

Several individuals have contributed to the editing of this volume. We gratefully acknowledge the labors of Sang Hyun Lee, Kenneth P. Minkema, Wilson H. Kimnach, Gerald R. McDermott, and Stephen J. Stein, each of whom played an important role in responding to papers at the conference. Two anonymous reviewers have also helped to improve these essays. And our editor, Barry Blose of the University of South Carolina Press, has emended what follows with impressive expertise. Last but not least, we offer a special word of thanks to Susanne Henry of Trinity Evangelical Divinity School for herculean secretarial labors on the volume's final drafts.

Introduction

David W. Kling and Douglas A. Sweeney

In the "Farewell Sermon" delivered to his Northampton congregation following his dismissal as their pastor in 1750, Jonathan Edwards reflected on how he wished to be remembered. Tellingly, he spoke not of his reputation in subsequent years of human history—whether among his parishioners, his ministerial colleagues, or those who would study him later—but about how he wanted to be remembered at the *end* of history—on judgment day. Simply put, this sermon makes clear that Edwards cared far more about how God would remember him than about how the rest of us would. In the light of eternity, what mattered most to him was not human vindication but divine approbation. At the end of time, Edwards averred, making reference to his recent firing, "all will be examined in the searching, penetrating light of God's omniscience and glory, . . . and all error, falsehood, unrighteousness and injury shall be laid open, stripped of every disguise; every specious pretense, every cavil, and all false reasoning shall vanish in a moment, as not being able to bear the light of that day."[1] To be sure, Edwards was a proud man (his detractors thought him haughty), interested throughout his life in cultivating a respectable reputation and in defending it doggedly when threatened with failure. But ultimately he believed that eternal memory, in which truth and justice prevailed, was much more important than historical memory, so full of biases and self-serving agendas.

Ironically, 250 years after Edwards delivered his "Farewell Sermon," an impressive group of scholars met in Miami to do the very thing that Edwards judged of no ultimate purpose, namely, to assess his historical legacy around the world. At an international conference held 9–11 March 2000, we gathered to discuss, not eternity and Edwards's ultimate fate, but the much more mundane and penultimate matter of the memory of Edwards in human history.

Why bother, one might well ask, to study this un-Edwardsian theme? Have American scholars not already paid too much attention to this otherworldly man, while neglecting all kinds of subjects more important for life in the here and now? We must admit that Edwards has already received far more than his fair share of scholarly attention, at least if fairness is understood in terms of equality. As the one referred to frequently now as "America's theologian," and perhaps this country's most prominent religious thinker, articles and books about Edwards continue to roll off the presses (and now, even websites) at a remarkable pace.[2]

But while Edwards himself continues to attract a remarkable amount of scholarly interest (considerably more so in the United States than elsewhere), sustained analysis of his historical influence lags far behind. Much work remains to be done on the long-term significance of his life and ministry, the dissemination of his many writings (both published and unpublished), his roles as a clerical and intellectual exemplar, his influence outside the world of religion, the appropriation and re-appropriation of his remarkably resilient cultural authority, and the convergence of these developments into discernible intellectual and ecclesiastical movements. We know a great deal, in other words, about this otherworldly man. But we still know precious little about his roles in shaping this world. Hence our call for a conference that began to assess these matters more comprehensively.

In some respects, the absence of a sustained analysis of Edwards's legacy is to be expected. Despite the (some would say disproportionate) proliferation of research on Edwards during the past half century, much work remains to be done on the sage of Northampton and Stockbridge. Edwards continues to appeal to so many in part because his life and work are so challenging, his thought so creative and elusive, as those who have spent much time on him will attest. His corpus is large, complicated, wide-ranging, and multi-faceted, attracting the attention of a broad range of interpreters—historians, theologians, philosophers, and biblical and literary scholars. The ongoing, definitive Yale edition of his works, scheduled for completion by the tercentenary of Edwards's birth in 2003, will comprise twenty-seven volumes in all—only about half of Edwards's corpus—grist for the mills of interested scholars for years to come.

This understandable preoccupation with Edwards's own personality, however, is not the only reason for the relative neglect of his legacy. Historiographical prejudice has contributed its share. Since the 1930s, especially, neo-orthodox theologians and secular scholars who followed their lead (such as Perry Miller, the famous founder of the Yale edition of Edwards's works) contended that Edwards's doctrinal legacy was squandered almost as soon as it was passed on. Although scholars of the 1940s and '50s were responsible for the resuscitation of Edwards as a subject worthy of study, by their account

Edwards's immediate followers failed to transmit his genius in any authentic way. Succeeding generations continued to claim Edwards's mantle, but it never quite fit.[3]

Beginning in the 1980s and continuing into the '90s, a small but significant group of historians has challenged this declension model. A number of revisionist works have argued convincingly for an enduring and vibrant Edwardsian legacy in the second half of the eighteenth century and especially the first half of the nineteenth century.[4] Moreover, national Jonathan Edwards conferences, beginning in 1984 at Wheaton College, and then in New Haven (1990), Bloomington (1994), and Philadelphia (1996), gave attention (some more, some less) to reassessing Edwards's legacy.[5] In particular, many of the papers presented at the meetings in Bloomington and Philadelphia contributed to the revision of our understanding of Edwards's legacy in the United States. But none of these added significantly to our knowledge of Edwards's legacy in other places.

With a growing conviction that vital Edwardsian cultural traditions did exist, then, both "at home" and abroad, over one hundred scholars gathered in Miami for a conference devoted to Edwards's historical memory around the world. These scholars built on foundations laid well in other recent bodies of literature that point to the importance of global perspectives even—and perhaps especially—for assessing evangelical leaders like Edwards. Recent analyses of the rise of modern world missions, for example, and of American religion in comparative perspective, have nudged American cultural historians out of their isolationist and exceptionalist cocoons. Most notably, the path-breaking work *Evangelicalism: Comparative Studies of Popular Protestantism in North America, the British Isles, and Beyond, 1700–1990* (1994) has urged us to move beyond "nation-specific accounts" of religious history and to explore those transatlantic connections that have played a critical role in "sustaining evangelicalism and explaining its development."[6] Unfortunately, however, as important as Edwards was in cultivating transatlantic connections, he was virtually ignored in this volume (as he has been in most of these larger literatures as well)—and not because he failed to exert any noteworthy popular appeal. Rather, as several essays in *Evangelicalism* make clear, Edwards's devotional and "affectional" writings enjoyed a widespread international appeal, among clergy and laity alike.[7]

Indeed, Edwards's example, thoughts, and writings infiltrated many regions around the world, not least his mother country of Great Britain. His regular correspondence with British friends and participation in many aspects of British culture, not to mention his Concert of Prayer with British Christians and eschatological concern with British history, offer an important reminder that Edwards was, after all, a British subject, and a prime example of the rich and complex Anglo American republic of letters. It is somewhat surprising that while scholars such as Norman Fiering have labored diligently to uncover the British sources of Edwards's thought, little attention has been given to Edwards's influence even on British evangelicalism.[8] Despite David Bebbington's observation in *Evangelicalism in Modern Britain* (1989) that Edwards was "the American theologian who stands at the headwaters of [British] Evangelicalism" and "the chief architect of the theological structures erected by Evangelicals in the Reformed tradition," scant attention has been directed toward a full assessment of Edwards's contribution to British life and thought.[9]

Moreover, it is well known that Edwards's *Life of Brainerd* and other theological treatises initially had a more receptive audience abroad than in America. Indeed, his *Life of Brainerd* and *Humble Attempt*, with its call for a United Concert of Prayer, directly inspired England's foray into overseas missions.[10] That Edwards was, in the words of Stuart Piggin in his essay in this volume, "massively constitutive of modern Protestant missions," has long been acknowledged but, until recently, insufficiently documented.[11] Historians of missions, including Andrew Walls in his acclaimed *The Missionary Movement in Christian History*, appreciate Edwards's impact, but a more complete story of Edwards's influence on modern missionary endeavor has yet to be chronicled.[12] In short, despite the recognition of evangelicalism's global reach and Edwards's transoceanic influence, no effort has been made to assess Edwards's international legacy in any kind of comprehensive way.

The essays in this volume, more than the contents of any other book to date, address the concerns mentioned above, contributing to the larger field of Edwards scholarship in two important ways. First, they represent the first major collection of essays dedicated exclusively to Edwards's legacy. Edwards scholarship has now matured to the point of necessitating a volume of essays devoted solely to this theme. In this volume Edwards is considered not as he wanted to be remembered by his God at the divine bar of eternal justice, but as mortal scholars have remembered and responded to him in history.

Second, the essays that follow move us further than any other single volume toward an assessment of Edwards's legacy outside of the United States. Each of the essays on Edwards abroad breaks new ground, whether focusing on the history of Edwards's publications around the world, his theological contributions to English and Scottish history, or his influence on the promotion of world missions. This recognition of Edwards's global impact—an impact that extends well into the twentieth century—portends the direction of future Edwards studies, and the essays in this collection signal a creative and important first step in that direction.

If the essays on Edwards abroad quite literally map new territory in Edwards studies, the first two groupings of essays on Edwards "at home" make clear that his life and American legacy continue to generate innovative scholarship. The most recent generation of Edwards scholars—in many respects a much more diverse group than earlier generations—demonstrates that Edwards is no longer the exclusive province of intellectual historians. Indeed, these essays demonstrate that Edwards is fair game for social historians, literary scholars, and comparativists of religion, and that Edwards's legacy may be fruitfully examined through the lenses of gender, family, and race.

In Part One, "Remembering Edwards's Ministry," four of the most insightful scholars at work in the field of religion and American culture contribute to the study of Edwards's legacy in American history and historiography. In the opening essay, George Marsden ruminates on the problems faced by Edwards's would-be biographers (Marsden has recently finished a biography of Edwards for Yale University Press). Considering the multitudinous ways in which modern scholars have remembered Edwards's life, he asks, "How does one do a comprehensive work that does justice to [it] all while retaining some intelligible coherence?" His answer: "The central theme for understanding Edwards . . . is encapsulated in his phrase, 'the divine and supernatural light.'"

Michael McClymond shifts our focus away from Marsden's historical quest to pursue a conjectural question. McClymond wonders aloud about what might have become of Edwards's work had he not received the vaccination that so tragically ended his life. What would Edwards have done? Would we remember him any differently? McClymond admits the usually limited value of such counterfactual musings. But in this case, he contends, there are "textual evidences from 1755–1758 that supply tantalizing glimpses into Edwards's authorial intentions at the end of his life." Among other things, these texts suggest "that Edwards's projected *A History of the Work of Redemption* was to be an expression of . . . a 'cultural turn' in his theology." Further, argues McClymond, "Edwards's theological legacy . . . would almost certainly have been quite different had he lived to complete and publish his magnum opus, and his work might have had influence on nineteenth-century missionary practice and might have helped to obviate the disastrous Fundamentalist-Modernist split of twentieth-century Protestantism."

Moving from the conjectural to the concrete, Catherine Brekus explores Edwards's theology of childhood and its transformation in nineteenth-century America. Although nineteenth-century Calvinist ministers traced many of their ideas back to Edwards, they tried to distance themselves from his view of infant damnation and children's depravity. At a time when liberals insisted that children were naturally innocent, Edwards's theology not only seemed harsh, but barbaric. By the mid–nineteenth century, very few Protestants, whether liberal or conservative, wanted to preserve his ideas about children. As Edwards had once feared, Calvinism had been profoundly transformed by its encounter with humanitarianism, sentimentalism, and the Enlightenment.

Ava Chamberlain reassesses Northampton's notorious "bad book" controversy in light of the reconfiguration of gender relations in eighteenth-century New England. Filling out the memory of modern historians as to the significance of this affair, she reminds us that it was "primarily about sex," not Edwards's patriarchal leadership style or the authority of the clergy. In spite of (or perhaps because of) Edwards's efforts to stem the rise of the ideology of separate spheres, and the false dichotomies, gender stereotypes, and double standards that would attend it, his own premodern views of sex would eventually contribute to his firing—notwithstanding the support he received from most of Northampton's women.

Part Two of this volume, "Edwards and American Culture," includes a broad sampling of innovative scholarship on Edwards's legacy in American history, primarily, though not exclusively, in the long nineteenth century. Mark Valeri places Edwards and his "New Divinity" followers within what he calls "a passage from a hierarchical and deferential discourse grounded in Puritan divinity to a liberal, democratic, and proto-capitalist discourse." Along the way, he flies in the face of a formidable body of existing literature that either "dismisses" Edwards's social thought "or highlights his antipathy toward the new economy." Valeri contends that Edwards facilitated a departure from puritan tradition and its communitarian values, one that "contributed to an alliance between evangelical religion and market culture." In sum, he writes that Edwards "brought the moral language of Calvinism into a discursive milieu that was congruent with the ethics of a market culture." Consequently, he enabled his followers to "support a political revolution in defense of New England's property rights and commercial aspirations."

James German extends Valeri's discussion into the post-Revolutionary period by examining the writings of Edwards's son, Jonathan Edwards Jr., the younger Edwards's most famous parishioner, Roger Sherman, and Sherman's colleague in national politics, Oliver Ellsworth. Together, their writings disclose "the emergence of an Edwardsian political economy premised on the reality of natural self-love rather than on the possibility of true virtue." These thinkers, of course, did not speak for all Edwardsians, especially Samuel Hopkins, who condemned "the love of self, *as self.*" But ultimately, "by legitimizing naturalistic political economy," these Edwardsians undermined the connection between theology and ethics in the realm of public life.

Perhaps more in keeping with the kind of legacy Edwards himself would have liked to bequeath, Charles Hambrick-Stowe discovers expressions of Edwardsian revivalistic piety between the Awakenings that crossed racial boundaries by highlighting the contributions of Samuel Hopkins, Sarah Osborn, and Lemuel Haynes. Hopkins denounced slavery by appealing to Edwardsian notions of "disinterested love." Osborn, a parishioner of Hopkins in Newport, Rhode Island, welcomed both free and enslaved blacks into her home during times of revival—despite increasing community criticism. And the Rev. Lemuel Haynes, a free black and Edwardsian-educated pastor in New England, "*embodied* the doctrine of disinterested benevolence." This trio of Edwardsians "connected the gospel of salvation in Jesus Christ with the single most crucial—and in their day neglected—issue of American history, the status of African Americans in this society."

Similar themes of Edwardsian piety and conviction were put to use in a quite different context, one of which Edwards himself had little knowledge, woman's fiction. Sharon Kim contests the memory of Edwards most common in American literature—that of the dour Puritan, the "man in black," popularized by nineteenth-century New England liberals. Focusing on Susan Warner's novel *The Wide, Wide World* (1850), a best-seller in its time but little known today, Kim shows how at least one popular female novelist and producer of woman's fiction "promoted a Christian belief that was both influenced by Edwards and consonant with his work," concluding that "the elegance and specificity with which Edwards described spiritual reality has contributed a valuable element" even to this unlikely literary genre.

Rounding out Part Two, in her wide-ranging and evocative essay Amanda Porterfield focuses on "expressions of feeling in American popular culture that some followers of Edwards might call spiritual." Indeed, according to Porterfield, Edwards's distinction "between self-love and love to something more [for Edwards, 'being in general'], can be found in a variety of places, many of which would not ordinarily be associated with Edwards or with Calvinist theology." And by connecting Edwards's thought with comments from Huck Finn, the writings of William James and the Dalai Lama, and the film *Runaway Bride,* Porterfield portrays Edwards as "a transitional figure" whose views on "love, happiness, and sincerity contributed to the development of an important tradition in American thought."

As alluded to above, the third and final part of the volume, "Edwards around the World," represents the most innovative contribution of this book of essays. Scottish historian David Bebbington, the keynote speaker at our conference, surveys Edwards's global impact with striking results. Noting that "Edwards's own reputation has extended to girdle the earth," he traces the "vicissitudes" of that reputation through what he suggests are its four phases. Along the way, he makes it clear that through all the ebb and flow of Edwards's influence he has been remembered outside America as much, if not more, than he has been here.

The Canadian historian D. Bruce Hindmarsh chronicles Edwards's impact upon English Methodists, Baptists, Congregationalists, and Anglican evangelicals. "To state it baldly," he concludes, "the Baptists championed Edwards, the Anglican evangelicals were ambivalent, and Wesley simply corrected him." But despite their varied appropriations, "all of the early English evangelicals found that Edwards's writings gave them hope—hope that [just as Edwards had seen revival] they might see revival, too." Indeed, "Edwards's example and his writing moved all these English evangelicals to affirm a larger role for human agency in evangelism and salvation."

Christopher W. Mitchell focuses on Edwards's side of the mutual benefits gained in an epistolary exchange with six Scottish correspondents. The exchange enabled Edwards to rise above his provincial surroundings and keep abreast of political news and intellectual and religious developments in other parts of the world—and to procure books. Such were the deep ties that when Edwards was dismissed from his Northampton pastorate his Scottish friends raised financial support to assist Edwards and his family, and invited him to Scotland. "The contributions to Edwards's thinking, writing, and spiritual well-being by his Scottish correspondents," concludes Mitchell, "are difficult to overestimate."

The appropriation of Edwards in Britain had far-reaching implications for the burgeoning missionary movement in the late eighteenth and early nineteenth centuries. Andrew Walls portrays Edwards as a transitional figure who lived before the emergence of the modern missionary movement and continued to think in terms of "Christendom," or the territorial principle of church in state. At the same time, Edwards was an evangelical, "radical" Christian in tension with the nominal faith of Christendom. Several generations later, Edwards's successors rejected the Christendom model, embraced the "missionary principle" of demonstration and persuasion, and appropriated Edwards for their own missionary ends. To be sure, Edwards's theology and call for prayer figured into the early missionary movement, but his *Life of Brainerd* had the most profound influence. The missionary movement remembered Brainerd, however, not as Edwards remembered him. For Edwards, Brainerd was an indefatigable minister who happened to work with the Native Americans; among the first missionary movement, Brainerd was recast as "a model missionary pioneer of the maritime age of missions."

Continuing the theme of Edwards and missions, Australian scholar Stuart Piggin argues that Edwards constructed a "new paradigm" for modern Protestant missions. Identifying seven facets of Edwards's missionary paradigm (theology, history, philosophy, pragmatics, practice, spirituality, and aesthetics), Piggin observes that the half century from 1740 to 1790 "is threaded through with many cords connecting Edwards with the founders of modern Protestant missions." Indeed, the early British missionary societies "were born in a world awash with Edwards." Piggin focuses on British missions to India, contending that Edwards's influence was twofold. First, his *Life of Brainerd* served as an ideal model of missionary piety, motivation, strategy, and saintliness. Second, his hostile (though occasionally temperate and open-ended) views toward Hinduism shaped later missionary attitudes.

Finally, in an important bibliographical essay, M. X. Lesser builds a compelling argument for "the timelessness of Jonathan Edwards" by tracing the publication history of Edwards's works abroad. Beginning in the 1730s and extending through the twentieth century, Edwards's writings (primarily from his Northampton years) proliferated in Britain and also made their way into translations in German, French, Dutch, Swedish, Welsh, Gaelic, Arabic, Choctaw, Chinese, and Korean. Additionally, the twentieth century witnessed articles and reviews about Edwards in nine languages. From Edwards's time and into our own, two venues—commercial and religious—published his works, an indication of Edwards's varied appeal and the uses (at times competing) to which he has been put through the centuries.

If the essays in this volume are a remarkable testament to Edwards's enduring legacy, then perhaps a few concluding words about Miami, the site of the conference that generated these essays, are in order. At first glance, Miami is a quite un-Edwardsian place for Edwards scholars to gather. Ever keen to his natural surroundings, Edwards would have felt alien in Miami's exotic subtropical climate with its lush greens and swaying palms. And yet if we are to take seriously his "Personal Narrative," Edwards would have relished this Florida environment, whose fierce lightning and thunderstorms lead the nation both in frequency and force, for he experienced in such magnificent displays of nature the very presence of God. Edwards described his own spiritual awakening—what he called "new dispositions, and that new sense of things" with its "inward, sweet delight in God and divine things"—as a new apprehension of the natural order.[13] Amid his internal transformation, the outward display of the Creator's atmospheric power bedazzled him.

> And scarce anything, among all the works of nature, was so sweet to me as thunder and lightning. Formerly, nothing had been so terrible to me. I used to be a person uncommonly terrified with thunder: and it used to strike me with terror, when I saw a thunderstorm rising. But now, on the contrary, it rejoiced me. I felt God at the first appearance of a thunderstorm. And used to take the opportunity at such times, to fix myself to view the clouds, and see the lightnings play, and hear the majestic and awful voice of God's thunder: which oftentimes was exceeding entertaining, leading me to sweet contemplations of my great and glorious God.[14]

In this sense Edwards may have been naturally "at home" in Miami. And yet the focus of the conference was not upon him but his legacy. Can Miami make any claim to Edwards's legacy? Surprisingly, yes, in both indirect and direct ways. First, if the books one owns and presumably reads have any influence —and this claim is vigorously made in several essays in this volume—then Edwards left his own mark, however slight, in Miami. In Coral Gables, the location of the University of Miami and the specific site of the Edwards conference, stands the historic home of George Merrick, the founder and planner of this so-called *city beautiful*. In 1898 his father, the Rev. Solomon Merrick, left Old Pilgrim Church in Duxbury, Massachusetts, and ventured to the frontier outpost village of Miami for the same reason that thousands left the northeast for the south: to escape frigid winters and the "New England Quinsy," a chronic type of rheumatism. This Yale graduate cultivated a fruit farm and served as the second pastor of the Coconut Grove Union Congregational Church (now Plymouth Congregational Church) from 1901 until 1907. Included among the works in the Reverend Merrick's theological library is *The Bible Hand-Book* (1883) by Joseph Angus (1816–1902), an English Calvinist Baptist and professed Edwardsian.[15] Merrick may not have owned works by Edwards, but he did own an influential work by someone who had—indeed, by someone whose writings bore an Edwardsian imprimatur.

A more direct Edwardsian legacy continues in today's Miami, a global city of the twenty-first century that is far removed from the village settled by New England Congregationalists a century ago. Among the many informal conversations that took place at the Edwards conference, one centered on plans to produce an anthology of Edwards's writings in Spanish. With clear instructional and theological purposes in mind, the person suggesting the project intended to make the anthology available not only to the primary target of Hispanic Christians at an educational center in Miami's "Little Havana," but also to readers in Spanish-speaking countries. Edwards thus continues to generate (in this case, favorable) interest in a world where the distinction between home and abroad is becoming increasingly blurred.

We began this introduction noting that partisans in Edwards's day voted him out of his Northampton parish. And we just now observed that partisans in our day plan to translate, publish, and disseminate his writings around the world. The essays that follow lie somewhere between these contrasting perspectives of censure and acclaim, offering a critical yet judicious appraisal of Edwards's legacy at home and abroad.

NOTES

1. "A Farewell Sermon," in *The Sermons of Jonathan Edwards: A Reader*, ed. Wilson H. Kimnach, Kenneth P. Minkema, and Douglas A. Sweeney (New Haven: Yale Univ. Press, 1999), 228. For the sake of scholarly convenience, the capitalization and punctuation of the Yale edition of Edwards's *Works* have been followed whenever possible. Unpublished manuscript material has been quoted literally.

2. The term is the title of Robert W. Jensen's book *America's Theologian: A Recommendation of Jonathan Edwards* (New York: Oxford Univ. Press, 1988). The current state of Edwards scholarship is discussed in two review essays: Michael J. McClymond, "The Protean Puritan: *The Works of Jonathan Edwards*, vols. 8–16"; and Roland A. Delattre, "Recent Scholarship on Jonathan Edwards," both in *Religious Studies Review* 24 (1998): 361–75. Indispensable bibliographical guides are the two volumes by M. X. Lesser, *Jonathan Edwards: A Reference Guide* (Boston: G. K. Hall and Co., 1981); and *Jonathan Edwards: An Annotated Bibliography, 1979–1993* (Westport, Conn.: Greenwood Press, 1994). On websites, see the Yale edition site: http://www.yale.edu/wje.

3. Edwards historiography is discussed at length by Douglas A. Sweeney, "Edwards and His Mantle: The Historiography of the New England Theology," *New England Quarterly* 71 (March 1998): 97–119; on neo-orthodoxy and Miller, see 107–11.

4. See Sweeney, "Edwards and His Mantle," 114–15 nn. 30, 31.

5. The books resulting from these conferences are *Jonathan Edwards and the American Experience*, ed. Nathan O. Hatch and Harry S. Stout (New York: Oxford Univ. Press, 1988); *Benjamin Franklin, Jonathan Edwards, and the Representation of American Culture*, ed. Barbara B. Oberg and Harry S. Stout (New York: Oxford Univ. Press, 1993); *Jonathan Edwards's Writings: Text, Context, Interpretation*, ed. Stephen J. Stein (Bloomington: Indiana Univ. Press, 1996); and *Edwards in Our Time: Jonathan Edwards and the Shaping of American Religion*, ed. Sang Hyun Lee and Allen C. Guelzo (Grand Rapids, Mich.: Eerdmans, 1999).

6. Mark A. Noll, David W. Bebbington, and George A. Rawlyk, eds., *Evangelicalism: Comparative Studies of Popular Protestantism in North America, the British Isles, and Beyond, 1700–1990* (New York: Oxford Univ. Press, 1994), 6. Cf. Thomas Bender, ed., *Rethinking American History in a Global Age* (Berkeley: Univ. of California Press, 2002), the most important recent call for a more cosmopolitan approach to the study of American history generally.

7. See Harry S. Stout, "George Whitefield in Three Countries," 64–66; Susan O'Brien, "Eighteenth-Century Publishing Networks in the First Years of Transatlantic Evangelicalism," 41, 43, 44, 45–46, 47.

8. Norman Fiering, *Jonathan Edwards's Moral Thought in Its British Context* (Chapel Hill: Univ. of North Carolina Press, 1981).

9. David Bebbington, *Evangelicalism in Modern Britain: A History from the 1730s to the 1980s* (1989; reprint, Grand Rapids, Mich.: Baker Book House, 1992), 5, 65.

10. Johannes van den Berg, *Constrained by Jesus' Love: An Inquiry into the Motives of the Missionary Awakening in Great Britain in the Period between 1698 and 1815* (Kampen: J. H. Kok, 1956), 92–93, 123; Sidney H. Rooy, *The Theology of Missions in the Puritan Tradition* (Grand Rapids, Mich.: Eerdmans, 1965), 292–93; Susan O'Brien, "A Transatlantic Community of Saints: The Great Awakening and the First Evangelical Network, 1735–1755," *American Historical Review* 91 (October 1986): 831; Joseph A. Conforti, *Jonathan Edwards, Religious Tradition, and American Culture* (Chapel Hill: Univ. of North Carolina Press, 1995), 68–69; Ronald E. Davies, "Jonathan Edwards: Missionary Biographer, Theologian, Strategist, Administrator, Advocate—and Missionary," *International Bulletin of Missionary Research* 21 (April 1997): 60.

11. For Edwards's influence upon the American foreign missionary movement via his New Divinity heirs, see David W. Kling, "The New Divinity and the Origins of the American Board of Commissioners for Foreign Missions," *Church History* 72, no. 4 (Dec. 2003), in press.

12. Andrew F. Walls, *The Missionary Movement in Christian History: Studies in the Transmission of Faith* (Maryknoll, N.Y.: Orbis, 1996), 66, 244.

13. Jonathan Edwards, "Personal Narrative," in *A Jonathan Edwards Reader,* ed. John E. Smith, Harry S. Stout, and Kenneth P. Minkema (New Haven: Yale Univ. Press, 1995), 281, 283.

14. Edwards, "Personal Narrative," 285.

15. Our thanks to David Bebbington, who espied the Angus book on a tour of the Merrick house and shared his find with David Kling. The full citation of this work is *The Bible Hand-Book* by Joseph Angus with revisions by F. S. Hoyt (Philadelphia: J. Fagan and Son, 1883). On Angus, see *The Blackwell Dictionary of Evangelical Biography, 1730–1860,* ed. Donald M. Lewis, 2 vols. (Oxford: Blackwell Publishers, 1995), 1:24.

Part One

Remembering Edwards's Ministry

THE QUEST FOR THE HISTORICAL EDWARDS
The Challenge of Biography

George M. Marsden

It seems difficult to believe, but the last full academic biography of Edwards published in the twentieth century was Ola Winslow's in 1940. After that, two half-biographies appeared, Perry Miller's in 1949 on aspects of Edwards's mind and Patricia Tracy's in 1979 on the social dynamics of his Northampton pastorate. Unfortunately these two "halves," although complementary, did not make a whole. In addition, Iain Murray produced a full biography published in 1987 for an admiring Reformed audience. Murray's work, which stands in the tradition of the seminal contribution of Edwards's great-grandson, Sereno Dwight, is well-researched and nicely done, but it is intended ultimately as hagiography, not as a critical academic work.[1]

Since scholarly interest in Edwards during the latter half of the twentieth century was greater than it ever had been, why was there no major life of Edwards? Part of the problem—I can tell you from now having completed the immodest and daunting task of writing a full biography—is the sheer immensity of the scholarship. Anyone working on Edwards confronts mountains of material. Very little in Edwards has not been studied and analyzed by someone. Often I have found what I thought was an original tidbit or insight, only to discover someone else has anticipated it. On the other hand, the magnitude of the scholarship is also a great asset. Any prospective biographer stands on the shoulders of a highly skilled company of predecessors.

Especially helpful is the *Works of Jonathan Edwards* project. Until now anyone who wanted to take on a comprehensive study of Edwards was confronted with climbing twin peaks: one mountain of Edwards's scholarship and another of Edwards's own writings. The latter was a task of a lifetime, due to the tedium of deciphering Edwards's handwriting. Now, thanks to the lifetime of work by Thomas Schafer, the research of George Claghorn on the letters, the immense contributions of others, and to the Edwards project, we have almost all of

Edwards's works available in transcription, if not yet in print. On a computer one can survey in minutes what would have consumed weeks or months twenty years ago. Taken together, the careful introductions to the volumes already offer the essential framework for a biography.

Yet even if one is working in such a fine community of colleagues and can begin to comprehend this immense mass of information, there is a more fundamental problem. What is the biography to be about? What is its core? How do you find a center or unifying theme? One can deal with Edwards as a theologian, a philosopher, an artist, a pastor, a preacher, an awakener, a leader of a party, a Calvinist, a Puritan, a biblicist, a millennialist, a missionary, an educator, an ascetic, a spiritual writer, a member of an elite clan, a family man, a gendered person, a personality, a colonial, an international, an eighteenth-century man, an anachronism, a modern man, a theologian for today, a universal man—I could add more. Everyone who has written on Edwards since at least Winslow has focused on one or two of these themes. The problem is how does one do a comprehensive work that does justice to all of these themes while retaining some intelligible coherence?

The challenges for the biographer are compounded by the elusiveness of Edwards's personality. Relative to the abundance of his writings, notebooks, sermons, and letters, we have amazingly few personal glimpses. As his cramped handwriting suggests, he seems extraordinarily guarded about revealing a private or personal side. Much of this is intentional. Edwards makes an early resolve "never to speak evil of any, except I have some particular good call for it."[2] So—much to the disappointment of biographers—he almost never speaks of personalities, except sometimes in his later years when there is more "good call for it." His sermons seldom have any personal reference. Even though in his theology he describes the universe as most essentially relationships among persons, in his writing, even in his letters, he deals almost entirely with principles.

Further, Edwards's personality is difficult to uncover because he is almost always assuming a role. These personae—of pietist, theologian, authoritative pastor, and so forth—were entirely real. We tend to think of role-playing as not genuine, but that is in part because we lack the eighteenth-century sense of status. Edwards, like most of his British contemporaries, thought that persons *should* define themselves by their status or roles. He was, moreover, a self-disciplined ascetic who willed himself into certain molds. So we seldom see the adult Edwards out of character.

Complicating the search for his personality is the fact that one of his religious principles was that personality should not be important. Although, like earlier Puritans, he might seem inordinately preoccupied with self-examination, his larger religious goal was to lose himself in God, to subordinate his will to God's. One result of this effort, even if he never entirely achieved his goal, is that our views of his personality are almost always refracted through his religious categories. Added to that is that he was unsociable and sometimes depressive. His tendencies toward depression are apparent from his earliest diaries to the last letter he wrote to the Princeton trustees describing "a low tide of spirits; often occasioning a kind of childish weakness and contemptibleness of speech, presence, and demeanor; with a disagreeable dullness and stiffness, much unfitting me for conversation."[3] In assessing Edwards's career, we must take into account that he must have been always subject to these "low tides." He was also, it seems, often physically ill.

Further, as Kenneth Minkema has shown, Edwards was his father's son. The Rev. Timothy Edwards was also strict, brittle, and unable to give up on an argument.[4] Jonathan was, in addition, reclusive and somewhat obsessive. His solution to most problems was to go off and write a treatise about it, and he could not bear to have someone else have the last word.

One must hasten to add that he also cultivated many admirable Christian virtues. Even though he lamented that he was "born to be a man of strife,"[5] he also worked hard to develop virtues, such as those described in *Religious Affections* as being "attended with the lamb-like, dove-like spirit and temper of Jesus Christ"[6] or practicing secret charity. Much in prayer and self-examination, he was, like many Calvinists, his own most severe critic, at least in some respects. He was constantly alert to the deceptiveness of the human heart. Despite his many conflicts, he seems to have been calm and controlled in his personal demeanor, dealing with people in the same way Samuel Hopkins says he broke the wills of his children, "with the greatest calmness."[7] The Rev. David Hall, one of his supporters on the council that approved his dismissal from the Northampton church, recorded in his diary: "I never saw the least symptoms of displeasure in his countenance the whole week but he appeared like a man of God, whose happiness was out of the reach of his enemies and whose treasure was not only a future but a present good, overbalancing all imaginable ills of life, even to the astonishment of many who could not be at rest without his dismission: it manifestly appeared to me."[8]

One way to try to get a balanced view of his personality is to take into account that in his closest relationships he was almost always surrounded by women. When he was growing up he had not only an authoritarian father, but also an impressive mother and ten sisters. His younger sister Jerusha, just the same age as Sarah Pierpont, may have been his original model of youthful piety. His continuing admiration for Sarah and his daughter Jerusha as spiritual exemplars is well known. One suspects that his female surroundings in his upbringing have to do with his extraordinarily sensitive nature and his insistence that true religion is seated in the affections. Many have commented that women were most frequently his models of true spirituality. He himself was capable of great religious ecstasies, which is not particularly a women's phenomenon and may be more related to the oscillations of a sometimes depressive personality. Yet his model of true piety as intense, but strictly disciplined according to intellectually exact principles, reflects a combination of sensitivities that reflected both sides of the expected gender roles of the times.

Edwards was greatly loved and admired by some men and women, and greatly despised by others. On the positive side were not only his immediate family but also a circle of protégés and disciples, mostly younger, although including some of the senior pastors of Boston, such as Thomas Prince. On the negative side were New England's Old Lights and eventually many of his townspeople and most of his extended family, all of which, he said, "hate me for my stingy principles, enthusiasm, [and] rigid proceedings."[9]

These widely contrasting assessments of Edwards's personality are best explained by viewing him as a leader of a partisan party. Such people are often viewed as harsh by their opponents, especially by those who have been subjected to scathing critiques over differences in principle. Those who share the party leader's principles, by contrast, view the leader as strong and heroic. Admirers also see a warm and personal side. Many Northampton people were sometimes enthralled by Edwards, at least so long as they shared his principles and could keep up with his strict expectations. Edwards also, as Hopkins reported, opened up with his close allies and admirers and among such could be "quite patient of contradiction" and "quite sociable and free with all."[10]

This brings us to the next step in the quest for the historical Edwards, to locate him in his own communities and traditions. Here the first job is to get beyond Perry Miller, who simultaneously did the most to promote Edwards studies over the past half century and the most to confuse the issues of biography. Miller's portrait is to Edwards what Shakespeare's *Hamlet* is to the actual Danish prince—a triumph of the imagination.

Miller distorted Edwards in several fundamental ways. Most important, he adopted the nineteenth-century model of the lonely genius and presented Edwards as a "backwoods adolescent" who "grasped in a flash" the implications of Locke and Newton for modern thought.[11] Miller simultaneously created an

Edwards essentially isolated from his own time and place and the first truly modern American. Thus he trumped the stereotype of Edwards as an anachronism, which had been the dominant view in the Progressive era—and is apparent in the otherwise sympathetic treatment of Winslow, who regretted that he spoke "through an outworn, dogmatic system" that "needed to be demolished."[12] For Miller it hardly mattered that Edwards was a theologian. "He was one of America's five or six major artists, who happened to work with ideas instead of with poems or novels." Further, Edwards's insight into science and psychology was "so much ahead of his time that our own can hardly be said to have caught up with him."[13]

Aside from the sheer wrongheadedness of most of this, the challenge it leaves us is to put Edwards back into the eighteenth century. Miller's emphasis on Locke and Newton did connect Edwards to the Enlightenment, even if Miller confused the nature of those connections. Miller pointed the way toward recognizing how engaged Edwards was with the thought of his own time, the more accurate detail of which has been filled in by William Sparkes Morris in *The Young Jonathan Edwards* and especially by Norman Fiering.[14] Any new synthesis of the Edwards scholarship, however, must draw not only on such work but also on the enhancements of our collective understanding of the eighteenth-century American colonies within the past fifty years. In order to get some new angles on Edwards I think the overarching question has to be: "What does an eighteenth-century Edwards look like?"

First, the extensive analyses by Morris, Fiering, and others of Edwards's intellectual roots underscore that Edwards was deeply grounded in traditions and intellectual currents beyond Locke and Newton. Further, his strongest and most explicit commitments were to the Calvinist-Protestant cause. He directed much of his intellectual energy toward refuting the intellectual trends of his day, which he designated collectively as "Arminian," and to analyzing the course of history that would bring the downfall of the papal Antichrist. In defending his heritage or in promoting a New Light/Pietist/evangelical/ Reformed agenda for awakening, Edwards was first of all a synthetic thinker. Contrary to Miller's representation, there is relatively little in Edwards for which there is not precedent in the writings of seventeenth-century Puritans or Reformed scholastics, or in early eighteenth-century sources. Rather than being a farm boy who grasped the future of Western thought in a glance by reading Locke and Newton, he was a provincial well connected to the formidable print culture of his day. He read widely and voraciously and borrowed freely. His originality was in the skill with which he marshaled his traditions to meet the challenges of the day. Seldom did he make an argument that rested substantially on an appeal to the authority of his predecessors—aside from biblical writers. Most of the extra-biblical sources for his thought, nonetheless, can be found in seventeenth-century or early-eighteenth-century writings. His genius was to pick and choose to fit the powerful logic of his own disputations.

Essential to understanding Edwards as an eighteenth-century Reformed Protestant is his biblicism. Again, this is a point that Miller—and Winslow and Tracy for that matter—ignore. Yet to live with Edwards day by day is to encounter someone who refracted virtually everything through "the prism of Scripture."[15] As Stephen Stein has shown, Edwards needs to be understood as standing in a tradition of biblical interpretation. He lived during the time of the "eclipse of the biblical narrative," but we must remember that, even among the educated, this was only a partial eclipse. Edwards was firmly committed to the tradition of those who took for granted the literal and typological interpretations of the Bible, that it was all of one piece, and that it provided a précis of all history. He was well aware of emerging biblical criticism and devoted a fair amount of space in his notebooks to arguments for biblical authenticity.[16]

Edwards's biblicism and his consequent view of history led Peter Gay to tag him as an "anachronism."[17] That seems a bit strong coming from someone who knows as much about the eighteenth century as anyone, since Edwards's view of Scripture was not so much different from that of Isaac Newton. It is true that Edwards remained conservative concerning Scripture and by the 1750s would have seemed out of date in some sophisticated European circles.[18] Yet many of Edwards's theological opponents also took much of Scripture pretty much at face value.

A related key to understanding Edwards is that he insisted on pursuing the implications of his biblically refracted beliefs to their logical conclusions. In his sermons he constantly reminded his parishioners that they truly lived on the edge of eternity and that it was utter folly to become preoccupied with mere worldly concerns or to be distracted by their lusts, desires, ambitions, or lethargy. Contrary to what some rehabilitators of Edwards might like to be the case, hellfire preaching was integral to Edwards's thought. It is indeed important to counter the impression—fostered by the notoriety of "Sinner in the Hands of an Angry God"—that hellfire was the *only* or almost the *principal* thing he was concerned about. Edwards preached on the full range of Reformed doctrines, of which eternal punishment was only a small part. Yet, because it was in Scripture and seemed useful to jolt people awake and to maintain the moral order, he regularly preached it. Further, we can understand his constant campaigns to curb the sexual looseness of his young people as, among other things, a literal application of New Testament admonitions. If he was convinced a principle was in Scripture, Edwards would not back off.

This brings us to the point that Edwards must be understood not only as an eighteenth-century man of thought but also as an eighteenth-century man of action. One of his principles was that true belief involves the affections and the will and hence is evidenced in action. As a result, even though Edwards was temperamentally reclusive and withdrawn, he was a leading figure in a number of causes. He was, as I have already suggested, very much a campaigner for a partisan party.

The party that he helped to shape combined the Reformed heritage with the awakening. Its antecedents can be found both in Puritanism and pietism and its parallels in the English awakening of Watts and Whitefield, the Scottish Reformed awakeners, and to a lesser extent the Wesleys. Edwards's party was part of an emerging transatlantic British evangelical synthesis, which is still with us. Edwards himself, however, was strictly Reformed and assumed that by force of logic the Reformed party would eventually dominate the entire worldwide awakening.

This movement, both before and after Edwards's time, had a paradoxical outlook that has often been noted. Aspects of it reflected Reformed establishmentarianism and cultural imperialism. Other aspects were anti-establishment, subversive, and invited individualism. Put another way, one side of the tradition followed the Old Testament, which was seen as providing a blueprint for building Christian nations. The other side was New Testament, building a believers' church in a hostile empire. The tragedy of Jonathan Edwards was that he—with his usual thoroughness—wanted to preserve all the benefits of both sides of the heritage.

His view of history, as well as his view of his own status, was thoroughly establishmentarian. The goal of his party was to bring the Protestant Reformation to its conclusion, reuniting Christendom through awakening and under sympathetic Protestant rulers. In his millennial views, he predicted that this would likely be accomplished at least by around the year 2000—which he thought could be the time the millennium itself would begin. In this perspective he could celebrate the Hanoverian monarchs as, at least, a good start and see God's hand in the triumph of colonial and other British arms over the French papists at Louisbourg.

Yet at the very same time he viewed Anglican England as deeply unfaithful, immoral, and corrupt, and he was thoroughly disgusted with the hypocrisy and lax morals of post-awakening New England. Especially he was so disillusioned with the often-awakened Northampton that he demanded that the church take a half step in a sectarian direction by requiring a standard of church membership that would better differentiate it from the less-than-Christian town.

That Edwards was willing to go down with the ship, taking his family with him, over the principle that he thought resolved this dilemma is a fascinating issue with many dimensions. I'll just mention a few. First, like a lot of early eighteenth-century figures, and like the seventeenth-century Reformed encyclopedists before him,[19] Edwards thought that he could formulate a comprehensive view of everything. He did not like loose ends. As David D. Hall has observed, the Puritan/pietist polity that he inherited had become terribly ad hoc and chaotic. Edwards was confident that logic could solve the problem—and he even had hopes that the Northamptonites would be convinced if only they would read his arguments. He also had great confidence that the Bible spoke on such matters, hence giving his logical expositions dogmatic authority. At the same time, as David Hall has also observed, he long had unrealistic hopes for the sustained moral reformation of the town. His elaborate Northampton Covenant of 1742, in which he used the enthusiasm of the town's recent great awakening to elicit elaborate promises of model behavior forever, seems utopian.[20]

When that failed, both sides were left disillusioned and—after the "Young Folks' Bible" case—embittered. Edwards then made his fateful half step in a sectarian direction, especially fateful because he was countering the views of his grandfather and ministerial predecessor, Solomon Stoddard. Yet he did so without ever intending to give up any of his grandfather's moral authority in the culture at large.

Edwards's establishmentarian side must be understood in the light of his social location. First of all, as an eighteenth-century British colonial living in a frontier town, Edwards lived virtually his whole life at the intersection of three cultures, the British, the French, and the Indian (if we may for the moment speak of each as one). These three were locked in desperate struggles for dominance and survival. We know how it turns out, but it was not at all obvious at the time. New England might have ended up like Quebec. Edwards's life was punctuated with devastating Indian warfare, from the deaths or captivity of his aunt and some of his Williams cousins in the Deerfield massacre (when he was an infant) to General Braddock's defeat (shortly before his death). Even in Northampton the hostile Indians often posed a real threat. In the mid-1740s, for instance, at the time when David Brainerd visited and died there, the Edwards lived in a fortified home. Stockbridge in the mid-1750s was much more dangerous.

Further, Edwards's patron, neighbor, and perennial ally in town and church was the great squire, judge, and military leader of the entire western Massachusetts region, Col. John Stoddard. "Perhaps never was there a man that appeared in New England," Edwards declared at Stoddard's funeral, "to whom the denomination *great man* did more properly belong." Stoddard was New England's chief negotiator with the Indians, and during King George's War in the 1740s he was in charge of defending the western frontier. In such company and when the international stakes were so high, it is easy to see why Edwards would be a thoroughgoing patriot, despite New England's and England's moral failings. As in the Old Testament, God might bless even a corrupt people if they had righteous leaders such as Stoddard.

The Stoddard connection also leads us to the immensely important point that Edwards was a leading figure in the aristocratic Williams-Stoddard clan.[21] This clan dominated the commercial, political, and ecclesiastical affairs of western Massachusetts. Contrary to the myth that originated from some misinterpretations by Sereno Dwight, Edwards was for many years a valued member of the Williams-Stoddard family empire. Edwards's role in helping the leaders of the clan in attempting to rid the county of the suspected Arminianism of Robert Breck in the 1730s is the best evidence of his early unity with the family. The Breck episode also counters the idea that the Williamses themselves were mostly Arminians. Some, especially the young Israel Williams, the leading candidate to be successor to John Stoddard after the latter's death in 1748, had a longstanding grudge against Edwards. Israel and his brother-in-law Jonathan Ashley of Deerfield did have religious differences with Edwards. But until Edwards betrayed the clan by attacking the revered Solomon Stoddard, Edwards had remained a member in good standing in the powerful family.

In the perspective of Edwards's ties to his extended family, we can better appreciate that he was an eighteenth-century British provincial aristocrat—a slaveholding Tory hierarchist—whose social views need to be understood according to the standards of his own day. Modern readers can be put off by his attitudes because they want him to be more of a post-Revolutionary American. Yet his untimely death in 1758 meant that he was entirely a pre-Revolutionary. True, one can find in Edwards the roots of more popular views—such as his spiritual egalitarianism. It is also true that his immediate successors, such as Samuel Hopkins and Jonathan Edwards Jr., turned his theology to the cause of antislavery. It is fair enough to point out these potentialities. Yet we also need to exercise the historical imagination to understand Edwards as a man of his own time, and we should not impose the standards of our time on people of his era.

Edwards's aristocratic establishmentarian outlook and his connection to John Stoddard are related to his international vision for his Reformed-pietist cause. In Edwards's view, the completion of the Reformation would depend in part on sympathetic Protestant rulers. Another of his important allies in this cause was Jonathan Belcher, governor of Massachusetts from 1730 to 1741 and of New Jersey from 1747 to 1757. The pious if sometimes wily Belcher was a great promoter of Whitefield, supported Indian missions, and became a valuable friend of the fledgling College of New Jersey. Though Edwards was on the fringe of the empire and part of a nondominant movement, he still had enough such connections to assume that, wherever possible, the clergy should work directly with the political establishment.

Edwards's millennialism has to be understood in this context. While hopes for world awakening were always central to his millennial concerns, as evidenced in his promotion of the international Concert of Prayer, his millennialism also always had a strongly political dimension. That is why, during King George's War in the 1740s, he began a notebook in which he kept a record of all the reports he could find of economic, military, political, and natural setbacks for Roman Catholic countries.

All of Edwards's principal activities were directed toward promoting the world Reformed awakening that would be first of all spiritual, but also political. His pastorate, his treatises on the awakenings, his mission work to the Indians, his treatises against false doctrines, and his work as an educator all fit this Reformed-pietist agenda.

The high value he placed on missions to the Indians is indicative of this concern. The greatest disaster for the New England Puritan project had been King Philip's War, which had virtually wiped out Reformed Indian missions for two generations. Edwards and his friends, including John Stoddard, Stephen Williams, David and John Brainerd, Eleazar Wheelock, Jonathan Dickinson, and others, dedicated themselves to regaining a foothold for this crucial work. All these projects were of one piece, part of a grand vision, which from a negative perspective could be seen as Reformed cultural imperialism, but in their own terms was the ushering in of the reign of God's beauty and love throughout the world.

After looking at all these dimensions of Edwards, the question remains for the biographer of how to tie them all together. What should be the central theme?

Here is my proposal: the central theme for understanding Edwards—and a theme that raises all the preceding above the merely mundane—is encapsulated in his phrase, "the divine and supernatural light."[22] The hub around which all his thought and action revolves is the question of whether people—himself and others—have been given the regenerating grace to see that light. If one has been given the eyes to see that perfect beauty of the light of God's love, epitomized in the sacrificial love of Christ, then all other loves are thrown into radically subordinate perspective. That new perspective has many intensely practical implications. The overarching question in all human relationships will be whether people have truly loving relationships to God. Nothing else should be nearly as important. If eternal destiny turns on being right with God, then that issue demands one's attention every waking hour. Like David Brainerd, one ought to be ready to give up all comforts of this life to be the agent through whom God saves souls. Awakening and regeneration, especially because they demand intense human effort yet are beyond human control, will be an obsession. Edwards's fervent concerns with awakening, or the experience of knowing the light of God's love, unite the theological and the practical, the personal and the global mission.

It is important to mention Edwards's brilliance in this connection. Edwards was not the first Christian or even the first New Englander to celebrate the beauties of the light of divine love. Yet there is a luminous clarity in his writing that raises his expositions of such themes above the ordinary. Edwards always wrote with remarkable precision, but sometimes on local controversies or millennial speculations that are no longer of great interest. When he applied his genius to some of the grand questions that have long been near the center of the Christian tradition, as in his great treatises, he left a legacy that transcends his time and place.

Nevertheless, when talking about biography, I think it is important to keep reminding ourselves—as I have been in this essay—that we are talking about an eighteenth-century person. Edwards was a biblical literalist who believed the earth was less than six thousand years old, who warned his parishioners of hellfire, and who expected deference to his authority as an aristocrat. Readers in the twenty-first century need the imagination to realize that none of these traits was especially remarkable in his time and place.

Or if Edwards's preoccupation with the "divine and supernatural light" and how people might see it is a useful unifying principle, that is also a helpful way of reminding us that study of Edwards also tells us something about eighteenth-century British and American culture. The "century of lights" fostered not only Enlightenment but also the New Lights. The fact that light was Edwards's favorite metaphor fits his time and also reminds us that what counted as "light" or true "enlightenment" in the eighteenth century was sharply contested.

At the same time, as the subject of Edwards on the beauty of divine light suggests, seeing him as situated in his own time and traditions should not diminish our ability to appreciate the genius of his insights into universal truths. While biographers need to depict him in his own time, they also have to convey enough of the grandeur to make the trip to the eighteenth century worth it for their readers.

NOTES

1. Sereno Dwight, ed., *Life of President Edwards, the Works of President Edwards: with a Memoir of His Life* (New York: S. Converse, 1829), vol. 1; Ola Elizabeth Winslow, *Jonathan Edwards, 1703–1758* (New York: Macmillan, 1940); Perry Miller, *Jonathan Edwards* (New York: William Sloane Associates, 1949); Patricia J. Tracy, *Jonathan Edwards, Pastor: Religion and Society in Eighteenth-Century Northampton* (New York: Hill and Wang, 1979); Iain Murray, *Jonathan Edwards: A New Biography* (Edinburgh: Banner of Truth Trust, 1987). M. X. Lesser, *Jonathan Edwards* (Boston: Twayne Publishers, 1988), provides a brief but useful overview of Edwards's life and work.

2. "Resolutions" (1722), #33, 26 December 1722, *A Jonathan Edwards Reader*, ed. John E. Smith, Harry S. Stout, and Kenneth P. Minkema (New Haven: Yale Univ. Press, 1995), 277.

3. Jonathan Edwards to the Trustees of the College of New Jersey, 19 October 1757, *Letters and Personal Writings*, ed. George S. Claghorn, *The Works of Jonathan Edwards*, vol. 16 (New Haven: Yale Univ. Press, 1998), 726.

4. Kenneth Pieter Minkema, "The Edwardses: A Ministerial Family in Eighteenth-Century New England" (Ph.D. diss., University of Connecticut, 1988).

5. John Searle to Jonathan Edwards, 4 June 1750, refers to this remark (Hartford Seminary Foundation, as transcribed by George Claghorn, Works of Edwards files).

6. Jonathan Edwards, *Religious Affections*, ed. John E. Smith, *The Works of Jonathan Edwards*, vol. 2 (New Haven: Yale Univ. Press, 1959 [1746]), 344.

7. Samuel Hopkins, *The Life and Character of Reverend Mr. Jonathan Edwards* (Boston: S. Kneeland, 1765), reprinted in *Jonathan Edwards: A Profile*, ed. David Levin (New York: Hill and Wang, 1969), 43.

8. Journal of David Hall, Massachusetts Historical Society, as quoted in Winslow, *Jonathan Edwards* (New York: Collier Books, 1961 [1940]), 236.

9. Jonathan Edwards to Thomas Foxcroft, 14 May 1749, *Letters*, 284.

10. Hopkins, *Life and Character of Edwards*, 42. The most positive assessment of Edwards's personality that we have from a non-admirer comes from the remarkable Abigale Williams Sergeant, who opposed his coming to Stockbridge. "Mr. Edwards is

now with us," she wrote to Ezra Stiles in February. "He has conducted [himself] with wisdom and prudence. . . . He is learned, polite, and free in conversation, and more catholic than I had supposed." Abigale Sergeant to Ezra Stiles, 15 February 1752, Stiles papers, Yale University, quoted in Murray, *Jonathan Edwards,* 362.

11. Miller, *Jonathan Edwards,* 52–53.

12. Winslow, *Jonathan Edwards,* 297–98

13. Miller, *Jonathan Edwards,* v and vi. Further, he says, the young prodigy "cast off habits of mind formed in feudalism, and entered abruptly into modernity, where facts rather than prescriptive rights and charters were henceforth to be the arbiters of human affairs" (77–78).

14. William Sparkes Morris, *The Young Jonathan Edwards: A Reconstruction* (Brooklyn: Carlson Publishing, 1991); Norman Fiering, *Jonathan Edwards's Moral Thought and Its British Context* (Chapel Hill: Univ. of North Carolina Press, 1981). Fiering says that "In general, Miller's discussion of Locke and Edwards on pp. 52–68 is probably the worst piece of writing he ever did, judged in terms of substance and interpretive accuracy" (36n.).

15. The phrase comes from Karl Dieterich Pfisterer, *The Prism of Scripture: Studies on History and Historicity in the Work of Jonathan Edwards* (Frankfurt: Peter Lang, 1975).

16. Jonathan Edwards, *Notes on Scripture,* ed. Stephen J. Stein, *The Works of Jonathan Edwards,* vol. 15 (New Haven: Yale Univ. Press, 1998), 1–34. Cf. Hans Frei, *The Eclipse of the Biblical Narrative: A Study in Eighteenth and Nineteenth Century Hermeneutics* (New Haven: Yale Univ. Press, 1974), 1–3.

17. Peter Gay, *A Loss of Mastery: Puritan Historians in Colonial America* (Berkeley and Los Angeles: Univ. of California Press, 1966), 88–117.

18. Robert E. Brown, *Jonathan Edwards and the Bible* (Bloomington: Indiana Univ. Press, 2002), is valuable in documenting Edwards's engagement with the biblical criticism of his era.

19. I am indebted on this point to David Hill Scott, "The 'Circle of Knowledge' and Jonathan Edwards's Integration of Reason and Revelation" (M. Div. thesis, Gordon-Conwell Theological Seminary, 1997).

20. Jonathan Edwards, *Ecclesiastical Writings,* ed. David D. Hall, *The Works of Jonathan Edwards,* vol. 12 (New Haven: Yale Univ. Press, 1994), 56. Hall's other observation was made at a session of the American Society of Church History, 8 January 2000.

21. On this connection see Kevin Michael Sweeney's very valuable dissertation, "River Gods and Related Minor Deities: The Williams Family and the Connecticut River Valley, 1637–1790" (Ph.D. diss., Yale University, 1986).

22. The phrase is from his 1734 sermon "A Divine and Supernatural Light, Immediately Imparted to the Soul by the Spirit of God, Shown to be Both a Scriptural, and Rational Doctrine," reprinted in virtually every collection of Edwards's works.

A Different Legacy?

The Cultural Turn in Edwards's Later Notebooks and the Unwritten *History of the Work of Redemption*

Michael J. McClymond

Historians have rules of procedure, and accordingly one is not supposed to ask about what might have happened in past times. The prohibition applies to a query such as the following: If Edwards had not received the smallpox inoculation that killed him and cut short his ambitious plans to write a comprehensive *History of the Work of Redemption,* then what might have been the outcome for his life and legacy? Philosophers use the term "counterfactual conditional" for an assertion based on a false or hypothetical premise. They have the logically odd status of being invariably true statements, since their protasis (the "if" part) is false by definition.[1] So, following this principle, one can construct an endless number of true, albeit whimsical, sentences, such as: "If there are married bachelors, then it will snow in Miami in July." A counterfactual conditional is thus unlike other assertions. It begins from a manifestly false premise—"if there had been no vaccination," although there *was* a vaccination, and it *did* end the life of Edwards—and then it springboards into uncharted territory: the realm of nonevents, or rather possible events. Those concerned with the actual and factual past have reason to resist the lure of conditional thinking.

"If there had been no vaccination. . . ." What justification could there be for pursuing such a line of inquiry? And how might one assess what Edwards might have written, but did not actually write? The answer lies in textual evidences from 1755–1758 that supply tantalizing glimpses into Edwards's authorial intentions at the end of his life. The relevant documents fall into three categories. The first is Edwards's well-known letter of 19 October 1757 to the trustees of the College of New Jersey, expressing his reservations about accepting their offer of the presidency of the college, and citing as a reason his desire to press forward with work on his planned publications.[2] Here he sets forth in considerable detail his plan for what he calls "a great work" entitled *A History of the Work of Redemption.* The second bit of documentary evidence rests in three notebooks pertaining to the history of redemption project described in the letter. John F. Wilson analyzed these notebooks in an appendix to volume 9 of Edwards's *Works,* and my case here partially rests on their contents.[3] The third category of evidence consists in the later "Miscellanies," especially as treated in Gerald R. McDermott's recent work, *Jonathan Edwards Confronts the Gods: Christian Theology, Enlightenment Religion, and Non-Christian Faiths.*[4]

In a nutshell, my argument is that the available evidence indicates that Edwards's projected *A History of the Work of Redemption* was to be an expression of what I am calling a "cultural turn" in his theology. With the phrase cultural turn, I am referring both to a preoccupation with "other" cultures—i.e., other than Anglo American, English-language, and Protestant—and an interest in identifying and describing an implicit divine presence and activity within Western cultures. Edwards's theological legacy, I contend, would almost certainly have been quite different had he lived to complete and publish his magnum opus, and his work might have had influence on nineteenth-century missionary practice and might have helped to obviate the disastrous Fundamentalist-Modernist split of twentieth-century Protestantism.

In making these claims, I should add a number of caveats, so as not to assert more than is warranted from the evidence. The cultural turn, though an intensification of Edwards's interest in cultural phenomena, was not a departure from his longstanding habits of thought. My book *Encounters with God* argued that Edwards's writings embody an "implicit apology" for Christianity that sought to reinterpret modern Euro-American culture so as to make it congruent with his theological convictions.[5] His intellectual engagement with what he called the "arts and sciences" was lifelong, and his later cultural turn was a long time in coming. A very early entry into Edwards's lifelong "Catalogue" of books indicates that he was interested in the "comparison of all Religions with the Xtian [i.e., Christian]" while still a student at Yale.[6] Furthermore, it is clear that the cultural turn did not involve any diminution of Edwards's commitment to biblical exegesis and the traditional sorts of typological interpretation. While the description of the projected *A History of the Work of Redemption* occupies the central place in the letter to the trustees, he refers also to "another great work," a *Harmony of the Old and New Testament* that exists in an impressive draft of five hundred manuscript pages, and which has recently become the subject of an illuminating essay by Kenneth P. Minkema.[7] The redemption notebooks, like the draft of the *Harmony,* contain traditional biblical material that I will not discuss here.

Nonetheless, with these qualifications in mind, there is good reason to speak of a cultural turn in Edwards's later writings. To build my case, I will turn to the textual evidences mentioned above, beginning with a consideration of the letter to the trustees in light of the redemption notebooks, and then the content of the redemption notebooks and the relevant material in the later "Miscellanies." By way of conclusion, I will offer some tentative assertions regarding the "what if?" question, that is, the intellectual legacy Edwards might have bequeathed had he lived to complete *A History of the Work of Redemption*.

The notebooks to the redemption project shed light on Edwards's letter to the trustees, and vice versa. The letter presents a formal statement regarding the governing principles of the "great work," while the notebooks provide further hints as to its possible content. A major benefit of the notebooks is in helping to establish a chronology as to when Edwards began preparing in earnest to write *A History of the Work of Redemption*. John F. Wilson, in his meticulous analysis of the notebooks' contents, concludes that Edwards wrote much of it very late in his life. The key arguments for this conclusion may be stated briefly. The three notebooks are designated "A," "B," and "C" by Wilson, and are respectively 123 pages long in manuscript, 32 pages, and 21 pages. "Notebook A" consists of parts bound together, and, in its present augmented form, it could not have been constructed before early 1755, since the notebook contains within it a draft of a letter dated 20 December 1754, and another dated 4 January 1755. "Notebook B" has inner pages that are entirely taken from Antoine Arnauld's *De la frequente communion*, a book received as a gift from John Erskine of Scotland. Without a reading knowledge of French and short on paper, Edwards turned this volume upside down and wrote in the bottom margin, occasionally writing down the sides of the pages as well. Edwards's letter to Erskine indicates that he received the Arnauld book in the spring of 1752, which is therefore the terminus a quo for the composition of "Notebook B." Edwards's biographer, Sereno Dwight, indicates that he wrote *Freedom of the Will* between November 1752 and April 1753. From July 1754 to January 1755, Edwards was too ill to keep up his correspondence, and hence was probably unable to engage in extensive reading and note-taking. Dwight says that Edwards composed the *End of Creation* and *Nature of True Virtue* in the spring of 1755. The later spring and summer of that year were not a propitious time for reading and research, since Stockbridge was under threat of a raid because of warfare in the interior. The composition of *Original Sin*, again according to Dwight, took place between the summer of 1756 and May 1757. There may be a reference to the text of *Original Sin* in the history of redemption notebooks, and this would argue for a very late date for some of the materials there, perhaps in the summer of 1757.[8]

Wilson summarizes his investigation of the dating of the notebooks as follows: "The cumulative evidence, then, suggests that Edwards began serious and concerted work on the notebooks for this project no earlier than the spring of 1755. It is also clear that he was very much at work on them through the summer of 1757, perhaps even as he received and pondered the invitation from the trustees of the College of New Jersey." This also has implications for interpreting the letter to the trustees: "The notebooks . . . give a context for the passage in the well-known letter to the trustees of the College of New Jersey. . . . The letter should be read quite literally as indicating that Edwards's intellectual energies were becoming centered on this project, and that accepting the trustees' invitation would require him to turn aside from that project in a far more immediate sense than has usually been thought to be the case." Thus the passage in the letter that speaks of *A History of the Work of Redemption* "should be seen as a summary outline of the proposed work, fuller and more systematically developed than any single comparable passage in the notebooks."[9]

If we consider the letter in Wilson's terms as a "summary outline of the proposed work," what do we see? Actually, we see a number of interesting things, if we read closely. The relevant section of the letter reads as follows:

> I have had on my mind and heart (which I long ago began, not with any view to publication) a great work, which I call *A History of the Work of Redemption*, a body of divinity in an entire new method, being thrown into the form of an history, considering the affair of Christian theology, as the whole of it, in each part, stands in reference to the great work of redemption by Jesus Christ; which I suppose is to be the grand design of all God's designs, and the *summum* and *ultimum* of all the divine operations and degrees; particularly considering all parts of the grand scheme in their historical order. The order of their existence, or their being brought forth to view, in the course of divine dispensations, or the wonderful series of successive acts and events; beginning from eternity and descending from thence to the great work and successive dispensations of the infinitely wise God in time, considering the chief events coming to pass in the church of God, and revolutions in the world of mankind, affecting the state of the church and the affair of redemption, which we have an account of in history or prophecy; till at last we come to the general resurrection, last judgment, and consummation of all things;

when it shall be said, "It is done. I am Alpha and Omega, the Beginning and the End" [Rev. 22:13]. Concluding my work, with the consideration of that perfect state of things, which shall be finally settled, to last for eternity. This history will be carried on with regard to all three worlds, heaven, earth and hell: considering the connected, successive events and alterations, in each so far as the Scriptures give any light; introducing all parts of divinity in that order which is most scriptural and most natural: which is a method which appears to me the most beautiful and entertaining, wherein every divine doctrine, will appear to greatest advantage in the brightest light, in the most striking manner, showing the admirable contexture and harmony of the whole.[10]

The letter is rich in "Edwardsisms," that is, terms with special meaning for him. These include such words and phrases as "history," "redemption," "*summum* and *ultimum*," "divine dispensations," and "beautiful and entertaining." Some of these serve as subject headings for entries in the "Miscellanies." Other phrases, such as "*summum* and *ultimum*," suggest a link with the treatise *End of Creation*, since these Latin terms seem to be functional equivalents for "chief end" and "ultimate end"—the topic of discussion in the very opening paragraph of *End of Creation*.[11] Like *End of Creation*, which moves from creation to consummation, Edwards's unwritten *A History of the Work of Redemption* was to be bracketed on either side by God's eternity. In fact, one might read *End of Creation* as supplying the "bookends" for the historical material to be included in the great work. Furthermore, the lengthy notebook entry "Miscellanies" 1263 seems to be relevant to the unwritten great work. This "Miscellanies" entry discusses the distinction between God's "natural" operations in history and God's "arbitrary" operations at the beginning and end of the world. Like *End of Creation*, it links redemptive history to creation and consummation, and so provides a conceptual scaffolding within which Edwards could have constructed his unwritten work.[12] The basic structure of *A History of the Work of Redemption* was to be an inverted parabola, something like an upside-down St. Louis arch, as suggested by phrasing of the letter, "beginning from eternity and descending from thence to the great work and successive dispensations of the infinitely wise God in time, considering the chief events coming to pass in the church of God, and revolutions in the world of mankind . . . till at last we come to the general resurrection, last judgment, and consummation of all things."

Since the title of the projected work, *A History of the Work of Redemption*, is identical to the title of Edwards's published sermon series, this might be taken as an indication the unwritten work was simply to be an expansion of the Northampton sermons, preached in the 1730s and published posthumously in 1777. Yet the reference to "a body of divinity in an entire [sic] new method" suggests something quite different from the sermons. Edwards knew very well what "body of divinity" signifies, and in theology this connotes a whole composed of interdependent members. Just as there is no human body, properly speaking, if there are no head, arms, or intestines, so there could be no "body of divinity" without a full treatment of all the major doctrinal loci—doctrine of God, anthropology, Christology, soteriology, ecclesiology, and eschatology. So if we take seriously the phrase "body of divinity," then it becomes clear that the sermons in the published *History of the Work of Redemption* barely begin to address the multifarious topics that Edwards intended to treat in his masterwork.

The phrase "entire new method" qualifies the words "body of divinity," and is then itself amplified with the words "being thrown into the form of an history." Here Edwards casts aside any reserve and plainly declares that he is going to do something unprecedented. The accent falls on the novelty of this new work. If Edwards's intention had been simply to expand and embellish the sermons later published as *A History of the Work of Redemption*, then it is hard to see how he could advance any claim to using an "entire new method." The published *History of the Work of Redemption*, as I have argued elsewhere, sits squarely within the well-established genre of the Christian "universal chronicle," as exemplified by such books as Augustine's *City of God* and Bishop Bossuet's *Discourse on Universal History* (1681). As C. A. Patrides has noted, there were some sixty universal chronicles written in western Europe by the year 1100, and a far greater number appeared in subsequent centuries up until the time of the Enlightenment.[13] It is therefore implausible to think a Christian universal chronicle, even done on a hitherto unrealized scale, would count for Edwards as a work written in "an entire new method." Only an ill-informed person would imagine this sort of sacred chronicle to be a methodological innovation.

When Edwards speaks of it being "thrown into the form of an history," the word "thrown" suggests a process of translation from one idiom to another. Edwards was well acquainted with the typical Protestant "body of divinity"— he told Bellamy that his favorite was Petrus Van Mastrict's *Theoretico-Practica Theologia* (1714)—and its essential structure was nonhistorical. The novelty of the unwritten work was its way of translating—or "throwing"—the traditional content of Protestant theology into an historical form. The timeless truths of the dogmaticians were to find expression in the form of narrative. In summary, then, the letter provides an outline of the proposed work, and from this brief summation it is clear that the "great work" was not to be simply an expansion of the sermon series preached in Northampton. Somehow Edwards intended to translate the content of traditional dogmatic theology into historical or narrative form. But how would he have done this? An examination of the contents of the redemption notebooks, with a sidelong glance at the "Miscellanies," provides a surprising answer: Edwards intended to bridge history and dogma through a pioneering effort in cultural analysis.

The notebooks to the redemption project, as already shown, reflect a very late stage in Edwards's life and show him hard at work in laying a foundation for his "great work." What may be surprising here is the degree to which he is concerned with cultural developments occurring outside the bounds of Christendom. He has much to say regarding "heathen" peoples and their relationship to the redemptive plan of God. He writes also of the "arts and sciences" in Western culture, and concerns himself with topics that seem to have little bearing on theology, for instance, the natural philosophy of Sir Isaac Newton. Cultural developments, he suggests, are a part of God's plan for history. This trend in Edwards's thinking becomes even more evident when one considers Edwards's intensive engagement with non-Christian religions in the later "Miscellanies," as documented in Gerald McDermott's recent book. Since the redemption notebooks are little known, I will cite passages that exemplify Edwards's style of thought.[14] These particular notebooks are regulative rather than substantive. That is, unlike most of the "Miscellanies," the entries are very brief and do not supply a fully developed argument that Edwards could insert into a later work. Instead the notebook entries for the redemption project supply major lines of argument and ultimate conclusions. They are Edwards's notes to himself, and they provide a concise summary of the major themes he envisaged as he prepared to write his *A History of the Work of Redemption*.

In the letter to the trustees, Edwards said nothing about the place of non-Christian religions and cultures within his "great work." The emphasis is on the "body of divinity ... thrown into the form of an history." When one looks at the redemption notebooks, a different picture emerges. It becomes clear that the gospel's "preparation"—a key word for Edwards—occurs among the "heathen" no less than among Israelites. So "the form of an history" that Edwards had in mind was not the traditional chronicle that follows the biblical narratives from Adam until Christ, and then recounts the history of Christianity from the apostles until the present day. Instead Edwards wished to expand this traditional Christian understanding of history with a full-scale consideration and critique of global religions and cultures in theological perspective. Of the three notebooks, the first and longest, "Notebook A," has most of the references to non-Christian religions and cultures. Edwards stresses the universal significance of the gospel as a message for all peoples. The "need" for Christ was apparent in all nations. An entry near the beginning of "Notebook A" makes this clear: "All Things ordered to shew the need of a [S]aviour from sin . . . among the Heathen." Again he writes, almost at the outset of the first notebook: "The Messiahs salvation was to be a general salvation of mankind of all nations. . . . It was not to remove the misery of men in one or two Branche[s] or in one or two nations but in all[.]"[15]

A part of the "preparation" for the gospel among non-Christians consisted in "traditions" that anticipated Christ's coming. This theme is especially clear in the later "Miscellanies," and the redemption notebooks supply a link between the "Miscellanies" entries on this topic and the great unwritten work. Edwards writes: "CONCERNING THE TRADITIONS among the HEATHEN & whether there was not a degree of Inspiration of some of the wise men among the Heathen. & whether those inspired Persons————were not good Men."[16] Evidently Edwards intended to discuss the "heathen traditions" in relation to Christ in his projected *A History of the Work of Redemption*. The final phrase in the quotation is surprising. The Puritan tradition was generally suspicious of supposed "good Men," and so Edwards's openness to finding them outside of Christendom is remarkable.

In "Notebook A," Edwards refers to a number of cultural developments as a part of God's providential plan. The invention of written language is one of these: "When speak[ing] of God then speak of the Invention of Letters as a great gift of God the special design of which was to prepare the way for the promoting the grand Designs of Redemption in the world."[17] One of the more interesting entries relates to Newtonian physics: "The true PHILOSOPHY of Sir Isaac Newton one thing to make way for the un[i]versal setting up of X [i.e., Christ's] kingdom."[18] Edwards's interest in Newtonian philosophy was nothing new, and the sixth volume of *The Works of Jonathan Edwards* provides plenty of evidence that he was engaged with natural philosophy in early life and even sought to find theological meaning through his scientific inquiries.[19] Yet what is striking about the notebook entry is the suggestion that Newtonian physics is a part of God's historical and providential plan. Modern science not only concurs with orthodox theology but also somehow promotes the advancement of Christ's kingdom. How Edwards would have argued to this conclusion is not at all clear, but one can see here the general tendency in "Notebook A" to view all aspects of human culture in relation to a divine redemptive plan. Edwards states his underlying principle in another entry: "All Truth tends to confirm and illustrate divine Truth. How Philosophy the more & more it is brought to perfection the more & more does become a Branch of Divinity. How all the sciences ... so far as they are truly understood and taught are like streams that empty themselves at least [last?] into divinity."[20] At the end of his life Edwards did not, as is sometimes claimed, abandon rational apologetics. Yet he had decided to subordinate rational argumentation to the constraints of historical narrative.

One thought-provoking entry in "Notebook A" pertains to the rise of skepticism in the modern era. While Edwards might simply have condemned this trend, instead he found something positive to say regarding it: "[PRE]SENT TIMES take notice of Gods End [in suf]fering such infidel Heretical sceptical [free]thinking spirit so exceedingly to prevail [in] this age ... How God hereby is preparing the way for the more abundant Manifestation of Truth."[21] Reading this entry at face value, it seems that even secularism is a part of God's providential plan. The word "preparing" is interesting in this context, inasmuch as Edwards typically uses it when there is some continuity or carryover between a religious or cultural development and the work of redemption. Thus certain "heathen traditions" are a "preparation" for the gospel in that they anticipate gospel teachings on the necessity of atonement, the doctrine of the Trinity, the indwelling Holy Spirit, etc. The later "Miscellanies" are especially rich in entries that discuss this sort of "preparation" for the gospel. Yet the question remains: What could Edwards have meant in saying that a "sceptical [free]thinking spirit" was "preparing" for an "abundant Manifestation of Truth"? The more conventional reading would be to see modern skepticism in contrast to gospel truth—the darkness that accentuates the vivid light that breaks forth during the eschaton. Yet another interpretation is possible. Skepticism itself might be a part of God's purpose. Edwards's use of the word "preparing" suggests that this latter reading is more likely. Elsewhere I have argued that the published *History of Redemption* sermons exhibit two distinct ways of construing the flow of history, a "contrast motif" and a "preparation motif," and generally this notebook entry seems to fit into the latter category.[22] Using Edwards's common image of "gradual" or stepwise progress, one could say that the redemptive work of God will build on Western secularism as well as "heathen traditions" outside of Christendom. One is struck by the analogy between Edwards's thinking and Dietrich Bonhoeffer's *Letters and Papers from Prison*. The brief statement in Edwards's notebook suggests that he, like Bonhoeffer, was struggling to find a way of understanding secularism not simply as sin and delusion but as an aspect of God's work in the world. Both Edwards and Bonhoeffer were prepared to undertake this sort of theological experiment, which, in Bonhoeffer's case, subjected the late thinker to a great deal of misunderstanding during the era of the so-called death of God theology during the 1960s.[23]

The last several hundred "Miscellanies" attest to the cultural turn in Edwards's later theologizing. John Wilson refers to the "Miscellanies" as "that storehouse of nuggets which he squirreled away against his future needs,"[24] and the content of many of the "Miscellanies" indicates that the writing of these entries was a part of Edwards's preparation for writing *A History of the Work of Redemption*. Since the final "Miscellanies" are still en route to publication in the Yale edition, their content is largely unknown except to scholarly specialists who have journeyed to the Beinecke Library. Yet those familiar with the transcriptions of the later "Miscellanies" will have been struck by the dozens and dozens of entries on non-Christian religions. Gerald McDermott's recent book provides a first attempt to map this terra incognita.[25] "At the time of his death," writes McDermott, Edwards "was still unsure how to explain fully the abundance of revelation given to the heathen."[26] His position regarding non-Christian religions cannot be reduced to a common denominator, but contains a number of distinct elements, as described by McDermott. Individual "pagans" may have received direct divine inspiration, non-Christian religions exhibited foreshadowings or "types" of biblical religion, and the common truths among world religions were due to traditions passed down by the founders of the nations, beginning with Noah's sons. In a separate line of argument, Edwards taught that Satan counterfeited true religion among the pagans, but God inverted the devil's work. The demand for human sacrifice—a diabolical deceit—helped to prepare the nations for the gospel. Yet Edwards provides differing theological appraisals of the non-Christian religions. Greece and Rome, along with China, receive favorable evaluation, while Islam and Native American religions come under censure.[27] Edwards drew heavily from the writings of "Chevalier" [Andrew Michael] Ramsay (1685–1743), and was fascinated by his assertions that the Chinese looking forward to a coming Messiah and that monotheism and even belief in a divine Trinity were widely diffused throughout the world's cultures. "By the end of his life," McDermott claims, "Edwards was entertaining conceptions that earlier Reformed thinkers would have abhorred."[28] Regarding salvation for those who had not heard of Israel's God or of Jesus, Edwards's position is unclear in the "Miscellanies," though McDermott argues that Edwards at least entertained the possibility that such persons could be saved.[29]

When one brings together the three elements of textual evidence considered here—the letter to the trustees, the redemption notebooks, and the later "Miscellanies"—a number of conclusions are in order. Immediately one is struck by the differences between the description of the "great work" in the letter to the trustees and what may be inferred from both the redemption notebooks and the later "Miscellanies." The letter underscores the novelty of Edwards's projected work, and yet its newness is explained in terms of methodology and not content. It is written with an "entire new method," says Edwards, "being thrown into the form of an history." Edwards speaks of it as a "body of divinity," and this traditional designation suggests that the content of the work was to be traditional even if the method was not. Yet when one looks at the redemption notebooks and the later "Miscellanies" it becomes apparent that the content of Edwards's *A History of the Work of Redemption* was to diverge from that of the standard Protestant "body of divinity." Perhaps Edwards judged that his brief letter to the trustees was not the proper context within which to expound the varied aspects of his revolutionary new approach to theology, and so mentioned only one of the innovations of the projected work, namely, its historical form.

The letter to the trustees presents a dilemma that cannot be resolved through a consideration of the letter alone. The issue is how he intended to transfer or translate the content of traditional theology into the form of historical narrative. In resolving this issue, the later notebooks are invaluable. Taken together, the redemption notebooks and the final "Miscellanies" indicate that Edwards was moving toward a kind of cultural analysis that included both empirical and normative aspects. He was not interested in Chinese or Greco-Roman history per se, but instead he wanted to scrutinize and evaluate these cultures theologically and assess the extent to which they presented an analogy to, anticipation of, or preparation for the coming of Christ. Likewise, Edwards's approach to the history of redemption during the church era also involved an evaluation in light of certain invariant theological principles. As "Notebook C" makes clear, Edwards was sharply critical of the Roman Catholic tradition, which he judged more harshly than many developments in the so-called heathen world. The point, though, is that he used a common approach for non-Christian societies and for the history of Christianity. He was developing a method that shuttled back and forth between fact and evaluation, description and assessment. Since Edwards's method followed the basic contours of the world's great civilizations—Greco-Roman, medieval Catholic, Islamic, Chinese, modern European, etc.—it is appropriate to speak of this as a cultural turn in Edwards's later thinking. And a part of that cultural turn was to look deeply into the increasingly secular society of his day to find God's presence and activity in unexpected places, such as Newtonian physics and skeptical philosophy. Culture, for the later Edwards, was the link between history and theology.

People tend to forget that the Fundamentalist-Modernist conflict in its final and divisive phase among the Presbyterians centered on the missionaries.[30] The conservatives, led by J. Gresham Machen, suspected that many missionaries sent overseas by their own denominations were failing to preach the gospel to non-Christians and instead had thrust themselves into various forms of humanitarian and educational endeavor. Fuel was added to the fire by the publication of William Ernest Hocking's *Re-Thinking Missions: A Laymen's Inquiry after One Hundred Years* (1932), a report that urged Christians not to claim exclusive validity for their own tradition but rather to work together with adherents of other religions in the pursuit of a unified religious truth. The Hocking report received a glowing review from Pearl Buck, the daughter of Presbyterian missionaries to China, author of the soon-to-be bestseller *The Good Earth* (1931), and a post-Christian: "I feel no need for any other faith than my faith in human beings."[31] Concerned over the Hocking report, disturbed by Pearl Buck's influence, and unconvinced by the Presbyterian Board of Foreign Missions's disavowals of Hocking's views, J. Gresham Machen launched an Independent Board of Presbyterian Foreign Missions "to promote truly Biblical and truly Presbyterian mission work."[32] He was censured by the Presbyterian denomination in 1934 and then suspended from ministry in 1936. This led to the formation of a new denomination, the Presbyterian Church in America—now the Orthodox Presbyterian Church.

From the standpoint of those whose outlook crystallized during the 1920s as "Fundamentalism," many of the missionaries were failing in their central task of preaching Christ crucified and calling men and women to repentance, faith, and conversion.[33] From the standpoint of those who became known as "Modernists," the objections of the conservatives exhibited a naivety regarding missionary practice and a refusal to enter into cultural engagement. Not everything in non-Christian societies was to be rejected as anti-Christian, and a proper appreciation of local cultures was a prerequisite to a deeper communication of the Christian message among non-Christians. At the core of this debate was a disagreement over how the gospel relates to cultures. Many conservatives did not see that it was necessary for the Euro-American missionary to link the Christian message to preexisting elements within non-Christian cultures. The gospel created its own point of contact within the hearts and minds of its listeners, and the missionary did not have to deliberate over how he or she might make the message culturally relevant. These conservatives objected to theological liberals who carried their cultural sensitivity to the point that they failed to present their hearers with any sort of spiritual challenge or call for transformation.

It is interesting to consider what might have happened in the nineteenth and early twentieth centuries if Edwards had left behind not only *The Life of David Brainerd* as a stimulus to missionary effort but *A History of the Work of Redemption* as an instructive example of cultural analysis. Edwards, as McDermott notes, may have pursued the study of non-Christian religions more intensively than any other person in colonial America,[34] and the writing of the masterwork would have carried Edwards yet further into the study of world religions and cultures. In all likelihood the specifics of Edwards's cultural critique in *A History of the Work of Redemption* would now be subject to withering criticism. When one examines the content of the later "Miscellanies," it is clear that Edwards's sources of information regarding non-Christian religions and cultures are woefully deficient by contemporary standards, and very little of what he gleaned from Theophilus Gale, "Chevalier" Ramsay, and other such sources would pass muster today among scholars of world history and comparative religions. But perhaps this is not the point. The power and influence of Edwards's masterwork would have endured simply because he attempted such a thing. And others might have been inspired to do likewise. The great sociologist Max Weber continues to exert widespread influence today through his massive cross-cultural analyses in *Economy and Society* (1922), and this despite the frequent criticisms he has drawn from regional specialists on China, India, ancient Israel, and medieval Europe. What made Weber exceptional was his thorough familiarity with a vast quantity of concrete empirical data, combined with an ability to formulate incisive theoretical principles on a high level of generality. Even those who reject many of Weber's specific judgments regarding particular cultures are inspired by his example and pursue sociological inquiry in the Weberian style and spirit.[35] From the evidence examined, it appears that Edwards's *A History of the Work of Redemption* was to be something like Weber's work in its global scope, attention to empirical detail, and theoretical elaborations. Unlike Weber's *Economy and Society*, the governing principles of the work were to be theological rather than sociological, and yet, like Weber's work, *A History of the Work of Redemption* was to work out a set of correspondences between empirical data and high-level generalizations.

Had Edwards not received the deadly inoculation shot, it seems likely that his "great work" would have provided his intellectual and cultural heirs with a model of cultural engagement that was rather different from any that they had encountered. On the one hand, Edwards was strictly orthodox in holding to a Calvinist conception of human sin and divine grace, together with the fundamental doctrines concerning God and Christ that he shared with Christians outside of the Reformed tradition. Yet, on the other hand, the unmistakable tendency of the later notebooks was toward an appreciation of God's presence and activity among non-Christian or "heathen" societies. This could arguably have had a direct influence on missionary practice in the nineteenth century among those conservative Protestants who were most likely to read his books, venerate his memory, and emulate his example. Since the later Edwards emphasized the congruence between non-Christian religions and the biblical message, Edwards's missionary disciples might have evolved a style of communication that was less confrontational and more dialogical. During the nineteenth century, J. Hudson Taylor's missionary colleagues regarded him as an oddball for adopting traditional Mandarin dress when he sought to evangelize the Chinese. In contrast, Matteo Ricci and a number of other seventeenth-century Jesuits approached Chinese culture with an erudition and cultural sensitivity that was rarely matched by Protestant missionaries until the twentieth century. Under the influence of Edwards's unwritten masterwork, there might have been a Protestant Ricci or two during the nineteenth-century heyday of Protestant foreign missions.

Toward the close of the nineteenth century, American theologians struggled with the question of where to find God in the midst of an emerging industrial and urban civilization, and this bore fruit in the Social Gospel message of Washington Gladden and Walter Rauschenbusch. One of the key disputes between the Social Gospel and its opponents concerned individual conversion and social change: Which of these two was more fundamental? In its early stages the movement sought to hold onto both the individualistic and the corporate aspects of the Christian message. In his 1875 speech on behalf of the Christian Labor Union, Jesse H. Jones spoke of "regeneration for the individual, reorganization for the community." Toward the end of the 1800s, there was increasingly strong rhetoric against religious individualism and in favor of what Newman Smyth—a Congregational minister in New Haven—called "a truer view of the solidarity of the race." By the time of the First World War, Walter Rauschenbusch was calling for "the fundamental step of repentance and conversion" for big businesses, which was "to give up monopoly power."[36] The possible relationship between Edwards's legacy and the Social Gospel movement is a complex issue, and there seem to be some basic differences between the two regarding the respective roles of human effort and divine initiative in inaugurating God's kingdom. Yet if Edwards's corpus of writings had included the monumental *A History of the Work of Redemption* as well as *Thoughts on the Revival* and *Religious Affections,* the debate over individual conversion and social change might have taken on a different character. Edwards's revival writings were the greatest sustained treatment of the theology of conversion by an American thinker, and the "great work" in its cultural analysis would probably have examined social change as an aspect of God's redemptive plan. A point of contact with the Social Gospel lay in Edwards's attentiveness to cultural trends as signs of God's presence and activity. The later notebooks suggest that Edwards may have been moving toward a more immanental understanding of God, like that of the Social Gospel thinkers.

An important question regarding *A History of the Work of Redemption* is what place Edwards would have assigned to America within the grand narrative. Despite Edwards's much celebrated and much maligned comments in 1743 regarding the possible commencement of the millennium in America, he seems to have distanced himself more and more from this statement in his later years.[37] His perspective became progressively more global. McDermott writes: "Edwards was not the provincial chauvinist he has been made out to be.... America for Edwards usually deserved condemnation, not celebration. The further he progressed in his career, the more distance he put between his country and the Kingdom of God."[38] In the three redemption notebooks, there is only one entry that specifically addresses America's role in God's plan, and what Edwards writes there is rather subdued: "I would humbly hope that I may reckon the SETTLEMENT OF NEW-ENGLAND as one Great Thing done to prepare the way for the introducing of Gospel Light into the American World."[39] He does not argue that America is a light to the nations, or that the eyes of other peoples are upon us. He merely asserts that New England is a means for the propagation of the gospel into other parts of the New World.

The muted nationalism of Edwards's later writings stands in contrast to the religious chauvinism so common in the later American tradition. Edwards's own grandson, the first Timothy Dwight, anonymously published an encomium to

America in 1771: "O land supremely blest! / To thee 'tis given / To taste the choicest joys of bounteous heaven; / Thy rising Glory shall expand its rays, / And lands and times unknown rehearse thine endless praise."[40] Here America, rather than God, becomes the object of "endless praise," and one wonders how Edwards might have reacted to this. During the late nineteenth century, the idea of America's providential role in God's plan became closely interwoven with the racial and ethnic notions of Anglo-Saxonism exemplified in Josiah Strong's *Our Country* (1885) and *The New Era* (1893). Strong intoned: "My plea is not, Save America for America's sake, but, Save America for the world's sake."[41] A widespread acceptance of Strong's way of thinking paved the way for war with Spain in 1898. Ultimately, the racial theories of Anglo-Saxonism, the rise of jingoistic nationalism, and the self-righteous style in foreign affairs did much to discredit providentialist thinking among American Christians in the twentieth century. The turn-of-the-century jingoists made it a lot less fashionable to invoke God on behalf of one's interpretation of history. The later Edwards did not seem to think, as Strong did, that the salvation of America would entail the salvation of the world. Instead the uncompleted *A History of the Work of Redemption* was designed to identify a particular work of divine providence in each particular society or culture. The "preparation" for the gospel among the Chinese was specific to the Chinese, and so on with all the other nations and cultures. There could be no single point of transmission for the gospel throughout the world, because the work of redemption was culturally specific to each people and region.

If we interpret the Fundamentalist movement of the twentieth century as an expression of militant antimodernism, then Edwards's efforts to identify and characterize God's activity within the seemingly secular spheres of culture—like Newtonian physics—might have helped to foster a theological style that was nonfundamentalistic. Edwards was reluctant to classify any major cultural development in Western society as wholly and irredeemably misguided. As noted above, Edwards's "Notebook A" contains one tantalizing statement in which he suggests that even modern skepticism is in some way "preparing" for the reception of God's truth. In contradistinction, the theological polemics of the Fundamentalists rested on black-and-white rhetoric, like that employed by the president of the World Christian Fundamentals Association who accused the liberals of using "that weasel method of sucking the meaning out of words, and then presenting the empty husks in an attempt to palm them off as giving the Christian faith a new and another interpretation."[42] On the other hand, Edwards's animosity toward Roman Catholicism showed no signs of abating during his later years, and this may require an adjustment of perspective regarding Edwards's commitment to cultural engagement and his search for common ground with those who believed differently than he did. The irony is that Edwards was willing to acknowledge spiritual truth and moral goodness among idolaters and pagans but not among Roman Catholics, who worshiped Jesus Christ and shared many of his basic theological convictions.

Edwards's possible legacy, as discussed, and Edwards's actual legacy differ in a fundamental way. His closest followers and advocates during the nineteenth century were primarily preoccupied with his arguments in favor of Calvinist doctrine, while the texts examined here—the letter to the trustees, the redemption notebooks, and the later "Miscellanies"—are virtually silent on this topic. Since *A History of the Work of Redemption* was to be a "body of divinity," it does not seem likely that the arguments of *Freedom of the Will* and *Original Sin* would have been left out of the great synthesis. On the other hand, the notebooks that provide the best clues as to the character of the unwritten work suggest that Calvinist doctrine was to play only a subordinate role. Mark Noll has scrutinized the nineteenth-century American thinkers who invoked Edwards's name on behalf of their ideas, and he concludes that the Princeton theologians were more accurate in their assessment of Edwards's doctrinal positions, while the New Englanders at Yale and Andover Seminary better understood the open-ended and exploratory character of Edwards's thinking. Yet the issues debated between the two groups centered almost entirely on theological anthropology—the freedom or bondage of the will, the imputation of Adam's sin, the presence or absence of a sin nature underlying individual acts of sin, and the defining marks of virtuous actions. *Freedom of the Will* drew no less than twenty-nine serious attempts at refutation during the nineteenth century, and other works were written to defend it. *The Nature of True Virtue* also engendered debate. The Princeton theologians criticized its "eccentric" theory of ethics, while those at Yale sought to defend it.[43] Among a less scholarly and more popular readership, Edwards continued to be known as the leading interpreter of colonial revivalism, and every American interpreter or practitioner of revivalism from the 1740s onward had to grapple with Edwards. Yet, in the nineteenth-century discussion of revivalism, just as in the Yale-Princeton debates, the concern was with Edwards's theological anthropology. Missing from the nineteenth-century debates and discussions was an awareness or appreciation for the history of redemption project to which Edwards was privately devoting his energies after he had completed *Freedom of the Will* and *Original*

Sin. Perhaps the surest assertion one can make regarding Edwards's theological legacy is that its center of gravity would have shifted toward historical and cultural issues and away from anthropological concerns if Edwards had lived to complete *A History of the Work of Redemption.*

As one gets further from Edwards's time, it becomes harder to make connections between Edwards's work and that of later thinkers. Yet it is quite clear that the twin themes of culture and narrative—both central to the projected "great work"—emerged as major topics in twentieth-century American theology. The theme of narrative went underground in New Haven for about two centuries, and then returned with a vengeance. During the 1930s and 1940s, when Perry Miller at Harvard was rehabilitating the study of American Puritanism and Edwards's place in the national culture, H. Richard Niebuhr at Yale was also reading Edwards. But while Miller's agenda was historical, Niebuhr's was theological, or rather ethical-historical-theological.[44] In the preface to *The Kingdom of God in America* (1937), Niebuhr spoke of the need to carry forward Edwards's *History of the Work of Redemption* and offered his book as a first step in that direction.[45] Niebuhr's *The Meaning of Revelation* (1941), with its stress on narrative, had a pervasive influence among faculty at Yale Divinity School, including Hans Frei, George Lindbeck, David Kelsey, and others. The narrative theology that took hold at Yale during the 1980s forged a union between theological reasoning and narrative form. While Karl Barth had something to do with this trend, it was H. Richard Niebuhr's reinterpretation of Edwards that served as the likely point of departure for the so-called new Yale School.[46] Regarding the theological theme of culture, the most prominent twentieth-century name is that of Paul Tillich. Despite the differences, far too numerous to indicate, between Edwards's and Tillich's approaches to culture,[47] both sought to identify an implicit divine presence in the "arts and sciences" of Western civilization. Tillich stated in a famous dictum that "religion is the substance of culture, and culture is the form of religion." Toward the end of his life, and following a visit to Japan, Tillich became increasingly interested in non-Western cultures and non-Christian religions, and so his "theology of culture" was gradually becoming a "theology of culture*s.*" If he had had the opportunity to rewrite his theology, Tillich indicated, he would have given a central place in it to a theology of world religions.[48] When one considers the unfinished *History of the Work of Redemption* alongside these mid- to late-twentieth-century trends in American theology, the effect is striking. Perry Miller, despite his hyperbolic claims for Edwards's modernity, may have been correct in insisting that Edwards anticipated a number of major intellectual movements long before they arrived. Had Edwards written and published his masterwork, these trends might have come sooner and stronger, with unforeseeable consequences for American Christianity.[49]

Some contrary-to-fact conditional questions are even more elusive than others. Yet one can pose them anyway: If Edwards had not received the fatal inoculation, would he have lived long enough to complete his projected work? Or if he had accepted the position at the College of New Jersey, would he have suffered the fate of all too many an academic administrator, who dreams of writing a great book but does not have time in which to do it? And what sort of influence would Edwards have exercised as the president of a fledgling college, destined to take its place as a leader in American education? And what would have been the result if Edwards's tenure at the College of New Jersey had delayed or prevented John Witherspoon from becoming his successor as president? Would Witherspoon's absence have altered the entire intellectual tradition at Princeton College, and perhaps throughout early America?[50] To answer these sorts of questions is to leap into empty space. This essay has followed, I hope, a safer course. The documents examined above show that Edwards in his later years was in the midst of an intellectual transition or "cultural turn," and that his projected unwritten work would have exemplified this new way of thinking and theologizing. This much can be reliably asserted from the sources at our disposal. The legacy that Edwards might have bequeathed, had he written and published his magnum opus, lies in the hazy realm of pure possibilities.

NOTES

1. The philosophical discussion of counterfactuals is quite complicated, as shown in R. S. Walters, "Contrary-to-Fact Conditional," in *The Encyclopedia of Philosophy*, ed. Paul Edwards, 8 vols. (New York: Macmillan/London: Collier Macmillan, 1967), 2: 212–16.

2. The letter is found in Jonathan Edwards, *Letters and Personal Writings*, ed. George S. Claghorn, *The Works of Jonathan Edwards*, vol. 16 (New Haven and London: Yale Univ. Press, 1998), 725–30.

3. John F. Wilson, "Appendix B: Jonathan Edwards's Notebooks for A History of the Work of Redemption," in Jonathan Edwards, *A History of the Work of Redemption*, ed. John F. Wilson, *The Works of Jonathan Edwards*, vol. 9 (New Haven and London: Yale Univ. Press, 1989), 543–56.

4. Gerald R. McDermott, *Jonathan Edwards Confronts the Gods: Christian Theology, Enlightenment Religion, and Non-Christian Faiths* (New York: Oxford Univ. Press, 2000).

5. Michael J. McClymond, *Encounters with God: An Approach to the Theology of Jonathan Edwards* (New York: Oxford Univ. Press, 1998), 101–4.

6. The unpublished "Catalogue" may not be a reliable indication of the books that Edwards actually read, but it shows what books were of interest to him. On the second page of the "Catalogue" we find an entry regarding an unnamed work, "a new comparison of all Religions with the Xtian, that I have seen at New Haven" (cited in Thomas H. Johnson, "Jonathan Edwards's Background of Reading," in *Publications of the Colonial Society of Massachusetts* 28 [1931]: 204).

7. Kenneth P. Minkema, "The Other Unfinished 'Great Work': Jonathan Edwards, Messianic Prophecy, and 'The Harmony of the Old and New Testaments,'" in *Jonathan Edwards's Writings: Text, Context, Interpretation*, ed. Stephen J. Stein (Bloomington and Indianapolis: Indiana Univ. Press, 1996), 52–65.

8. Wilson, "Appendix B," in Edwards, *Works* 9:546–47, 550–55.

9. Ibid., 9:553, 555.

10. Edwards, *Works*, 16:727–28.

11. I am indebted to Professor Thomas Schafer for pointing out in conversation that Edwards customarily used Latinate English terms and phrases with a precise sense of their original meaning in Latin. Thus "arbitrary" does not signify "capricious" but rather something "depending on the will" (Lat. *arbitrium*, "will"). "Gradual," in reference to redemptive history, means "occurring in steps" (Lat. *gradus*, "step"). So "*summum* and *ultimum*" denote that which is "highest" and that which is "furthest" or "last." A discussion of "chief" or "highest ends" and "ultimate ends" occurs at the beginning of *End of Creation*, and the distinction plays a role throughout the argument of the treatise (Jonathan Edwards, *Ethical Writings*, ed. Paul Ramsey, *The Works of Jonathan Edwards*, vol. 8 [New Haven: Yale Univ. Press, 1989], 405). Hence it is plausible to suppose that the phrase in the letter, "*summum* and *ultimum*," provides a link between the unwritten masterwork and the published *End of Creation*.

12. McClymond, *Encounters*, 110.

13. Ibid., 66.

14. I am indebted to Dr. Kenneth Minkema, executive editor of *The Works of Jonathan Edwards*, for supplying me with transcriptions of Edwards's redemption notebooks, cited below as "Notebook A," "Notebook B," and "Notebook C."

15. Edwards, "Notebook A," 1–2. The same idea crops up repeatedly in the first notebook. In "Notebook A," 107, Edwards intends to "shew also how all Things among the Heathen shewed the need of such a Saviour to save the Nations from their sins."

16. Ibid., 4.

17. Ibid.

18. Ibid.

19. See Jonathan Edwards, *Scientific and Philosophy Writings,* ed. Wallace E. Anderson, *The Works of Jonathan Edwards,* vol. 6 (New Haven and London: Yale Univ. Press, 1980).

20. Edwards, "Notebook A," 8.

21. Ibid., 19–20.

22. McClymond, *Encounters,* 71–73.

23. "Notebook B" and "Notebook C" are less pertinent to the argument presented here. "B" is largely devoted to the sort of biblically based and typological reasoning found in the published *History of Redemption* sermons. "C" is most devoted to anti-Catholic polemics. It contains numerous historical extracts from Archibald Bower's *History of Popery* (7 vols., London: n.p., 1748–1766) treating such matters as the rise of priestly celibacy, episcopal and papal authority, the veneration of saints and images, the taking of oaths in the name of saints and holy objects, purgatory, and the collection of church taxes.

24. Wilson, "Appendix B," in Edwards, *Works,* 9:554.

25. See my review of Gerald R. McDermott, *Jonathan Edwards Confronts the Gods: Christian Theology, Enlightenment Religion, and Non-Christian Faiths* (New York: Oxford Univ. Press, 2000), in *The Journal of Religion* 81 (2001), 478–80.

26. McDermott, *Jonathan Edwards Confronts the Gods,* 224; see also 206.

27. Ibid., 176–93 (Greece and Rome), 207–16 (China), 166–75 (Islam), and 194–206 (Native American religions).

28. Ibid., 221.

29. Ibid., 4n. 3, 9, 143–45, 193, 216.

30. See the recent in-depth article by Bradley J. Longfield, "For Church and Country: The Fundamentalist-Modernist Conflict in the Presbyterian Church," *Journal of Presbyterian History* 78 (2000): 35–50; and John R. Fitzmier and Randall Balmer, "A Poultice for the Bite of the Cobra: The Hocking Report and Presbyterian Missions in the Middle Decades of the Twentieth Century," in *The Diversity of Discipleship: The Presbyterians and Twentieth-Century Christian Witness,* ed. Milton J. Coulter, John M. Mulder, and Louis B. Weeks (Louisville: Westminster John Knox Press, 1991), 105–25.

31. Pearl Buck, writing in 1939, quoted at http://www.kirjasto.sci.fi/pearlbuc.htm; 30 March 2002.

32. J. Gresham Machen, *Christianity Today* 4 (June 1933): 10–13; cited in Longfield, "For Church and Country," 47.

33. The Hocking Report said that "the time has come to set the educational and other philanthropic aspects of mission work free from organized responsibility to the work of conscious and direct evangelism." Missionaries were to serve "largely without any preaching, to cooperate whole-heartedly with non-Christian agencies for social improvement" (William Ernest Hocking, *Re-Thinking Missions: A Laymen's Inquiry*

after One Hundred Years [New York: Harper and Brothers, 1932], 326; cited in Fitzmier and Balmer, "Poultice," 108).

34. McDermott, *Jonathan Edwards Confronts the Gods,* 6.

35. For a contemporary appraisal of one aspect of Weber's legacy, see David Noel Freedman and Michael J. McClymond, eds., *The Rivers of Paradise: Moses, Buddha, Confucius, Jesus, and Muhammed as Religious Founders* (Grand Rapids, Mich.: Eerdmans, 2001), including my conclusion, "Prophet or Loss?: Reassessing Max Weber's Theory of Religious Leadership" (613–58), and the four responses by scholars of Judaism, Buddhism, Confucianism, and Islam (659–84).

36. Jesse Henry Jones, *Equity* 2, no. 5 (June 1875): 17; Newman Smyth, *Old Faiths in New Light* (New York: Scribner, 1879), 141); Walter Rauschenbusch, *A Theology for the Social Gospel* (New York: Macmillan, 1917), 117; cited in Charles Howard Hopkins, *The Rise of the Social Gospel in American Protestantism, 1865–1915* (1940; reprint, New Haven: Yale Univ. Press, 1967), 47, 62, 232.

37. See the text and discussion in McClymond, *Encounters,* 74–75.

38. Gerald McDermott, *One Holy and Happy Society: The Public Theology of Jonathan Edwards* (University Park: Pennsylvania State Univ. Press, 1992), viii.

39. Edwards, "Notebook A," 35.

40. Quoted in Ernest Lee Tuveson, *Redeemer Nation: The Idea of America's Millennial Role* (1968; reprint, Chicago: Univ. of Chicago Press, 1980), 104.

41. Strong is quoted in Sydney Ahlstrom, *A Religious History of the American People* (New Haven: Yale Univ. Press, 1972), 733–34.

42. Quoted in Walter Lippmann, *A Preface to Morals* (1929; reprint, New York: Macmillan, 1935), 30–31.

43. Mark Noll, "Jonathan Edwards and Nineteenth-Century Theology," in *Jonathan Edwards and the American Experience,* ed. Nathan O. Hatch and Harry S. Stout (New York: Oxford Univ. Press, 1988), 260–87.

44. H. Richard Niebuhr spoke of Edwards in a letter to his son in 1958: "I am a petty believer alongside him and an undisciplined one. But I feel nearer to him as theologian than to any others except for Luther & Calvin & maybe Augustine. Except for the problem of demythologizing his hell I can take him almost straight" (Richard R. Niebuhr, "Foreword," in H. Richard Niebuhr, *Theology, History, and Culture: Major Unpublished Writings,* ed. William Stacy Johnson [New Haven and London: Yale Univ. Press, 1996], x). See also in this volume Niebuhr's 1958 address, "The Anachronism of Jonathan Edwards," 123–33.

45. "Hence my greatest hope is that such a work as this may serve 'even as a stepping stone' to the work of some American Augustine who will write a *City of God* that will trace the story of the eternal city in its relations to modern civilization instead of to

ancient Rome, or of Jonathan Edwards *redivivus* who will bring down to our own time the *History of the Work of Redemption*" (H. Richard Niebuhr, *The Kingdom of God in America* [New York: Harper and Brothers, 1937], xvi.)

46. H. Richard Niebuhr emphasized the importance of narrative in the chapter "The Story of Our Life" in *The Meaning of Revelation* (New York: Macmillan, 1941), 43–90, and called for a universal history of God's redeeming work: "The Christian community must turn ... from the revelation of the universal God in a limited history to the recognition of his rule and providence in all events of all times and communities" (87). Continuing Niebuhr's legacy is Hans Frei's *The Eclipse of Biblical Narrative: A Study in Eighteenth and Nineteenth Century Hermeneutics* (New Haven and London: Yale Univ. Press, 1974). Essays reflecting the major trends in narrative theology are contained in Stanley Hauerwas and L. Gregory Jones, eds., *Why Narrative?* (Grand Rapids, Mich.: Eerdmans, 1989). Karl Barth's approach to narrative is treated in David Ford, *Barth and God's Story: Biblical Narrative and the Theological Method of Karl Barth in the "Church Dogmatics"* (Frankfurt am Main, Bern: Peter Lang, 1981). Regarding recent theology at Yale, see Mark I. Wallace, *The Second Naivete: Barth, Ricoeur, and the New Yale Theology,* 2nd ed. (Macon, Ga.: Mercer Univ. Press, 1995).

47. A key difference between Edwards and Tillich concerns the nature of divine revelation, which Tillich held as a universal feature of all human experiences and cultures, and which Edwards saw as specific to particular times, places, and persons. See Tillich's essay, "The Significance of the History of Religions for the Systematic Theologian," in *The Future of Religions,* ed. Jerald C. Brauer (New York: Harper and Row, 1966), 80–94. H. Richard Niebuhr was closer in spirit to Edwards when he wrote that "revelation" is an "intelligible event which makes all other events intelligible" (*The Meaning of Revelation,* 93). Both Edwards and Niebuhr sought not only to recount biblical history but also to use the narratives and ideas of the Bible to interpret world history generally. Edwards, Niebuhr, and Niebuhr's successor, Hans Frei, were all tied to the texts and themes of the Bible in a way that Tillich was not.

48. On Tillich's theology of Western culture, see his early German work, translated as *The System of the Sciences According to Objects and Methods,* translated with introduction by Paul Wiebe (Lewisburg, Pa.: Bucknell Univ. Press, 1981), and *Theology of Culture,* ed. Robert C. Kimball (New York: Oxford Univ. Press, 1959). On Tillich's approach to non-Christian religions, see the aforementioned essay "The Significance of the History of Religions for the Systematic Theologian," and *Christianity and the Encounter of the World Religions* (New York: Columbia Univ. Press, 1963).

49. One line of inquiry that arises out of Edwards's cultural turn is the following: If Edwards had intensively pursued the study of non-Christian religions and cultures in writing *A History of the Work of Redemption,* might this have gradually reshaped

Edwards's theological method in some fashion? Would he have begun to see theology as conditioned by cultural context and qualified by human limitations and biases? If this had occurred, then Edwards would have shared in the opportunities and dilemmas of many late-nineteenth-century and twentieth-century theologians.

50. I am indebted to John F. Wilson, of Princeton University, for suggesting some of these truly imponderable conditional questions in personal correspondence with the author. My thanks are also due to him for reading through an earlier draft of this essay, and making numerous helpful suggestions.

Remembering Jonathan Edwards's Ministry to Children

Catherine A. Brekus

During the late 1820s, Sereno Dwight, the great-grandson of Jonathan Edwards, decided to publish a ten-volume collection of Edwards's collected works. At a time when liberal Protestants attacked Calvinism as arbitrary and cruel, Dwight wanted to portray Edwards as a devout minister who had been persecuted for defending religious truth. But when Dwight reread *Some Thoughts Concerning the Present Revival,* he found a passage that troubled him. In a paragraph defending the doctrine of original sin, Edwards had written: "As innocent as children seem to be to us, if they are out of Christ, they are not so in God's sight, but are young vipers, and are infinitely more hateful than vipers, and are in a most miserable condition, as well as grown persons." Although Dwight deeply admired Edwards's theology, he feared that these words might heighten anti-Calvinist sentiment or harm his great-grandfather's reputation. Deciding to make a small (but momentous) editorial change, he omitted Edwards's original description of children as "young vipers." His new, edited version sounded distinctly softer: "Innocent as children seem to be to us, yet, if they are out of Christ, they are not so in the sight of God; but are in a most miserable condition." The Edwards who could calmly describe children as "young vipers" was not the man whom he wanted to remember.[1]

In hindsight, Dwight had good reason to edit Edwards's writings. During the nineteenth century, Edwards's critics used his harsh language to ridicule Calvinism for its "barbarism." In 1890, in a particularly biting critique, Oliver Wendell Holmes painted a vivid portrait of a stern, grim-faced Edwards telling his son that God despised him. "I can imagine Jonathan Edwards in the nursery with his three-year-old child upon his knee," he wrote. "The child looks up to his face and says to him,—'Papa, nurse tells me that you say God hates me worse than He hates one of those horrid ugly snakes that crawl all round. Does God hate me so?'" A hardhearted Edwards replies, "Alas! my child, it is but too true. So long as you are out of Christ you are as a viper, and worse than a viper, in his sight." When Sarah Edwards ("one of the loveliest of women and sweetest of mothers") comes into the nursery, she finds her child crying. "What is the matter, my darling?" she asks. His reply is devastating: "Papa has been telling me that God hates me worse than a snake." Holmes ended this vignette by assuring his readers that "Poor, gentle, poetical, sensitive, spiritual, almost celestial Mrs. Jonathan Edwards" would never have allowed such "poison to rankle in the tender soul of her darling."[2] Writing at a time when middle-class Protestants elevated mothers as patient, nurturing, and even "celestial," Holmes simply could not imagine that Sarah Edwards had subscribed to her husband's outrageous doctrine of infant depravity.

In the new, humanitarian climate of nineteenth-century America, few Protestants—whether liberal or conservative—wanted to preserve Edwards's unflinching view of children's sinfulness. While liberal Unitarians condemned Edwards for his "false theology," his Calvinist supporters tried to ignore, repress, or modify his beliefs in order to make them appear less cruel.[3] Ironically, even the clergymen who fought over his mantle found it hard to stomach his image of children as "young vipers." In the hundred years after his death, they waged an ultimately futile battle to reconcile their softer, more sentimental view of childhood with his vision of God's utter sovereignty. To be sure, Edwards's theology of children was more complicated and ambivalent than they seem to have recognized: he not only saw children as sinners, but as potential saints. Yet as eighteenth- and nineteenth-century Americans became increasingly committed to the virtues of compassion, benevolence, and sympathy, almost no one wanted to remember his ideas about children. By examining how Edwards's theology was remembered (and distorted), we can see how deeply Calvinism was challenged and transformed by its encounter with the Enlightenment.

Edwards's Theology of Children

If someone could travel back in time to tell Jonathan Edwards that American Calvinists would eventually reject his view of children's depravity as cruel and unfair, he would certainly be disappointed, but not surprised. Even during his own life, his understanding of original sin and infant damnation caused controversy and contention. On one hand, he simply echoed traditional Puritan assumptions about children. Theologically, the Puritans fed their children a steady diet of catechisms and books warning them not to provoke God's wrath. In the best-selling book *The Day of Doom*, which was published in 1662, Michael Wigglesworth imagined an angry God condemning sinners—even infants—to "endless pains, and scalding flames." (Echoing Augustine, however, he hastened to add that children would have "the easiest room in Hell.") When Puritan children recited the alphabet using the *New England Primer,* they learned that "U" stood for "Upon the Wicked God shall rain an horrible Tempest." The Puritans, as many historians have lamented, raised their children in a climate of fear.[4]

Yet even in comparison to earlier Puritans, Edwards's emphasis on childhood depravity sounded particularly severe. Even though earlier Puritans had defended the doctrines of infant damnation and predestination, they had also offered a more comforting message. Indeed, many seem to have believed that their *own* children were safe from God's punishments. Identifying themselves as the "new Israel," they claimed that God had entered into a special covenant with them that extended to their descendants as well. In theory, a sovereign God could choose to save or damn anyone whom he pleased, but according to seventeenth-century Puritan ministers, in practice he almost always decided to show compassion to the children of the covenant. As Cotton Mather explained, "The children of Godly Parents, we are bound in a Judgment of Charity to reckon, as much belonging upon the Lord, as Themselves."[5] Proud of their status as God's chosen people, the Puritans reassured themselves that most (if not all) of their own children had been predestined for salvation.

In contrast, Edwards did not use his sermons to reassure parents, but to shatter their complacency. Privately, he seemed to share Cotton Mather's assumption that "the infants of the godly that die in infancy are saved," but publicly he warned parents not to underestimate God's hatred of sinners, no matter how young.[6] If they truly believed what they heard in church every Sunday—"that every one that has not been born again, whether he be young or old, is exposed every moment to eternal destruction, under the wrath of Almighty God"—then they had to face the possibility that their own children might be "the heirs of hell."[7] Perhaps Edwards took a gentler tone during his private pastoral visits, but during his Sunday sermons he tried to jolt parents into confronting the hard truths about sin and damnation. For example, in a sermon based on Ephesians 6:4, "And, ye fathers, provoke not your children to wrath; but bring them up in the nurture and admonition of the Lord," Edwards asked parents to imagine how they would feel if their children died young. Would they be filled with remorse if they were suddenly forced to watch their "Children in their death bed in the sensible approaches of death . . . Gasping and dying"? If they had neglected the duties of family prayer or Bible reading, would they spend the rest of their lives in terror that their children had been "Cast, Gone down into Hell"?[8]

Although one recent historian has described Edwards as "the most eloquent defender of divine punishments, pain, and torment in American history," he was not a sadist who took pleasure in terrorizing children.[9] Rather, he was a devout Calvinist who was deeply ambivalent about the currents of thought known as the "Enlightenment." During the seventeenth and early eighteenth centuries, moral philosophers such as the third earl of Shaftesbury and Francis Hutcheson began to question traditional beliefs in human depravity, forging a new, more optimistic understanding of human nature. For example, Shaftesbury challenged the doctrine of original sin by claiming that humans are not intrinsically selfish, but benevolent: they possess an inherent "moral sense" that helps them distinguish virtue from vice. Similarly, Hutcheson praised humans as essentially good, not evil. Rather than being motivated solely by self-interest, they were also guided by "natural" feelings of altruism. By the mid-eighteenth century, as historian Norman Fiering has argued, most people believed that human nature was "irresistibly compassionate": in other words, they believed that God had designed humans to respond to suffering with instinctive sympathy and compassion.[10]

The emergence of this modern, humanitarian sensibility inevitably challenged traditional Christian understandings of God. It was hard to imagine why a benevolent God would allow humans to suffer—or worse, *delight* in their suffering. While John Locke denied that a compassionate God would subject sinners to eternal tortures in hell, John Tillotson rejected the Calvinist faith in predestination. "This doctrine cannot be of God," he protested, because "God is good and just." Rejecting Calvinism as arbitrary and cruel, these men created a more liberal understanding of both humanity and God.[11]

In this new intellectual climate, the doctrine of infant damnation appeared particularly brutal. As early as 1740, John Taylor, a Presbyterian minister in Norwich, England, insisted that a compassionate God would never condemn infants to eternal punishment. "Consider seriously what a God he must be," he protested, "who can be displeased with, and curse his innocent Creatures, even before they have a Being. *Is this thy God, O Christian?*" Troubled by this question, Experience Mayhew, a missionary to Native Americans, attacked the doctrine of imputation as "one of the grossest of all absurdities." Infants could not be guilty of a sin they had not personally committed.[12]

Although both Taylor and Mayhew were identified with the liberal wing of Calvinism, more orthodox ministers also found it difficult to defend the doctrine of infant damnation. In 1757, when the Rev. Samuel Webster published a treatise against original sin protesting the belief that "perfectly *innocent* and *blameless*" infants would be "*tormented with fire and brimstone*," the Rev. Peter

Clark, a conservative, could manage only a lame response. At first he denied that he or other Calvinists held such a hard view: "tho we don't ... hold Infants to be perfectly innocent ... yet neither do we hold Infants liable, eventually, to the Punishment of Hell thereafter." According to him, Calvinists did not teach the doctrine of infant damnation, but only the "eternal Privation of Life." Although nonelect infants would not rejoice in heaven, they would not suffer eternal torments.[13] The problem with this argument, as the Rev. Charles Chauncy pointed out in a caustic rebuttal, was that it was untrue and, furthermore, it undermined the doctrine of original sin: Calvinists taught that "mankind *universally,* infants as well as others, are liable to the damnation of hell-fire, on account of *Adam's* first Sin."[14] Trying to rectify his mistake, Clark decided to evade the issue altogether, solemnly concluding that God's relationship to children was beyond human comprehension. People should not be "ever-busily inquisitive into the future State of Infants, in which we have no Matter of Concern," he insisted. "Whether all, or how many few are saved? Who are they? And what their State is? Which are all Questions, that it can be of no Use or Profit to us to have resolv'd."[15] Faced with Webster's outraged questions about the fate of "tender Infants," Clark hid behind ambivalent language. In a particularly confusing sentence, he hesitated to "either affirm, or deny" that infants as well as adults inherited the stain of original sin.[16]

In contrast, Edwards spoke plainly—more plainly than anyone else dared. In order to defend traditional Calvinist teachings, he became a crusader against what he perceived as maudlin views of children's innocence. For example, in response to John Taylor's argument that sin was the product of bad example, not inherent depravity, he claimed that children's daily lives told a darker story. "The influence of bad example, without corruption of nature, will not account for children's universally committing sin, as soon as capable of it," he explained. Citing a long list of biblical examples, he argued that God had never treated children as blameless innocents. For example, during the destruction of Sodom, God had decided to rescue Lot, but he had allowed countless numbers of infants to perish. God had also destroyed thousands of children in the flood, saving only Noah and his family, and he had slain all the first-born children in Egypt. From Edwards's viewpoint, the evidence was irrefutable: the faith in children's innocence was not just misguided, but blasphemous.[17] Since infants inherited the stain of original sin, they were as guilty as adults. It was "exceeding just" that "God should take the soul of a new-born infant and cast it into eternal torments."[18]

Besides criticizing John Taylor, Edwards also found fault with the views of Isaac Watts, a British evangelical whose published sermons and hymns were popular in America. Disturbed by the idea of infant damnation, Watts wondered whether God sentenced infants outside of the covenant to annihilation, not everlasting punishment. According to Edwards, this line of thought smacked of irrationality: "To think of poor little *infants* bearing such torments for Adam's sin, as they sometimes do in this world, and these torments ending in death and annihilation, may sit easier on the imagination, than to conceive of their suffering eternal misery for it. But it does not at all relieve one's *reason*." No matter what anxious parents wanted to believe, there was no scriptural warrant for Watt's ideas about annihilation.[19]

Yet because Edwards insisted that humans were responsible for their own sinfulness, he never argued that infants were born essentially evil. In response to liberals who accused Calvinists of making God the author of sin, Edwards insisted that humans were morally neutral at birth, not depraved. He described sin as privative: it was the inevitable result of human frailty after Adam's fall. As Edwards explained, Adam had been created with divine as well as natural principles, but because of his sin, he had lost his holiness—and his ability to control his passions. As a result, infants came into the world without the "superior" principles that would have curbed their natural selfishness. Without God's indwelling spirit, they inevitably fell into corruption.[20]

By explaining that humans begin to sin "immediately, as soon as they are capable of it," Edwards implicitly raised questions about the moral status of infants. When exactly did children become capable of committing sin? In a footnote to his tract *Original Sin*, he offered two different explanations for human depravity: "either . . . men are born guilty, and so are chargeable with sin before they come to act for themselves, or else commit sin immediately, without the least time intervening after they are capable of understanding their obligations to God, and reflecting on themselves." Although the two possibilities led to the same conclusion—"infinite guilt"—they had different implications for understanding children's nature. Like Augustine, who saw infants as "non-innocent," Edwards may have imagined children as tending toward sin, but not as corrupt as adults. Indeed, he testified that "dispositions to evil are commonly much stronger in adult persons, than in children, when they first begin to act in the world as rational creatures." Nevertheless, he concluded that even if infants were not actively sinful at the very moment of birth, it ultimately made no difference. As he explained, if the "time of freedom from sin be so small," then it was "not worthy of notice."[21]

During special religious meetings that he held for children (probably those aged six and older), Edwards tried to convince them to repent and seek God's grace. Although many of the parents in his congregation objected to "frighting poor innocent children with talk of hell fire and eternal damnation," Edwards refused to sugarcoat the truth. "A child that has a dangerous wound may need the painful lance as well as grown persons," he explained. "And that would be a foolish pity, in such a case, that would hold back the lance, and throw away the life."[22] Because he believed that children sometimes "needed" to be hurt, he deliberately exploited their fears of darkness, "monsters," abandonment, and death. In a particularly frightening sermon, Edwards warned children that unless they were "born again," their parents would stop loving them. It was impossible for saints to love sinners: if Christ sentenced them to eternal punishment in hell, their parents would not "be grieved," but would "praise God for his justice."[23] Painting a graphic picture of parents looking down at their children in hell, he explained: "When they shall behold you with a frightened, amazed countenance, trembling and astonished, and shall hear you groan and gnash your teeth; these things will not move them at all to pity you, but you will see them with a holy joyfulness in their countenances, and with songs in their mouths."[24] In other words, according to Edwards, children's worst nightmares were not just fantasies, but accurate depictions of their future anguish. They would spend eternity in a dark pit; they would be tormented by monsters; and no matter how much they wept for mercy, they would be utterly alone, forsaken by their parents.

This was the Edwards whom later nineteenth-century evangelicals wanted to forget and liberals loved to hate: the stern, uncompromising Edwards who insisted that all humans, even children, were guilty of original sin. Yet there was also another, more complicated side to Edwards's view of children that both his supporters and his critics chose to ignore. Echoing Augustine, Calvin, and the Puritans, he claimed it was possible for God to choose even the tiniest infants for salvation. "As to the Time of bestowm[en]t of Conv[ersion]," he explained, "when G[od] hath a design of mercy, he sometimes bestows it on Persons when young or Even in childhood."[25] Even though infants or small children would not realize they had been spiritually reborn, they would learn to "exercise grace gradually as they exercise their reason."[26] As they grew to maturity, their virtuous actions would reveal them as God's elect.

In his sermons to children, Edwards always tempered his emphasis on God's anger by imagining joyful children in heaven. Paradoxically, he plumbed the depths of hell in order to help them imagine the soaring beauty of God's grace—a beauty they could not fully see without the "new sense." His sermons were analogical: he showed children the ugly horrors of the "bottomless pit" in order to give them a brief taste of heaven's "sweetness." If they stubbornly refused to repent, they could be thrown into hell at any moment, but if they were born again, they would be safe in the shelter of Christ's love. With plain, childlike language, Edwards promised them eternal life and magnificent rewards in heaven. They would sleep with angels watching over them; they would no longer fear thunder and lightning; they would "triumph over" the most horrible monster of all, the devil; and most important, they would no longer be afraid of death. Safe with Christ, they would feast on sumptuous food and be crowned with a "glorious crown" that would be "a thousand times more excellent than the best crown that is worn by any king or queen."[27]

Without intending it, Edwards preached a potentially subversive message about children's value in the eyes of God. Undermining the traditional hierarchies of age and wealth, he insisted that Christ loved even the poorest or humblest child. "Christ is ready to receive little children into communion with him, even the poor children of poor parents," he promised. "Those that are despised in the world, Christ don't despise them." Although some adults—particularly those who had not yet been "saved"—measured children's worth according to their age or their social standing, Christ saw only their religious devotion. God's world, according to Edwards, was a topsy-turvy world where children could be superior to adults. Ironically, even though he hoped to strengthen the traditional, patriarchal family, he also implicitly undermined it. On one hand, he insisted that "good" children would never tell lies, play on the Sabbath, or challenge the authority of their parents. Preaching a message of social control, he commanded them to be obedient. "Nothing has a greater tendency to bring a curse on persons, in this world, and on all their temporal concerns," he admonished, "than an undutiful, unsubmissive, disorderly behaviour in children towards their parents."[28] Yet at the same time, he also insisted that children could be better Christians than adults. Despite children's youth, "many of them have more of that knowledge and wisdom, that pleases him and renders their religious worship more acceptable, than many of the great and learned men of the world."[29]

Because of his genuine belief that children could be converted, Edwards gathered them together in special meetings to listen to their questions, catechize them, and explain the gospel to them in clear, simple language. In 1734–1735, during the height of the revival in his congregation, he also admitted twenty children (defined as those under the age of fourteen) into church membership. Although Edwards stopped welcoming children as members when the revivals cooled, perhaps because some of them lost their fervor, his brief experiment marked a sharp break with the Puritan custom of limiting church membership to adolescents and adults.[30]

Edwards's attitude toward Phebe Bartlet, a four-year-old girl in his congregation, demonstrates his remarkable faith in children's genuine piety. When Phebe's parents wondered whether she had been "born again," he made a personal visit to their house to speak with her. As her parents explained, Phebe had been so distraught by the thought of her sinfulness that she had feared she might "go to hell," but one afternoon, as she "continued exceedingly crying, and wreathing her body to and fro, like one in anguish of spirit," she had suddenly fallen silent. Turning to her mother with a smile, she had proclaimed, "Mother, the kingdom of heaven is come to me!" Although Edwards admitted that earlier Puritans had thought it was "a strange thing, when any seemed to be savingly wrought upon, and remarkably changed in their childhood," he was absolutely convinced that Phebe had been reborn in Christ.[31] Despite her youth, she was a symbol of God's extraordinary grace.

As the story of Phebe Bartlet illustrates, Edwards created a double image of children as both sinners and saints. Since children, like adults, were fully human, they were tainted with original sin, and yet also capable of genuine faith. Perhaps not surprisingly, when Edwards's Northampton parish decided to dismiss him, many "youth" remained supportive.[32]

The Battles over Children's Nature

Given the complexity of Edwards's theology, he could have been remembered as one of the first ministers to treat children as religious equals. After all, few other clergymen dared to elevate a four-year-old girl as an icon of true piety—a judgment that some of his colleagues must have found ludicrous at the time. Yet by 1758, the year that Edwards died, his ideas about children were increasingly under attack, and later in the nineteenth century he was mostly remembered for his rigid defense of orthodoxy, not his compassion. In the fevered imagination of the American public, Edwards had become a hard-hearted disciplinarian—a man who supposedly taught bereaved parents that "Hell is being paved with infants' skulls."[33]

How and why did this happen? The answer is twofold. First, the intellectual revolution that began during Edwards's life only accelerated after his death. Although historians have not fully explained why Americans began to question Calvinist understandings of original sin, predestination, the atonement, and free will, it is clear that they were in search of new models for understanding both humanity and God. Influenced by the "moderate" strand of Enlightenment thought—as represented by thinkers such as John Locke and Francis Hutcheson—they increasingly placed humans, not God, at the center of the universe. In the words of historian Elizabeth Clark, Protestants "shifted their focus from the drama of God, the sovereign judge, sentencing the depraved human to an afterlife of unremitting suffering, to that of God, the benevolent father, working for his children's physical and spiritual well-being. The purpose of worship shifted from the glorification of God to the salvation and celebration of man."[34] Unlike earlier Christians, who had accepted suffering as a just penalty for sin, many now found it shocking—even obscene—to imagine that a compassionate, benevolent God would allow countless numbers of people to spend eternity in pain. Just as Edwards had feared, his ideas had been eclipsed by the rise of a new, humanitarian sensibility.

Second, and coupled with the Enlightenment, the American Revolution led to a new faith in human goodness and rationality. Understandably, the men and women who had triumphed over the British and created a new republic found it hard to accept the Calvinists' stark view of human sinfulness. Although Congregationalists and Presbyterians continued to attract converts, they were dwarfed by the Methodists, whose doctrine of free will helped to make them the fastest-growing denomination in the new republic. According to popular Methodist preachers, such as Benjamin Abbott and Lorenzo Dow, it was absurd to believe that humans were helpless to influence whether they were saved or damned. "You will if you will, you won't if you won't," went one satirical piece of verse. "You're damned if you do, and you're damned if you don't." In a culture that prized self-reliance, freedom, and individualism, Edwards not only seemed anachronistic, but reactionary. As one historian has noted, "Edwards's thought, and the New England theology which stemmed from it, was ill-suited to express the growing democratic ideals of this period."[35]

The Unitarians, who prided themselves on their theological liberalism, were especially forceful in their denunciations of Calvinism. To be sure, they were a minority of Christians in the early nineteenth century (and they made few converts outside of New England), but because they included some of the leading intellectuals of the day, including William Ellery Channing and Theodore Parker, they exerted a disproportionate influence on public opinion. Besides denying the doctrine of the trinity, Unitarians complained that the beliefs in predestination and total depravity had the effect of making God into a tyrant. In an article in the *Christian Examiner,* a popular Unitarian journal, Edwards was caricatured as a hellfire preacher who had portrayed both humanity and God in "horrifying" terms:

> Construct in imagination the picture of horrors which human life is, according to the scheme of a Jonathan Edwards. A relentless Sovereign throned in the distant sky; a ruined, reprobate, and helpless race, struggling and weeping

across the earth; a bottomless, roaring hell, opening its jaws underneath; the thunders and lightnings of condemnation, rolling and flashing throughout the scene; the immense majorities of dying souls, dropping into the brimstone gulf; while a few favorites, by a mechanical device, are caught up in glory! Is this a view which any kind and healthy heart can credit or can endure?[36]

By insisting that Calvinism was neither "kind" nor "healthy," Unitarians tried to discredit it in the public imagination.

Debates over children's nature were especially heated in the early nineteenth century for political as well as theological reasons. Anxious about the fate of the new republic, which seemed perilously fragile in its early years, Americans grappled with deeply theological as well as political questions: Were ordinary people virtuous enough to govern themselves? Were humans born essentially good, or prone to sin? Could they be entrusted to withstand the temptations of power? On one side stood liberals such as William Ellery Channing, who urged people to "have faith in the child. . . . Believe in the greatness of its nature."[37] If educated correctly, children would naturally mature into virtuous citizens. On the other side stood conservatives who argued that children were naturally selfish and aggressive, suggesting the need for a strong, centralized government. "I have been employed in the education of children and youth more than thirty years," wrote Timothy Dwight, a Federalist and Jonathan Edwards's grandson. "Yet among the thousands of children, committed to my care, I cannot say with truth, that I have seen *one*, whose native character I had any reason to believe to be virtuous." Using Edwardsian language, he concluded that a child was a "depraved being" who needed to be led to "real virtue."[38]

By the 1820s, however, growing numbers of ministers hesitated to use Dwight's blunt language of depravity. While some were doubtlessly influenced by the romantic faith in children's innocence, others seem to have censored their real views out of fear of alienating people in the pews. As one writer admitted, he cringed to hear indulgent parents calling their children "little doves," "harmless creatures," or "pretty innocents," but he found it difficult to speak his mind. At a time when William Wordsworth, the romantic poet, imagined infants coming into the world "trailing clouds of glory," and scores of other writers celebrated them as virtual angels, or, to use a favorite nineteenth-century word, cherubs, few ministers dared to suggest that infants were not spotlessly innocent.[39]

To answer popular objections to the idea of infant damnation, Congregationalists and Presbyterians began to craft a new defense of original sin.

Nathaniel William Taylor, the architect of the "New Haven theology" and a professor at Yale, suggested that infants were not depraved from the very moment of conception, but rather, they began to sin as soon as they became "moral agents." As we have seen, this argument echoed the letter of Edwards's teachings, but not the spirit. Although Edwards had debated over whether infants were sinful at the moment of birth, he had also insisted that they committed their first sin almost immediately. In contrast, Taylor was deliberately vague about the timing of infants' moral accountability. Although admitting that they began to sin "very early," he also hesitated to speculate about timing: "I *do not know,* the precise instant," he concluded. Most important, he assured his congregation that if a child died before becoming a moral agent, he or she would be "saved through the redemption that is in Christ Jesus."[40] As his critics pointed out, this argument created a conundrum: Why would a dying infant need to be redeemed by Christ if he or she were not stained by sin? Nevertheless, Taylor's ideas had a profound effect on the way future ministers handled the question of innate depravity.

Influenced by Taylor's theology, Lyman Beecher, one of the most powerful clergymen of his time, tried to settle the debates over infant damnation by making the ludicrous claim that Calvinists had never believed in it. "FUTURE PUNISHMENT OF INFANTS NOT A DOCTRINE OF CALVINISM," trumpeted the headline of his 1828 article. In a bold attempt to rewrite New England's history, Beecher insisted that Calvinists had never taught "the monstrous doctrine that infants are damned, and that hell is doubtless paved with their bones." After spending fifty years in the ministry and reading "the most approved Calvinistic writers," Beecher swore that he had "never seen or heard of any book which contained such a sentiment, nor a man, minister, or layman, who believed or taught it." Of course, Beecher had a point: no one had been grotesque enough to describe infant carcasses in hell. But he deliberately misrepresented the Calvinist tradition by insisting that ministers had only suggested that infants *could* be damned, not that those outside of the covenant necessarily *would* be. "What does Edwards say?" Beecher asked. "Simply and only, as all the Reformers had said, that infants are *exposed* justly to eternal death on account of original sin; but that they *suffer* this deserved punishment HE DOES NOT SAY." Unfortunately for Beecher, his Unitarian critics responded by publishing a lengthy rebuttal of his claims. After quoting extensively from Edwards's works, they concluded, "The doctrine of Edwards is that INFANTS are just as guilty as Adam himself was; that they consequently deserve the full punishment threatened him for his disobedience: that this punishment is death—death temporal and eternal, perfect, helpless, never ending misery." Forced to concede that his argument applied mostly to his own contemporaries, not to the past, Beecher rarely (if ever) invoked Edwards's ideas about children again.[41]

Of course, it is important to emphasize that many Congregationalist and Presbyterian clergymen continued to identify themselves as Edwardsians, and neither Beecher nor Taylor spoke for their entire denominations. Indeed, Taylor was chastised for suggesting that infants were as holy as Adam before the fall or as Jesus in the manger, and Beecher was attacked by "Old School" Presbyterians who accused him of straying too far from orthodox understanding of original sin. Although he was eventually acquitted, in 1834 the Presbytery of Cincinnati investigated charges that he had made misleading statements about the doctrine of innate depravity.[42] "INFANTS ARE SINNERS," insisted Gardiner Spring, the minister of the Brick Presbyterian Church in New York, capitalizing his words for emphasis. Rejecting Taylor's argument about moral agency, he explained, "If infants belong to the *children of men;* if they have a *heart* and soul; then from the moment they are human and descendants of Adam, they are sinners."[43]

Yet even ministers who tried to be faithful to Edwards's legacy tended to shy away from his frank language about the possibility of children's damnation. While Gardiner Spring insisted that "sin in an infant is as *really* ill-deserving, as it is in an adult," he also assured parents that God was too compassionate to allow a child to suffer. "That the grace of God, through Jesus Christ, rescues all infants from perdition, I do not deny, but fondly hope," he wrote. "That it rescues untold millions, I have not a doubt."[44] Although he would have strenuously denied the charge, his language linked him as much to the sentimental writers of his age as it did to Edwards.

While other theologians gradually chipped away at Edwards's theology, Horace Bushnell shook its foundations with the publication of his influential book *Christian Nurture* in 1847. Like Edwards, Bushnell was a Congregationalist who denied "the radical goodness of human nature," but he also argued that almost all children, if carefully nurtured, had the capacity to become faithful Christians. As he explained, a child could "grow up a Christian, and never know himself as being otherwise."[45] On one hand, Bushnell's emphasis on the organic unity of the family echoed seventeenth-century covenant theology: just as Puritan parents had hoped that the covenant extended to their progeny, Bushnell claimed that Christian parents almost always succeeded in raising pious children. But in a crucial difference, Bushnell did not believe that sinners needed to be "born again" during a climactic conversion experience—an experience that almost always involved psychological pain. Rejecting Edwards's faith as gloomy and morbid, he condemned Calvinists for tormenting impressionable young children with threats of hell—a criticism that other liberals quickly echoed.

As Protestants battled over children's nature, they turned to fiction, a genre that allowed them to spread their ideas to a broad reading public. The two most popular novels in the nineteenth century, *The Wide, Wide World*, which was published in 1850, and *Uncle Tom's Cabin*, published in 1852, offered sharply divergent images of children. Susan Warner, the author of *The Wide, Wide World,* was a Presbyterian who seems to have been influenced by Edwards's theology, and she portrayed her main character, ten-year-old Ellen Montgomery, as "hardened by sin." Even though Ellen is a sweet, loving child, she must learn how to subdue her "strong passion" and "strong pride" as she grows to adulthood. Again and again, Ellen learns the agonizing lesson that "the root of evil was in her own heart."[46] Since the narrative structure of the book pointed to Ellen's eventual embrace of Christianity, readers never had to confront the possibility that she might not be saved. Nevertheless, Warner offered a far more negative picture of children's sinfulness than any other sentimental writer of her generation.

More typical was Harriet Beecher Stowe, whose novel *Uncle Tom's Cabin* sold more copies than any other book in nineteenth-century America. Although Stowe was the daughter of Lyman Beecher, she rejected her father's Calvinist faith in favor of a more liberal creed, and instead of joining the hairsplitting debates over when children began to sin, she emphasized their essential goodness. Even Topsy, a "naughty" slave child who lies and steals, misbehaves because of a long history of neglect and abuse, not innate depravity. When she is treated with love, she begins "striving for good." Another child in the book, five-year-old Evangeline, is a "bright angel" who is "almost divine." As one of the most "Christ-like" characters in the novel, she boldly testifies against the dehumanization of slavery. Because of her purity, her patience, and her innocent wisdom, she serves as a model for adults to emulate.[47]

Ironically, "Little Eva" bore a striking resemblance to the precocious, pious Phebe Bartlett: both of them were surprisingly wise beyond their years; both devoted their lives to Christ; and both served as symbols of true religion. Yet even though Stowe could have used Bartlett's story to illustrate that even Edwards—the formidable defender of children's depravity—had sometimes glimpsed children's goodness, she had little sympathy for his theology. In a later novel, she maligned his sermons as "so terrific in their refined poetry of torture, that very few persons of quick sensibility could read through them without agony."[48]

Given this condemnatory language, it is not surprising that Edwards's remaining defenders in the nineteenth and twentieth centuries searched for ways to make him seem more enlightened and modern. Since he had been a devoted father to his eleven children, some portrayed him as a loving patriarch who had mixed doctrinal rigor with warmth and affection. For example, the novelist Jeremiah Rankin created a fictionalized portrait of Edwards's family that emphasized his kindness. Others tried to counter negative images by perpetuating Lyman Beecher's earlier strategy of misrepresentation and evasion. As late as 1901, for example, a Presbyterian minister quoted selective passages from Edwards's writings in order to prove that he had been grossly misrepresented: not only had he never preached infant damnation, but he had believed in "the salvation of all dying in infancy." Apparently this minister believed that Edwards could remain relevant only if he were stripped of his true theological convictions.[49]

Almost seventy years ago, historian Joseph Haroutunian condemned nineteenth-century Calvinists for diluting Edwards's piety with moralism: their history was "a history of degradation," a history of corruption and failure.[50] By trying to make Calvinism more rational and humanitarian, they had destroyed Edwards's vision of a sovereign, majestic God who had created the world for *his* glory, not the glory of humanity. Although historians have rightly questioned Haroutunian's value judgments—for one thing, many would see the transformation of Calvinism as an improvement, not a decline—he identified one of the most important religious developments in American history. As the controversies over children's nature reveal, nineteenth-century Protestants were deeply ambivalent about Edwards's theology. Like Sereno Dwight, who found it hard to imagine that his great-grandfather had genuinely viewed children as "little vipers," future Calvinists looked back at his world across a gulf that they found almost impossible to bridge. "For his day and ours," one scholar commented in 1953, "original sin, infant damnation, and divine sovereignty had become too strong a dose for those whose personal security rested in the ordered amiability of the natural world, the innate virtue of men, and the tender rational benevolence of a loving heavenly Father."[51]

Many Protestants continued to celebrate Edwards as a famous revivalist and as a brilliant intellectual, but in a world where "Little Eva," not Phebe Bartlet, had won the battle for America's religious imagination, few wanted to remember his theology of childhood.

Notes

I would like to thank Kenneth Minkema for his help with this essay. I am also indebted to Marcia Bunge and all the participants in the project on The Child in Christian Thought, which was funded by the Lilly Endowment.

1. Cf. Sereno Dwight, ed., *The Works of President Edwards with a Memoir of His Life* (New York: S. Converse, 1829), 4:164, with Jonathan Edwards, *Some Thoughts Concerning the Present Revival* (1742), in Jonathan Edwards, *The Great Awakening,* ed. C. C. Goen, *The Works of Jonathan Edwards,* vol. 4 (New Haven: Yale Univ. Press, 1972), 394. This omission was repeated in later reprints of Dwight's edition. For example, see Jonathan Edwards, *Some Thoughts Concerning the Present Revival,* in *The Works of Jonathan Edwards,* ed. Sereno E. Dwight, revised and corrected by Edward Hickman (Edinburgh: Banner of Truth Trust, 1974), 1:393.

2. Oliver Wendell Holmes, *Over the Teacups* (Boston: Houghton, Mifflin, 1890), 249–50.

3. William Ellery Channing lamented that Edwards had wasted his intellectual brilliance on defending a "false theology." See his "Remarks on National Literature," *Christian Examiner* 7 (January 1830): 269–95.

4. Michael Wigglesworth, *The Day of Doom: or, A Poetical Description of the Great and Last Judgement* (1662; reprint, Tucson, Ariz.: American Eagle Publications, 1991), 30, 66; *The New England Primer* (Boston: S. Kneeland and T. Green, 1727). For a longer discussion of Edwards's attitude toward children, see Catherine A. Brekus, "Children of Wrath, Children of Grace: Jonathan Edwards and the Puritan Culture of Child Rearing," in *The Child in Christian Thought,* ed. Marcia Bunge (Grand Rapids, Mich.: Eerdmans, 2001), 300–328.

5. Cotton Mather, *Help for Distressed Parents* (Boston: Harris, 1695), 13, quoted in Peter Gregg Slater, *Children in the New England Mind* (Hamden, Conn.: Archon Books, 1977), 29. Slater claims that "although Puritan clergymen . . . allowed in their theology for the possibility, even the likelihood, that some infants were damned, when they discussed specific children the presumption was almost always made that heaven was the destination." See Slater, *Children in the New England Mind,* 40. See also C. John Somerville's *The Rise and Fall of Childhood* (Beverly Hills: Sage Publications, 1982), which argues that seventeenth-century Puritans were less harsh in their attitudes toward children than their eighteenth-century descendants (124–25). As Harry S. Stout has reminded us in his *The New England Soul: Preaching and Religious Culture in Colonial New England* (New York: Oxford Univ. Press, 1986), printed sermons are not necessarily representative of what ministers actually said in the pulpit. Since there are thousands of unpublished Puritan sermons in archives, it is impossible to make definitive statements about them as a whole. Nevertheless, it is significant that clergy rarely spoke

about infant damnation in their published sermons. For another study of Puritan attitudes toward children, see Sandford Fleming, *Children and Puritanism: The Place of Children in the Life and Thought of the New England Churches, 1620–1847* (New Haven: Yale Univ. Press, 1933).

6. Jonathan Edwards, "Miscellanies," no. 849, quoted in Jonathan Edwards, *Original Sin,* ed. Clyde A. Holbrook, *The Works of Jonathan Edwards,* vol. 3 (New Haven: Yale Univ. Press, 1970), 27n.

7. Edwards, *Works,* 4:394.

8. Jonathan Edwards, "Sermon on Ephesians 6:4," February 1748, Edwards MSS, Beinecke Rare Book and Manuscript Library, Yale University.

9. Philip Greven, *Spare the Child: The Religious Roots of Punishment and the Psychological Impact of Physical Abuse* (New York: Knopf, 1991), 57. See also Philip Greven, *The Protestant Temperament: Patterns of Child-Rearing, Religious Experience, and the Self in Early America* (New York: Knopf, 1977).

10. Norman Fiering, "Irresistible Compassion: As Aspect of Eighteenth-Century Sympathy and Humanitarianism," *Journal of the History of Ideas* 37 (April–June 1976): 195–218. On Shaftesbury, see D. P. Walker, *The Decline of Hell: Seventeenth-Century Discussions of Eternal Torment* (London: Routledge and Kegan Paul, 1964). For a broad overview of the intellectual challenge posed by deists and other Enlightenment thinkers, see Henry F. May, *The Enlightenment in America* (New York: Oxford Univ. Press, 1976).

11. Tillotson is quoted in Norman Fiering, *Jonathan Edwards's Moral Thought and Its British Context* (Chapel Hill: Univ. of North Carolina Press, 1981), 228. See also Jonathan Edwards, *Sermons and Discourses 1723–1729,* ed. Kenneth P. Minkema, *The Works of Jonathan Edwards,* vol. 14 (New Haven: Yale Univ. Press, 1997), 29. On the growth of a new humanitarian sensibility in mid-eighteenth-century America, see Karen Haltunnen, "Humanitarianism and the Pornography of Pain in Anglo American Culture," *American Historical Review* 100, no. 2 (April 1995): 303–34; Elizabeth B. Clark, "The Sacred Rights of the Weak: Pain, Sympathy, and the Culture of Individual Rights in Antebellum America," *Journal of American History* 82, no. 2 (September 1995): 463–93; and Ava Chamberlain, "The Theology of Cruelty: A New Look at the Rise of Arminianism in Eighteenth-Century New England," *Harvard Theological Review* 85, no. 3 (1992): 335–56.

12. John Taylor, *The Scripture-Doctrine of Original Sin Proposed to Free and Candid Examination* (London: J. Wilson, 1740), 151; and Experience Mayhew, *Two Sermons on the Nature, Extent and Perfection of the Divine Goodness* (Boston: D. and J. Kneeland, 1763), 62–63, cited in H. Shelton Smith, *Changing Conceptions of Original Sin: A Study in American Theology Since 1750* (New York: Charles Scribner's Sons, 1955), 24.

13. [Samuel Webster], *A Winter's Evening Conversation upon the Doctrine of Original Sin* (Boston: James Parker and Co., 1757), 6, 27–28; [Peter Clark], *The Scripture-Doctrine*

of Original Sin, Stated and Defended. In a Summer Morning's Conversation, between a Minister and a Neighbor (Boston: S. Kneeland, 1758), 115, 7–8.

14. [Charles Chauncy], *The Opinion of One that Has Perused the Summer Morning's Conversation, Concerning Original Sin, Wrote by the Rev. Peter Clark* (Boston: John Green and Joseph Russell, 1758), 5.

15. [Peter Clark], *Remarks on a Late Pamphlet, Intitled "The Opinion of One that has Perused the Summer Morning's Conversation"* (Boston: Edes and Gill, 1758), 33, 42.

16. Webster, *Winter Evening's Conversation,* 7; and Clark, *Remarks on a Late Pamphlet,* 39–40. See also [Samuel Webster], *The Winter Evening Conversation Vindicated; Against the Remarks of the Rev. Mr. Peter Clark of Danvers* (Boston: Edes and Gill, 1758), and Peter Clark, *A Defense of the Principles of the "Summer Morning's Conversation—Concerning the Doctrine of Original Sin"* (Boston: Edes and Gill, 1760). See also the helpful accounts of this pamphlet war in Slater, *Children in the New England Mind,* 52–57, and Smith, *Changing Conceptions of Original Sin,* 37–59.

17. Edwards, *Works,* 3:200, 216, 217–18.

18. Jonathan Edwards, *The "Miscellanies" (Entry Nos. a–z, aa–zz, 1–500),* ed. Thomas A. Schafer, *The Works of Jonathan Edwards,* vol. 13 (New Haven: Yale Univ. Press, 1994), 169.

19. Edwards, *Works,* 3:410.

20. Ibid., 3:50–51.

21. Ibid., 3:134, 135 n., 50–51, 137. See also Slater, *Children in the New England Mind,* 60–62. On Edwards's attitudes toward older converts, see Kenneth P. Minkema, "Old Age and Religion in the Writings and Life of Jonathan Edwards," *Church History* 70, no. 4 (December 2001): 674–704. On Augustine, see Martha Ellen Stortz, "'Where or When Was Your Servant Innocent?': Augustine on Childhood," in *The Child in Christian Thought,* 78–102.

22. Edwards, *Works,* 4:394. See also Jonathan Edwards, "Sermon on Ephesians 6:4," February 1748, Edwards MSS, Beinecke Library, Yale University.

23. Jonathan Edwards, MSS sermon on 2 Kings 2:23–24.

24. See Jonathan Edwards, "The End of the Wicked Contemplated by the Righteous: or the Torments of the Wicked in Hell, No Occasion of Grief to the Saints in Heaven," quoted in *Jonathan Edwards: A Profile,* ed. David Levin (New York: Hill and Wang, 1969), 223. This sermon echoed Wigglesworth's *Day of Doom.*

25. Jonathan Edwards, "Sermon on John 3:8," December 1734, Edwards MSS, Beinecke Library, Yale University. Many scholars have argued that Edwards was influenced by Enlightenment thought. See Perry Miller, *Jonathan Edwards* (1949; reprint, Amherst: Univ. of Massachusetts Press, 1981); Fiering, *Jonathan Edwards's Moral Thought,* and James Hoopes, "Jonathan Edwards's Religious Psychology," *Journal of American History* 69, no. 4 (March 1983): 849–65.

26. Edwards, *Works,* 13:389.

27. Jonathan Edwards, "Children Ought to Love the Lord Jesus Christ Above All" (1740), MSS sermon, Beinecke Library, Yale University, scheduled to be published in Jonathan Edwards, *Sermons and Discourses, 1739–42,* ed. Nathan O. Hatch and Harry S. Stout, *The Works of Jonathan Edwards,* vol. 22 (New Haven: Yale Univ. Press, 2003).

28. Edwards, "Children Ought to Love the Lord Jesus Christ Above All." The quotation is from Jonathan Edwards, *Farewell Sermon,* in *Jonathan Edwards: Representative Selections,* rev. ed., edited by Clarence H. Faust and Thomas N. Johnson (New York: Hill and Wang, 1962), 198.

29. Edwards, *Works,* 4:408.

30. For statistics on the ages of new members in Edwards's church, see Minkema, "Old Age and Religion in the Writings and Life of Jonathan Edwards," 688.

31. Edwards, *Works,* 4:158. See also his letter to Thomas Prince, where he marveled that "we had the most wonderful work among children that ever was in Northampton," in Edwards, *Works,* 4:548.

32. Jonathan Edwards, "Letter to the Reverend Thomas Gillespie" (1751), in Jonathan Edwards, *Letters and Personal Writings,* ed. George C. Claghorn, *The Works of Jonathan Edwards,* vol. 16 (New Haven: Yale Univ. Press, 1970), 386.

33. C. S., "Jonathan Edwards," *Hampshire Gazette* (2 October 1887): 3.

34. Elizabeth B. Clark, "The Sacred Rights of the Weak: Pain, Sympathy, and the Culture of Individual Rights in Antebellum America," *Journal of American History* 82, no. 2 (September 1995): 471.

35. Clyde A. Holbrook, "Jonathan Edwards and His Detractors," *Theology Today* 10, no. 3 (October 1953): 394. On populist challenges to Calvinism in the nineteenth century, see Nathan O. Hatch, *The Democratization of American Christianity* (New Haven: Yale Univ. Press, 1989).

36. "Strength and Weakness of the Popular Religion and of Liberal Christianity," *Christian Examiner* 64, no. 2 (March 1858): 211, 217

37. William Ellery Channing, "The Sunday School," in *The Works of William E. Channing* (Boston: James Munroe, 1845), 4:357.

38. Timothy Dwight, *Theology Explained and Defended* (New York: Harper and Bros., 1857), 432; and Timothy Dwight, "On Education," *Christian Spectator* 2 (July 1820): 350. The latter essay was published posthumously.

39. Crispus, "On the Education of Children," *Panoplist* 10 (September 1814): 394. William Wordsworth, "Ode: Intimations of Immortality," *The Norton Anthology of English Literature,* 4th ed., gen. ed. M. H. Abrams (New York: W. W. Norton, 1979), 2:215.

40. Nathaniel William Taylor, *Concio ad Clerum: A Sermon Delivered in the Chapel of Yale College, September 10, 1828* (New Haven: Hezekiah Howe, 1828), 23–24. For two

good discussions of Taylor, see Smith, *Conceptions of Original Sin,* 86–109, and Allen C. Guelzo, *Edwards on the Will* (Middletown, Conn.: Wesleyan Univ. Press, 1989). As Guelzo explains, Taylor shifted the burden of proof onto those who believed in infant damnation, "forcing them to show first how the infants had become guilty, rather than by challenging the unbelievers to show how they could logically be innocent" (263).

41. Lyman Beecher, *Sermons Delivered on Various Occasions* (Boston: T. R. Marvin, 1828), 17, quoted in Slater, *Children in the New England Mind,* 83; Lyman Beecher, "Future Punishment of Infants Not a Doctrine of Calvinism," *Spirit of the Pilgrims* (January, February, March 1828): 89–90; "Dr. Beecher Against the Calvinistic Doctrine of Infant Damnation," *Christian Examiner and General Review* 5, no. 4 (July/August 1828): 338; Lyman Beecher, "Dr. Beecher's Reply to the *Christian Examiner,*" *Spirit of the Pilgrims* 3 (April 1830): 181–95. For a helpful discussion of "the disappearance of infant damnation," see Slater, *Children in the New England Mind,* 49–92.

42. Smith, *Changing Conceptions,* 131–32.

43. Gardiner Spring, *Dissertation on Native Depravity* (New York: J. Leavitt, 1833), 6, 23, quoted in Smith, *Changing Conceptions,* 135.

44. Spring, *Dissertation on Native Depravity,* 52, 67.

45. See Horace Bushnell, *Christian Nurture* (New York: Charles Scribner, 1861; reprint, Cleveland Ohio: Pilgrim Press, 1994), 22, 10; and Margaret Lamberts Bendroth, "Horace Bushnell's *Christian Nurture,*" in *The Child in Christian Thought,* 350–64.

46. Susan Warner, *The Wide, Wide World* (1850; reprint, New York: Feminist Press, 1987), 38, 181, 161. See Sharon Kim, "Beyond the Men in Black: Jonathan Edwards and Nineteenth-Century Woman's Fiction," in this volume.

47. Harriet Beecher Stowe, *Uncle Tom's Cabin* (1852; reprint, New York: Penguin Books, 1981), 443, 231, 410, 411.

48. Harriet Beecher Stowe, *The Minister's Wooing* (Hartford, Conn.: Stowe-Day Foundation, 1978), 337.

49. Jeremiah Rankin, *Esther Burr's Journal* (Washington, D.C.: Howard Univ. Press, n.d.). John W. Stagg, "Three Maligned Theologians," *Presbyterian Quarterly* 55 (January 1901): 45. Stagg made the same claim about William Twisse and John Calvin.

50. Joseph Haroutunian, *Piety versus Moralism: The Passing of the New England Theology* (New York: Henry Holt and Company, 1932), xxii. Historians have debated over the persistence of Edwardsianism in nineteenth-century America. For a small sampling of this work, see Ann Douglas, *The Feminization of American Culture* (New York: Knopf, 1977); Frank Hugh Foster, *A Genetic History of the New England Theology* (New York: Garland Publishing, 1987); and Joseph Conforti, *Jonathan Edwards, Religious Tradition, and American Culture* (Chapel Hill: Univ. of North Carolina Press, 1995). Conforti argues that the "Edwardsian and Calvinist traditions" persisted until the Civil War,

"long after their alleged demise" (4). As he admits, however, nineteenth-century theologians appropriated some pieces of Edwards's theology while ignoring others, "reinventing" him to serve their own needs. For an overview of changing ideas about human nature, see Merle Curti, *Human Nature in American Thought: A History* (Madison: Univ. of Wisconsin Press, 1980).

51. Holbrook, "Jonathan Edwards and His Detractors," 386.

Bad Books and Bad Boys

The Transformation of Gender in Eighteenth-Century Northampton, Massachusetts

Ava Chamberlain

In the spring of 1744, clergyman Jonathan Edwards learned that a number of boys in his parish "had Books in keeping, which they improved to promote lascivious and obscene Discourse among the young People." Because the boys were subject to the discipline of the church, Edwards put the matter to the brethren, who appointed a committee to investigate the incident. The committee ultimately secured confessions and promises to reform from several of the accused, thus bringing the matter to an apparently satisfactory conclusion. According to an account written by fellow minister Samuel Hopkins some fifteen years later, however, this minor disciplinary proceeding occasioned a major controversy, which drove a wedge between the minister and his parishioners. In Hopkins's opinion, the so-called bad book affair "seemed in a great Measure to put an end to Mr. Edwards's Usefulness at Northampton, and doubtless laid a Foundation" for the congregation's 1750 vote to dismiss him.[1]

Ever since Hopkins's early assessment, scholars have been trying to understand how such a powerful and successful clergyman as Edwards could have been so summarily ousted from Northampton, and many have followed Hopkins's lead in attending to the specifics of the bad book affair. A majority of the boys implicated in the scandal were members of Northampton's elite, Hopkins observed; he also noted that Edwards failed to discriminate between witness and suspect as he announced the list of persons requested to appear before the committee.[2] Seizing upon this putative oversight, subsequent Edwards biographers have magnified its importance. Sereno Dwight identifies it as the probable reason why Edwards lost support for his prosecution of the case. Although in Hopkins's account it appears that Edwards read the names only to the brethren who had authorized the investigation, James R. Trumbull describes the list as bursting "like a bomb" upon the congregation when Edwards read it "from the pulpit." Likewise, Ola E. Winslow faults Edwards for his "tactlessness in giving premature publicity to an unsorted list of names," though she moves beyond the details of the case to discern a larger pattern of behavior connecting it directly with Edwards's dismissal. Patricia Tracy has been the first to stray from Hopkins's script. Since in manuscript the list clearly distinguishes between witness and suspect, she doubts that Edwards would have carelessly implicated the innocent. In lieu of the traditional interpretation, then, she treats the episode as a sign of Edwards's declining authority in Northampton and as an example of the loss of ministerial influence being felt in parishes throughout New England in the mid–eighteenth century.[3]

To be sure, the bad book affair signaled a society in transition, but the nature of the shift was more widespread and more profound than that identified by Tracy. The bad book affair was primarily about sex, sex and speech, reading and talking about sex. If it had occurred seventy-five or even fifty years earlier, it would have generated little debate, not because ministers had more power then—although they did—but because the gender relations that characterized Puritan society during the first century of settlement supported disciplining men and boys for their sexual offenses. During Edwards's lifetime, however, men's and women's roles in New England society were changing. The alliance between male and female, revealed in the early Puritan image of woman as "helpmeet," was giving way to a more rigid, gendered definition of rights and responsibilities and the general understanding that the sexes were spiritually equal was being replaced by a conviction of their difference.[4] Although the essentialization of gender difference would not fully manifest itself until after the Revolution, recent historians have identified the period between 1680 and 1720 as a crucial turning point in the emergence of this new paradigm.[5] In the 1740s, more than a generation after the onset of this transitional period, Jonathan Edwards planted his feet firmly in Puritan traditionalism and squared off against his opponents, youthful males eager to carve out new prerogatives for themselves in the face of shifting public opinion. As the church and the community took up sides in the controversy, Edwards came to find that even with God on his, it was becoming increasingly difficult to hold his own against the fickle will of the majority.

Events relating to the bad book episode fall into two distinct phases. In the first, a group of Northampton's adolescent boys secretly circulated among themselves a number of popular medical texts containing detailed descriptions of the structure and function of women's reproductive anatomy. The boys then used their newly acquired knowledge of women's bodies to taunt and ridicule adolescent girls. According to testimony, such behavior had been occurring for as long as five years. When Edwards became aware of the boys' conduct, he asked the brethren of the church to initiate an investigation, and they complied. The case entered its second phase when a number of the brethren who had initially supported the action, some of whom were evidently parents of the accused boys, "altered their Minds . . . and declared, they did not think [it] proper to proceed as they had done." Before the committee even met, reported Hopkins, "the Town was suddenly all on a Blaze."[6] As the committee met to obtain testimony, the accused compounded their offense by speaking contemptuously of the committee's members and playing childish games during its proceedings, thus bringing upon themselves the further charge of contempt for authority. Of the three extant confessions, in fact, two address that charge alone, to the exclusion of the original indictment of lascivious speech. Only one boy confessed to the original offense.

Edwards named on his list ten boys suspected of passing around bad books and mocking girls, but subsequent testimony suggested that as many as ten additional boys were originally involved.[7] All but one of the boys on the list were church members, most having joined during the 1734–35 Connecticut Valley awakening.[8] Although two were the sons of deacons, it is clearly an exaggeration to describe the majority as "members of the oldest and most influential families in the town."[9] It is also something of an exaggeration to call the offenders boys. With an average age of twenty-four, they were approaching the outer limit of youth, that transitional stage of life, defined in the eighteenth century as spanning the years from about fifteen to twenty-five, in which young people were expected to make choices concerning marriage and career that would characterize their adulthood.[10] None of the accused boys, however, was married, and none owned property. They, like many young men in New England, were in a state of protracted adolescence, having been forced by an increasing scarcity of land to delay marriage and household formation. Since, on average, Northampton "youth" were not marrying until the age of 28.6 years in this time period, the "boys" were not yet worrying themselves about adult responsibilities.

Although defined as transitional, youth was also a stage marked by its own distinctive ethos. Recent scholarship suggests that the adolescent or "youth" culture Edwards described in *A Faithful Narrative,* the 1737 treatise in which he traced the spiritual transformation of the very same youths he later condemned for their licentiousness, was thriving not only in Northampton before the 1734–35 Connecticut Valley awakening but throughout New England prior to the Revolution.[11] When he first assumed the pastorate, Edwards noted that "licentiousness for some years greatly prevailed among the youth of the town." Many of the young people were "very much addicted to night-walking, and frequenting the tavern, and lewd practices." They would frequently "get together in conventions of both sexes, for mirth and jollity, which they called frolics; and they would often spend the greater part of the night in them, without regard to any order in the families they belonged to."[12] Although youths were viewed as more tractable than adults and, therefore, more easily converted, they were also considered more susceptible to the sins of pride and sensuality. In colonial adolescent culture, adult critics maintained, pride displayed itself in contempt for authority, rebellion against family government, boasting, Sabbath breaking, and blasphemy, while sensuality encouraged company keeping, reveling, drinking, masturbation, and fornication.[13] In their night walking, frolicking, and tavern haunting, of course, Northampton's young people were committing the trespasses characteristically associated with their stage of life.

In the latter part of the seventeenth century, Anglo American magistrates and clergy embarked upon a general campaign to reform the morals of the citizenry. Adolescent culture was, according to Richard Gildrie, but one manifestation of a broader "profane" lifestyle that persons of all ages and classes embraced. Reformers viewed the "hedonistic individualism" of this lifestyle, which encouraged "deliberate and open defiance of official standards of conduct," as a threat to the social order. Although youth was commonly viewed as a time for temporary indulgence in profane activities, New England clergy struggled to prevent this brief flirtation from hardening into a permanent habit by frequently preaching on the sins of youth and on the importance of strong family government.[14] By the 1720s, however, reformers believed that their efforts, which had relied upon government-enforced laws against vice and upon the voluntary activity of moral reform societies, had largely failed to achieve their intended effect. Adopting a new approach, they urged that a "lasting reformation could come about only as consequence of a revival of religion through the outpouring of God's grace."[15] Eighteenth-century revivalists, therefore, targeted young people not only to bring the next generation into the church but also more effectively to address the sins of youth.

In his 1737 *A Faithful Narrative,* Edwards heralded the success of his efforts to reach Northampton's youth. On "the evening after the Sabbath, and after our public lecture," which had been "especially the times of their mirth and company-keeping," the young people began to meet in groups for "social religion." Soon thereafter "a young woman, who had been one of the greatest company-keepers in the whole town," was converted, and by the end of the awakening, he estimated, "by far the greater part of persons in this town, above sixteen years of age, are such as have the saving knowledge of Jesus Christ."[16] In his account of the 1740–42 revival in Northampton, Edwards again stressed the role of young people. Although the previous awakening had effected "a very great alteration among the youth of the town, with respect to reveling, frolicking, profane and unclean conversation, and lewd songs," since that time there had been a "very lamentable decay of religious affections." The first sign of a "visible alteration," he indicated, was "more seriousness and religious conversation, especially among young people." Gradually, this "engagedness of spirit about the things of religion" became "very general amongst young people and . . . religious subjects almost wholly took up their conversation when they were together."[17] At the peak of the revival in 1742, Edwards led his congregation in a public renewal of their covenant, a strategy commonly advocated by the earlier generation of reformers to root out immoral behavior.[18] For their part, as Edwards reported, Northampton's adolescents vowed to avoid "any youthful diversions and pastimes, in meetings or companies of young people," and "all freedoms and familiarities in company" that tend "to stir up or gratify a lust of lasciviousness."[19]

The bad book episode is evidence that Northampton's youth culture continued to thrive despite Edwards's protracted campaign against it. Although the adolescent members of his congregation may have temporarily shifted the focus of their activities from sex to religion during the revivals, the behavior alleged in the case suggests that they never wholly abandoned those "diversions" tending to "gratify a lust of lasciviousness." Sexual reading was not the most common expression of youths' susceptibility to the sin of sensuality, but in the late seventeenth century, as the commercial press in London began producing medical texts for a general audience, there is evidence that at least some fell into the hands of adolescents.[20] Unlike elite medical literature, which was written in Latin and inaccessible to the lay reader, the new, popular medical texts were written in a plain style and sold for a modest price. Steady offerings in the cheap print trade, they supplied both adolescents and adults with a readily available source for information on such subjects as reproductive anatomy, the means of conception, the signs of pregnancy, and the best methods of overcoming barrenness. Magistrates and clergy worried that readers would misuse the books by treating them as pornography or gleaning from them information about prohibited practices, such as abortion and masturbation. Sexual reading was, then, one aspect of the profane lifestyle that received widespread attention during the moral reform campaigns of the seventeenth and eighteenth centuries. But despite legal restrictions and the efforts of such reformers as Cotton Mather, notes David Hall, "the wrong kinds of books seeped into New England."[21]

Testimony from the bad book case indicates that the boys were circulating among themselves copies of at least two popular medical texts. Elizabeth Pomeroy reported finding hidden "in their house up the chimney" a book entitled *The Midwife Rightly Instructed.*[22] Published in London in 1736, the book was written by surgeon Thomas Dawkes, who was convinced that "rash, and ignorant Midwives" commit "daily Mischiefs." To correct that unfortunate state of affairs, he proposed that midwives be trained by men, who could provide them with "the true and solid principles of their Art," and not by women, who taught by experience. To display the benefits of such enlightened instruction, the text assumes the form of a conversation between the author and a young woman training to be a midwife. Having framed the book in this fashion, Dawkes is careful to avoid "any Expressions which wou'd clash with the Principle of [female] Modesty" or be "an Indignity to their Chastity." He does not include "a Description of any Parts of the Body, unnecessary to be known by a Woman," or "a Representation in Figures, of the Parts themselves." He does, however, think a well-trained midwife should have a "Knowledge of those Parts of the Body, which are concerned in Delivery," and in addition to this provocative topic, he describes for his pupil such things as the proper manner of examining a pregnant woman, the different possible positions of the fetus in the womb, the various stages of labor, and the best method of delivering a healthy infant.[23] Given that childbirth was one of the few realms of human experience in colonial New England reserved to women alone, *The Midwife Rightly Instructed* would have offered Northampton's adolescent boys a glimpse of this fascinating and forbidden territory.[24]

The testimony also specifies that the boys possessed a copy of the most notorious and successful of the popular medical texts, which they referred to simply as "Aristotle." John Lancton "boasted that he had read Aristotle," while several others declared that they "wanted Aristotle, intended to find it."[25] The book's full title is *Aristotle's Masterpiece: or, the Secrets of Nature Displayed in all the Parts thereof.* First published in 1684, this pseudo-Aristotelian text "was the single most popular book about reproduction" in eighteenth-century England and America.[25] Often bound together with three other texts attributed to the "Famous Philosopher," the *Masterpiece* exists in three distinct versions, which were issued in a large number of different editions throughout the eighteenth and nineteenth centuries.[27] Editors of the book recognized its erotic potential and commonly warned in their introductions of the possibility of abuse if it "should fall into the Hands of any Obscene or Wanton Person."[28] Unlike Thomas Dawkes, however, they did not hesitate to include detailed descriptions of the structure and function of both male and female reproductive organs as well as discussions of such titillating subjects as the signs of virginity, the means of assuring sexual satisfaction in marriage, and why abstinence from sex causes a mysterious ailment, called "greensickness," in young women. Some editions of the text also contained a frontispiece depicting a naked, hairy woman, lurid illustrations of monstrous births, and a fold-out representation of the "form of the child in the womb." Despite their professed moral scruples, the *Masterpiece*'s editors undoubtedly recognized the potential of such material to increase sales dramatically.

Northampton's adolescent boys treated *Aristotle's Masterpiece* and *The Midwife Rightly Instructed* not as medical texts but as pornography. They were clearly aware that their possession of these books was illicit. Someone, presumably Ebenezer Pomeroy, Elizabeth's brother, hid Dawkes's manual, as she had testified, "on the backside of the chimney on the press." Noah Baker concealed the contraband "between his coat and the lining." And Oliver Warner offered to show the *Masterpiece* to a friend for the exorbitant sum of "ten shillings in money." Although Ebenezer Bartlet said he "sat 'till midnight reading one of them books," collective reading of the texts was preferred to private, for it enhanced the titillation of the activity. Boys gathered in small groups—generally between two and five, of shifting composition—and apparently took turns reading juicy bits from the books for the entertainment of their companions. Rebecca Strong discovered Charles Wright and Timothy Root "with a book that they were provoked about." Mary Downing witnessed Oliver Warner and "one or two" other boys "reading amongst them in a book" at her mother's house. Bathsheba Negro testified that she had seen Noah Baker, Timothy Root, and Elkanah Burt "reading in a book that they called 'the bible' in a laughing way." "All read in it," she reported, but "Timothy Root read most," and it was he who called it the "young folks' bible."[29]

In their communal sharing of books, Northampton's sexually curious adolescents were participating in a form of entertainment popular in eighteenth-century New England. Jane Kamensky observes that Puritans "conceived of the Bible more as oral performance than as written text," and this conflation of the spoken and written word meant that "a great many more people *heard* books than *read* them."³⁰ In adapting that practice to their own ends, however, Edwards's young parishioners set their culture apart from, indeed in opposition to, the dominant culture. Timothy Root expressed this subversive intent when he called a sex manual the "young folks' bible," for this label simultaneously affirmed and undermined the authority of the text on which Puritan New England was founded.

Although all those accused of participating in the ritual of transgressive reading were male, gender exclusivity did not characterize the social occasions at which the books were read. Only two boys appear to have testified before the investigating committee about their cohorts' misbehavior. The large majority of the witnesses were girls, and they were able to testify because they were present at the scene of the crime. Edwards's list of witnesses contains the names of seven adolescent girls and two young married women, and records indicate that as many as ten additional women and girls were party to the readings. Their presence, of course, increased the books' already potent sexual charge. In this context, reading became flirting, even incipient foreplay. Bathsheba Negro, for example, described how Timothy Root laughingly read a book "before her [and] Naomi Warner." He was "ready to kiss them," she states, "and catch[ed] hold of the girls and shook 'em."³¹ In this statement, similar to that made by other girls, Bathsheba describes the boys as active participants and the girls as passive observers or victims.³² These gender roles reflect the "sex-linked patterns of sociability" inherent in colonial society. For the boys to read, snigger, and tease while the girls voiced ineffectual protests fulfilled the expectations of a culture that viewed men's "carnal, sensual" nature as requiring "restraint" and women's "weak, unstable" nature as needing "protection."

More revealing than the female protestations of modesty, however, are the aggressive ways in which the boys used their newfound knowledge to harass and degrade the girls. From their reading, they constructed an image not only of "what the girls was" but of "what nasty creatures they was." They "run upon the girls ... boasting how much they knew about them," it was reported. They bragged that they "knew about girls, knew what belonged to girls as well as girls themselves," and even claimed to "know as much about ye as you, and more too." John Lancton humiliated a group of girls by talking to them "about the things that was in that book in a most unclean manner a long time." When Mary Downing "checked him" for talking "exceeding uncleanly and lasciviously," he simply laughed. When he heard Joanna Clark groan at a gathering "last lecture day night," Ebenezer Pomeroy insinuated that she was pregnant. "I believe you need the old granny," he jeered; "I have read in a book about that."

Oliver Warner taunted several girls with his apparent ability to detect that they were menstruating. "When does the moon change girls? Come, I'll look at your [face] and see whether there be a blue circle 'round your eyes. . . . I believe it runs." With this verbal penetration of the girls' bodies, the boys crossed the line separating playful from actionable speech, and although the courts in New England no longer paid much attention to such offenses, Edwards was unwilling to "let boys be boys."

Learning of the boys' misconduct, Edwards first, according to Hopkins, made some discreet inquiries to substantiate the rumors. Finding several persons willing "to testify, that they had heard one and another from time to time talk obscenely; as what they were led to by reading a Book or Books, which they had among them," he then requested that the brethren of the church "look into the Matter."[33] In notes he made during the case, Edwards observed that he thought the boys' behavior "a scandalous offense," and he defended his judgment with a long list of scriptures. Colossians 3:8, which commands the saints to put all "filthy communication out of your mouth," stipulated that it "would be unclean" for "young men" to talk about "these things needlessly." Similarly, "foolish talking" is "one thing reckoned gross" by Ephesians 5:3–5 and in some circumstances even "excludes [the perpetrator] out of the kingdom of heaven."[34]

The records of the case do not state the precise nature of the allegations made against the boys. It appears, however, that they were accused not of sexual reading per se but of sexual speech. Edwards's notes focus on the boys' "filthy communication," and Oliver Warner's use in his confession of the quasi-legal phrase "very unclean and lascivious expressions" also suggests that the young men were charged with some form of lewd speech. Nevertheless, it is likely, given the interrelations among private reading, communal reading, and speech, that the charge implicitly incorporated whatever additional offenses may have related to the boys' possession and consumption of illicit books.[35]

The affair entered a second phase because many Northampton residents did not share Edwards's judgment of the boys' behavior. Although the church brethren "with one consent, and much Zeal, manifested it to be their Opinion, that it ought to be enquired into," when the matter was brought into family and community circles, that consensus rapidly broke down. Hopkins may not have exaggerated when he quipped that many of the brethren "condemned what they had done, before they got home to their own Houses." Prior to the first meeting of the investigating committee, "a great Number of Heads of Families altered their minds" and decided "that their Children should not be called to an Account in such a way for such things." When the committee finally did convene, some of the accused "refused to appear" and "others that did appear, behaved unmannerly, and with a great Degree of Insolence, and contempt of the Authority of the Church."[36] While waiting to be interviewed, a number of the boys entertained themselves by playing "leap frog" and "dancing in the lot."[37] As the door of the committee room cracked open, Simeon Root, "in a loud and earnest manner" and "with an air of contempt," announced, "What do we here? We won't stay here all day long!" Simeon's brother Timothy similarly confirmed his propensity for ungoverned speech when he professed he would not "worship a wig" and asserted he did not "care a turd" or "a fart" for any of the committee members. Declaring that he "ben't obliged to wait any longer on their arses," Timothy, along with Simeon and a couple of other boys, further exhibited his disrespect for the committee's proceedings by running off to the local tavern to have "a mug of flip."[38]

While the boys' original misbehavior reflected their adolescent susceptibility to the sin of sensuality, their conduct during the committee proceedings involved the second of youth's sins, that of pride. Unregulated speech characterized both episodes, but by compounding the nature of their offense, the boys may have delivered to the committee a more socially acceptable means of disciplining them. With the testimony of such town elites as Colonel John Stoddard, Captain Roger Clapp, and Deacon Ebenezer Pomeroy weighing against them, Timothy and Simeon Root admitted to being "guilty of scandalously contemptuous behavior toward the authority of the church." Although they resolved to behave themselves "more humbly, meekly and decently" and to treat their superiors "with due honor and respect," absent from their confessions is any mention of "those foul expressions" that had occasioned the proceedings.[39] Only one of the boys implicated in the original scandal confessed to the charge of lascivious speech, and his admission is, in its wording, grudging and insincere. Oliver Warner appears to have confessed that he uttered "certain very unclean and lascivious expressions" and to have promised "to avoid all lascivious, vain and light conversation" in the future. But he also protested that he did "not remember my using those expressions" and stated that he acknowledged them only because two witnesses "so positively and constantly declare that I did utter those expressions."[40] The confession's explicit reference to the dual testimony suggests, moreover, that it was only through the application of the "two-witness rule," a traditional provision of both the colonial legal system and Congregational church discipline, that Oliver Warner felt compelled to make even this obviously lame admission.[41]

The goal of church disciplinary proceedings was confession, which allowed the offending member to reclaim his or her status within the community of the faithful. That Edwards secured three confessions indicates that he maintained a level of community support sufficient to bring the bad book affair to a successful conclusion. That the confessions were incomplete and possibly insincere, however, reflects the widespread criticism of his prosecution of the case.

The list of disputed points Edwards compiled during the case suggests that the controversy focused on the distinction between private and public offense. A long-standing principle of Congregational church discipline, which Edwards cites as the "rule in the eighteenth of Matthew," stipulated that private offenses should be addressed first in private conference and only dealt with publicly if private means proved unsatisfactory.[42] The parents of the accused boys evidently maintained that their sons had committed "a private offense" and that Edwards should "have gone and talked privately with them" before initiating public disciplinary proceedings, which, in any case, were justifiable only if prompted by a specific complaint, of which there was none. Edwards disagreed with both positions. To deny a church the power "to meddle without a complaint," he wrote, is to strip the church of its "power of authoritative inquiry" and its "power of self-preservation." According to his interpretation of scripture, a complaint was necessary "only in the two instances of personal injury and private offense." The boys' reading and talking about sex, Edwards strenuously maintained, was "not a private offense." Offenses "become public," he asserted, not only "by [there] being a great many witnesses" to them but also "by the fame of them." Since the boys' behavior had become the subject of widespread gossip—even Edwards had heard the rumor—it could not be classified as a private offense. Furthermore, his preliminary questioning of the boys "could not" have been "done privately," for without a public "search" and the opportunity to encounter witnesses "face to face," he could not discover which boys were implicated in the scandal.[43]

In colonial New England, according to Mary Beth Norton, the boundary between public and private was far from exact. Although the colonists acknowledged "the theoretical opposition *public/private,*" they "found it extremely difficult to draw a clear line between the two" because "the meaning of *private* was by no means fixed." An expansive meaning of "public," which considered relations among family members and a wide range of sexual and moral behaviors subject to public regulation by both church and state, predominated during the first century of settlement. In this period, "private" signified, quite simply, all that was "not public," but the broad scope of the public realm left the private little room. Edwards's assertion that the boys' actions became public "by the fame of them" signals that he was using a traditional form of the public/private distinction, which equated public with "widely known" and private with "concealed, secret."[44] His campaign to supervise the morality of his parishioners also displayed his continuing commitment to a worldview in which the meaning of privacy was so ambiguous that all actions were potentially subject to public scrutiny. This worldview shaped the brethren's initial support of Edwards, but when they left the meetinghouse, it came into conflict with a new worldview that was emerging in the midst of the colonists' everyday sociability.

The narrow and contested zone of privacy that had characterized the Puritan period began to expand in the eighteenth century and to distinguish itself more precisely from the public sphere, thereby shielding many areas of human activity previously regulated by church and state from the scrutiny of the public authorities. "The mission of governing the tongue," Jane Kamensky notes, "passed from the sphere of law to the sphere of etiquette" and "had become by the mid–eighteenth century a private matter, an exercise in self-control."[45] According to Cornelia Hughes Dayton, the developing ethic of privacy also encouraged "middling and elite families" to claim "the right to keep private the premarital sexual lapses of their young people." As Dayton has demonstrated, the "single standard" of godly behavior that Puritan legislators had tried to apply to "men and women in the areas of sexual and moral conduct" began in the 1690s to give way to a double standard, which "taught young men that their sexual irresponsibility was forgivable while it held women to a higher standard of sexual virtue."[46] This incipient double standard transformed the court's approach to a variety of sexual wrongdoing, particularly fornication and rape. No longer willing to accept a woman's testimony at face value, judges began to require corroborating evidence to prove paternity or sexual assault. Men routinely refused to confess when accused of such offenses and hired lawyers able to manipulate the increasingly complex legal system to help them escape conviction. By mid-century, criminal courts had virtually ceased prosecuting men for fornication, which had the effect of rendering premarital pregnancy essentially "a woman's crime."[47]

Placing the bad book affair in the context of this developing double standard reveals that the case set the town ablaze precisely because the offenses were gendered. Taking a traditional stance, Edwards aligned himself with those evangelicals Dayton has characterized as wishing "to return to a single standard akin to that of the seventeenth century," a standard that insisted "on chastity for both sexes and proper public contrition from all sinners, no matter their social rank."[48] His critics, however, were committed to a more modern conception of gender, which privatized and generally condoned—with a sly wink and a nod—male sexual license. Because the language expressing this new gender ideology had yet to be fully articulated in the 1740s, those supporting the boys resorted to a form of discourse that had commonly mediated disputes over privacy in the previous century. In other words, Edwards's critics followed a pattern displayed by Anne Hutchinson, who accused the Bay ministers during her trial of "a Breach of Church Rule, to bringe a Thing in publicke before they have delt with me in private."[49] But when Northampton's parents argued that their sons' sex talk was a private offense that should have been handled privately, they applied to "private" a meaning not available in Hutchinson's Boston.

Three other cases of church discipline in 1740s Northampton illustrate Edwards's ineffectuality as he struggled to defend an outmoded ideology of gender and to use the powers of his office to compensate for the court's diminishing role in the regulation of morals. In all three Edwards tried to discipline members of his congregation for sexual misconduct, and in all three the original offense was followed by an additional charge of contempt for authority or of attempting to evade responsibility and punishment. The first case dates from 12 June 1743 when, according to Northampton church records, Samuel Danks was excommunicated for the sin of fornication and for "contempt of the authority of the church."[50] Although nothing more is known of this case, the contempt charge and subsequent excommunication suggest that Danks did not willingly submit to discipline. The second case occurred in February 1747, when Thomas Wait was accused of both fornication and falsehood. Not only did he refuse to confess his sin, but he publicly denied fathering Jemimah Miller's child, which she had put to him, as was the custom, "in time of travail."[51] Wait contested the charges, arguing that the woman's word should not be accepted as true without corroboration. The church evidently supported the traditional view that a woman in labor would not lie and found Wait guilty. Wait, nevertheless, continued to deny his culpability, for he requested an appeal of the church's verdict to a council of ministers in April 1747.[52]

A more complex and well-documented fornication case began sometime prior to February 1748 when Martha Root gave birth to twins, one of whom died, and named Elisha Hawley, son of one of Northampton's wealthiest and most prominent families, as the father.[53] Elisha's brother Joseph was a young attorney eager to make a reputation for himself, and with his assistance Elisha went to great lengths to avoid accepting any financial or moral responsibility for the child. Insisting upon his paternity, Martha brought a civil suit against

Hawley, and in May 1748 she was awarded a monetary settlement of £155.[54] Edwards, however, evidently thought that the required payment was an insufficient penalty, for the church brethren proceeded to excommunicate Elisha for the sin of fornication and to determine it his duty to marry Martha. Like Thomas Wait, the Hawleys appealed this judgment to a council of ministers, which convened in June 1749. Edwards prepared for this meeting the equivalent of a legal brief, and both he and Joseph Hawley presented to the council their respective arguments on the "obligation of a man to marry a virgin that he hath humbled."[55] Although the council accepted without dispute the judgment that Elisha Hawley was guilty of fornication and determined him "bound in conscience" to marry the mother of his child, they stopped short of declaring it "his duty" to marry her; moreover, they recommended that, "upon his making a penitent confession of the sin of fornication," his excommunication be lifted and he be accepted back into the fellowship of the church.

The three fornication cases over which Edwards presided conform closely to the pattern Cornelia Hughes Dayton associates with the emergence of a sexual double standard in colonial New England, and the bad book episode follows the same sequence of events. In each, although Edwards's attempt to apply a single standard was generally supported by the church brethren, it aroused opposition in the larger community. Buoyed by that turn of events, the men charged with sexual misconduct did not humbly submit to the discipline of the church but vigorously protested the proceedings against them. This pattern indicates that the bad book affair was not an isolated event but, instead, was yet another battle in the campaign waged over the new, emergent ethic of privacy.

To describe the bad book affair simply as a manifestation of Edwards's declining ministerial authority is, thus, incomplete, for such an interpretation fails to consider changes in the underlying social forces that specified the nature of that authority. In his 22 June 1750 "Farewell Sermon" to the Northampton church, Edwards reflected on the controversies that had hindered his efforts to reform the town's youth. From the outset of his ministry, he explained, he had "had a peculiar concern for the souls of the young people." He sincerely "sought the good and not the hurt of our young people" and found it "a thing exceeding beautiful" if they "could be persuaded, when they meet together, to converse as Christians" and to avoid "impurity, levity and extravagance." For his efforts, however, he had received not his congregation's respect but "their reproach." His campaign "for the suppressing vice among our young people," he observed, gave "great offense" and was the occasion "by which I became so obnoxious." He nevertheless addressed to the young people one last warning "against frolicking" and "some other liberties commonly taken by young people in the land." Only the prospect of an eventual eschatological vindication tempered the obvious futility of this final warning. On Judgment Day, he predicted, it would appear that "the things I have taught you were true" and "the counsels I have given you were good." People might speak out "in justification of such liberties and customs, and may laugh at warnings against them," Edwards cautioned, "but God will approve and confirm" the besieged minister's efforts "in that day when we shall meet before him."[56]

Edwards struggled to preserve within his congregation the gender relations that characterized the premodern worldview of Puritan New England, but despite threats of divine judgment, his position was rapidly losing support in the broader society. He made himself "obnoxious" by rejecting the new laissez-faire approach to male sexual ethics and waging an extended campaign premised on the belief that men should be held publicly accountable for behaviors increasingly considered matters of private morality. Gender-related conflict was, therefore, a defining feature of Edwards's ministry in the 1740s. Although this conflict does not directly explain why his congregation voted to dismiss him, it does indicate that one issue that helped to undermine his tenure in Northampton was gender. When, in the final controversy over church membership, Edwards altered long-standing policy and demanded that his parishioners subject their personal piety to public scrutiny, the vast majority of his parishioners decided that he must go. In this last stand, the majority of Edwards's supporters were women.[57] Perhaps they sensed that the newly emerging configuration of public and private space would offer men vastly greater liberties than it would women.

NOTES

The New England Quarterly 75 (June 2002) for "Bad Books and Bad Boys: The Transformation of Gender in Eighteenth-Century North Hampton," by Ava Chamberlain. Copyright held by *The New England Quarterly*. Reproduced by permission of the publisher and the author.

 1. Samuel Hopkins, *The Life and Character of the Late Reverend Mr. Jonathan Edwards* (Boston: S. Kneeland, 1765), 53–54, 55.

 2. The brethren "chose a Number of Men, to assist their Pastor in examining into the Affair. Upon which Mr. Edwards appointed the time for their meeting at his House: and then read a Catalogue of the Names of young Persons, whom he desired to come to his House at the same time. Some were the accused, and some Witnesses; but it was

not then declared of which Number any particular Person was" (Hopkins, *Life of Edwards,* 54).

3. Sereno E. Dwight, *The Life of President Edwards* (New York, 1830), 299–300; James Russell Trumbull, *History of Northampton, Massachusetts, from Its Settlement in 1654,* 2 vols. (Northampton: Gazette Printing, 1898), 2:202; Ola Elizabeth Winslow, *Jonathan Edwards, 1703–1758* (1940; reprint, New York: Collier Books, 1961), 207; Patricia J. Tracy, *Jonathan Edwards, Pastor: Religion and Society in Eighteenth-Century Northampton* (New York: Hill and Wang, 1979), 160–64, 193.

4. On the image of helpmeet, see Laurel Thatcher Ulrich, *Good Wives: Image and Reality in the Lives of Women in Northern New England, 1650–1750* (1980; reprint, New York: Vintage Books, 1991), 35–50, 106–17; on spiritual equality, see Amanda Porterfield, *Female Piety in Puritan New England: The Emergence of Religious Humanism* (New York: Oxford Univ. Press, 1992).

5. See Cornelia Hughes Dayton, *Women before the Bar: Gender, Law, and Society in Connecticut, 1639–1789* (Chapel Hill: Univ. of North Carolina Press, 1995), as well as her earlier essay "Turning Points and the Relevance of Colonial Legal History," *William and Mary Quarterly* 50 (January 1993): 7–17. See also Mary Beth Norton, *Founding Mothers and Fathers: Gendered Power and the Forming of American Society* (1996; reprint, New York: Vintage Books, 1997). In an earlier essay ("The Evolution of White Women's Experience in Early America," *American Historical Review* 89 [June 1984]: 593–619), Norton maintained that the transitional period began as early as the 1660s, but she later called "that date twenty years too early" (*Founding Mothers,* 416n. 27).

6. Hopkins, *Life of Edwards,* 54.

7. The fragmentary manuscripts that document this incident are housed at the Franklin Trask Library, Andover Newton Theological School, Newton Centre, Massachusetts. They include a list of witnesses/suspects; documents entitled "Here Are Included the Testimonies against Oliver Warner, given in the Spring, in the Year 1744" and "Papers Concerning Young Men's Reading Midwives' Books, Their Contempt of the Church, etc."; draft and final versions of excerpts from the testimony transcripts; the confessions of Timothy and Simeon Root; a draft version of Oliver Warner's confession; and Edwards's notes outlining issues in dispute in the controversy and defending his actions. All quotations from these manuscripts are by permission of the Franklin Trask Library, Andover Newton Theological School, and are taken from a transcription (cited as "Bad Book Papers") supplied by *The Works of Jonathan Edwards,* New Haven, Connecticut. Some of these documents are published in *A Jonathan Edwards Reader,* ed. John E. Smith, Harry S. Stout, and Kenneth P. Minkema (New Haven: Yale Univ. Press, 1995), 172–78, and in Thomas H. Johnson's "Jonathan Edwards and the 'Young Folks' Bible,'" *New England Quarterly* 5 (January 1932): 37–54. In addition, there is a letter

from Edwards to Dorothy Danks Hannam, 26 March 1744 (*Letters and Personal Writings*, ed. George S. Claghorn, *The Works of Jonathan Edwards*, vol. 16 [New Haven: Yale Univ. Press, 1998], 143), asking for information about the incident.

8. Church membership information is taken from Kenneth P. Minkema's "Annotated Church Membership Records from Northampton, Connecticut, 1677–1760," unpublished manuscript.

9. Trumbull, *History of Northampton*, 2:202.

10. Youth was one of four "ages of man" that, eighteenth-century Puritans agreed, formed the human life course. For the boys' average age, see Tracy, *Jonathan Edwards, Pastor*, 162; for a definition of adolescence, see Roger Thompson's "Adolescent Culture in Colonial Massachusetts," *Journal of Family History* 9 (summer 1984): 127n. 1.

11. On colonial adolescent culture, see Ross W. Beales, "In Search of the Historical Child: Miniature Adulthood and Youth in Colonial New England," *American Quarterly* 27 (October 1975): 379–98; N. Ray Hiner, "Adolescence in Eighteenth-Century America," *History of Childhood Quarterly* 3 (fall 1975): 253–80; Gerald F. Moran and Maris A. Vinovskis, "Troubled Youth: Children at Risk in Early Modern England, Colonial America, and Nineteenth-Century America," in their *Religion, Family, and the Life Course: Explorations in the Social History of Early America* (Ann Arbor: Univ. of Michigan Press, 1992), 141–80; and Thompson, "Adolescent Culture," the substance of which is also found in chapter 5 of his *Sex in Middlesex: Popular Mores in a Massachusetts County, 1649–1699* (Amherst: Univ. of Massachusetts Press, 1986).

12. Jonathan Edwards, *A Faithful Narrative of the Surprising Work of God*, in *The Great Awakening*, ed. C. C. Goen, *The Works of Jonathan Edwards*, vol. 4 (New Haven: Yale Univ. Press, 1972), 146.

13. Hiner, "Adolescence in Eighteenth-Century America," 260–61; see also Moran and Vinovskis, *Religion, Family, and the Life Course*, 151–52.

14. Richard P. Gildrie, *The Profane, the Civil, and the Godly: The Reformation of Manners in Orthodox New England, 1679–1749* (University Park: Pennsylvania State Univ. Press, 1994), 9, 43, 106–7.

15. Michael J. Crawford, *Seasons of Grace: Colonial New England's Revival Tradition in Its British Context* (New York: Oxford Univ. Press, 1991), 23.

16. Edwards, *Works*, 4:147–49, 158.

17. Edwards to Rev. Thomas Prince, 12 December 1743, Edwards, *Works*, 16:115–17; see also Jonathan Edwards, *Some Thoughts Concerning the Present Revival of Religion*, in Edwards, *Works*, 4:326.

18. According to Crawford, "prayer for revival gradually took the place of covenant renewal" in the decades following the turn of the eighteenth century. Although common during the campaign for the reformation of manners, only Edwards's "account of

the New England revivals of the 1740s mentions renewal of covenant" (*Seasons of Grace,* 181).

19. Edwards to Prince, 12 December 1743, Edwards, *Works,* 16:123–24.

20. Thompson reports two incidents of adolescent group reading of a sex manual in *Sex in Middlesex,* 85–86, 87.

21. David D. Hall, *Worlds of Wonder, Days of Judgment: Popular Religious Belief in Early New England* (1989; reprint, Cambridge: Harvard Univ. Press, 1990), 54. On the cheap print trade in New England, see also Bruce C. Daniels, *Puritans at Play: Leisure and Recreation in Colonial New England* (New York: St. Martin's Griffin, 1995), 40, and *A History of the Book in America,* vol. 1: *The Colonial Book in the Atlantic World,* ed. Hugh Amory and David D. Hall (Cambridge: Cambridge Univ. Press, 2000), 335, 387, 391–93.

22. "Testimonies against Oliver Warner," in "Bad Book Papers."

23. Thomas Dawkes, *The Midwife Rightly Instructed: or, the Way, which all Women desirous to learn, should take, to acquire the True Knowledge and be Successful in the Practice of, the Art of Midwifery* (London: J. Oswald, 1736), iv, xv, xvii, xxxi, xviii, 4, and passim. Thomas H. Johnson, who first attempted to identify the bad book, incorrectly concluded that *The Midwife Rightly Instructed* was a variant of the title of one of the Aristotle texts discussed below ("Jonathan Edwards and the 'Young Folks' Bible,'" 52–54). But as Mary Fissell has shown, the boys were reading at least two and possibly three different popular medical texts (Mary E. Fissell, "Making a Masterpiece: The *Aristotle* Texts in Vernacular Medical Culture," in *Right Living: An Anglo-American Tradition of Self-Help Medicine and Hygiene,* ed. Charles E. Rosenberg [Baltimore: Johns Hopkins Univ. Press, 2003]).

24. See Ulrich, *Good Wives,* 126–35.

25. "Testimonies against Oliver Warner," in "Bad Book Papers."

26. Fissell, "Making a Masterpiece."

27. The three versions of *Aristotle's Masterpiece* were first issued in 1684, 1697, and 1702, respectively (Fissell, "Making a Masterpiece"). The collected edition, entitled *The Works of Aristotle: The Famous Philosopher,* appeared in 1733 and, in addition to the *Masterpiece,* contained *The Problems of Aristotle, Aristotle's Last Legacy,* and *Aristotle's Complete and Enlarged Midwife.* Because all of the Aristotle texts share a great deal of common material, a general notion of what the boys were reading can be acquired from any of these titles.

28. Introduction to *Aristotle's Master-Piece: or, the Secrets of Generation Displayed in all the Parts thereof* (London: Printed for W. B., 1694; reprinted, New York: Garland Publishing, 1986).

29. "Testimonies against Oliver Warner," in "Bad Book Papers." Bathsheba Negro, a church member, is identified in Oliver Warner's confession as "Maj. [Ebenezer] Pomeroy's

servant." As her name suggests, Bathsheba was an African-American slave. Her presence at the gatherings adds a racial dimension to the episode that, while intriguing, is beyond the concerns of the present investigation.

30. Jane Kamensky, *Governing the Tongue: The Politics of Speech in Early New England* (New York: Oxford Univ. Press, 1997), 14, 31.

31. "Testimonies against Oliver Warner," in "Bad Book Papers."

32. In his account of the bad book affair, Trumbull notes that "Sarah Clarke, daughter of Ebenezer, was one of those accused of reading bad books" (203n. 1). Because her name appears as neither suspect nor witness in Edwards's records of the case, however, Trumbull's claim cannot be confirmed.

33. Hopkins, *Life of Edwards*, 54.

34. Edwards's notes defending his actions, in "Bad Book Papers."

35. Oliver Warner's confession, in "Bad Book Papers." Similarly, Hopkins describes the boys as using the books "to promote lascivious and obscene Discourse among the young People" (*Life of Edwards*, 53–54).

36. Hopkins, *Life of Edwards*, 54. On the tendency of "collectivities of men" in colonial New England to believe in "the necessity of achieving consensus within their own ranks," see Norton, *Founding Mothers*, 217–22.

37. "Papers Concerning Young Men's Reading Midwives' Books," in "Bad Book Papers."

38. Fair copy of the testimonies, in "Bad Book Papers." According to Bruce Daniels, flip, which "became New England's most popular mixed drink in the eighteenth century," was a mixture of "two-thirds beer, sweetened with sugar, molasses, dried pumpkin, and a measure of rum" (*Puritans at Play*, 154–55).

39. Confession of Timothy and Simeon Root, in "Bad Book Papers." In the fair copy of the testimonies, Timothy Root is reported to have admitted to the original offense: "As to those foul expressions, I have full remembrance of them."

40. Draft of Oliver Warner's confession, in "Bad Book Papers." Kamensky observes that failure to remember was a common way "those called upon to apologize appear deliberately to have flouted the conventions of penitential discourse" (*Governing the Tongue*, 145).

41. Oliver Warner's confession names Joanna Clark and Bathsheba Negro as testifying that they had heard him "utter certain very unclean and lascivious expressions," specifically those comments in which he referred to menstruation. Of all the talk generated by the boys' illicit reading, only that cryptic comment referring to the moon and blue circles under the eyes was successfully sanctioned. The two-witness rule is defined in the *Cambridge Platform*, which states, referencing Matt. 18:16, that for private offenses "if the offender heare not his brother, the brother offended is to take with him one or two more, that in the mouth of two or three witnesses, every word may be established"

(Williston Walker, *The Creeds and Platforms of Congregationalism* [New York: Charles Scribner's Sons, 1893], 227); see also Dayton, *Women before the Bar*, 30.

42. Edwards's notes defending his actions, in "Bad Book Papers." This rule is grounded in Matt. 18:15–17 and is also articulated in the *Cambridge Platform* (Walker, *The Creeds and Platforms of Congregationalism,* 227). In October 1731 the Hampshire County Ministerial Association reaffirmed this rule in its determination that a church should use "private admonition" before it makes offenses public "matters of church discipline" (Tracy, *Jonathan Edwards, Pastor,* 256n. 36).

43. Edwards's notes defending his actions, in "Bad Book Papers." In August 1749, according to the Northampton church records, the church endorsed Edwards's position by voting "that any 'public fame of scandal in the church' might be brought to the church by the pastor for their deliberation, even if there was no complaint" (Tracy, *Jonathan Edwards, Pastor,* 167).

44. Norton, *Founding Mothers,* 22, 24, 21, 169, 383; see also her discussion of the case of Anne Eaton, 165–80.

45. Kamensky, *Governing the Tongue,* 190, 182.

46. Dayton, *Women before the Bar,* 215, 10, 229; see also her article "Taking the Trade: Abortion and Gender Relations in an Eighteenth-Century New England Village," *William and Mary Quarterly* 48 (January 1991): 19–49.

47. Laurel Thatcher Ulrich, *A Midwife's Tale: The Life of Martha Ballard Based on Her Diary, 1785–1812* (New York: Knopf, 1990), 148; see also Carol F. Karlsen, *The Devil in the Shape of a Woman: Witchcraft in Colonial New England* (1987; reprint, New York: Vintage Books, 1989), 194–202.

48. Dayton, *Women before the Bar,* 208.

49. Quoted by Norton, in *Founding Mothers,* 389; see "A Report of the Trial of Mrs. Ann Hutchinson before the Church in Boston, March, 1638," in *The Antinomian Controversy, 1636–1638: A Documentary History,* ed. David D. Hall (Middletown, Conn.: Wesleyan Univ. Press, 1968), 353. See also Norton's analysis of Anne Hutchinson's trial generally, in *Founding Mothers,* 359–99.

50. Records of the First Church of Northampton, microfilm copy, vol. 1, p. 25, Forbes Library, Northampton, Massachusetts.

51. Thomas Wait to Edwards, 9 March 1746/47, Beinecke Library, Yale University. A 1668 Massachusetts law codified the "practice of asking unwed mothers to name the father of their child during delivery." This man "would be judged the 'reputed father' of her child and required to pay for its support" (Ulrich, *A Midwife's Tale,* 149).

52. Edwards to Rev. Robert Breck, 7 April 1747, Edwards, *Works,* 16:222. There is no record of the council's decision.

53. For two recent accounts of the Hawley-Root case, see Kathryn Kish Sklar's "Culture versus Economics: A Case of Fornication in Northampton in the 1740s," *University*

of *Michigan Papers in Women's Studies* (May 1978): 35–56, and Tracy's *Jonathan Edwards, Pastor,* 164–66.

54. As criminal prosecutions for fornication decreased for men, it became more common for women to bring civil suits to force their lovers to pay child support; see Dayton, *Women before the Bar,* 218–22.

55. Edwards's "brief" is housed in the Franklin Trask Library, Andover Newton Theological School, Newton Centre, Massachusetts. Permission to quote courtesy of the Franklin Trask Library and transcription supplied courtesy of *The Works of Jonathan Edwards,* New Haven, Connecticut.

56. Jonathan Edwards, "A Farewell Sermon Preached at the First Precinct in Northampton, After the People's Public Rejection of Their Minister . . . on June 22, 1750," in *The Sermons of Jonathan Edwards: A Reader,* ed. Wilson H. Kimnach, Kenneth P. Minkema, and Douglas A. Sweeney (New Haven: Yale Univ. Press, 1999), 234–35.

57. The vote was 230 in favor of dismissal and 23 opposed, with only male church members voting (Winslow, *Jonathan Edwards, 1703–1758,* 235–36). In a letter to one of his Scottish correspondents, Edwards remarks on the gendered nature of the factions in Northampton. "The people of Northampton are hitherto destitute of a minister," he writes. "But the major part of 'em seem to continue without any relentings or misgivings of heart concerning what has been done; at least the major part of the leading men in the congregation. But there is a number whose hearts are broke at what has come to pass; . . . and there are more women of this sort than men" (Edwards to Rev. John Erskine, 15 November 1750, Edwards, *Works,* 16:363–64).

PART TWO

Edwards and American Culture

Jonathan Edwards, the Edwardsians, and the Sacred Cause of Free Trade

Mark Valeri

On 1 February 1775 Jonathan Edwards the Younger, pastor of the White Haven Church in New Haven, urged his parishioners to revolutionary action against Great Britain. Among the many reasons he gave, he emphasized British violation of the natural rights of Americans. Chief among these rights was the freedom to engage in commerce without interference. Rebellion was a moral duty because "the court of Great Britain" had "laid the most burdensome restrictions on our trade, whereby we are restrained from carrying on free trade," especially with "those foreign parts where we could [trade] to the greatest advantage." Edwards mentioned excise taxes, port bills, trade restrictions, monopolies, and unfair navigation courts. He especially fumed against the "vast train of collectors, comptrollers," and other royal officials who clogged up exchange and received salaries from fees levied on merchants. These measures, he griped, artificially raised the prices of goods over their market values.[1]

Previous discussions of religion and the American Revolution rarely have noted the remarkable conjunction between commercial and revolutionary sensibilities represented by the political preaching of Jonathan Edwards Jr. Other paradigms exist for explaining the patriotism of New England clergy: fears of Anglicanism, popular resentment against social elites, or republican politics and the language of liberty. However useful, these paradigms do not account for the economic motives for the likes of Jonathan Edwards Jr. to support Independence.[2] What *was* the son of Jonathan Edwards doing, arguing that New Englanders ought to sacrifice themselves for the sake of a market economy?

The question, of course, assumes that one does not readily associate the Edwards family with the culture of the market in the eighteenth century. Indeed, much of the existing commentary, particularly on Jonathan Edwards Sr. (hereafter, simply Edwards), dismisses his social thought out of hand or highlights his antipathy toward the new economy. Edwards has been read as the proponent of a theology of transcendence and an evangelical piety that led to a thorough rejection of market culture. From this perspective, he appears as a throwback to the communal ethic of Puritanism. In Perry Miller's trenchant, even if problematic, treatment, Edwards appears as a prophetic critic of the self-satisfied, bourgeois ethos of provincial New England.[3]

To be sure, there have been several recent efforts to connect Edwards and his fellow evangelicals to the market in terms of a generalized social ethos. That is, many scholars have described Edwards as promoting a religious style and theological system that indirectly contributed to a modern, capitalistic personality. Social historians of the eighteenth-century revivals have argued that New Lights such as Edwards transmitted an individualistic, incipiently democratic, and definitively commercial religiosity. Several intellectual historians have contended that the Calvinist doctrines of original sin and divine providence, however unattached to specific economic ideas, implied the inevitability and legitimacy of market laws. Cultural historians have begun to explore how the rhetorical techniques and publication strategies of popular revivalists promoted market-like attitudes toward social mobility, communication, and consumption.[4]

Such work has helped us to see possible connections between popular evangelicalism and liberal economic culture; but it omits consideration of how Edwards's quite formidable thought fits into the picture. In many ways, Edwards still vanishes—a negligible character at most—from the story of American Protestantism and commerce. This paper attempts a reconsideration of Edwards, his followers, and a market culture in eighteenth-century New England. In contrast to much of the existing literature, which stresses Edwards's affinity with Puritanism, it emphasizes how some of the post-Puritan aspects of Edwards's ethical writings contributed to an alliance between evangelical religion and market culture.[5]

The discussion below suggests that Edwards brought the moral language of Calvinism into a discursive milieu that was congruent with the ethics of a market culture. It draws on the observation that Edwards participated in the rapidly expanding market of ideas in the world of eighteenth-century Anglo America letters. His participation in this cosmopolitan culture modeled—one might even say legitimated—similar efforts by his followers. To be sure, Edwards was not a prophet for the market. He was a transitional figure between his Puritan forebears, who disapproved of the market in their day, and his late-eighteenth-century followers, New Divinity men such as his son, who came to support a political revolution in defense of New England's property rights and commercial aspirations.

This is not to suggest that one can draw straightforward and unambiguous corollaries between Edwards's theology, new social and moral theories, and a market culture. Edwards criticized theological or ethical assertions that contradicted orthodox Christian teaching, and he devoted much of his writing to exegesis of the Bible with interpretive strategies that resisted many contemporary moral assumptions. Moreover, he often preached against market behaviors. He set the organic obligations of Christian virtue against self-motivated economic activity, warning his people against using supply and demand as the only criteria for determining their prices. Edwards can be described as a republican social theorist with an egalitarian and communal ethic at odds with the market.[6]

Yet intellectual historians who have given close attention to Edwards's ethics offer the possibility of an alternative reading. Edwards can be situated in what Robert Wuthnow has described as an Enlightenment "community of discourse." That term allows for ideological conflict—between, say, New Lights and rationalists—within a shared set of linguistic and theoretical assumptions. These conceptual frameworks encompass beliefs about the goals of social order and the grammar, or rules and norms of argument (what counts as valid), in public speech.[7] This reference to discursive communities helps us to recover the relation between religion, economics, and political change. It helps us to understand the so-called long eighteenth century in New England as a passage from a hierarchical and deferential discourse grounded in Puritan divinity to a liberal, democratic, and protocapitalist discourse.[8]

One can pursue such a reading with an initial observation: Edwards wrote much of his theology using basic terms and definitions that could be thought of as "rational" in the sense of having universal currency among British and European writers of his day. Edwards participated in a conversation with philosophers such as Locke, Leibniz, and Malebranche about fundamental epistemological questions. He used their terms, accepted their rules of logic, and employed their modes of analysis. Even as he attempted to improve on them, he set aside traditional Puritan suspicions against contemporary metaphysics as a source for ethical categories.[9]

To put this in a slightly different framework, Edwards used the theoretically laden language of virtue, benevolence, and moral fitness. In one of his more striking meditations, he explained that these moral idioms were the valid terms of religious ethics, because those "abstract ideas which we call universals" (and the implied "we" is the Anglo-European philosophical community of his day) communicated moral truths that crossed national, social, and cultural boundaries. Technical, generalized, or abstract language approximated a form of pure speech. This helps to explain why Edwards, who was so concerned for everyday moral experience, often wrote prose that was nearly void of concrete social reference. He argued at great length about the nature of true virtue, with heady references to "being-in-itself," and did not mention one specific deed, because he was searching for a universal moral terminology.[10]

Edwards furthermore saw in such a universal language the possibility for a conversation between Calvinism and new ethical theories that were derived from observable laws of social order and harmony. To be sure, he always attempted to turn the ethics of the Enlightenment to apologetic purposes. In a technical sense, he claimed that only the regenerate had a true realization of the meaning of experience in the world: the dependence of all beings on the most high and omnipotent God-in-Christ. He asserted that only true believers could discern rightly the relationship between the natural moral law and divine command. Yet Edwards held that writers such as Hugo Grotius (a natural law theorist), Samuel Clark (a rational idealist), and Francis Hutcheson (a proponent of the Moral Sense school of ethics) could say quite a bit that was useful and true, even if it was inadequate for an orthodox theology. In his striking introduction to *The Nature of True Virtue,* Edwards made this very point: he agreed with even "considerable Deists" about the definitions of essential moral terms such as "the universal system of existence," "virtue," "benevolence," and "love."[11]

Intellectual historians have told us this much about Edwards; but they have yet to consider how his conversation with Enlightened interlocutors implicated him in cultural expressions that also—in different contexts—legitimated many aspects of the market. Under pressure from commercial forces, communities that previously had been knit together by scriptural assumptions were compelled to articulate a new means of social integration.[12] Seventeenth-century Puritans immersed themselves in biblical motifs and metaphors, especially those reflected in the language of covenant. Godly moralists stressed the role of the clergy in interpreting scriptural rules, applying them quite directly to local circumstances, and nurturing a community of discipline to enforce them.[13]

Edwards, in contrast, was more than willing to write in an analytical vein, consider abstract moral categories, and urge individuals to see themselves as linked to a far-flung community in terms of universal laws that stood alongside evangelical imperatives. More often than not, Edwards looked to the evangelical church as the ultimate expression of this society. As he informed one of his Scottish correspondents, "the Church of God, in all Parts of the World, is but one. The distant members are closely united in one Glorious Head. This Union is very much her Beauty."[14] The logic of Edwards's comments, however, can be correlated with a version of cosmopolitan culture that was less evangelical and more commercial. In both Edwards's and the rationalists' accounts, people from distant lands could share moral ideas through a contemporary discourse; this discourse flowed through networks of communication that spread far beyond local societies. The very notion of such an invisible, global communion aligned Edwards with his contemporaries who viewed the exchange of knowledge in the market as a means of a moral society that transcended local, organic communities with their customary obligations.

Indeed, Edwards became a highly visible participant in the transatlantic commerce of ideas that was crucial to the development of a modern economic culture. To locate him here, in what Jürgen Habermas has described as the public sphere, is to suggest yet another connection between his theology and commerce.[15] Edwards was both a producer and a consumer in the international market. His accounts of revivals and reflections on them were exported to Scotland, printed there, and imported back to New England. Notably, he and his publishers conformed their narratives to contemporary standards of taste and reasonableness; they did not emphasize the visions, trances, and other evangelical excesses that appeared in private accounts of revivals. Even in his treatment of the Bible, which ostensibly contained a language peculiar to the saints, Edwards used (which is to say consumed) a striking array of modern sources. He considered how recent scientific and philosophical conventions, including those proposed by deist and other rationalist writers, affected the language of biblical interpretation. He roamed the disciplinary forefronts of textual and historical criticism, reading the latest works on astronomy, geology, antiquity, and philosophy of history. Edwards certainly did not jettison a fully Calvinist interpretation of Scripture, replete with notions of providential intervention into history, miracles, the cosmic struggle between God and Satan, and millennial speculations. Yet his scriptural notes and citations, often used for his weekly preaching, drew on the latest insights coming from the transatlantic republic of letters: scientific societies, learned clubs, and recent publications.[16]

To refer to Edwards as producer and consumer of the new moral discourse is not to claim that he endorsed any commercial system per se. His specific economic recommendations were few and far between. Yet they did reveal something of the effect of his conversation with progressive social theorists. To give one example, Puritan moralists often critiqued commercial innovations, such as rapidly fluctuating prices, consumption of luxury goods, and treating credit as a commodity for profit. From their perspective, a simple reading of biblical injunctions against usury forbade such market practices. Edwards, in contrast, rarely focused on such specific rules. He stressed the pursuit of virtue within the market. This did not mean that people had a warrant to play the market without regard for moral restraints. Edwards contended in a 1747 sermon that merchants should not always raise their prices to the highest possible profit margin. The problem with such inflationary tactics, he argued nonetheless, was not that they necessarily violated the Bible or were inherently vicious. Rather, they were bad because they hampered trade. They impeded a material means of social integration. Inflation constrained commerce when currency underwent constant devaluation, as it did during the mid–eighteenth century in Massachusetts. Warnings against inflation should not be taken to contradict the axioms of the market: "'tis no rule that men are bound to by, that in their dealings with their neighbours they must dispose of what they have in terms proportionably easy with those on which they came by 'em." Merchants may make a healthy profit from their wares and even price their goods according to current taste and fashion. To deny them this right, he shuddered, "would in Effect make all things common," which was "not agreeable to the design of the world," that is, to nature.[17]

Edwards sought to subject economic rules to this fundamental law: God designed economic exchange between free individuals to benefit all of society. Commerce is "one of those Improvements of Human society that are much for the Benefit of mankind when duly and properly managed," he noted. Or, as he put it more tellingly, "buying and selling is one exercise in society."[18]

Eighteenth-century moralists who employed similar formulations often found them compatible with the dictates of a market economy. Proponents of a liberal economic order saw the principles of the market not as ethical innovations but as natural and moral laws. They were descriptions of the way people *were* organized into a society. It was just this line of reasoning, according to Joyce Appleby, that convinced English theorists of the benefits of free-market exchange on a worldwide scale. In this intellectual milieu it was possible for merchants and ministers to conceive of individuals who followed rational modes of economic exchange, i.e. the profit motive, and yet who were united into an international and benevolent community.[19]

The potential for sociability according to rational economic laws certainly intrigued Edwards. On the rare occasions that he commented on the future of economic exchange, he foresaw that the spread of "knowledge and trade" would go hand in hand with "prosperity" and social union on a universal scale, as temporal affairs moved toward "one orderly, regular, beautiful society."[20] He culled from Boston newspapers and the *Scotch Magazine* the latest financial news, looking for signs of the progress of the market. He noted that the mercantilist taxation policies of the French monarchy signaled economic and social disaster. Conversely, news that the Pope had begun to encourage manufactures, abolish many Holy Days (thereby increasing the number of work days), and reform regressive economic laws in the papal states took Edwards aback. He could not fathom a reconciliation between false doctrine and commercial success.[21]

As a transition figure, Edwards conveyed no small amount of ambivalence toward a liberal commercial order. He did not follow Enlightenment moral rules all the way to a laissez-faire ethics. He fussed and fumed against avaricious merchants and self-legislating individuals. Yet he did set a discursive precedent for later American Calvinists who came to embrace the market. In line with the latest rules for social analysis he held that the chief end of public moral laws was social union on an international scale. He saw commerce as one potential link in a network of sociability. In the end, nonetheless, he was hardly confident that a market economy necessarily led to solidarity. He never deemed it a moral law in such terms.

Edwards's colleagues and followers, however, used the same language, the same discursive assumptions, to determine that the market did produce social solidarity and therefore was a moral law. They were true to his moral method and vocabulary (even if they did not reach the theological sophistication of Edwards) while expressing a level of confidence in the market that he never had. It was not just that Edwards's fellow evangelicals employed the latest in communication techniques, engaged in commercially oriented publishing, and were active agents in the transatlantic market of ideas.[22] They invested such networks with high moral purpose.

One might consider, for example, the efforts of Thomas Prince Jr., a close associate of Edwards who was instrumental in printing Edwards's works. In 1743 Prince began to produce a new serial publication, *The Christian History*. He designed it as a medium for knowledge about the revivals, and gave much attention to Edwards's role in them. During the same year, another periodical appeared in Boston. Benjamin Franklin promoted *The American Magazine and Historical Chronicle*, a vehicle for rational writers and economic progress.[23]

Although *The Christian History* and *The American Magazine* were intellectual competitors, they adopted the same layout, used the same editorial strategies, and produced parallel tables of contents. Just as Franklin's serial gave notice about current events in faraway places, such as China and St. Petersburg, Prince brought his readers news from New York, New Jersey, Georgia, England, and Scotland. *The American Magazine* included testimonials to literati such as Alexander Pope; Prince offered short biographies of New Light preachers. *The American Magazine* provided extracts from religious and moral essays on happiness or religious superstition; *The Christian History* excerpted sermons and treatises on the New Birth. *The American Magazine* printed letters with personal advice on marriage or business; letters in *The Christian History* recounted the moral virtues of local revivals. Finally, while Franklin reprinted historical writings by political commentators, Prince reprinted the historical reflections of Puritan divines.[24]

The format and content of these magazines can be traced to a common model: English publications such as Edmund Cave's *The Gentleman's Magazine*. Printed in London beginning in 1731, and widely imported into America, *The Gentleman's Magazine* mapped out perfectly the visual apparatus for a serial that promoted Enlightenment morals, progressive politics, and a market economy. Cave placed beneath the title an illustration of one of the great gates to inner London and its markets. A table of contents lay below the illustration. It included essays on scientific discoveries and voyages to distant lands, extracts from moral writings (the editors favored selections from Shaftesbury, Pope, Tindal, Woolston, and Swift), historical excerpts, and weekly notices of bankruptcies, values of the most popular stocks, and prices of staple goods, such as wheat or copper.[25]

News from distant lands, excerpts from scientific and moral essays of rationalist writers, letters about political or social affairs, and the promotion of success in a commercial order brought *The American Magazine* and *The Gentleman's Magazine* within the sphere of the emergent print culture of the eighteenth century. As David Hall has contended, the growth of such publications helped to form a transatlantic network of sociability. The exchange of Enlightenment ideals and fashionable commodities united producers and consumers. Boston and Philadelphia were too distant from the London exchange to warrant weekly updates in stock prices; but *The American Magazine* still announced its commercial orientation. In place of *The Gentleman's Magazine*'s picture of St. John's Gate, it presented a prospect of Boston harbor: wharves, docks, and ships, all situated in the New World by the images of an Indian, tobacco, and American flora. Intended as an item for popular consumption, *The American Magazine* fit well within the cultural matrix of the market.[26]

One can locate Prince's *Christian History*, just as one can Edwards's thoughts on commerce, in the same discursive milieu. Focused as it was on the preached word that stimulated revivals, *The Christian History* omitted the visual imagery of market gates, ships, and wharves. Yet the appeal to popular consumption in the use of extracts, the rapid and serial publication of news and ideas, the promotion of an international network of knowledge and experience, and the conviction that the present moment reflected the truth of universal verities marked Prince's New Light magazine as much as it did Cave's or Franklin's. Edwards envisioned an international society bound together by the latest moral philosophy, returned to Calvinism. Prince offered a popular vehicle to spread such bonds. In the process, Prince also joined Edwards in contributing to the creation of a modern public sphere. Edward Cave and his American imitators made progressive ideas accessible to a widespread audience through the treatment of news as a commodity and a corresponding diffusion of a wide array of new knowledge.[27]

Prince, like Edwards, did not advocate rationalist religion; but he, also like Edwards, did accept the same conventions as his more cosmopolitan models. No less than *The American Magazine, The Christian History* attempted to certify itself as intelligible and appealing to the common person, as a way for individuals to be united into a far-flung community, as employing universally acknowledged language, and as the reflection of a new and sociable moral conscience.

As if to make explicit this implicit connection between religion, printing, and a market culture, Thomas Prince's father, Thomas Prince Sr., previously had produced a manual for American merchants, *The Vade Mecum for America*. It offered what his son's *Christian History* lacked: lists of currency values and their relation to standard measures of goods, tables of simple and compound interest rates, meeting times for civil courts in all the colonies (the sites of negotiation between merchants and their debtors or creditors), dates and locations for trading fairs, descriptions of intercolonial and local roads, and even a gazette of streets in Boston, lest out-of-town merchants lose their way. Furnished with the *Vade Mecum* in one pocket, and the latest installment of *The Christian History* in another, the evangelical merchant belonged to a vast network of religious and commercial connections.[28]

Over the course of the 1750s and 1760s the next generation of evangelicals, Edwards's closest adherents, revealed the full implication of this initial, theoretical rapprochement between Calvinists and the market. Joseph Bellamy, to illustrate, has been noted for his turn to moral law, the orientation of his moral theology around the concept of natural law, and his engagement with English rationalists, Scottish Moral Sense theorists, and Leibnizian authors, such as Christian Wolff. Bellamy modeled for dozens of Calvinists the possibility of natural theology as an apology for Reformed teaching. He also taught his students to shape the moral demands of Christianity around the concept of law. By the early 1770s, these so-called New Divinity men, or Edwardsians, had so thoroughly accepted the foundational discourse of the Enlightenment that they took the concept of natural rights as the political and economic application of natural and revealed truth.[29]

The evidence for this is their preaching in support of Independence from Britain during the 1770s. They joined other Americans who legitimated the Revolution as a defense of their natural rights to free trade.[30] Claims about the laws of nature, natural rights, and British violation of those rights appear repeatedly in Edwardsian preaching during the 1770s—more often than fears of an Anglican episcopate. Edwards the Younger urged his people in 1775, for instance, to understand the imperial crisis as a contest that pitted "natural means" of resistance against the violations of natural law. "Encroachment on our natural rights as men, and such infringements on the laws of justice and equity," he asserted, "we are bound to oppose." His people were justified in "all" their "exertions in favour" of their "common rights and liberties." So too Nathaniel Niles, who, like Edwards the Younger, was one of Bellamy's students. Niles described British trade policies as a violation of a "sacred contract." As he put it, in a truly free society "every individual would choose to move in his proper sphere" without social coercion of the sort imposed by the imperial government. Britain's denial of America's rights to free trade, through excise taxes, port bills, and monopolies, amounted to a heinous crime.[31]

From the Edwardsians' perspective, then, violent resistance to Britain was a necessary corollary to love for the universal principles of law and liberty. Levi Hart, Bellamy's son-in-law, equated the Lords of Trade with "Banditti or pirates" who would rob Americans of their economic prerogatives. He claimed that British mercantile policy amounted to "oppression and violence," which in their natural tendency led to "the utter ruin of society" and therefore merited swift and violent opposition. Bellamy complained that the British "ministry" was "angry" with New England "more than with any [other] part of America" because Yankee merchants insisted on free commerce when Parliament "would have our money in ways in which we ask to be independent." Bellamy drew the unavoidable conclusion. He led the leaders of his congregation to sign a 1776 town covenant in which they claimed that the British government had violated the laws of nature, becoming "unnatural Enemies." The people of Bethlehem, like those in Edwards's New Haven, promised to arm themselves in defense of their "Invaluable Rights and Privileges."[32]

According to the Edwardsians, then, the War for Independence was morally reasonable in that Britain had violated natural economic laws. Parliament taxed them without their consent. It also had impeded the market in America. The revolutionary sermon by Jonathan Edwards Jr. cited at the start of this paper serves to illustrate dozens of New Divinity statements that linked natural law, political rights, and economic freedom. Not usually given to creativity, Edwards Jr. was so enraged by attacks on American commerce that even he raised his rhetoric to an ingenious level. The Navigation Acts, he asserted, amounted to nothing less than the tool of "the great whore of Babylon," which "would suffer none either to buy or sell, save that he had the mark, the name of the beast." "We may expect" that such a beast, Edwards Jr. concluded, would not stop until it either had "taken absolutely all our property" or had been defeated by an aroused populace.[33]

What allowed the New Divinity men to join non-Calvinists in the effort to defend New England's commercial prerogatives? Both groups shared a common public discourse, despite their theological controversies. Recent attempts to link Edwardsian theology to the market in different terms—such as particular Calvinist doctrines—cannot fully explain the eventual alliance of Calvinists and non-Calvinists in patriotic fervor. Nor can they account for the permutations in the long relationship between Reformed teaching and commerce. After all, Reformed doctrine in itself—notions of original sin, the evil of self-love, or divine sovereignty—did not always imply a convergence between Calvinism and the market. Through the seventeenth century, the most staunch Calvinists in England, New England, and the Netherlands were frankly opposed to the basic tenets of a market economy.

The alliance between Calvinists and a new economic order, I suggest, may be traced in part to the ways in which Jonathan Edwards introduced his followers to the eighteenth-century public sphere: the transatlantic market of ideas. In his day, Edwards never found an easy or obvious correlation between Calvinism, the new philosophical idiom, and commerce. In their day, however, the New Divinity Men found that a rational, public discourse was inseparable from the moral axioms of the market. When they took up new rules for public morality—a language quite different from traditional Puritan moral writing—they found a correlation between Calvinism and commerce.

One must allow, of course, that they sometimes differed from each other in their enthusiasm for certain kinds of markets. From the precincts of coastal New Haven, Edwardsian Benjamin Trumbull applauded a profitable engagement in transatlantic exchange on a grand scale. From the rural hamlet of Bethlehem, Bellamy, in contrast, cast a rather critical eye on Boston's mercantile culture even as he revered the localized markets of western Connecticut.[34] All of this is to suggest that even proponents of an Enlightened Calvinism could muster some critical assessment of the market's potential for sociability, and in some circumstances or at some point judge it as a failure. But in 1776 that day was far off. For the generation of Jonathan Edwards Jr., the promise of social solidarity lay with a free market. This explains how the defense of New England's economic liberties with their very lives appeared to be a sacred duty.

NOTES

1. Jonathan Edwards Jr., sermon on Ecclesiastes 4:1, 1 February 1775, Jonathan Edwards Jr. papers, Hartford Seminary library, manuscript #166.2735.75777.

2. For a statement that captures existing positions on religion and the American Revolution, see J. C. D. Clark, *The Language of Liberty, 1660–1832: Political Discourse and Social Dynamics in the Anglo-American World* (New York: Cambridge Univ. Press, 1994). The title of my essay takes its cue from one influential formulation in this literature: Nathan O. Hatch, *The Sacred Cause of Liberty: Republican Thought and the Millennium in Revolutionary New England* (New Haven: Yale Univ. Press, 1977).

3. Perry Miller, *Jonathan Edwards* (New York: W. Sloane Associates, 1949). Joseph Haroutunian, *Piety Versus Moralism: The Passing the New England Theology* (New York: H. Holt, 1932), makes the distinction between Edwards and his followers quite explicit in these terms.

4. See Richard L. Bushman, *From Puritan to Yankee: Character and the Social Order in Connecticut, 1690–1765* (Cambridge: Harvard Univ. Press, 1967); Gordon S. Wood, "Religion and the American Revolution," in *New Directions in American Religious History*, ed. Harry S. Stout and D. G. Hart (New York: Oxford Univ. Press, 1997), 173–205; Harry S. Stout, *The Divine Dramatist: George Whitefield and the Rise of Modern Evangelicalism* (Grand Rapids, Mich.: Eerdmans, 1991); Frank Lambert, *Pedlar in Divinity: George Whitefield and the Transatlantic Revivals, 1737–1770* (Princeton: Princeton Univ. Press, 1994); Frank Lambert, *Inventing the "Great Awakening"* (Princeton: Princeton Univ. Press, 1999); William K. Breitenbach, "Unregenerate Doings: Selflessness and Selfishness in New Divinity Theology," *American Quarterly* 34 (1982): 479–502; and James D. German, "The Social Utility of Wicked Self-Love: Calvinism, Capitalism, and Public Policy in Revolutionary New England," *Journal of American History* 82 (1995): 965–98. Economic historians who address religion in the eighteenth century (they are few and far between) tend to merge a generalized notion of Puritanism with Bushman's description of New Lights. See, for example, Margaret Ellen Newell, *From Dependency*

to Independence: Economic Revolution in Colonial New England (Ithaca, N.Y.: Cornell Univ. Press, 1998).

5. Although Charles L. Cohen may have coined the phrase "post-Puritan," I use it here in a different sense: see Charles L. Cohen, "The Post-Puritan Paradigm of Early American Religious History," *William and Mary Quarterly,* 3rd ser., 54 (1997): 695–722.

6. For Edwards's antimarket statements, see Mark Valeri, "The Economic Thought of Jonathan Edwards," *Church History* 60 (1991): 37–54; and Gerald McDermott, *One Holy and Happy Society: The Public Theology of Jonathan Edwards* (University Park: Pennsylvania State Univ. Press, 1992).

7. See Robert Wuthnow, "Protestants and Economic Behavior," in *New Directions in American Religious History,* ed. Harry S. Stout and D. G. Hart (New York: Oxford Univ. Press, 1997), 260–95. For the idea of Enlightenment conceptual frameworks and discursive communities, see Robert Wuthnow, *Communities of Discourse: Ideology and Social Structure in the Reformation, the Enlightenment, and European Socialism* (Cambridge: Harvard Univ. Press, 1989), esp. 1–22.

8. See T. H. Breen and Timothy Hall, "Structuring Provincial Imagination: The Rhetoric and Experience of Social Change in Eighteenth-Century New England," *American Historical Review* 103 (1998): 1410–39; and Christopher Grasso, *A Speaking Aristocracy: Transforming Public Discourse in Eighteenth-Century Connecticut* (Chapel Hill: Univ. of North Carolina Press, for the Omohundro Institute of Early American History and Culture, 1999).

9. See, for ample evidence of this, Leon Chai, *Jonathan Edwards and the Limits of Enlightenment Philosophy* (New York: Oxford Univ. Press, 1998). As critics of Catholicism, seventeenth-century Calvinists had minimized Aristotelian assumptions about nature and stressed the knowledge of the divine will chiefly in scriptural history. Edwards thus stands as a contrast to Puritanism. For an interesting, even if overstated, comparison of Edwards to Catholic Aristotelians such as Aquinas, see Anri Morimoto, *Jonathan Edwards and the Catholic Vision of Salvation* (University Park: Pennsylvania State Univ. Press, 1995).

10. Jonathan Edwards, "The Mind," 41, in *Scientific and Philosophical Writings,* ed. Wallace E. Anderson, *The Works of Jonathan Edwards,* vol. 6 (New Haven: Yale Univ. Press, 1980), 359–60. For "being" and virtue, see Jonathan Edwards, "The Nature of True Virtue," in *Ethical Writings,* ed. Paul Ramsey, *The Works of Jonathan Edwards,* vol. 8 (New Haven: Yale Univ. Press, 1989), esp. 539–60.

11. Edwards, *Works,* 8:541. Recent literature is replete with examples of how Edwards engaged the writings of non-Calvinist moralists and used many of their idioms. For theological concepts, see Michael J. McClymond, *Encounters with God: An Approach to the Theology of Jonathan Edwards* (New York: Oxford Univ. Press, 1998), esp. 93–104;

and Sang Hyun Lee, *The Philosophical Theology of Jonathan Edwards* (Princeton: Princeton Univ. Press, 1988). For epistemology, see Chai, *Jonathan Edwards*. For moral language (especially the language of virtue, benevolence, and social union), see Norman Fiering, *Jonathan Edwards's Moral Thought and Its British Context* (Chapel Hill: Univ. of North Carolina Press, for the Institute of Early American History and Culture, 1981). For Edwards and other religious traditions, including deism, see Gerald R. McDermott, *Jonathan Edwards Confronts the Gods: Christian Theology, Enlightenment Religion, and Non-Christian Faiths* (New York: Oxford Univ. Press, 2000).

12. This is apparent from the discussion in Bushman, *Puritan to Yankee*.

13. See, for Puritan biblicism, Theodore Dwight Bozeman, *To Live Ancient Lives: The Primitivist Dimension in Puritanism* (Chapel Hill: Univ. of North Carolina Press, for the Institute of Early American History and Culture, 1988); and William Hunt, *The Puritan Moment: The Coming of Revolution in an English County* (Cambridge: Harvard Univ. Press, 1983), 87–155.

14. Edwards as quoted in James Robe, ed., *Christian Monthly History* 2, no. 8 (Edinburgh, 1745), 235, cited and quoted in Susan O'Brien, "Eighteenth-Century Publishing Networks in the First Years of Transatlantic Evangelicalism," in *Evangelicalism: Comparative Studies of Popular Protestantism in North America, the British Isles, and Beyond, 1700–1990*, ed. Mark A. Noll, David W. Bebbington, and George A. Rawlyk (New York: Oxford Univ. Press, 1994), 38–57, quote from 39.

15. Jürgen Habermas, *The Structural Transformation of the Public Sphere: An Inquiry into a Category of Bourgeois Society,* trans. Thomas Berger (Cambridge: Massachusetts Institute of Technology Press, 1991). David S. Shields, *Civil Tongues and Polite Letters in British America* (Chapel Hill: Univ. of North Carolina Press, for the Institute of Early American History and Culture, 1997), shows how Habermas's "public sphere" can be modified and complicated to fit the eighteenth-century American setting.

16. For Edwards as producer of internationally exchanged print accounts, see Susan O'Brien, "Eighteenth-Century Publishing Networks in the First Years of Transatlantic Evangelicalism." There is much evidence for Edwards's and his Scottish correspondents' growing concern to distinguish their revivals from evangelical excesses; see C. C. Goen, "Editor's Introduction" to Jonathan Edwards, *The Great Awakening,* in *The Works of Jonathan Edwards,* vol. 4, (New Haven: Yale Univ. Press, 1972), 32–83; and, for one trenchant example, Edwards to William McCulloch, 12 May 1743, in Jonathan Edwards, *Letters and Personal Writings,* ed. George S. Claghorn, *The Works of Jonathan Edwards,* vol. 16 (New Haven: Yale Univ. Press, 1998), 105–7. For Edwards and biblical criticism, see Robert E. Brown, *Jonathan Edwards and the Bible* (Bloomington: Indiana Univ. Press, 2002).

17. Edwards, sermon on Ezekiel 22:12, 1746/47, Beinecke Library, Yale University.

18. Ibid.

19. Joyce Oldham Appleby, *Economic Thought and Ideology in Seventeenth-Century England* (Princeton: Princeton Univ. Press, 1978).

20. Edwards, *An Humble Attempt to Promote Visible Union* [Boston: D. Henchman, 1747], in Jonathan Edwards, *Apocalyptic Writings,* ed. Stephen J. Stein, *The Works of Jonathan Edwards,* vol. 5 (New Haven: Yale Univ. Press, 1977), 338–39; and Jonathan Edwards, *A History of the Work of Redemption,* ed. John F. Wilson, *The Works of Jonathan Edwards,* vol. 9 (New Haven: Yale Univ. Press, 1989), 483–84.

21. Edwards, "Apocalyptic Notebook," in Edwards, *Works,* 5:255–74, esp. 255–56, 272, 275.

22. See especially Harry S. Stout, *The Divine Dramatist: George Whitefield and the Rise of Modern Evangelism* (Grand Rapids, Mich.: Eerdmans, 1991), 113–32; Frank Lambert, *Pedlar in Divinity: George Whitefield and the Transatlantic Revivals, 1737–1770* (Princeton: Princeton Univ. Press, 1994), 52–94; and Frank Lambert, *Inventing the "Great Awakening"* (Princeton: Princeton Univ. Press, 1999), 83–179.

23. *The Christian History* was published in Boston. The first intercolonial American imprint, *The American Magazine* was published in Boston, Newport, New Haven, New York, and Philadelphia.

24. *The Christian History* 53 (3 March 1743/4), title page; *The American Magazine* (November 1744), title page.

25. *The Gentleman's Magazine* (March 1743), title page.

26. See David D. Hall, "The Atlantic Economy in the Eighteenth Century" and "Learned Culture in the Eighteenth Century," in *A History of the Book in America, Volume One: The Colonial Book in the Atlantic World,* ed. Hugh Amory and David D. Hall (New York: Cambridge Univ. Press, 2000): 152–62, 411–33. In "Social and Literary Form in the *Spectator,*" *Eighteenth-Century Studies* 33 (1999): 21–42, Scott Black contends that *The Spectator,* which was similar in content and form to *The Gentleman's Magazine,* should be read in such a way.

27. Habermas, *The Structural Transformation of the Public Sphere;* see Shields, *Civil Tongues.* For a recent study that analyzes Cave's magazine from the perspective of Habermas, see Edward Larkin, "Inventing the American Public: Thomas Paine, the *Pennsylvania Magazine,* and American Revolutionary Discourse," *Early American Literature* 33 (1998): 250–76. For a recent study of the meaning of print culture for the revivals, with attention to Prince, see Lambert, *Inventing the "Great Awakening."*

28. [Thomas Prince], *The Vade Mecum for America* (Boston: S. Kneeland and T. Green, 1731), passim.

29. See Mark Valeri, *Law and Providence in Joseph Bellamy's New England: The Origins of the New Divinity in Revolutionary New England* (New York: Oxford Univ. Press, 1994).

30. For material here and below on the New Divinity, see Mark Valeri, "The New Divinity and the American Revolution," *William and Mary Quarterly*, 3rd ser., 46 (1989): 741–69.

31. Jonathan Edwards Jr., sermon on Luke 22:36, 30 April 1775, Jonathan Edwards Jr. papers, Hartford Seminary, 166.2735.75785; and Edwards Jr., sermon on Ecclesiastes 7:14, 31 August 1774, Edwards Jr. papers, 166.2735.75758; Edwards Jr., sermon on Judges 12:5–6, 22 December 1775, Edwards Jr., papers, 166.2735.75816; Nathaniel Niles, *Two Discourses on Liberty* (Newbury-Port, Mass.: I. Thomas and H. W. Tinges, 1774), 23, 27.

32. Levi Hart, sermon on 1 Kings 8:23–25, 24 May 1774, Levi Hart papers, Connecticut Historical Library, Hartford; Joseph Bellamy, sermon on Hosea 2:5–8, 25 June 1775, Joseph Bellamy papers, Sterling Library, Yale University; Andrew Martin et al., Bethlehem Town Covenant, 18 July 1776, Connecticut State Library, Revolutionary War Records, ser. 1, vol. 5, part 1, Connecticut State Library, Hartford.

33. Jonathan Edwards, sermon on Ecclesiastes 7:14, 31 August 1774, Jonathan Edwards papers, 166.2735.75758.

34. Valeri, *Joseph Bellamy's New England*, 76–109; German, "The Social Utility of Wicked Self-Love."

The Political Economy of Depravity
The Irrelevance (and Relevance) of Jonathan Edwards

James D. German

"What is government," asked James Madison (as Publius), "but the greatest of all reflections on human nature?" For learned Americans of the revolutionary and early national periods, the science of government was rooted in antecedent knowledge about the nature of the human person. Political economy was a branch of moral philosophy. It appeared as such in leading systematic treatises, such as the influential *System of Moral Philosophy* by Francis Hutcheson, and in the organization of college curricula, most notably at Princeton under the instruction of John Witherspoon.[1]

The derivation of political economy from premises about human nature was not restricted to representatives of Scottish thought, such as Hutcheson and Witherspoon. Hutcheson's most powerful critic in America, Jonathan Edwards, left a substantial body of writing that assessed the moral potential of the human person from which his followers deduced conclusions about the possibilities of social life. For those men and women who thought about public life in Edwardsian terms, *Freedom of the Will* and the dissertation *On the Nature of True Virtue* were seminal texts. In the former work, Edwards directed his argument against timid Calvinists who, in fear of a mechanistic determinism that undermined moral accountability, retreated from the Reformed doctrine of God's sovereignty in election and reprobation. Edwards reconciled the Calvinist doctrine of God's eternal decree with human moral responsibility by distinguishing between the natural ability that humans have to do good and their moral inability to do good. People are free to act according to their inclinations but, without supernatural regenerating grace, they are wholly inclined to evil. In the latter text, Edwards preserved a sphere for uniquely gracious ethics by demonstrating that the natural sources of virtue celebrated by various British thinkers of the eighteenth century, particularly Hutcheson, all fell short of true virtue, which he defined as the disinterested love of being-in-general. At best, aesthetic appreciation, natural affection, pity, and conscience were the products of merely natural—as opposed to genuinely moral—inclinations. At worst, they were the expressions of a wicked self-love that diametrically opposed the good of others.²

Edwards's towering accomplishment made the essential Calvinist doctrines that underlie evangelical preaching—depravity, election, regeneration—intellectually respectable, even formidable, in the age of the Enlightenment. But what did Edwards's conception of human nature offer to the righteous when they thought about political economy? Many fine historical works show how Edwardsianism provided moral and intellectual support for corporate, or communal, conceptions of social order. The prescription of disinterested love as the highest virtue and the proscription of selfishness as the source of vice pointed New Divinity preachers toward the celebration of selfless public spirit and the condemnation of ambition and avarice. It made them suspicious of individualism in politics and economics, pitting them successively against loyalists, antifederalists, and democratic republicans, as well as against certain economic activities—commerce, consumption, banking, and manufacturing—that grew out of and rewarded self-interested behavior and created invidious distinctions in communities. Edwardsian corporatism, in this view, coincided with and mutually reinforced the ethical ideals of the Puritan community, civic humanism, Protestant communalism, and an agrarian *mentalité*.³

New Divinity ministers often followed Edwardsian premises about human nature to communitarian conclusions. But other, quite contrary possibilities also lay embedded in Edwards's moral philosophy. While the New Divinity clergyman might wax ecstatic with millenarian hope for a Christian community of men and women regenerated by God's grace, the Edwardsian statesman of the Revolutionary era faced the task of constructing a political and economic order consistent with human nature as he found it, not as he hoped it might become. The key question for Edwardsian statesmen was this: What does Edwards's moral philosophy suggest about the possibilities of human nature, apart from grace? The answer: truly virtuous behavior is a moral impossibility. Unregenerated men and women will not—indeed cannot—choose either to love God supremely or to love their neighbors as themselves. Ubiquitous self-love leading to self-interested action is the irreducible fact of social life. Thus, Edwardsian thinkers directed their attention to the moral possibilities of counterfeit virtue. Because Edwards taught them that every action that passed for moral—certainly every action that was socially useful—could arise from purely natural motives, some Edwardsians in the Revolutionary era came to believe that true virtue was unnecessary in political and economic life. In his critique of naturalistic ethics, Edwards ironically opened the door to naturalistic political economy. The writings of the Jonathan Edwards Jr., the younger Edwards's most famous parishioner, Roger Sherman, and Sherman's protégé, friend, and collaborator in Connecticut and national politics, Oliver Ellsworth, reveal the emergence of an Edwardsian political economy premised on the reality of natural self-love rather than on the possibility of true virtue.[4]

In April 1775, a few days before events at Lexington and Concord marked the beginning of armed struggle against Britain, the task of preaching the annual sermon at the New Haven Freeman's meeting fell to the younger Edwards. The several political sermons he had preached to his separatist White Haven congregation in New Haven since his ordination in 1769 had been the standard fare of the evangelical New England pulpit. Understood as God's sovereign judgment on sin, public calamities called for genuine repentance and true religion. His sermon to the assembled freemen that election day must have sounded most peculiar. His text—"Let every soul be subject unto the higher powers. For there is no power but of God: the powers that be are ordained of God. Whosoever therefore resisteth the power, resisteth the ordinance of God"—provided an unlikely vehicle for encouraging the patriot resistance that Edwards was known to support. After noting that "scarce anything new" could be said about "the nature of civil government, and the extent and limits of the authority of magistrates," his sermon made two points, both negative. The first point was that his text merely "gives *the general rules of obedience and submission*," and should be interpreted like any other text "expressed in general and absolute terms." Similar texts included Jesus' command to turn the other cheek when smitten and Paul's demand that servants obey their masters. "Who ever understood these words in the most literal and extensive sense?" Edwards Jr. asked. Christians were neither obligated "to suffer every ruffian to beat and mangle" them nor, if captured and enslaved by Indians, to passively submit. Analogously, the text did not enjoin "passive obedience and non-resistance to our rulers in all cases." Without further elaboration on what the text did enjoin, Edwards Jr. moved to his second point, "the immediate business of the day," about which he offered some specific electoral advice. He urged the freemen to reject any candidate who opposed the nonimportation and nonconsumption recommended by the Continental Congress, who doubted the necessity of the defensive preparations enacted by the Connecticut General Assembly, or who argued that Americans should seek to redress their grievances "by barely petitioning" the king. He cautioned them against voting for a certain "farmer"—doubtless loyalist Joshua Chandler from North Haven

Parish—who "goes round among the farmers and tells them that it is by all means best to send a farmer to the Assembly, and not one that lives in the town or city." Choose instead, Edwards Jr. said, the "real friends to your country and its constitution." He did not say, because he did not need to say, who those friends were. The voters knew that one candidate for the Governor's Council, Roger Sherman, a prominent New Haven merchant, used all his influence as a member of both Congress and Council to defend American liberties. They also knew that Sherman was a member of the White Haven Church and a dear friend of Edwards Jr.[5]

In the genre of New England political sermons, the younger Edwards's discourse is remarkable for what it did not say. It does not center on a national covenant, on God's sovereignty, or on virtue, neither true nor civic. He neither helped his audience make sense of the imperial crisis nor gave them positive directions from Scripture or reason about how they should proceed. Utterly failing to "invest contemporary experience with the weight of myth," he merely pointed to Sherman, his pious laymen, and said, follow him into rebellion and revolution. This endorsement was based on Edwards's recognition that Sherman had mastered both theology and political economy. Two decades later, at Sherman's funeral, Edwards Jr. remarked that his favorite parishioner had been an able defender of "the peculiar doctrines of grace." In the "general course" of their "long and intimate acquaintance," Edwards Jr. confessed, he had been "much improved" by Sherman's "observations on the principal subjects of doctrinal and practical divinity." However so great his theological abilities, Edwards Jr. recognized that Sherman's "proper line was politics." Sherman "was qualified" for "usefulness and excellence" as a political thinker, Edwards Jr. thought, "especially by his knowledge of human nature."[6] As political economy was a branch of moral philosophy, Sherman's genius, as the younger Edwards saw it, resided in his ability to apply Edwardsian conceptions of human nature to political discourse.

No less than the freemen of New Haven, historians of the revolutionary era could profitably heed the younger Edwards's advice and follow Sherman. The social and political significance of the elder Edwards's thought might be found not so much in the political preaching of New Divinity clergy—which frequently took Edwardsian theological premises to communitarian or traditionalist conclusions in political economy—as in the moral arguments and assumptions of pious politicians. Understanding how men like Sherman read and appropriated Edwards, how Edwardsianism shaped their conception of political economy, and how it colored their conversations with the freemen who made them political leaders may reveal more about the political and economic legacy of Edwards than the volumes of sermons delivered on fast, thanksgiving, and election days.

Sherman's two extant contributions to theological discourse—*A Short Sermon on the Duty of Self-Examination, Preparatory to Receiving the Lord's Supper,* published in 1789, and an unpublished correspondence with Samuel Hopkins in 1790—provide a point of entry into his Edwardsian world of pious politics. In the *Short Sermon,* he argued that communicants should examine their "knowledge of the Gospel-scheme of salvation" as defined by Edwardsian theology, the sincerity of their repentance from sin, the quality of their "faith in Jesus Christ," the character of "their love to God and man," and the extent of their "obedience to the commands of God." On one level, the *Short Sermon* served as an argument in support of the younger Edwards's controversial position of refusing the Lord's Supper to members of New Haven's First Church, where opponents to the elder Edwards's theology had filled the pulpit since the Great Awakening.[7] But more importantly, Sherman's *Short Sermon* expresses the piety of a layman who measured his thoughts, affections, and actions against the standard of Edwards's theology.

This very piety precipitated Sherman's controversy with Samuel Hopkins. Sherman read Hopkins's *Inquiry into the Nature of True Holiness* and a manuscript version of his as yet unpublished *Dialogues between a Calvinist and a Semi-Calvinist.* He objected to two propositions he found in those works. The first was Hopkins's equation of selfishness with self-love. While Hopkins acknowledged that it was appropriate to love self (in due proportion to one's worth on the scale of being) as part of one's love to being-in-general, he condemned "the love of self, *as self,*" as inherently sinful. Sherman objected that self-love was a natural rather than a moral principle. In depraved beings, he granted that self-love was the source of all wickedness. But in the righteous, he argued, self-love was the measure of the love owed to one's neighbor. As Sherman did not know how to measure the value of himself and his neighbor on the scale of being, he thought it safest to wish the greatest possible happiness for both.[8]

Hopkins replied that a distinct love of one's self was superfluous in the righteous, insofar as they had sufficient grounds to love themselves as part of being-in-general. He insisted that righteous self-love was impossible (which, in his terms, it was, as his definition of self-love excluded the love of being-in-general). And he argued that Sherman's position could not account for the origin of evil. "Is it not perfectly unaccountable," he asked, "that selflove, if it be a perfectly innocent and good affection, should be positive, productive source or fountain of moral evil?" Sherman's reply betrayed some impatience with Hopkins. He saw little "force" in Hopkins distinction between the Christian who regulated her self-love by her love of being-in-general and the Christian who loved herself as part of being-in-general. Without quibbling, he merely noted that Hopkins's definition of self-love was unusual. Citing Edwards's *Original Sin,* his *Sermons,* and Hopkins's *Sin, the Occasion of Great Good,* Sherman argued that Hopkins blurred the crucial distinction between "positive causes" and "occasions." Sin originated not in an evil principle of self-love in either Adam or subsequent sinners, but rather in absence of the divine principle of holiness that regulated the natural principle of self-love. Depravity existed not in principles, he reminded Hopkins, but in exercises; not in self-love per se, but in the unrestrained exercise of self-love.[9]

Sherman's second objection centered on Hopkins's peculiar formula that in order to be saved one must be willing to be damned. The proposition "that a person ought to be willing to be fixed in a State of eternal enmity to God from a principle of Supreme love to him," Sherman thought absurd. Moreover, his belief that self-love was a natural principle led him to conclude that "it is naturally impossible for any moral agent to be willing to be separated from all good, to all evil." True to Edwards, Sherman admitted that God's glory required the eternal damnation of sinners and that "absolute submission to the will of God" in this, as in all else, was a Christian duty. But again, he thought Hopkins had confused essential Calvinist distinctions. Christians were to submit to God's "providential will" so far as it was revealed in Scripture and by events, but "no particular person while in a State of probation can know that it is the providential will of God that he shall finally perish." At the same time, the Christian knows that it is God's "prescriptive will, *that he should turn and live.*" This scriptural prescription, argued Sherman, was as inconsistent with a willingness to be damned as it was consistent with a natural principle of self-love.[10]

Sherman's stated concern with both of Hopkins's propositions lay in the bad effects that they might have in causing sincere Christians to doubt "their good estate." The ground for this concern is obvious. If self-love was sin, and if a willingness to be damned was evidence of genuine repentance and sincere faith, then Sherman, by the standards of his *Short Sermon,* was unfit for Christian communion. In his public life, according to his biographer, he had aggressively pursued every political and economic opportunity to his advantage.[11] Just as he been unwilling to endure the poverty and obscurity to which he was born in this world, so too was he unwilling to be damned in the next. But

Sherman also recognized that Hopkins's critique of self-love subverted the political economy that he and other Edwardsian statesmen had worked out through the course of the Revolution. This political economy, derived (as the younger Edwards recognized) from premises about human nature articulated in the moral philosophy of the senior Edwards, received its fullest explication in arguments that Sherman and his long-term Edwardsian collaborator, Oliver Ellsworth, made in support of the Federal Constitution.

Ellsworth's world, like Sherman's, was largely defined in Edwardsian terms. As a boy, he had prepared for college in the home of Joseph Bellamy. After graduating from the College of New Jersey in 1766 (a year behind the younger Edwards), he studied theology under John Smalley, one of Bellamy's protégés, with the intention of becoming a minister. Like many promising young men of his generation, he became a lawyer instead. Not surprisingly, he took Sherman, more than twenty years his senior, for his model. John Adams remarked that he "never knew two men more alike." Through his political career, Ellsworth remained an active member of his church in Windsor and a supporter of its evangelical ministers. After retiring from politics in 1801, he served on the board of the New Divinity–sponsored Connecticut Missionary Society. By 1787, he and Sherman had spent countless hours together in the Connecticut Assembly, on the bench of the Connecticut Superior Court, in the Continental Congress, and at the Constitutional Convention. Each wrote a series of essays urging ratification of the Constitution.[12] Their arguments, much like those of Madison, Hamilton, and Jay, centered on the singular accomplishment of the convention in creating a constitution that was consistent with the self-interested nature of human beings, particularly with their natural inclination to ambition and avarice.

Sherman's seven essays on the Constitution addressed what he termed the "sublimity of *nonsense* and *alarm*" that antifederalists "thundered" against the Constitution, particularly regarding "a *bill of rights,* the *liberty of the press, rights of conscience, rights of taxation and election, trials in the vicinity, freedom of speech, trial by jury,* and a *standing army.*" Sherman surely knew of one argument, consistent with an Edwardsian ethic of true virtue, that he could have used to show that the Constitution provided sufficient safeguards against self-interested tyrants. The delegates to the federal convention shared the conviction that the relatively large size of the electorate for House members, combined with indirect election or appointment of other federal officers, would serve to filter talent and virtue, allowing only the best to rise to the top. But rather than talking about the possibilities of a virtuous magistracy, Sherman, following

James Madison, thought it safer to assume its viciousness. Mere "paper protection" of rights was no protection against tyranny, he argued, "your stipulation is not worth even the trouble of writing." Given the ambition of men, the sovereign state preserved the rights of its citizens only when "the *rulers were interested* in preserving" those rights. Sherman's proof lay in the Constitution of Connecticut, where, he observed, the General Assembly was "not only supreme in the usual sense of the word," but that it exercised "*literally, all the powers of society.*" If it wanted, it could maintain a standing army in peacetime, annul jury trials, silence the press, levy whatever onerous taxes it pleased, and even repeal the state's Bill of Rights. Nevertheless, the rights of Connecticut's citizens remained "perfectly safe." "What forms your security under the General Assembly?" Sherman asked. "Nothing save that the interest of the members is the same as yours." In his mind, the "sole question" regarding rights concerned the structure of representation. "If the members of Congress are to be interested just as you and I are," Sherman concluded, "we shall be . . . safe."[13] Edwardsian moral philosophy taught Sherman to expect the ubiquity of self-love, and hence of self-interest, in public life. In the world as Sherman found it, virtue, whether residing in the magistracy or the citizenry, provided a less adequate safeguard for liberty than individual self-interest.

As Sherman's essays centered on aligning self-interested ambition with public interest, Ellsworth's were chiefly concerned with enlisting avarice in service of the common good. Like Sherman, Ellsworth rejected true virtue as a foundation for political economy. "The business of a civil government," he believed, was "to protect the citizen in his rights, to defend the community from hostile powers, and to promote the general welfare." The state had "no business to meddle with the private opinions of the people," but only with how they demeaned themselves as citizens. His essays focused on the political and social conditions that encouraged socially useful behavior. "The love of wealth," argued Ellsworth, "is a passion common to all men, and when justly regulated it is conducive to human happiness." The just regulation of this passion began with the "Author of our Nature," who "wisely ordered" that the "blessings of this world should be acquired by our own application in some business useful to society." Wise governments can cooperate with providence, encouraging industry by "good laws," specifically those that protect the "wealth" that industry naturally produces.[14] The adoption of the Constitution would create political and economic conditions in which commerce would flourish, thereby encouraging industry not merely in the merchant, but also in the farmer and manufacturer.

Ellsworth emphasized that Connecticut's farmers would be among the chief beneficiaries of the enhanced commercial intercourse the Constitution promised. He assumed as a "fixed truth that the prosperity and riches of the farmer must depend on the prosperity of . . . trade," insofar as agricultural profits hinge on "a ready demand and generous price" for surplus produce. This occurs only "where trade flourishes, and when the merchant can freely export the produce of the country to such parts of the world as will bring the richest return." No less than farmers, merchants are motivated by the "desire of gain [that] is common to mankind," such that they will purchase little when they "are shut out from nine-tenths of the ports in the world." In this way, "every foreign prohibition on American trade is aimed in the most deadly manner against the holders and tillers of the land." The creation of "such a national government as will make the country respectable" will enrich farmers. In a similar vein, Ellsworth argued that the development of certain manufactures would also increase agricultural profits. Cloth, particularly wool and linen, could be produced and sold competitively, which would "increase our wealth by increasing the labour of the people, and saving the surplus of our earnings for a better purpose than to purchase the labour of the European nations." He praised, and predicted fine profits for, the recently established Hartford Broadcloth Mill (in which he happened to be an investor). But ultimately, he argued, the economic benefits of manufactures would be reaped by the farmers who produced the wool and the flax that supported textile manufacturing. With the adoption of the Constitution, Ellsworth concluded, "the sources of wealth are open to us, and there needs but industry to become as rich as we are free."[15]

If the protection of wealth and the promotion of commerce and manufacturing, through the mechanism of natural self-interest, encouraged industry, the failure of the state to protect the property interests of its citizens promoted vicious selfishness, resulting in private and public injustice. For Ellsworth, this explained both the disorder of the 1780s and why antifederalists preferred that disorder to a sound constitutional order. Echoing Locke, Ellsworth argued that "we combine in society, with an expectation to have our persons and properties defended against unreasonable exactions." When a society fails to "insure justice from the public and between individuals," he continued, "the common duties of humanity will gradually go out of use." As they find that their government does not provide the "expected protection of their interests," some individuals, "tho' otherwise honest, become desperate." Their natural self-love—the innocent inclination that formed the original ground of social union—turns into vicious selfishness, as they determine to "share by the spoils of anarchy" those things that they would otherwise "wish to acquire by industry." Among the "several classes of men" who opposed the Constitution from "selfish" motives were debtors and the politicians who courted their votes. Lacking sufficient "resolution to be either honest or industrious," debtors had "long been upheld by the property of their creditors and the mercy of the public." By electing legislators who enacted "paper money and tender acts," they daily destroyed "a thousand honest men." Because their success in "oppressing" others depended on the weakness of the state, they preferred "the shadow of government to the reality." It was not the self-interest of debtors, or of the politicians they elected to office, that was the problem. Rather political and economic conditions bent self-interest from honest industry to the "indolence and knavery" that sought to "establish iniquity by law."[16] Ellsworth looked for a constitutional (rather than a moral) solution that would displace selfishness and restore natural self-interest as the ruling passion in public life.

Ellsworth's analysis of debtor antifederalism shows how Edwards's distinction between natural ability and moral inability made it possible for Edwardsian politicians to embrace naturalistic explanations of vice. Although New Divinity preachers, following their Puritan forebears, could (and often did) identify the moral causes of public disorder, Edwards's theology allowed (but by no means required) their politically minded followers to revise and even reverse the causal relationship. Bad policy promoted vicious behavior. Edwardsian politicians knew that the mere identification of social conditions that encouraged agents to behave wickedly in no way freed those agents from moral responsibility, any more than the doctrine of original sin freed sinners from moral responsibility. Edwards's moral philosophy thus allowed statesmen to argue that the political conditions that promoted immoral behavior should be changed, without admitting that those conditions provided any justification for immoral behavior. The necessity that made debtors support paper money and tender laws was wholly moral, not natural. And this public injustice, like all sin, had its uses. In the "general policy" of Rhode Island, notorious for its fiscal irresponsibility in the 1780s, Ellsworth found confirmation of the "sentiment thrown out by some of our adventurous divines"—Bellamy and Hopkins—"that the permission of sin is the highest display of supreme wisdom." Rhode Island's "apostacy from all the principles of good and just government" served as an illustration of "unrighteousness in the essence, in effects, and in its native miseries," and hence as a demonstration of the necessity of constitutional reform.[17]

For Sherman and Ellsworth, Edwardsian moral philosophy opened the door to naturalistic political economy. Natural self-interest—ambition and avarice—

formed the cement of society. A wise policy steered self-interest into socially useful courses, while a foolish one encouraged its degeneration into vicious selfishness.

Of course, nothing in Edwards's writings compelled New Divinity preachers to walk through this door into the world of modern liberal political theory. Some clergymen used Edwards's notion of true virtue to update the vocabulary, but not necessarily the content, of the political economy of John Winthrop's "Model of Christian Charity." Ellsworth's theological teacher, John Smalley of New Britain Parish in Farmington, for instance, had established an international reputation as an able exponent of Edwards's theology by 1769, when he published two sermons explicating the distinction between natural and moral inability. But his theology did not lead him into patriot, let alone liberal, political discourse. In the early 1770s, while the younger Edwards encouraged New Haven freemen to follow patriot leaders into resistance and revolution, Smalley dismissed parliamentary taxation as trifling, suggested that the patriot leadership was poorly informed, and expressed outraged surprise that his parishioners responded to the call from Boston for armed resistance to the Coercive Acts. "What! Will you fight against your King?" he exclaimed. He publicly pondered whether he could, and should, forbid the militia to muster.[18]

In Farmington, just as in New Haven, the laity, as much as the clergy, inherited the political and social legacy of Edwards. Farmington's leading patriot, John Treadwell, a member of both the Connecticut General Assembly and the Farmington Sons of Liberty, was as thoroughly steeped in Edwardsian thought as Smalley, Sherman, Ellsworth, and the younger Edwards. He counted *Freedom of the Will,* as taught by Naphtali Daggett, among the two most important books he read as a student at Yale. Farmington patriots—Treadwell almost certainly among them—forced Smalley to publish a clarification—or more accurately, a retraction—of his political statements in the *Connecticut Courant,* effectively ensuring his silence on public issues for the duration of the Revolutionary War. After 1783, Smalley continued to insist on the virtually unrestricted obligation of subjects to obey magistrates. And where Smalley decried commerce, manufacturing, and the pursuit of pecuniary advantage as evidence of human depravity, Treadwell, albeit with more ambivalence than Sherman or Ellsworth, advocated policies that promoted economic diversification and development. But theology became his first love. Treadwell went on to draft an Edwardsian *Summary of Christian Doctrine* for the Connecticut Missionary Society, and to argue about the finer points of New Divinity theology against both the younger Edwards and Smalley in the pages of the *Theological Magazine* and the *Connecticut Evangelical Magazine.* As a member of Connecticut's upper house, as a judge, and eventually as governor, Treadwell's career suggests that historians might find the political and economic meaning of the New Divinity in the pious politician, rather than in the political preacher. In matters of intellectual leadership, as Edmund Morgan observed, the revolutionary clergy had lost the initiative to lawyers.[19]

Did those pious lawyers, Sherman and Ellsworth, speak with an authentically Edwardsian voice? Or did they merely manipulate Edwards's thought to suit their own political ends? Anachronistic questions about how Edwards might have responded to the changed political and economic circumstances of the Revolutionary era are pointless. We simply do not know—cannot know—how his supple and fluid mind might have engaged the public issues that confronted his followers after his death. By the Revolution, Edwards was a corpus of writing to be used and appropriated by those who found him useful and appropriate.[20]

While some Edwardsian clergymen, such as Smalley, Bellamy, and Hopkins, seem to have resisted the liberal and capitalist conclusions that Sherman and Ellsworth reached, others embraced them. By the early 1790s the younger Edwards had gone from merely endorsing Sherman as a candidate for public office to extending the line of Edwardsian political and economic analysis that Sherman initiated. His writings during the last decade of his life both demonstrate the authentically Edwardsian grounding of the political economy articulated by Sherman and Ellsworth and illustrate the tendency of the course they charted to wash Edwardsians into the mainstream of public discourse in the early republic.

A few years after the private argument between Sherman and Hopkins about self-love, the younger Edwards vindicated his parishioner's position in an attack on Hopkinsianism published in the *Theological Magazine*. He began with the observation that although self-love had become the subject of disquisition "in all discourses concerning the nature of virtue or vice, benevolence, [and] public spirit . . . no subject is less understood." Edwards Jr. could make no more sense of Hopkins's phrase "the love of self, *as self*," than could Sherman. If by self-love, Hopkins meant the love of one's own happiness, or benevolence to one's self, then in a regenerate person, whose highest happiness consisted in benevolence to being-in-general, self-love became the equivalent of "benevolence itself." Thus, Edwards Jr. reasoned, purportedly wicked self-love must have its object in "those appetites and affections which are merely private and personal, centering in him who is the subject of them, and not aiming at the good of others." It is essentially the complacence that is "enjoyed in eating and drinking, in honor, personal ease, and in intercourse with the opposite sex." Like Sherman, Edwards Jr. thought that Hopkins's notion of "*Loving self as self*" was nonsensical. How does one love food, drink, ease, or honor "*as self*?" If self-love consisted in such appetites, then it could neither be more "virtuous nor vicious" than those appetites themselves. But morality did not inhere in appetites, but solely in the manner of their exercise. The love of wine, for example, could variously be exercised virtuously, innocently, or viciously. Likewise, "the sinfulness of self-love depends not on the nature of it, but entirely on the degree." To Hopkinsians who complained that this turned well-regulated vice into virtue, Edwards Jr. pointed out that they affirmed that to love oneself according to one's "capacity and importance in the general system" was holy while to love oneself more than one's "capacity and importance" warranted was vicious. "Now what is this," he asked, "but a well regulated self-love?" And how was one to love oneself as part of universal being? Did it require him "to choose and wish for roast beef and a glass of wine" as he does "a dose of ipecacuanha, merely because it is useful to some other purpose?" The confusion that resulted from Hopkins's false distinction between love of self as self and love of self as part of being was compounded by his false conflation of self-love and selfishness. Following Sherman, Edwards Jr. cited *True Virtue* to demonstrate that self-love, or a "man's regard to his confined private self" so far "as was consistent with the general good" was neither selfishness nor benevolence.[21]

This principle of natural self-love shaped the way Edwards Jr. thought about public life through the 1790s. Specifically, he celebrated the public happiness that resulted from what (in his evangelical preaching) he termed the "splendid sins" that arose "from a wrong principle of heart, from mere self-love or some more depraved appetite." In his 1791 commencement address at Yale, he contemplated "the pleasures resulting to the benevolent mind from viewing the progress of manufacturers in this country." After noting the developments in agriculture, iron making, and shipbuilding, Edwards Jr. (like Ellsworth) celebrated New England's future in textiles. Manufacturing was "richly beneficial to the *poorer* class or citizen," thought Edwards Jr., as it offered employment to "multitudes, who, would otherwise . . . be idle, vicious and miserable." Although Edwards Jr. could contemplate the progress of manufacturing with benevolence, he recognized that the impulses that drove industry—"the requisitions of necessity and pride"—were hardly virtuous. When "excessively indulged," he told his students at Union College, pride degenerated into vice—the several forms of *ambition* and *avarice*—but when "controlled by the dictates of wisdom," pride was "greatly productive of good to mankind." Whether considered as a natural or a vicious instinct, pride demanded "numerous articles," chiefly "ornamental," that "necessity" had forgotten. Thus, pride was "*rarely,* perhaps *never,* gratified, without contribution to the happy subsistence of numbers." Pride increased the demand for goods and services, and hence served as a spur to industry and became a source of wealth to the poor. Luxury, for those who could afford it, became a positive social good. Where was true virtue in this political economy? Outside of and above the ordinary business of society, the "benevolent mind" found pleasure in observing baser passions providentially "regulated, so as to feed the hungry, clothe the naked, employ the idle, and prevent them from the practice of vice and wickedness."[22]

Although Edwards Jr., following Sherman and Ellsworth, came to recognize that natural self-love functioned as a useful and necessary principle in regulating social behavior, he did not embrace the liberal notion that the rational pursuit of self-interest in this world was a sufficient motive to ensure public happiness. A general belief in a future state of punishments and rewards served as a necessary ancillary encouragement to moral action. Economic self-interest sometimes led people into theft and fraud as well as into productive labor. It might never direct them to perform acts of kindness, gratitude, or mercy. The state, through its distribution of punishments and rewards, could not provide sufficient encouragement to all socially useful actions. The magistrate neither rewards virtue in general nor punishes vice in general. At best, he affords protection only to those perfect rights of men—to life, liberty, and property—and only when the violation of those rights is public and legally proven. The law can neither stop wicked individuals from violating the rights of others when the prospect of detection and punishment is remote nor compel them to regard the imperfect rights of others—to duly express gratitude, kindness, and mercy they owe. A rationally self-interested man, constrained only by the fear of the law, will lie, cheat, and steal when he thinks he can get away with it, will pay his debts and fulfill his contracts only to the extent that he fears prosecution, and by his unkindness and ingratitude foment strife, contentions, and lawsuits.[23] The fear of hell and the hope of heaven extended the utility of self-interest from this world into the next.

Which religion best persuades its devotees of final judgment? Dismissing Islam and paganism as improbable candidates for the religion of Connecticut, Edwards Jr. turned to a comparison of the utility of deism and Christianity. Explicitly following David Hume, Edwards Jr. doubted that natural religion could establish either the moral perfections of God or the certainty of a future state. Apart from the certainty of a moral God, there could be no grounds to suppose that vice would be punished and virtue rewarded. Insofar as Christianity established the goodness of God and promised final judgment, it provided the most firm foundation for the moral action necessary to public happiness. For Connecticut, Edwards Jr. concluded, the "belief in Christianity" was "necessary to political prosperity."[24]

The younger Edwards's auditors and readers could not have confused the politically useful virtue that arose from a fear of punishment or hope of reward with the true virtue that his father had defined as the essence of genuine religion. At the heart of the evangelical preaching of the New Divinity lay a sharp contrast between the "servile fear of God" that sprang from a deluded hope of his favor and the disinterested love for God because of his intrinsic greatness and goodness. The former remained rooted in self-love and did not indicate the gracious work of the Holy Spirit in the heart.[25] But the younger Edwards recognized that the bare belief of the truth of religion in the head—what in theological terms was sometimes called historical faith—was socially useful even in the absence of the power of vital religion in the heart. In God's provident design, counterfeit religion, no less than counterfeit virtue, had its public uses.

Edwards Jr.'s conclusions broke no new ground in political economy. Indeed, his work, along with that of Sherman and Ellsworth, shows how Edwardsians participated in the larger project, first defined by the Scotsman—the errant Calvinist—David Hume, to reduce politics to a science. Hume decried selfishness while arguing that governments should be constructed as though men were knaves; he described how the ordinary, irreducible passions of avarice and ambition could promote industry and wealth; he showed that luxury, commerce, and refinement contributed to human happiness; and he judged religious beliefs by their public utility, apart from a consideration of their truth or falsity. Hume's *Essays* were very much discussed in the early republic. They shaped the mind of Madison at the Constitutional Convention and informed the thought of Hamilton as he formulated his reports on public credit, banking, and manufacturing. Perhaps Sherman took Hume from Convention and Congress to Edwards Jr., where he found a warmer reception than he (and we) might have expected. The elder Edwards's efforts to undermine the ethics of the Scotsman Francis Hutcheson ironically led Edwardsians to embrace much of the political economy of Hutcheson's best reader. By legitimizing naturalistic political economy, Edwardsianism rendered its supernaturalism in theology and ethics irrelevant to public life. Herein lies its significance.[26]

Notes

I am indebted to Gerald McDermott, Mark Valeri, Thomas Clark, and Krista Medo for their critical comments on this essay and am grateful for the financial support of the Pew Program in Religion and American History, the Beinecke Rare Book and Manuscript Library at Yale University, and the Research Services Council of the University of Nebraska at Kearney.

1. [John Jay, James Madison, Alexander Hamilton], *The Federalist,* ed. Benjamin Fletcher Wright (Cambridge: Belknap Press of Harvard Univ. Press, 1961), 356; Francis Hutcheson, *A System of Moral Philosophy, In Three Books,* 2 vols. (London: A. Millar, 1755). Book One concerns the "constitution of human nature," the "supreme good," and the "supreme happiness of mankind." Book Two considers "special laws of nature ... previous to civil government." Book Three (vol. 2:212–347) closes with an analysis of civil polity. Jack Scott, ed., *An Annotated Edition of Lectures on Moral Philosophy by John Witherspoon* (Newark: Univ. of Delaware Press, 1982; originally published in *The Works of Rev'd John Witherspoon,* ed. Ashbel Green, 4 vols. [Philadelphia: William W. Wood, 1802], 3:269–374). Witherspoon's seven lectures on politics and jurisprudence were preceded by nine lectures on ethics.

2. Jonathan Edwards, *A Careful and Strict Enquiry into the Modern Prevailing Notions of that Freedom of Will, Which is Supposed to be Essential to Moral Agency, Verture and Vice, Reward and Punishment, Praise and Blame,* ed. Paul Ramsey, *Works of Jonathan Edwards,* vol. 1 (New Haven: Yale Univ. Press, 1957), 156–62; Jonathan Edwards, *Ethical Writings,* ed. Paul Ramsey, *Works of Jonathan Edwards,* vol. 8 (New Haven: Yale Univ. Press, 1989), 609–18. The literature on Edwards is voluminous. I have depended most heavily on Allen C. Guelzo, *Edwards on the Will: A Century of American Theological Debate* (Middletown, Conn.: Wesleyan Univ. Press, 1989), esp. 17–53; and Norman Fiering, *Jonathan Edwards's Moral Thought and Its British Context* (Chapel Hill: Univ. of North Carolina Press, 1981), esp. 322–61.

3. Gerald R. McDermott, *One Holy and Happy Society: The Public Theology of Jonathan Edwards* (University Park: Pennsylvania State Univ. Press, 1992), 93–116; Mark R. Valeri, *Law and Providence in Joseph Bellamy's New England: The Origins of the New Divinity in Revolutionary America* (New York: Oxford Univ. Press, 1994), 76–109; Joseph A. Conforti, *Samuel Hopkins and the New Divinity Movement: Calvinism, the Congregational Ministry, and Reform in New England between the Great Awakenings* (Grand Rapids, Mich.: Eerdmans, 1981).

4. For standard biographies of the younger Edwards, Sherman, and Ellsworth, see: Robert L. Ferm, *Jonathan Edwards the Younger, 1745–1801: A Colonial Pastor* (Grand Rapids, Mich.: Eerdmans, 1976); Christopher Collier, *Roger Sherman's Connecticut: Yankee Politics and the American Revolution* (Middletown, Conn.: Wesleyan Univ. Press,

1971); and William Garrott Brown, *The Life of Oliver Ellsworth* (New York: Macmillan, 1905). Donald Weber, *Rhetoric and History in Revolutionary New England* (New York: Oxford Univ. Press, 1988), 46–73, and William Casto, "Oliver Ellsworth's Calvinism: A Biographical Essay on Religion and Political Psychology in the Early Republic," *Journal of Church and State* 35 (1994): 507–26, contain important analyses, respectively, of Edwards and Ellsworth.

5. Romans 13:1–2. Jonathan Edwards Jr., "Submission to Rulers," in *The Works of Jonathan Edwards, D.D. Late President of Union College. With a Memoir of his Life and Character, by Tyron Edwards,* 2 vols. (Andover: Allen, Morrill, and Wardell, 1842), 2:238–46. Compare with Jonathan Edwards, Fast Sermon of April 1771, and Fast Sermon of April 1772, in Edwards-Chapin Collection, Box 1, Uncataloged MS Vault 803, Beinecke Rare Book and Manuscript Library, Yale University, New Haven, Connecticut; and Weber, *Rhetoric and History,* 51–62. Chandler had served several terms as a selectman and currently sat as a delegate to the General Assembly. He lost his seat in 1775, and his farm in 1777, when he, by then an open loyalist, left New Haven for good. Sherman's work in the Continental Congress is described in Collier, *Roger Sherman's Connecticut,* 94–100. Oscar Zeichner, *Connecticut's Years of Controversy, 1750–1776* (Chapel Hill: Univ. of North Carolina Press, 1949), 190–92.

6. The typical function of the New England political sermon is described in Harry S. Stout, *The New England Soul: Preaching and Religious Culture in Colonial New England* (New York: Oxford Univ. Press, 1986), 285–87; and Barry Alan Shain, *The Myth of American Individualism: The Protestant Origins of American Political Thought* (Princeton: Princeton Univ. Press, 1994), 7. Quotation from Weber, *Rhetoric and History,* 73. Jonathan Edwards Jr., "God a Refuge and Help," in *Works of Jonathan Edwards, D.D. Late President of Union College,* 2:182–83.

7. [Roger Sherman], *A Short Sermon on the Duty of Self-Examination, Preparatory to Receiving the Lord's Supper* (New Haven: Abel Morse, 1789), 3–9. Edwards's position on noncommunion is discussed in the letter from White Haven Deacon David Austin to Roger Sherman, 10 Feb. 1790, Roger Sherman (1721–1793) Collection, Manuscripts and Archives, Yale University Library, New Haven, Connecticut; and in Ezra Stiles, *The Literary Diary of Ezra Stiles,* ed. Franklin Bowditch Dexter, 3 vols. (New York: Charles Scribner's Sons, 1901), 3:344. The First Church's ministers were Joseph Noyes, Chauncey Whittelsey, and James Dana. Dana, the central figure in the Wallingford Controversy of 1758 and critic of the senior Edwards in *An Examination of the Late Reverend President Edwards's "Enquiry on Freedom of Will,"* (Boston: Daniel Kneeland, 1770), had been installed as pastor at the First Church in 1789.

8. The *Inquiry* and the *Dialogues* are both reprinted in Samuel Hopkins, *The Works of Samuel Hopkins, D.D.,* 3 vols (Boston: Doctrinal Tract and Book Society, 1854,

reprinted, New York: Garland, 1987), 3:5–141, 143–57. Roger Sherman to Samuel Hopkins, 28 June 1790, Roger Sherman (1721–1793) Collection; Sherman chiefly objected to section 4 of Hopkins's *Inquiry,* in *Works of Samuel Hopkins,* 3:22–30 (quotation from page 23). See William Breitenbach, "Unregenerate Doings: Selflessness and Selfishness in New Divinity Theology," *American Quarterly* 34 (winter 1982): 479–502, for a trenchant analysis of Hopkins on self-love.

9. Samuel Hopkins to Roger Sherman, 2 Aug. 1790, Roger Sherman (1721–1793) Collection; Roger Sherman to Hopkins, Oct. 1790, ibid. The texts Sherman referred to are Jonathan Edwards, *Original Sin,* ed. Clyde Holbrook, *Works of Jonathan Edwards,* vol. 3 (New Haven: Yale Univ. Press, 1970), 380–88; Jonathan Edwards, "Men Naturally God's Enemies," in *The Life and Character of the Late Reverend Mr. Jonathan Edwards, President of the College at New Jersey, Together with a Number of his Sermons on Various Important Subjects,* [ed. Samuel Hopkins] (Boston: S. Kneeland, 1765), 104–64, esp. 118–19; and (I think) less plausibly, Samuel Hopkins, *Sin Thro' Divine Interposition, an Advantage to the Universe,* in *Works of Samuel Hopkins,* 2:509.

10. Roger Sherman to Samuel Hopkins, 28 June 1790, Roger Sherman (1721–1793) Collection; Roger Sherman to Hopkins, October 1790, ibid.

11. Collier, *Roger Sherman's Connecticut,* esp. 3–40.

12. A compelling case for the centrality of the New Divinity in Ellsworth's life appears in Casto, "Oliver Ellsworth's Calvinism," *Journal of Church and State* 35 (1994): 507–26. For Adams on Sherman and Ellsworth, see John Adams to John Sanderson, 19 Nov. 1822, quoted in Collier, *Roger Sherman's Connecticut,* 284. Sherman's pseudonymous essays, published as "Letters of a Countryman" and as "A Citizen of New Haven," first appeared in the *New Haven Gazette* from 14 November 1787 through 25 December 1787. Ellsworth's pseudonymous essays, published as "Letters of a Landholder," first appeared in the *Connecticut Courant.* Both were reprinted contemporaneously, and in Paul Leicester Ford, *Essays on the Constitution of the United States, Published during its Discussion by the People, 1787–1788* (Brooklyn: Historical Printing Club, 1892).

13. Ford, *Essays on the Constitution,* 218–21. For a discussion of this "filtration of talent," see Gordon S. Wood, *The Creation of the American Republic, 1776–1787* (Chapel Hill: Univ. of North Carolina Press, 1969), 511–12. According to Wood, the most complete statement of this notion came from Connecticut. See William Pitt Beers, *An Address to the Legislature and People of the State of Connecticut* (New Haven: T. and S. Green, 1791), 18–29. Compare Sherman with Madison on "parchment barriers" in *Federalist* 48 and his observation that "ambition must be made to counteract ambition" in *Federalist* 51. *The Federalist,* 343, 356.

14. Ibid., 171–72, 200.

15. Ibid., 140, 201–2.

16. Ibid., 143–46, 179–80.

17. Ibid., 196–97. For an explicit New Divinity argument that debt arises from moral—rather than natural—inability, see John Smalley, Sermon of 6 July 1783, John Smalley Sermons, Folder 1, Beinecke Rare Book and Manuscript Library, Yale University, New Haven, Connecticut. Ellworth's references are to Joseph Bellamy, *The Wisdom of God in the Permission of Sin, Vindicated* (Boston: S. Kneeland, 1760); Samuel Hopkins, *Sin Thro' Divine Interposition, an Advantage to the Universe* (Boston: Daniel and John Kneeland, 1759).

18. John Smalley, *The Inability of the Sinner to Comply with the Gospel, His Inexcusable Guilt in Not Complying with it, and the Consistency of These with Each Other, Illustrated, in Two Discourses on John 6:44* (Boston: John Kneeland, 1772); *Connecticut Courant,* 17 Oct. 1774.

19. Denison Olmsted, *Memoir of John Treadwell, LL.D., Late Governor of Connecticut* (Boston: T. R. Marvin, 1843), 7–12; *Connecticut Courant,* 10 Oct. 1774; John Smalley, Sermon of 6 July 1783, John Smalley Sermons, Folder 1, and Smalley, Sermon of 23 March 1800, John Smalley Sermons, Folder 3, Beinecke Rare Book and Manuscript Library; John Smalley, "On the Evils of a Weak Government," *Sermons, On Various Subjects, Doctrinal and Practical* (Middletown, Conn.: Hart and Lincoln, 1814), 10–14; [John Treadwell], *A Summary of Christian Doctrine and Practice: Designed Especially for the Use of the People in the New Settlements of the United States of America* (Hartford, Conn.: Hudson and Goodwin, 1804); Treadwell, "Sketches of the Town of Farmington," Treadwell Papers RG 69:25, Box 2, Connecticut State Library, Hartford, Connecticut; [Treadwell], Untitled Reply to [Jonathan Edwards Jr.], "The Proof of the Moral Perfections of God, from the Light of Nature," *Theological Magazine* (March–April 1796), 1:382–88; [Treadwell], "The Natural Evidence of the Goodness of God," *Connecticut Evangelical Magazine* 2 (May 1802): 401–10; [Treadwell], "The Work of God Perfect" *Connecticut Evangelical Magazine* 2 (June 1802): 458–65, 3 (July 1802): 15–21, 3 (August 1802): 41–47; [Treadwell], "Thoughts on the Inability of Sinners," *Connecticut Evangelical Magazine* 6 (April 1806): 361–69, 7 (Sept. 1806): 88–95, 7 (Dec. 1806): 201–5; Edmund S. Morgan, *The Challenge of the American Revolution* (New York: Norton, 1976), 61.

20. Joseph A. Conforti, *Jonathan Edwards, Religious Tradition, and American Culture* (Chapel Hill: Univ. of North Carolina Press, 1995), esp. 5–10, makes a persuasive case for a "post-Geertzian" reading of Edwards's legacy that acknowledges the selective appropriation and ongoing reconstruction of his ideas by his cultural heirs.

21. [Jonathan Edwards Jr.], "Of Self-Love," *Theological Magazine* 2 (1797): 357–60; *Theological Magazine* 3 (1798): 371–75. Cf. Edwards, *Works,* 8:577. The elder Edwards had further developed this position in his Charity Sermons, especially "Charity contrary to a Selfish Spirit" (Edwards, *Works,* 8:254–59).

22. Jonathan Edwards Jr., "False Refuges Unsafe," in *Works of Jonathan Edwards, D.D. Late President of Union College,* 2:327–28; Edwards Jr., "An Oration for Commencement, Y[ale] C[ollege], 1791, On the Pleasures Resulting to the Benevolent Mind from Viewing the Progress of Manufacturers in this Country," Edwards-Chapin Collection, Box 1, Folder 5; Edwards Jr., "Ethical Observations," ibid.

23. Jonathan Edwards Jr., "The Belief in Christianity Necessary to Political Prosperity," *Works of Jonathan Edwards, D.D. Late President of Union College,* 2:185–88.

24. Ibid., 2:202–4. Edwards apparently accepted Hume's notion that God's goodness cannot be known from nature in his published argument with Treadwell. See Edwards Jr., "The Proof of the Moral Perfections of God, from the Light of Nature," *Works of Jonathan Edwards, D.D. Late President of Union College,* 2:471–90.

25. Jonathan Edwards Jr. "Remarks on the Improvements made in Theology by his Father, President Edwards," *Works of Jonathan Edwards, D.D. Late President of Union College,* 1:490. Cf. Samuel Hopkins's argument in the debate about "unregenerate doings." Samuel Hopkins, "Enquiry Concerning the Promises of the Gospel," in *Works of Samuel Hopkins,* 3:233–37, 261–75; Samuel Hopkins, *The True State and Character of the Unregenerate,* in *Works of Samuel Hopkins* (Boston, 1854), 3:293–98, 308–16.

26. For a succinct discussion of the significance of Hume's essays in the early republic, see Stanley Elkins and Eric McKitrick, *The Age of Federalism* (New York: Oxford Univ. Press, 1993), 92–114. David Hume, *Political Essays,* ed. Knud Haakonssen (Cambridge: Cambridge Univ. Press, 1994), 4–15, 24–27, 46–50, 51–57, 105–14.

All Things Were New and Astonishing

Edwardsian Piety, the New Divinity, and Race

Charles E. Hambrick-Stowe

As the historical memory of Jonathan Edwards helped shape religious and cultural life in the New Republic—a process which is the subject of this book—an Edwardsian form of piety took root and became part of America's spiritual inheritance. In this context, the term "Edwardsian piety" does not refer directly to that sense of divine excellence expressed in the writings of Jonathan Edwards himself—"the manifestation of his internal glory," the "communication of the infinite fulness of God to the creature," the personal "inward, sweet sense" of Christ—or in the experience of the godly Sarah Edwards. It rather has to do with the devotionalism of Edwardsians, those who carried the essence of his evangelical Calvinist Christianity into the very different social setting of the Revolutionary and Early National periods in the new United States. Joseph A. Conforti has linked the publication and distribution of Edwards's "devotional-inspirational" writings by his New Divinity followers with the creation of an enduring religious tradition in American culture. "The *Life of Brainerd*, like Edwards's *Personal Narrative* and 'Resolutions,' enabled leaders of the Second Great Awakening to shape and popularize an Edwardsian brand of piety that addressed the concerns and needs of evangelical Protestantism" in the New Republic. At the heart of this piety, along with its revivalism, was the identification of "true holiness as radical disinterested benevolence." As Conforti notes, historians have recognized the connection between this "doctrine of disinterested benevolence ... especially as it was reformulated by Edwards's New Divinity disciples" and the missionary movement, temperance, abolitionism, and other social reform causes that characterized the antebellum period in the north.[1]

The "distinguishing signs" (to use Edwards's term, from his reflections on the Great Awakening) of such piety were manifest long before the antebellum period, however, and even before the advent of the Second Great Awakening, in the decades between the supposed waning of the revivals associated with the Great Awakening and the reappearance of similar social-spiritual phenomena after the achievement of American independence. During the 1760s and 1770s, Edwardsian revivalistic piety found vital expression in ways that made possible its survival in the New Republic. And at least one of the "works of God" among New England Congregationalists in this tradition during the Revolutionary period may be (in another word associated with Edwards) as "surprising" today as it was then—the operation of God's Spirit across racial lines.

Race could scarcely be considered a front-burner issue for Edwardsians of the second half of the eighteenth century. The movement's primary concerns were theological, pastoral, and spiritual. Moreover, not many Euro-Americans yet felt their consciences pricked by the fundamental evil of slavery, and few if any were close to imagining the possibility of actual, equal, full citizenship for vast numbers of African Americans. Yet, by connecting some dots—drawing the lines among three notable Edwardsians—a pattern emerges which does involve inter-racial salvation and fellowship and which begins to look something like an enduring American spiritual inheritance. These three may have been out ahead of many of their colleagues on the matter of race, but there is no question that they were exemplary New England evangelicals in the Edwardsian tradition. Samuel Hopkins, trained for the ministry by Edwards, pastor in Great Barrington, Massachusetts, and then of First Congregational Church in Newport, Rhode Island, was, according to Conforti his biographer, "the most important Calvinist theologian in New England between Jonathan Edwards and Nathaniel Taylor." Sarah Osborn, also of Newport, whom historians Jon Butler and Harry S. Stout of Yale have called "one of the most powerfully gifted female preachers in colonial American history," was an amazingly prolific writer, popular devotional leader, and teacher. And Lemuel Haynes, influenced directly by Hopkins and at least indirectly by Osborn, is recognized as "the first black to be ordained by any religious organization in America" and a champion of orthodoxy on the theologically dangerous northern New England frontier.[2]

Early in 1776, prior to the Declaration of Independence, Samuel Hopkins published *A Dialogue Concerning the Slavery of the Africans,* in which he stated that it was "the Duty and Interest of the American States to emancipate all their African Slaves." Hopkins employed republican rhetoric in his argument for civil liberty—he can sound very Jeffersonian when he wants to—but it was his religious faith, his theology, that impelled him to this unusually bold stand. Born in Connecticut in 1721, Hopkins came of age during the spiritual revivals known as the Great Awakening. He graduated from Yale College in 1741, studied for the ministry in Edwards's Northampton parsonage, and then devoted his career to advancing the evangelical Calvinism he had learned from his great mentor. For twenty-six years Hopkins served as pastor of the Congregational church in Great Barrington, in western Massachusetts. He and other students of Edwards, notably Joseph Bellamy and Jonathan Edwards Jr., developed a school of thought within Congregationalism that opposed the trend toward softer, more Arminian views of human ability and divine benevolence. Edwardsians, or Hopkinsians as some began to call them, upheld a system of doctrines which they termed Consistent Calvinism. They proclaimed a very high view of God's sovereignty, the abject sinfulness of humanity, the gospel of redemption by the mediating death and resurrection of Jesus Christ, a personal experience of conversion through repentance and acceptance of Christ, and the hope that God would use the preaching of this gospel to revive churches and communities as had occurred during the Great Awakening of the 1730s and early '40s. Detractors who considered these views extreme branded them with the epithet "New Divinity," and it stuck as a party label, like "Puritan" two centuries before. Enough parishioners agreed with the more liberal view that in 1769 Hopkins was dismissed by his congregation. A year later, thanks to the persistent lobbying of Sarah Osborn and her "Religious Female Society," Newport's small and struggling First Church called Hopkins as pastor. Second Congregational Church, with future Yale president Ezra Stiles as pastor, was the large, urbane, prestigious church in town. First Church, despite its name, stood at the working-class margins of Newport's mercantile society. In Newport Hopkins saw the slave trade in operation firsthand and was horrified. There Hopkins felt God's hand lead him to attack white ownership of blacks as "an open violation of the law of God" and "a very great and public sin."[3]

Hopkins's denunciation of slavery was no mere local pronouncement. He addressed *A Dialogue Concerning the Slavery of Africans* to "the Honourable Members of the Continental Congress, Representatives of the Thirteen United American Colonies" (as they were still called). Written in the form of a highly charged conversation between a gentleman who defends slavery as necessary and good from the biblical, economic, and humanitarian viewpoints and an abolitionist, the treatise anticipates many of the issues in the debate as it heated up two generations later. In 1776 Hopkins was concerned with the contradiction of Anglo Americans rising up against British tyranny with the banner of liberty while erecting their society on the backs of African slaves. British oppression of the colonies, he states, "is lighter than a feather, compared to [the] heavy doom" of blacks in America, and "may be called liberty and happiness when contrasted" with slave experience. Like Isaiah with Assyria, Hopkins identified Britain's harsh colonial policy as God's hand of judgment. Slavery was "a sin which God is now testifying against in the calamities he has brought upon us" and "consequently must be reformed, before we can reasonably expect deliverance, or even sincerely ask for it." Hopkins of course was far from a Tory. He and his New Divinity colleagues were zealous patriots, and he paid the price when British troops marched into Newport and pillaged the town, including his church and parsonage. But he broadened the struggle for independence to include a Christian vision of freedom for all of humanity. He denounced American liberty as hollow, hypocritical, as long as blacks were held as property. And Hopkins was concerned about evangelism. The evils of slave-trading and slave-holding by those who called themselves Christians naturally resulted in "the greatest and most deep-rooted prejudices against the Christian religion" among blacks "and bar the way to that which is above all things desirable, their coming to the knowledge of the truth that they might be saved."[4]

New Divinity believers—in the forefront of the new missionary movement as it was spreading from England and the Continent to the American churches—based their mission on the doctrine of "disinterested benevolence." They were "disinterested" not in the sense of being apathetic but rather deeply sympathetic, denying one's self out of love for the other, simply for the sake of the other, with absolutely nothing personally to gain. Developing ideas broached in the 1740s and '50s by Jonathan Edwards, Hopkins and his colleagues rejected the Enlightenment notion that human beings are naturally good, that we instinctively choose the best course for ourselves and for society. In the Age of Reason European philosophers and American Founding Fathers elevated enlightened self-interest to the height of virtue. In 1776 not only Hopkins's *Dialogue* and Jefferson's Declaration but Adam Smith's *Wealth of Nations* appeared before the public. In the rising economic system of capitalism, as Conforti puts it, "self-love replaced the moral sense as the primary natural faculty influencing and controlling human behavior.... Rationalists contended that self-love did not conflict with the public good." For them, the greatest good is achieved through the composite of individuals pursuing "life, liberty, and ... happiness." In contrast, according to Mark Valeri, the New Divinity "turned a Calvinist doctrine of human nature into a critique of the rising culture of commerce." For Hopkins, it was not only his Calvinist doctrine of Original Sin that proved the liberals wrong. The persistence of American slavery, and its justification as necessary and good—this was the most damning evidence that self-interest is the very definition of sin. As Hopkins straightforwardly stated, "moral depravity, or sin, consists in self-love." For Anglo Americans truly to embrace the common good of all, African Americans would need to be included in that "all."[5]

Hopkins's two-volume magnum opus was his 1793 *System of Doctrines*. Here he argued that commitment to "the publick interest, the greatest good and happiness of the whole" defines the Christian life. Of course he did not deny personal and family needs, but stated that one's own "happiness" must be pursued not "any farther than it is consistent with the greatest interest and happiness of the whole" and only in ways that are "really included in it, and serve to promote it." Such righteousness is beyond the reach of sinners, however, for we are by nature "wholly corrupt" in our selfishness. New Divinity insisted that we "must be renewed by the spirit of God, in order to [become] in the least degree virtuous and holy." That this ethic of personal and social holiness operated solely by God's grace and not by human ability is explicit in Hopkins's arrangement of topics. It follows chapters on the person and work of Christ, "the application of redemption" to God's people, the regeneration of the soul by the Holy Spirit, and the experience of conversion. So "disinterested benevolence" is part of the doctrine of sanctification. Hopkins recognized that this gospel was alien to late-eighteenth-century Enlightenment rationalism and the ways this philosophy seemed to be influencing American popular culture in the optimistic New Republic. "The more men are inclined to embrace and be satisfied with a selfish religion, the more careful and zealous should publick teachers be, to oppose it, and detect the delusion, and preach up that pure and undefiled religion, which consists in renouncing self, and the exercise of disinterested affection."[6]

Historians used to portray the New Divinity as a futile attempt by an out-of-touch scholastic clergy to preserve the stale doctrines of a bygone day. Edwards's vital piety had declined into arid moralism. More recently, historians have described the movement as part of a family of "vital nineteenth-century Edwardsean traditions" that shaped a new American evangelical culture. According to the new historians, it "spread because of its sensitivity to the human dilemmas of life in late colonial New England." The New Divinity fashioned from Edwardsian Calvinism "a theology of revival" and a "social agenda of revival" which was not a hoary theological relic but rather a broad-based movement addressing the social context of the day.[7] It is certainly true that this revived evangelical Calvinism was alive among the members of Newport's First Church before the arrival of Samuel Hopkins—he did not introduce it there. Edwardsianism, it should now be evident, was as much a movement of the laity as of the clergy. Sarah Osborn, for example, launched a spiritual revival—and connected the doctrine of disinterested benevolence with the presence of Africans in American society—long before she persuaded her church to call Samuel Hopkins.

Sarah Osborn's faith was rooted in the New England Puritanism of the seventeenth century. Born in London in 1714, she immigrated to Massachusetts as a child with her parents, and to Rhode Island when she was a young teen. Mission-minded Connecticut and Massachusetts Congregationalists had been founding churches in Rhode Island since the 1690s. The Newport church suffered schism in 1728, however, when the majority rejected the venerable pastor Nathaniel Clap's traditional Puritanism in favor of a milder theology more in tune with the town's commercial culture. Unlike her parents, who separated and went with Second Church, young Sarah stayed with Clap in the now-decimated First Church. Clap had led her to Jesus her Savior. Clap brought evangelists George Whitefield and Gilbert Tennent to Newport, sparking New England's Great Awakening and the revival of Sarah's own faith in Christ. Within the rhythms of Puritan spirituality, exemplified in Clap's ministry, she began to construct her life as a schoolteacher, neighborhood devotional group leader, and organizer of the "Religious Female Society." She embraced the theology that was being expressed by Hopkins, Jonathan Edwards Jr., and Joseph Bellamy which would soon be called the New Divinity. About the time these pastors first appeared in print, Sarah Osborn published her own defense of Calvinist orthodoxy, *Nature, Certainty and Evidence of True Christianity* in 1755. Like her learned contemporaries, she disparaged the theology of human goodness with its "hateful principle of self-love," preaching that salvation comes when God leads "me to throw down the Weapons of my Rebellion" and personally "surrender to Christ as mediator." Like the great pastor-theologians, she upheld sanctification as a life of "disinterested benevolence." Like them, she worked and prayed that the Great Awakening would not fade into history. Then in 1766 and 1767, while First Church endured the lackluster ministry of Clap's successor, Sarah Osborn was at the center of a fresh revival in Newport. Attendance at the prayer groups meeting in her home—every night but Saturday—exploded so that "the House will not contain them," as many as 525 people a week.[8]

The outbreak of revival coincided with Sarah Osborn's breaking of the color barrier by welcoming blacks into her home. She already had had to defend herself against the charge of "moving beyond my line" by leading groups of men and older teenage boys. "I by no means set up for their instructor," she insisted, they simply came. In the spring of 1765, "several Ethiopians . . . having their liberty to go where they like on Lords day Evenings have ask'd Liberty to repair to our House for the benefit of family prayer, reading, etc. and I Have thot it a duty to Encourage them." In addition to Bible study and prayer, she taught them to read and write. By June of 1766 an Ethiopian Society of free blacks organized and met at her house every Tuesday evening, while another forty-two blacks who were still slaves gathered with her on Sunday evenings. The ladies and gentlemen of Newport were scandalized, accusing her of "keeping a Negro House." Her evening guests "seem . . . to refresh, recruit and enliven my Exhausted spirits," she wrote, justifying her ministry to a pastor friend. These were "sweet refreshing Evenings" to her soul, and the experience was contagious. The presence of blacks may have had a magnetic effect on white youth, as suddenly large numbers of "white Lads and Neighbors daughters also [began to] press in" on Sunday and Tuesday evenings. She admitted, "I was affreightened at the throng and Greatly feared that it would be as the river Jordan overflowing all the banks." She felt compelled to explain that the blacks were not "lifted up with Pride," that her spiritual leadership was acceptable because technically servants were like "children" in a household "though for stature men and women," that the blacks "call it School" rather than "Meeting," and that some of the blacks were starting prayer groups in the households where they served. Since "God Himself has thus employed me," she argued, "who would advise me to shut up my Mouth and doors and creep into obscurity?" Inside the Osborn home—and no doubt inside Sarah Osborn herself, for she was not without her own ambivalent racial feelings—Newport was turning upside down. With weekly groups of women and men, male and female teens, free blacks and slaves, and with blacks and whites meeting together, Sarah Osborn was at the heart of what she called (echoing Jonathan Edwards's words at the start of the Great Awakening) an "astonishing" and "surprizing" work of God. She wrote in 1767, "Last Summer all things were new and astonishing to me."[9]

In 1769 Samuel Hopkins became Sarah Osborn's pastor. She engineered this call and supported him through the tense beginning of his Newport ministry, and when the British forced him to flee during the Revolution she once more kept the church going. After her death in 1796 Hopkins published her spiritual autobiography and "Extracts from her Diary" and other biographical material as *Memoirs of the Life of Mrs. Sarah Osborn* (Worcester, 1799). It was Osborn's ministry in her home and through the Religious Female Society that placed Hopkins in direct contact with blacks and awakened him to the slavery issue. Osborn was the theologian who, by conducting racially integrated religious gatherings, made the connection between New Divinity doctrine and salvation for African Americans. If she could not hope to force major social change by pressing on from spiritual to civil freedom, the acts of teaching black people to read, praying with them, receiving inspiration and encouragement from them, and becoming their friend were in themselves stunningly bold. The witness of these black Christians combined with that of Sarah Osborn brought Hopkins to the point, on the eve of American independence, where he would address his *Dialogue Concerning the Slavery of the Africans* to the Continental Congress.[10]

Congress did not listen to Samuel Hopkins. But he was heard in other quarters. "A young Mollato," as he called himself in the introduction to a poem he wrote on the Battle of Lexington, would soon employ many of Hopkins's arguments in his own written attack on slavery. Lemuel Haynes, born in 1753 in Hartford but abandoned by his white mother, was raised in a pious evangelical household in Granville, western Massachusetts. Though he was indentured as a servant, the couple embraced him with extraordinary, one might say "disinterested," love. Lemuel internalized the words of Scripture and of sermons by famous preachers like George Whitefield as he heard and read them by the fireside in family devotions. A member of the local militia company, he marched in the April 1775 Lexington Alarm and subsequent siege of Boston. In 1776 Haynes enlisted in the Continental Army, serving in the Ticonderoga campaign, but a case of typhus cut short his military career. His poem is a conventional celebration of New England virtue and valor ("One Son of Freedom could annoy / A Thousand Tyrant Fiends")—until the final stanza, when suddenly young Haynes turns Hopkinsian.

> Sin is the Cause of all our Woe
> That sweet deluding ill
> And till we let this darling go
> There's greater Trouble still.

New Divinity Congregationalists brought this critical-mindedness to their patriotism. And the fact that Haynes was black put a sharper edge on his words. The Founders little imagined the "greater Trouble" that awaited the Republic because of their failure to deal with slavery in their generation.[11]

In 1776, sometime after the Fourth of July, Pvt. Lemuel Haynes wrote his essay "Liberty Further Extended: Or Free thoughts on the illegality of Slave-keeping." Just as Hopkins addressed himself to Congress, Haynes began by quoting Congress: "We hold these truths to be self-Evident, that all men are created Equal, that they are Endowed By their Creator with Ceartain unalienable rights." Citing Acts 17:26 (God "hath made of one blood all nations of men for to dwell on all the face of the earth"), Haynes posited that "Even an affrican, has Equally as good a right to his Liberty in common with Englishmen." Haynes was certainly instructed—and inspired—by Hopkins's work emanating from Rhode Island. But Haynes's prose rises to greater heights as he, Moses-like, identifies himself with his people in his "main proposition"— "That an *African,* or in other terms, *that a Negro may Justly Chalenge, and has an undeniable right to his Liberty*" and that "*Consequently, the practise of Slavekeeping, which so much abounds in this Land is illicit.*" Lemuel Haynes the "African" stood up to "Justly Chalenge" the foundations upon which his New Republic was being erected. No New Divinity preacher ever attacked the power of sin with greater prophetic force. "O! what an Emens Deal of Affrican-Blood hath Been Shed by the inhuman Cruelty of Englishmen! that reside in a Christian Land! ... O ye that have made yourselves Drunk with human Blood! altho' you may go with impunity here in this Life, yet God will hear the Crys of that innocent Blood, which crys from the Sea, and from the ground against you, Like the Blood of Abel ... *vengence! vengence!* What will you Do in that Day when God shall make inquisision for Blood? he will make you Drink the phials of his indignation which Like a potable Stream shall Be poured out without the Least mixture of mercy; Believe it, Sirs, their shall not a Drop of Blood, which you have Spilt unjustly, Be Lost in forgetfullness. But it Shall Bleed affresh, and testify against you, in the Day when God shall Deal with Sinners."[12]

Lemuel Haynes was long looked upon as a kind of Uncle Tom in black American history. "Liberty Further Extended" was discovered in manuscript and published in the *William and Mary Quarterly* only in 1983. Before that he was assessed simply as an intelligent free black who somehow made good as a Congregational pastor. It was even assumed that his New Divinity theology masked his blackness. Now we see that the New Divinity was central to his spiritual identity and gave him a language to "Justly Chalenge" his society. John Saillant has suggested that we could trace "the Revolutionary origins of Black Theology" to Haynes's "black Calvinism." He was raised on Edwardsianism and studied it formally after his discharge from the army. Urged by friends to prepare for the ministry, he apprenticed with several New Divinity pastors in Connecticut, one of whom secured him a teaching job. By the end of 1780 he was licensed to preach and became the supply pastor of his home church. He married a white schoolteacher who was a parishioner. After five years the church applied to the Litchfield (Connecticut) Association for Haynes's ordination to the ministry. He was ordained on 9 November 1785, at Torrington, where he had also done some preaching. Haynes attracted a wide audience, leading one neighboring congregation to complain "that their people would go away from home, and especially to hear that colored man preach." On an evangelistic tour of Vermont he continued to impress white Congregationalists with his blend of sound theology and powerful preaching. In 1788 Rutland's West Parish called him as pastor. West Parish was the evangelical Calvinist congregation created when the local church split along lines identical to those in Newport. Of course it was Edwardsian-Hopkinsian Congregationalists, not the more theologically liberal church, who welcomed the black pastor.[13]

Haynes served the West Rutland church for thirty years, gaining a reputation as a defender of Calvinist orthodoxy and as a sought-after evangelist who toured for the Connecticut Missionary Society. Vermont, and the northern frontier of New England generally, was tough territory for the New Divinity, with intense competition from Free Will Baptists, Universalists, and freethinkers attracted to the antireligious rationalism of Ethan Allen, war hero and author of *Reason, the Only Oracle of Man*. Haynes's most famous encounter with religious liberalism came in 1805 when he debated the leading Universalist, Hosea Ballou. Haynes's rebuttal—a witty lampoon of "Universal Salvation" as "a very ancient doctrine" introduced by Satan in the Garden of Eden (when the serpent lied to Adam, "Ye shall not surely die")—was published and remained in print for decades. Revival sometimes resulted from his ministry to the extent that he was able to report, "The Holy Spirit came down like a mighty rushing wind, bearing away all opposition." In 1804 he wrote, "The alteration in this state within the last two or three years is surprising. Thousands have been converted. The call almost everywhere now is—*preach! preach!*" Haynes received recognition from colleagues. He served as moderator of the Vermont General Convention and trustee of the Vermont Missionary Society, was active in Federalist Party politics, and was an intimate friend of Vermont's antislavery governor and of the U.S. senator who introduced the bill to abolish the slave trade. Middlebury College awarded him an honorary master's degree, and he preached by invitation at Yale College.[14]

Like Edwards at Northampton and Hopkins at Great Barrington before him, in 1818 Lemuel Haynes suffered the indignity of being dismissed from his long-term pastorate. His outspoken Federalist politics and his unswerving theological orthodoxy and moral-spiritual rigor had eroded support within the congregation. Race also played a role, as upwardly mobile members began to feel less than respectable with a black pastor. A friend of Haynes's reported some years after the event: "He subsequently used to say, he lived with the people in Rutland thirty years, and they were so sagacious that at the end of that time they found out he was a *nigger,* and so turned him away." In his farewell sermon Haynes never mentioned race, but he did imply that the official complaints were "the *pretended* reasons" and that "the truth" was "kept out of sight, to escape censure." Nevertheless, he spoke with gracious charity: "My dear brethren and friends, I did not realize my attachment to you before the parting time came. Many disagreeable things have taken place; but still I feel my heart going out towards this people.... You will accept my warmest gratitude for the many instances of kindness shown me." Lemuel Haynes here *embodied* the doctrine of disinterested benevolence. From 1818 until his final illness at age eighty in 1833, Haynes then pastored in Manchester, Vermont, and Granville, New York.[15]

When Samuel Hopkins published his comprehensive *System of Doctrines* in 1793, Haynes joined other evangelical Congregationalists in viewing this work as an authoritative formulation of theology in the Edwardsian tradition. Listed at the front of volume one among the more than one thousand subscribers who financially enabled its publication is the name "Rev. Lemuel Haynes, Rutland." The subscription list, organized by state, is a nine-page "Who's Who" of New Divinity pastors and lay leaders, many of them with titles like Captain or Esquire or Deacon. The names of fourteen women are sprinkled among the long columns of type, until we come to the list for Hopkins's own state of Rhode Island. There, mingled alphabetically among the names of men (seven clergy, twenty-seven lay), are ten women—including of course Sarah Osborn. These ten would be the leading members of Osborn's Religious Female Society. Then—and no such category exists for any state other than Rhode Island—there is a list of "Free Blacks" (seventeen African American women and men: thirteen from Newport, four from Providence). Since they have been forgotten, let them be memorialized here:

>   Prince Amy
>   Mrs. Wishee Buckminster
>   Lincoln Elliot
>   Newport Gardner
>   Mrs. Jenny Gardner
>   Mrs. Priscilla Freeman
>   Robert Keith
>   Congo Jenkins

Adam Millar
Solmar Nubia
Mrs. Obour Tanner
Zingo Stevens
Mrs. Duchess Quamine
Cato Coggeshall
Cato Mumford
Nimble Nightingale
Bristol Yamma

These African American Christians—black Edwardsians—had first gathered in the flush of revival twenty-five years earlier in Sarah Osborn's parlor. In Rhode Island blacks and women combined to account for twenty-seven of the sixty-one New Divinity subscribers to Hopkins's *System of Doctrines,* a remarkable 44 percent participation rate. The presence of these names on the subscription list makes in its own way a theological statement, albeit unintended, as forceful as any of Hopkins's arguments for the sovereignty of God or the doctrine of disinterested benevolence in the text itself.[16]

The New Divinity movement, or at least these three Edwardsians, connected the gospel of salvation in Jesus Christ with the single most crucial—and in their day neglected—issue of American history, the status of African Americans in this society. And they did it in the Revolutionary period traditionally thought of as being between the two Awakenings. They passed on the flame, as it were, of the Edwardsian "theology of revival" and its "social agenda." In vital ways, they kept the spirit of the earlier revivals alive, applied their evangelical Calvinism to the new social context, and made it possible for Edwardsian piety to flourish in the early nineteenth century.

This is not to say that Hopkins and Osborn were unambiguous in their personal feelings toward blacks; the more modern acceptance of general racial equality no doubt eluded them as it did other white eighteenth-century Americans. This would be a step beyond their friendship with exemplary individual black Christians like Lemuel Haynes and those Rhode Islanders listed in the front matter of Hopkins's *System of Doctrines.* In fact, New England Congregationalism failed to become the vehicle for mass evangelism of African Americans. More broadly, Congregationalism soon lost its evangelical force, as its zeal for revival was muted with the rise of a more reserved theological liberalism by about the middle of the nineteenth century. Although Jonathan Edwards and his New Divinity heirs were instrumental in articulating and transmitting that "religion of the heart" which, in the words of David Kling, "remains to this day as a central feature of American Evangelicalism," the essence of revival-oriented heart religion was disseminated in many new, often quite different, directions. As Kling states, "there was no birthright to the language, no designated heir to the affections." Other Christians in the post-Revolutionary United States besides those New England Congregationalists who were the biological children of the Puritans were also starting to make the connection between the Great Commission and the presence of blacks in American society. Some more evangelical groups began to seek out and to embrace African American converts warmly—and even adopted some worship practices with roots in Africa. Critics of early Methodism, John Wigger has argued, were particularly "disturbed by the increasingly African-American character of Methodist worship" in the 1790s and the first decade or so of the 1800s. It was the evangelicalism of these upstart Methodist and Baptist movements—which, as Joseph Conforti shows, appropriated the spiritual legacy of Jonathan Edwards in their own ways—and then much later Pentecostalism, that provided the most conducive setting for American blacks to marry African identity with the gospel.[17]

To leap ahead by a full century, in 1907 Elder Charles H. Mason returned from Azusa Street in Los Angeles to his Church of God in Christ congregation in Memphis, full of "the overflowing joy of the glory of the Lord." Although he had gone west with some skepticism to investigate reports of an outpouring of Holy Spirit baptism unprecedented since Pentecost, when he saw what was happening he "knew it was right." In that pivotal Pentecostal revival, Mason recalled, "everything was new to me and to all the saints." He and thousands of others had been drawn from across the United States, some even from abroad, to the emotionally explosive services being led by William J. Seymour and other Spirit-ordained evangelists, black and white, male and female. The meetings were held in a rundown former African Methodist Episcopal Church building that had been used for a stable before it was resurrected as the Apostolic Faith Gospel Mission. Mason, an African American preacher raised in the southern holiness tradition, never would have thought of himself as an Edwardsian, and the all-night meetings with their tongues-speaking and ecstatic behavior was probably beyond anything imagined by the enthusiasts of New England's Great Awakening. But Mason carried with him on that train back to Memphis something of "America's spiritual inheritance." In his Pentecostal awakening the language of piety we associate with Edwards, Osborn, Hopkins, and Haynes gained fresh currency. And is there not in Mason's language of spiritual rebirth in a shockingly inter-racial setting an echo from Sarah Osborn's report of the 1766 Newport revival—"all things were new and astonishing"?[18]

NOTES

1. Jonathan Edwards, *Two Dissertations, I. Concerning the End for Which God Created the World. II. The Nature of True Virtue* (Boston: S. Kneeland, 1765), 107; Jonathan Edwards, *Letters and Personal Writings,* ed. George S. Claghorn, *The Works of Jonathan Edwards,* vol. 16 (New Haven: Yale Univ. Press, 1998), 792–93. Edwards's "Personal Narrative," a window into his spiritual life, is also published in John E. Smith, Harry S. Stout, and Kenneth P. Minkema, eds., *A Jonathan Edwards Reader* (New Haven: Yale Univ. Press, 1995), 281–96. Joseph A. Conforti, *Jonathan Edwards, Religious Tradition, and American Culture* (Chapel Hill: Univ. of North Carolina Press, 1995), 2, 64; Jonathan Edwards, *A Treatise Concerning Religious Affections,* ed. John E. Smith, *The Works of Jonathan Edwards,* vol. 2 (New Haven: Yale Univ. Press, 1959), 191.

2. Joseph A. Conforti, "Samuel Hopkins (1721–1803)," in *Makers of Christian Theology in America,* ed. Mark G. Toulouse and James O. Duke (Nashville: Abingdon Press, 1997), 73; see also Joseph A. Conforti, *Samuel Hopkins and the New Divinity Movement* (Grand Rapids, Mich.: Eerdmans, 1981). Jon Butler and Harry S. Stout, eds., *Religion in American History: A Reader* (New York: Oxford Univ. Press, 1998), 129; introduction to Charles E. Hambrick-Stowe, "The Spiritual Pilgrimage of Sarah Osborn (1714–1796)," in *Religion in American History,* ed. Butler and Stout, 130–41 (orig. *Church History* [December 1992], 408–21); Sarah Osborn, "Extracts from [a] Diary," in *The Living Theological Heritage of the United Church of Christ,* vol. 3, *Colonial and National Beginnings,* ed. Charles Hambrick-Stowe (Cleveland, Ohio: Pilgrim Press, 1998), 158–62; Helen MacLam, "Black Puritan on the Northern Frontier: The Vermont Ministry of Lemuel Haynes," in *Black Preacher to White America: The Collected Writings of Lemuel Haynes, 1774–1833,* ed. Richard Newman (Brooklyn, N.Y.: Carlson, 1990), xix; see also John Saillant, "Lemuel Haynes and the Revolutionary Origins of Black Theology, 1776–1801," *Religion and American Culture: A Journal of Interpretation* 2 (winter 1992): 79–102; and John Saillant, "Lemuel Haynes (1753–1833)," *Makers,* ed. Toulouse and Duke, 97–100.

3. Samuel Hopkins, *A Dialogue Concerning the Slavery of the Africans* (Norwich, Conn.: Judah P. Spooner, 1776), 11; William Breitenbach, "Piety *and* Moralism: Edwards and the New Divinity," in *Jonathan Edwards and the American Experience,* ed. Nathan O. Hatch and Harry S. Stout (New York: Oxford Univ. Press, 1988), 177–204; Charles Sellers, *The Market Revolution: Jacksonian America, 1815–1846* (New York: Oxford Univ. Press, 1991), 206–7.

4. Hopkins, *Dialogue,* 37, 11, 19–20.

5. Conforti, *Samuel Hopkins,* 112–14; Samuel Hopkins, *The System of Doctrines, Contained in Divine Revelation* (Boston: Isaiah Thomas and Ebenezer T. Andrews, 1793), 1:545; Mark Valeri, *Law and Providence in Joseph Bellamy's New England* (New York: Oxford Univ. Press, 1994), 6; David W. Kling, *A Field of Divine Wonders: The New Divinity and Village Revivals in Northwestern Connecticut, 1792–1822* (University Park: Pennsylvania State Univ. Press, 1993), 243.

6. Hopkins, *System of Doctrines,* 1:545–47, 560, 566.

7. Conforti, *Jonathan Edwards, Religious Tradition, and American Culture,* 10; Valeri, *Law and Providence,* 7; Kling, *A Field of Divine Wonders,* 74, 88; Harry S. Stout, *The New England Soul: Preaching and Religious Culture in Colonial New England* (New York: Oxford Univ. Press, 1986), 6. These authors effectively refute the famous thesis of Joseph Haroutunian, *Piety versus Moralism: The Passing of the New England Theology* (New York: Henry Holt and Co., 1932).

8. Mark A. Peterson, *The Price of Redemption: The Spiritual Economy of Puritan New England* (Stanford, Calif.: Stanford Univ. Press, 1997), 189; Hambrick-Stowe, "Spiritual Pilgrimage of Sarah Osborn," in *Religion in American History,* ed. Butler and Stout, 130–31. On issues of religion and society in colonial Rhode Island, see Sydney V. James, *John Clarke and His Legacies: Religion and Law in Colonial Rhode Island, 1638–1750,* ed. Theodore Dwight Bozeman (University Park: Pennsylvania State Univ. Press, 1999). Sarah Osborn, *Nature, Certainty and Evidence of True Christianity* (Boston: S. Kneeland, 1755), 5–6; Sarah Osborn and Susanna Anthony, *Familiar Letters, Written by Mrs. Sarah Osborn, and Miss Susanna Anthony, Late of Newport, Rhode-Island* (Newport, R.I.: Newport Mercury, 1807), 110–11.

9. Mary Beth Norton, "'My Resting Reaping Times': Sarah Osborn's Defense of Her 'Unfeminine' Activities, 1767," *Signs: Journal of Women in Culture and Society* 2 (1976): 518–26, 529.

10. Osborn and Anthony, *Familiar Letters,* 31; Sellers, *Market Revolution,* 206.

11. Lemuel Haynes, "The Battle of Lexington," in *Black Preacher,* ed. Newman, 13, 15.

12. Lemuel Haynes, "Liberty Further Extended," in *Black Preacher,* ed. Newman, 17–19, 22–23.

13. Saillant, "Lemuel Haynes and the Revolutionary Origins of Black Theology," *Religion and American Culture* 2, no. 1 (winter 1992): 79; "Lemuel Haynes," in *Makers,* ed. Toulouse and Duke, 97–100; MacLam, "Black Puritan," in *Black Preacher,* ed. Newman, xxi–xxv.

14. MacLam, "Black Puritan," in *Black Preacher,* ed. Newman, xxii–xxxiv; Lemuel Haynes, "Universal Salvation," in *Black Preacher,* ed. Newman, 105–11.

15. MacLam, "Black Puritan," in *Black Preacher,* ed. Newman, xxxiv–xxxv; Lemuel Haynes, "A Black Puritan's Farewell," in *African American Religious History: A Documentary Witness,* 2nd ed., ed. Milton C. Sernett (Durham, N.C.: Duke Univ. Press, 1999), 52–60.

16. Hopkins, *System of Doctrines*, xi, xv.

17. Conforti, *Jonathan Edwards, Religious Tradition, and American Culture*, passim; Kling, *A Field of Divine Wonders*, 243; John H. Wigger, *Taking Heaven by Storm: Methodism and the Rise of Popular Christianity in America* (New York: Oxford Univ. Press, 1998), 118–24, chap. 6. On American evangelicalism and black religious experience, see Sylvia R. Frey and Betty Wood, *Come Shouting to Zion: African American Protestantism in the American South and British Caribbean to 1830* (Chapel Hill: Univ. of North Carolina Press, 1998), esp. chap. 5.

18. Elsie W. Mason, "Bishop C. H. Mason, Church of God in Christ," in *African American Religious History*, ed. Sernett, 323; Vinson Synan, *The Holiness-Pentecostal Tradition: Charismatic Movements in the Twentieth Century* (Grand Rapids, Mich.: Eerdmans, 1997 ed.), 70–71, 92–106, 125–27; Edith L. Blumhofer, *Restoring the Faith: The Assemblies of God, Pentecostalism, and American Culture* (Urbana and Chicago: Univ. of Illinois Press, 1993), 73–74.

Beyond the Men in Black

Jonathan Edwards and Nineteenth-Century Woman's Fiction

Sharon Y. Kim

Jonathan Edwards and woman's fiction are not often linked, except perhaps as antitheses. Also known as domestic or sentimental fiction, this genre originated among New England liberals who used it to undermine Edwardsian Calvinism and to popularize Unitarian and Arminian views.[1]

It is in part the medium of woman's fiction that helped to distort Edwards's image and give him a less-than-flattering legacy in nineteenth-century literature—namely, the men in black—anachronistic, overly rational clergymen. With names like Dr. Bland, Dr. Grey, and Dr. Scarsley, these men could read the Bible in Hebrew and Greek but were often painfully out of touch with the rest of humankind. They would face grieving families at funerals and speak about predestination or hell. They would be preoccupied with doctrinal matters irrelevant to the needs of normal people.[2] As scholarly lore would have it, women novelists opposed these dogmatic Calvinists with warmhearted, moral women. In *The Gates Ajar* (1869), for example, Elizabeth Stuart Phelps contrasts a beautiful, compassionate Aunt Winifred with the churchmen whose theology cannot comfort the narrator when her brother dies. While the narrator loves Aunt Winifred, she observes her minister one day and muses: "I wondered whether Dr. Bland thought it wicked to smile in church. No, of course he has too much sense. I wonder what it is about Dr. Bland that always suggests such questions."[3] As in many of these novels, Phelps's narrator shows a desire to be charitable; she notes her minister's sense and often says that he is a good man. Beneath this kindness, however, lies a portrait of a man who seems to disapprove of smiling in church and has a less than sanguine effect upon others.

Harriet Beecher Stowe presents the most detailed descriptions of these men in her novel *Oldtown Folks* (1869). While Stowe praises Edwards as one of "those brave old thinkers who had broken up the crust of formalism and mechanical piety," she notes that "New England theology in particular, with its intense clearness, its sharp-cut crystalline edges and needles of thought, has had in a peculiar degree the power of lacerating the nerves of the soul, and producing strange states of morbid horror and repulsion."[4] Her character Dr. Moses Stern, a visiting Edwardsian minister, doesn't just wear nineteenth-century black or even eighteenth-century black. He still wears seventeenth-century clerical dress, buckles and all, and constantly reiterates "the most unpopular and unpleasant points of Calvinism" whether anyone wants to hear him or not. "He moved among men," writes Stowe, "But seemed not of men," and his Calvinist theology was a system "calculated, like a skillful engine of torture, to produce all the mental anguish of the most perfect sense of helplessness with the most torturing sense of responsibility."[5]

I would like to move beyond the men in black by focusing upon an obscure female author, Susan Warner, who sought to promote, not undermine, a Calvinistic Christianity. Her most famous work, *The Wide, Wide World* (1850), outsold all others of her time except *Uncle Tom's Cabin* (1851–1852); it was read in at least six other countries and translated into four other languages.[6] *The Wide, Wide World* tells the story of ten-year-old Ellen Montgomery, later orphaned, who must live with a crabby aunt in the backwoods of New York state. Through everyday trials and adventures, Ellen adjusts to life in the country and begins to grow into a young woman, helped by Alice Humphreys and Alice's brother John, a handsome young clergyman. *The Wide, Wide World* bears all the marks of a sentimental novel, including the orphaned heroine and numerous tear-filled scenes. Contrary to critical opinion, however, Warner does not portray the "feminized" or watered-down religion associated with this genre. In 1850, Susan Warner was a confirmed member of the Mercer Street Presbyterian Church, zealously evangelical, with a formidable knowledge of the Bible.[7] Warner would have benefited from the changing views of women's nature, sphere, and roles, popular revivalism, and romantic evangelicalism which marked this period; yet she was not part of the often anti-Calvinist bent of these movements.[8] In striking contrast to Stowe and most other women novelists, Warner actively affirmed such difficult Calvinist doctrines as natural depravity and predestination. She somehow managed to present these beliefs in an engaging manner, enough to appeal to a wide readership that included such disparate people as Louisa May Alcott, Henry James, and Vincent Van Gogh. Van Gogh, in fact, liked the book so much that he gave copies of it as gifts to family and friends.[9] While virtually unknown today, Warner wrote nearly thirty novels before her death in 1885. Especially through *The Wide, Wide World,* she strongly influenced the development of the domestic novel and the religious novel; she may even have influenced the writings of Henry James, as discussed below. Although an unlikely descendant and ally, Warner has created for Edwards a more positive legacy in nineteenth-century literature than an engine of torture or the men in black.

Warner owned at least two works by Jonathan Edwards, *A History of the Work of Redemption* (1739) and *Some Thoughts Concerning the Present Revival of Religion in New England* (1742), which she had a particular interest in reading since her beloved minister recommended it.[10] In fact, at a time when Warner lacked the money to mend a simple dress, she still decided to purchase the *Thoughts Concerning the Present Revival*.[11] While Warner does not mention Edwards directly, Edwards would have shaped her understanding of Christianity through her personal readings, her denomination, and her minister, Dr. Thomas Skinner. A New Divinity minister with a "perfectly infectious" smile and "sunny gladness . . . overspreading his whole face,"[12] Skinner admired Edwards and often incorporated Edwards's writings into his own. In a response to a woman's conversion narrative, for example, he comments, "We may see in the history of this person how completely the sinner is in the hands of God." He later specifies in capital letters that a sinner is "A SINNER IN THE HANDS OF AN ANGRY GOD."[13] In works such as "The Old in the New" and "Discourse, Delivered in the Mercer-Street Church," Skinner quotes Edwards and refers to him as an exemplar of Christianity.[14] Warner eagerly looked forward to learning from Skinner, whether through sermons, Bible studies, or personal conversations. Her understanding of Christianity would thus have had a distinctly Edwardsian tone. Some Warner works, like *The Word* (1865) or *Trading* (1872), contain explicit teaching about typology and redemption history congruent with, if not shaped by, Edwards's *History of the Work of Redemption*. I will focus, however, on Warner's most influential novel, *The Wide, Wide World*.

While *The Wide, Wide World* is not baldly denominational, Warner's Calvinistic beliefs affect both its values and its construction. Consider her belief in natural depravity. Much as she loves her daughter, Mrs. Montgomery tells her frankly, "The Lord Jesus is far, far more worthy of your affection than I am, and if your heart were not hardened by sin you would see him so."[15] Unlike Stowe's Evangeline, who is naturally ethereal and pure, Ellen has a distinctly sinful nature. For Warner, the sweetest child is still a sinner, "hardened by sin," until she truly becomes a Christian. In an age when children often died, this idea was a bitter pill to swallow, and popular women writers often shunned it. Warner, however, expressed it plainly in her novel through dialogue and characterization.

Further, since Warner believed in natural depravity, she often explained personal suffering as God's way of chastising sin and promoting faith. Early in the novel, Mrs. Montgomery understands that without affliction, earthly loves could choke her devotion to God and prevent her spiritual life from growing (56–57), and this explanation for suffering recurs throughout *The Wide, Wide World*. Ultimately, Ellen does not suffer because of evil men or social injustice; she suffers because there is something wrong with her—her faith is imperfect, or she does not love God enough. For this reason, despite the genuine meanness of some characters, such as Aunt Fortune or Mr. Saunders, Ellen herself must bear some responsibility for her trials. Warner's characters thus suffer in a profoundly different manner than the heroines of more liberal fiction.

Warner also emphasizes the determinism of God, with which contemporaries like Melville bitterly struggled. Early in the novel, Ellen says that she cannot change her wrong tendencies. "You cannot help it, I know, my dear," said Mrs. Montgomery, with a sigh, "except by His grace who has promised to change the hearts of his people—to take away the heart of stone and give them a heart of flesh" (38). In this scene and similar scenes, Warner shows that becoming a Christian depends completely upon the grace of God. Far from being a problem for Warner, this concept heightens the preciousness of faith in the novel. Further, every major plot event, particularly the painful ones, such as the death of Mrs. Montgomery, becomes evidence for the sovereignty of God, and Warner often turns them to the glory of God. One episode deserves mention because it cuts so strongly against sentimental convention. John Humphreys rescues Ellen from a childhood enemy, who has intercepted her as she rides alone on an empty road. After seeing that Ellen is safe, John explains that he would not have been on the road at that time had he not been unwillingly detained by a friend. John attributes this delay explicitly to God, who has inconvenienced John's schedule but enabled him to help Ellen. In fact, John almost rides past Ellen and her enemy, since Ellen's face is turned away and he doesn't recognize her. But, "*some strange notion crossing his mind*" (400, italics added), John wheels his horse around. Again, instead of simply making John a hero, Warner attributes John's act of heroism to the providence of God, highly unusual in the sentimental novel.

The principal link between Edwards and Warner, however, is not the theological framework of American Calvinism but rather an identical manner of conceiving of and pursuing an authentic relationship to God. The search for true Christianity appears frequently in Edwards's writing and much Puritan writing. What is true salvation? What is a true conversion? What is a true

Christian life? What does it mean to worship in spirit and in truth? From his *Thoughts* on the First Great Awakening to "Directions for Judging of Persons' Experiences" (n.d.) to *The Nature of True Virtue* (1765), Edwards took pains to separate the truth from similar but false ideas. This careful specification appears in one of his most beautiful sermons, "A Divine and Supernatural Light" (1734). As Edwards explains, the divine light is not merely conviction about sin or comprehension of Christian matters; nor is it the twinge of conscience, an impression upon the imagination, or a sensation of religious feeling. All of these belong to the realm of common grace, available even to an unregenerate man. In these cases, the Spirit of God acts upon the natural man without essentially changing him. With the divine light, however, the Spirit of God imparts a new, supernatural principle. It is a spiritual faculty through which a Christian can sense spiritual truths in spiritual terms. It provides "a true sense of the divine excellency of the things revealed in the Word of God, and a conviction of the truth and reality of them, thence arising.[16]

Edwards's *Treatise Concerning Religious Affections* (1746) goes into an extended series of distinctions showing what can and cannot rightly be called a sign of the work of God's spirit, but his autobiographical "Personal Narrative" ca. 1739) offers concrete details that clarify what he means by divine light. Again, Edwards makes a series of distinctions between true spiritual religion and close imitations that others might mistake for it. As he explains, his childhood delight in prayer, abundant concern with pious duties and the soul, frequent religious talk, and even "two more remarkable seasons of awakening" in his later life were not the same thing as the "inward, sweet delight in God and divine things" or the "inward, sweet sense" of these things that he later experienced.[17] Edwards writes that he had often prayed and been earnest about religious matters, yet the real spiritual life only arrived when he received that inward sense of God and divine things. This sense exceeds human imagination, emotion, or reason.

In their pursuit of God, the Puritans did not seek sublime or mystic visions as much as they did greater understanding of Scripture. Most of their epiphanies thus involve a remembrance of a Bible verse or a sudden realization of its meaning. For example, after Jonathan Edwards one day reads 1 Timothy 1:17: "Now unto the King eternal, immortal, invisible, the only wise God, be honor and glory forever and ever, Amen," he writes: "As I read the words, there came into my soul, and was as it were diffused through it, a sense of the glory of the Divine Being; a new sense, quite different from anything I ever experienced before.[18] Edwards has read and understood this verse before, but now he *truly* understands it, so much so that it is as if he had never understood it before. God does not physically appear and speak to Edwards. Rather, a new sense opens up; it comes into the soul; it is diffused through the soul, and—the vital, implicit fact—God makes it do so. He experiences the divine and supernatural, superseding what had been normal religious devotion and normal comprehension of the Bible. Edwards describes this light in terms of marvel and delight.

One word occurs several times in these two accounts, "sense." As Edwards believed, any reasonable person can understand Christian teaching or imitate Christian modes of thought, but the regenerate believer will possess a qualitatively different principle of perception. Paul writes in 1 Corinthians 2:14, "the natural man receiveth not the things of the Spirit of God . . . neither can he know them, because they are spiritually discerned." Thus, evidence of supernatural discernment could show that an individual not only knew about the right biblical teachings but possessed their spiritual fulfillment. For Edwards, the spiritual life is not a figurative concept or a trope for the postconversion experience. Because it allows the believer to sense the things of God, the spiritual life makes the understanding and experience of spiritual things practically empirical.[19]

It is just this type of empiricism that Warner found attractive in her minister. "Dearest Annie," she wrote to her sister. "You and I know, by *experience*, too little of this. If I could only see things as Dr. Skinner sees them! What beauty and glory, to *his* eye, beam from passages where I was never struck by anything particularly. It is a happiness to know at any rate that the source of his light is open to me too."[20] Warner describes Dr. Skinner as one who has experienced the spiritual reality referred to in the Bible, and the mark of this experience is that he can see the beauty and glory contained in the Bible, just as Edwards received that new sense of the glory of the Divine Being. Warner sought this type of faith in her own life and sought to portray it in her novels.

The spiritual moments in *The Wide, Wide World* thus take a similar form to those recorded in Edwards's writings. Without any direct visions or words from God, Ellen has several epiphanies that indicate a new, spiritual life. John tells Ellen one day that a true Christian has "a change wrought in them by the Holy Spirit,—the change that makes them different from others, and different from their old selves." "Do all Christians have it?" Ellen asks. And John replies, "Certainly. None can be a Christian without it" (352). Ellen's epiphanies occur mostly while reading or remembering verses from the Bible. One night, for example, Proverbs 8:17 comes to Ellen's mind: "I love them that love me, and they that seek me early shall find me" (261–62). Suddenly, Ellen understands the meaning of that promise and its particular fulfillment in her life. Although she had often read that verse, she now has a deep sense of its truth and reality, a perception that brings her to tears. In another episode, Ellen reads the story of Lazarus in John 11, and Warner writes: "She read it as she never had read it before;—she found in it what she never had found before. . . . On the love of Christ, as there shown, little Ellen's heart fastened" (430). These moments match Edwards's specification in *A Treatise Concerning Religious Affections* that the affection not arise merely from the "occasion" of "Scripture, remarkably brought to the mind" or "the sudden and unusual manner of its coming into the mind" but the glory and excellency of Christ, revealed in the Scripture.[21]

These moments also demonstrate a spiritual perception that Ellen has lacked before becoming a Christian. Warner thus emphasizes the "change" that John mentions, the difference between new self and old self, Christian and non-Christian. The change offers the most graphic evidence of the Holy Spirit because it distinguishes knowledge of the Bible from actual participation in what the Bible expresses—the letter of Christianity from its spirit. In language reminiscent of Edwards's, John teaches Ellen that the Bible shows "signs" by which she can know if the Holy Spirit has set its "mark" upon her (352), the hope being that she has indeed been changed in her essential nature. As Edwards writes in his *Treatise Concerning Religious Affections:* "But all spiritual discoveries are transforming; and not only make an alteration of the present exercise, sensation and frame of the soul; but such power and efficacy have they, that they make an alteration in the very nature of the soul. . . . Such power as this is properly divine power, and is peculiar to the Spirit of the Lord: other power may make a great alteration in men's present frames and feelings; but 'tis the power of a Creator only that can change the nature, or give a new nature."[22]

One such epiphany occurs after Ellen examines herself carefully and believes that she has indeed become a Christian. Ellen feels much joy, tinged with sadness that her mother has died before seeing her become a Christian:

> Weeping with mixed sorrow and thankful joy, Ellen bent her head upon her little Bible to pray that she might be more changed; and then, as she often did, raised the cover to look at the texts in the beloved handwriting.
> "I love them that love me, and they that seek me early shall find me."
> Ellen's tears were blinding her. "That has come true," she thought.
> "I will be a God to thee and to thy seed after thee."
> "That has come true too!" she said, almost in surprise . . .

> —And then, as by a flash, came back in her mind the time it was written; she remembered how when it was done her mother's head had sunk upon the open page; she seemed to see again the thin fingers tightly clasped;—she had not understood it then; she did now! "She was praying for me," thought Ellen,—"she was praying for me! she believed that would come true." (352)

Like Edwards's reading of 1 Timothy 1:17, this realization is unpremeditated, sudden, and closely tied to the Bible. Further, the spiritual event takes place in the midst of a physical action (reading) and a mental one (thinking about the verses) but surpasses them. When Ellen reads the first verse, she thinks, "That has come true," and after the second, "That has come true too!" In themselves, these rapid thoughts already add to Ellen's knowledge, but anyone can make such deductions. It is the flash—"she had not understood it then; she did now! 'She was praying for me'"—that exceeds reason. No logical connection exists between reading the inscribed verses, the memory of her mother's head sinking to the page, and prayer. How does Ellen know? Warner implies that since Ellen has learned to love and trust God herself, she can recognize the identical spiritual attitude, seen but not understood in the past, in her mother. After this realization, Ellen knows that a bond once lacking between herself and her mother has suddenly been formed. Before, they had had a close relationship as mother and daughter. Now, they have a spiritual kinship as women who know the same God. Warner describes this as a "link of communion" (353).

Ellen's epiphany is itself linked to Mrs. Montgomery's experience while writing the verses for her daughter. The first verse, "I love them that love me; and they that seek me early shall find me," comes from Proverbs 8:17. Mrs. Montgomery had quoted it in a previous scene (39), urging Ellen to give her full love to God. No doubt, Mrs. Montgomery inscribes the verse as a reminder of that conversation, one that would be repeated every time Ellen opened her Bible. Ellen's mother consciously chooses Proverbs 8:17 for instructional purposes.

The second verse, however, is God's word to Mrs. Montgomery: "This [Proverbs 8:17] was for Ellen; but the next words were not for her; what made her write them?" Warner asks (42). Unlike the first inscription, the second verse, from Genesis 17:7, is written without contrivance and defies the methodical didacticism that Ellen's mother had planned. Mrs. Montgomery suddenly understands the promise of God contained in the Bible verse, "I will be a God to thee and to thy seed after thee." She knows and believes that Ellen will one day become a Christian. Immediately, Mrs. Montgomery bows in fervent prayer. Ellen sees this action but supposes "that one of her mother's frequent feelings of weakness or sickness had made her lean her head upon the Bible, and she thought no more about it" (42).

This scene shows its kinship to Puritan epiphany through its close connection to the Bible, the sudden charge of meaning given to a familiar verse, and the fact that Ellen, an unregenerate person, cannot understand what has just happened; she doesn't even realize that her mother has prayed.[23] However, when Ellen understands both the verses and her mother's prayer, the promise of Genesis 17:7 is fulfilled, and Mrs. Montgomery's epiphany while writing the verse finds its completion in Ellen's comprehension of it. Ellen shows that she knows and follows the same God as her mother. The link of communion falls into place.

Through these moments, Warner engages in a meticulous specification concerning Christianity, reminiscent of Edwards. She emphasizes how this type of Christianity supersedes what is normally taken as religious experience; she also goes out of her way to distinguish between the conventions of the sentimental novel (such as the mother-daughter bond) and the true life of faith. Just as Edwards's "Personal Narrative" helps to show in concrete terms what he delineates in "A Divine and Supernatural Light," Warner uses literary realism to show her beliefs as they would play out in everyday life. In sermon form, if the events of the novel were condensed into instructive points, her novel might read something like this: What is true Christianity? First, what it isn't. It is not childhood innocence. It is not church-going, reading the Bible, singing hymns, understanding or affirming Christian doctrine, or having a Christian mother. It is not sentimental attachments or a liking for a handsome young clergyman. It is not an effect of the imagination or the intellect or a general religiousness. It is not good behavior or temperance. It is not Catholicism. Second, positively, what it is. It is a true sense of the reality and truth of the divine things revealed in the Word of God; it comes from no natural means but only by the Spirit of God. It is a new life and principle different from the old. It emerges most beautifully in times of trial and loss. It results in greater love for God above all else, a practical love for others, and a purified heart toward the world.

Because Warner wanted to show that a regenerate believer has a qualitatively different life than the nominal Christian, the story of Ellen's growth entails a marked change in perception and character. The Bible-reading Ellen at the beginning of the novel is not the Christian Ellen at novel's end. This sense of a pilgrim's progress, a dynamic change in the inner life, forms one of the principal contributions of the Puritan tradition to the novel and is part of Warner's legacy among the women writers of her day.

Catharine Sedgwick, for example, wrote some of the earliest examples of woman's fiction, starting with *The New England Tale* in 1825. Interestingly, as Nina Baym remarks, all of Sedgwick's heroines prior to 1850 exhibit very little if any change in character; they have no flaws and thus remain static. Her last novel, published in 1857, however, contains for the first time a flawed heroine who must learn and grow.[24] Scholars classify Warner as a descendant of Sedgwick's, but Warner read two of Sedgwick's novels only after she had written *The Wide, Wide World*, and then she found them "dismally poor."[25] More than Sedgwick influencing Warner, it may be that the success and power of Warner's work, which focuses intently on a young girl's spiritual growth, moved Sedgwick to tell a different kind of tale.

The notion of character and progress links Warner more directly with the most famous of domestic novels, Louisa May Alcott's *Little Women* (1868). On a rare, precious day off from work, Jo March chooses to read *The Wide, Wide World*, which she's read before, and enjoys crying over the voluminous novel. Just as Warner incorporates Bunyan's *Pilgrim's Progress* into her work as a parallel to Ellen's life, Alcott makes *Pilgrim's Progress* the structural metaphor for her novel, titling chapters after episodes in Bunyan's allegory and chronicling the passage from girlhood to womanhood of the four March girls. The conversations between Marmee and Jo, and the moments in which Jo and Amy are encouraged to rely upon that "Friend" who is in heaven, resemble similar moments in Warner's novel. An older woman counsels the younger women as they go through various hardships; the tone of intimacy and understanding, along with the rounded characterization of the women, allows the scenes to avoid a clumsy didacticism.

Warner had a stronger influence upon Maria Cummins's *The Lamplighter* (1854), the wildly popular novel that prompted Hawthorne's cranky remark about "scribbling women" and which Joyce brutally satirized in the "Nausicaa" episode of *Ulysses*.[26] The title, opening scene, and controlling metaphor of *The Lamplighter* come directly from the opening scene of *The Wide, Wide World*, in which Ellen watches a lamplighter at work in the city. Cummins's novel also follows the basic plot pattern of its forebear—an orphan girl, a father lost at sea, the overcoming of adversity, the growth into womanhood. More significantly, Cummins imitates the Puritan-like spiritual moments seen in Warner: "Gertrude had often found in time and the soothing influences of religious faith some alleviation to her trials; but never until this night, did she feel a spirit not of earth, coming forth from the very chaos of sorrow into which she was plunged, and enkindling within her the flame of a higher and nobler sensation than she ever yet had cherished."[27] Cummins describes the "spirit not of earth" that Gerty feels for the first time, even though she has had religious experiences before. Although Cummins places a Unitarian and romantic inflection upon this scene, she adopts the passage into a deeper spiritual experience from Warner. In addition to these popular women writers, Warner also sparked imitation among lesser known authors, such as Julia Dorr, whose *Farmingdale* (1854) borrows the mean aunt, orphancy, and trials in the countryside from Warner and was marketed explicitly to compete with *The Wide, Wide World*.[28]

Warner inspired not only the domestic novelists but other religious writers as well. Scholars often note the "Puritan antipathy" toward novels that persisted into the nineteenth century.[29] The traditional view that novels were fictitious, immoral, corrupting, and a waste of time was probably compounded by the express anti-Calvinist intent of many popular nineteenth-century novels. Many New Divinity ministers, for example, criticized or disdained the novel. When *The Wide, Wide World* appeared, however, thousands of readers responded warmly to the lifelike characters and what they commended as the "fine spirit of evangelical truth."[30] Many sent letters to Warner explaining how her novel had helped them spiritually, even, in some cases, helping to spark conversion.[31] Perhaps more significantly, Dr. Skinner himself encouraged Warner. Skinner remarks in a letter that most novels promote the cause of "irreligion," yet Warner's novel was different: "The spirit in your book is the spirit of the gospel. The teaching of it, is the teaching of the Evangelical Pulpit. . . . It requires good judgment, and taste, to teach religion, by fiction; and hence the frequency of failure. So much are you to be congratulated at your success."[32] Warner's ability to combine faith and literary realism opened the way for other religious writers, such as her sister Anna—who wrote numerous novels but is most famous for the hymn "Jesus Loves Me, This I Know"—and Martha Finley. Finley wrote the popular and relentlessly Calvinistic Elsie Dinsmore books, extending Warner's influence to didactic children's literature. In *Elsie Dinsmore,* the main character encounters a Christian woman for the first time in a moment of great distress. This scene imitates the first time Warner's heroine in *The Wide, Wide World* meets a Christian woman other than her mother. Even the names are similar: Ellen meets Miss Alice, Elsie meets Miss Allison. Further, as one scholar notes, one of Finley's most famous scenes, in which a young girl faints at a piano rather than perform on the Sabbath, is taken, "minus the doctrinal subtleties," from Warner's *Melbourne House* (1865).[33] Warner also wrote books for children, such as the *Tales Illustrating the Lord's*

Prayer series (1873–1877) and *Trading*, which contains discussions of Old Testament types of the messiah and their New Testament fulfillment.

Finally, I wish to hint at a more surprising literary influence. Henry James's *Washington Square* (1881) follows a moral structure that strongly resembles those of some later Warner novels, such as *Diana* (1877). Both *Diana* and *Washington Square* contain female protagonists who have lost one parent and maintain a tense, perhaps antagonistic, relationship with the other. Both center upon renunciation—the heroines do not marry the man they love but years later encounter him again and reaffirm their decisions. Both Warner and James examine the moral and psychological effects of Victorian renunciation. Warner, however, moves from renunciation into a complex meditation upon marriage, which through typology recreates in the nineteenth century the Puritan bridal-passion discussed by Amanda Porterfield.[34]

In *The Spoils of Poynton* (1896), James names his heroine Fleda, perhaps after Fleda Ringgan of Warner's second novel, the best-seller *Queechy* (1852). James's Fleda has the simple beauty, keen perception, and humorous independence common to woman's fiction, including Warner's. But she is marked most strongly by the highly developed conscience and scrupulosity central to a Warner heroine. Just as a Warner novel is built specifically to make subtle distinctions in spiritual and moral matters, *The Spoils of Poynton* hinges upon Fleda's extreme moral scrupulosity. Like an engine of torture, this scrupulosity forces Fleda into an excruciating test of her moral character, which she passes. However, her exacting conscience prevents Fleda from marrying the man she loves and uselessly condemns herself, her lover, and his mother to unfulfilled lives. This is perhaps James's critique of the Warner heroine—she has principles that go so far beyond the norm that only she can live up to them, at the cost of needless suffering to herself and others. As a literary critic, James was familiar with Warner's work, reviewing several of her novels in print, and even citing Warner as a corrective to the "great brilliancy and great immorality" of the French realists.[35] James's debt to George Eliot's *Middlemarch* (1871–1874) has already been noted in discussions of *The Portrait of a Lady* (1881). His debt to the less esteemed American women novelists in depicting the workings of the female soul has yet to be fully explored.[36]

Warner's treatment of female psychology, particularly in the context of a moral dilemma, is one way in which Warner took the spiritual life described by Edwards and expressed it in the medium of nineteenth-century fiction. Warner's way of imagining this religious realism—scenes, characters, and plots—helped to shape what would become the conventions of the popular sentimentalist genre. Initially, Warner enjoyed both popular and critical success. In the postbellum years, however, changing definitions of high culture and literature served to exclude much religious, domestic, and popular fiction. Warner's novels, once reviewed alongside the works of Hawthorne, fell increasingly into neglect.

The changing reviews of Warner in the *New York Times* serve to illustrate these shifting standards. When *The Wide, Wide World* first appeared, the *New York Times* praised the novel as a great work, the kind produced only once in an age.[37] By the end of that century, nostalgia would eclipse artistic merit in assessments of Warner's work. An 1898 article notes "certain charming pictures of rural life, with characters cleverly hit off, sentiment which is genuine, and a refreshing clearness" but lingers most over how the reader "recalls stolen hours on the farm, perhaps, and a flavor of lilacs steals up from somewhere; or he remembers how his mother used to laugh and weep [with Warner's heroine]." While the writer calls Warner a "pioneer," noting the "freshness and originality" of *The Wide, Wide World,* he states, "Frankly, it is difficult to understand today why that book should have had so widespread and persistent popularity."[38] By 1910, the *New York Times* would view Warner favorably only for nostalgic reasons, using terms like "quaintness" and "antiquation." A review of Warner's biography states: "The life it chronicles, the temper in which it is written, have an odd and rather pathetic flavor of survival in this bustling and skeptical day."[39]

Jane Tompkins discusses Warner's fading and wryly comments: "If the religious views that characterized the attacks on *The Scarlet Letter* in the 1850s had dominated literary criticism after the war, Hawthorne would have done well to experience a religious conversion."[40] While Tompkins discusses many factors in the decline of sentimental fiction, and Warner's in particular—including Warner's geographical separation from the Boston literati, her decision to publish through a religious publisher, and perhaps the prejudices of male critics—it is most likely Warner's commitment to religion that most precipitated her exclusion from the literary canon. Not only did Warner portray religious characters, she wrote from an unambiguous and unconflicted religious perspective, one increasingly viewed as incompatible with literary art. Whatever the reasons that Warner was mostly forgotten, she still had a distinct influence upon several genres of nineteenth-century fiction.

Through Susan Warner, Jonathan Edwards bequeathed more to nineteenth-century literature than a traumatic theology or an emotionally stunted minister. In her later years, Warner occasionally satirized some men in black, such as the stupefied elders of *Daisy Plains* (1886), but she never used these men as a means of undermining a rigorous religion. In all of her novels, the most mature, compassionate, and attractive characters quote the Bible, discuss theological matters, and actively, scrupulously instruct others. Warner differed from most writers of popular sentimental fiction, who were mostly post-Calvinist or anti-Calvinist, promoting a religion of the heart but dissolving spiritual or biblical rigor. In her most famous and influential novel, *The Wide, Wide World,* Warner portrayed and promoted a Christian belief that was both influenced by Edwards and consonant with his work. The elegance and specificity with which Edwards described spiritual reality has contributed a valuable element even to the genre of nineteenth-century woman's fiction.

NOTES

1. See Ann B. Douglas, *The Feminization of American Culture* (New York: Avon Books, 1978), 80, passim; David S. Reynolds, *Faith in Fiction: The Emergence of Religious Literature in America* (Cambridge: Harvard Univ. Press, 1981), 96–122, esp. 106. I adopt the term "woman's fiction" from Nina Baym's seminal work, *Woman's Fiction: A Guide to Novels by and about Women in America: 1820–1970* (Chicago: Univ. of Illinois Press, 1993).

2. This characterization is essentially the female and literary response analogous to the anti-Calvinist complaints developed by male religious leaders, which Nathan O. Hatch summarizes as attacking Reformed orthodoxy's "implicit endorsement of the status quo, its tyranny over personal religious experience, its preoccupation with complicated and arcane dogma, and its clerical pretension and quest for control." (Nathan O. Hatch, *The Democratization of American Christianity* [New Haven: Yale Univ. Press, 1989], 171.)

3. Elizabeth Stuart Phelps [Ward], *The Gates Ajar* (Boston: Fields, Osgood and Co., 1869), 66.

4. Harriet Beecher Stowe, *Oldtown Folks,* ed. Henry F. May (Cambridge: Belknap Press of Harvard Univ. Press, 1966), 71. Stern was based upon Nathaniel Emmons.

5. Ibid., 403.

6. Edward Halsey Foster, *Susan and Anna Warner* (Boston: Twayne Publishers, [1978]), 35. For the listing of translations, see Dorothy Hurlbut Sanderson, *They Wrote for a Living: A Bibliography of the Works of Susan Bogert Warner and Anna Bartlett Warner* (West Point, N.Y.: Constitution Island Association, 1976), 20.

7. Warner experienced conversion in her early twenties, joined the Mercer Street Presbyterian Church in 1844, and served as a fund-collector for missions. She was also a Visitor for the New York City Tract Society. She joined a Methodist church in the early 1860s.

8. See Douglas, *Feminization of American Culture;* Martha Tomhave Blauvelt and Rosemary Skinner Keller, "Women and Revivalism: The Puritan and Wesleyan Traditions," in *Women and Religion in America,* ed. Rosemary Radford Ruether and Rosemary Skinner Keller (San Francisco: Harper and Row, 1983), 2:316–31; Cathy N. Davidson, *Revolution and the Word: The Rise of the Novel in America* (New York: Oxford Univ. Press, 1986), 40–54; William G. McGloughlin, ed., *The American Evangelicals, 1800–1900* (New York: Harper and Row, 1968); George M. Marsden, *The Evangelical Mind and the New School Presbyterian Experience: A Case Study of Thought and Theology in Nineteenth-Century America* (New Haven: Yale Univ. Press, 1970).

9. J. Van Gogh-Bouger, ed., *The Letters of Vincent Van Gogh* (Boston: Houghton Mifflin Co., 1927), 1:63, 67, 80, 108. I discuss Alcott and James below.

10. Warner owned two copies of *A History of the Work of Redemption,* which was published posthumously after 1753, though preached as a series of sermons in 1739.

11. Anna Warner, *Susan Warner* ([New York.: G. P. Putnam's Sons, 1909]), 232–33.

12. Susan Warner, quoted in Anna Warner, *Susan Warner,* 219.

13. Dr. Thomas Harvey Skinner, *Another Voice from the Grave!* (Boston: M. Crocker for Armstrong, 1819), 14, 16.

14. Dr. Thomas Harvey Skinner, "The Old in the New: or, The Position and Policy of the Presbyterian Church" (Saint Louis: White, Woods and Co., 1855) [no page numbers for this text]; Dr. Thomas Harvey Skinner, "Discourse, Delivered in the Mercer-Street Church" (New York: Leavitt, Trow and Co., 1845), 14, 17.

15. Susan Warner, *The Wide, Wide World* (New York: Feminist Press, 1987), 38. All other references to this text will be to this edition.

16. Jonathan Edwards, "A Divine and Supernatural Light, Immediately Imparted to the Soul by the Spirit of God, Shown to be Both a Scriptural and Rational Doctrine," in *A Jonathan Edwards Reader,* ed. John E. Smith, Harry S. Stout, and Kenneth P. Minkema (New Haven: Yale Univ. Press, 1995), 111.

17. Edwards, "Personal Narrative," in *A Jonathan Edwards Reader,* ed. Smith et al., 281, 283, 284.

18. Ibid., 284.

19. See also Thomas A. Schafer, introduction to Edwards, *The "Miscellanies,"* ed. Thomas A. Schafer, *The Works of Jonathan Edwards,* vol. 13 (New Haven: Yale Univ. Press, 1994), 49–52.

20. Anna Warner, *Susan Warner,* 236.

21. Jonathan Edwards, *A Treatise Concerning Religious Affections,* ed. John E. Smith, *The Works of Jonathan Edwards,* vol. 2 (New Haven: Yale Univ. Press, 1959), 142–43.

22. Ibid., 2:340.

23. All of the elements of epiphany in *The Wide, Wide World* together align it more specifically with the Puritan epiphany than with the Wesleyan elements of the general evangelical epiphany. See Blauvelt and Keller, "Women and Revivalism."

24. Baym, *Woman's Fiction,* 61.

25. Anna Warner, *Susan Warner,* 305; Foster, *Susan and Anna Warner,* 53. Foster suggests that Susan Warner may have read one Sedgwick novel as a child, but Warner's extant journals, which record her daily readings, show no record of this. Since some of Warner's journals were destroyed, it is unclear whether or not Warner read Sedgwick's early novel, though she certainly preferred the novels of Maria Edgeworth and Sir Walter Scott.

26. Hawthorne complains of the "d——d mob of scribbling women," authoresses who sell innumerable editions to a tasteless public but fail to achieve true art. (Nathaniel Hawthorne to William D. Ticknor, 19 Jan. 1855, letter 779 of *The Centenary Edition of the Works of Nathaniel Hawthorne: The Letters, 1853–1856,* ed. Thomas Woodson, James A. Rubino, L. Neal Smith, and Norman Holmes Pearson [Columbus: Ohio State Univ. Press, 1987], 17:303–4.)

27. Maria Cummins, *The Lamplighter,* ed. Nina Baym (New Brunswick, N.J.: Rutgers Univ. Press, 1988), 104–5.

28. An advertisement printed with the book, for example, states that *Farmingdale* "Excels in interest, and is quite equal in its delineation of character to, 'The Wide, Wide World.'" (Caroline Thomas [Julia Caroline Dorr], *Farmingdale* [New York: D. Appleton and Company, 1854].)

29. Herbert Ross Brown, *The Sentimental Novel in America: 1789–1860* (New York: Harper and Brothers, 1940), 15. In addition to Reynolds and Davidson, see also William Gilmore, *Reading Becomes a Necessity of Life: Material and Cultural Life in Rural New England, 1780–1835* (Knoxville: Univ. of Tennessee Press, 1989), 39–40; David W. Kling, *A Field of Divine Wonders: The New Divinity and Village Revivals in Northwestern Connecticut, 1792–1822* (University Park: Pennsylvania State Univ. Press, 1993), 224. Warner and her circle still held these views of the novel. Olivia Phelps Stokes writes that Warner's sister gave her a look of "troubled surprise" when Stokes referred to Susan's works as novels. "In her younger days," explains the biographer and friend, "many persons holding strict ideas kept aloof from novels." Warner herself once wrote in her journal: "One thing I ought never to do, at least for some time, and that is, to read novels. I know they have done me mischief enough already." Like many a female novelist in the nineteenth century, Warner takes a negative view of novels within her own novel. John, for example, asks Ellen not to read any novels, and Ellen replies, "I never do, John" (564). For Warner, as perhaps for Edwards who read Richardson's *Pamela,* the novel was not so much a generic prose form as it was a subject matter and perspective. This

distinction is sometimes lost in scholarly treatments of attacks against the novel. (Olivia Egleston Phelps Stokes, *Letters and Memories of Susan and Anna Bartlett Warner* [New York: G. P. Putnam's Sons, 1925], 14; Anna Warner, *Susan Warner*, 155.)

30. "Alice's Admirer" to Susan Warner, 1 March 185—, Warner House Collection, Constitution Island Association, West Point, New York.

31. "I owe my change of heart and life to the influence of the Wide, Wide World[—] my first convictions of sin were the result of reading the conversations of John and Ellen," wrote one. (Unknown, letter to Susan Warner, 1863, Warner House Collection.) Anna Warner also notes that many could "trace their heart conversion" to the blessing of God upon *The Wide, Wide World* (Anna Warner, *Susan Warner*, 264).

32. Dr. Thomas Harvey Skinner to Susan Warner, 24 June 1851, Warner House Collection.

33. Jane Weiss, "'Many Things Take Up My Time': The Journals of Susan Warner" (Ph.D. diss., City University of New York, 1995), 354.

34. Amanda Porterfield, *Feminine Spirituality in America: From Sarah Edwards to Martha Graham* (Philadelphia: Temple Univ. Press, 1980), 19–50.

35. Henry James, "The Schönberg-Cotta Family," review of *The Schönberg-Cotta Family*, by Elizabeth Rundle King, *Nation*, 14 Sept. 1865, 345.

36. Alfred Habeggar focuses more heavily on the biographical influences informing James's appropriation of woman's fiction as well as the sexual dimensions of woman's fiction. Describing these women and James's relationship to them in terms of an agon, Habeggar does not analyze James's novels themselves for the positive contributions made by the women novelists, particularly with respect to the depiction of a character's interior life. (Alfred Habeggar, *Henry James and the "Woman Business"* [New York: Cambridge Univ. Press, 1989].)

37. Helen Papashvily, *All the Happy Endings* (New York: Harper and Brothers, 1956), 2.

38. Edgar Mahew Bacon, "Susan Warner," *New York Times Book Review*, 3 Sept. 1898, 588.

39. "Susan Warner and Her Work," *New York Times Book Review*, 5 Mar. 1910, 122.

40. Jane Tompkins, *Sensational Designs: The Cultural Work of American Fiction, 1790–1860* (New York: Oxford Univ. Press, 1985), 31.

Gary Marshall's *Runaway Bride* in Light of *The Religious Affections* and *The Nature of True Virtue*

Reflections on Popular American Culture

Amanda Porterfield

In Gary Marshall's 1999 film, *The Runaway Bride,* Richard Gere plays Ike Graham, a hard-boiled metropolitan newspaper columnist notorious for his criticism of the fair—or, as he would say, *unfair*—sex. Julia Roberts plays Maggie Carpenter, a flirtatious hardware store owner in an outlying town who is notorious for fleeing a series of grooms. Ike writes a story about Maggie's leaving seven men heartbroken at the altar, claiming that she proves his view of womanhood's essentially feckless nature. In retaliation, Maggie gets Ike fired by threatening to sue the newspaper for falsehood and slander—she has only run away from *three* weddings, not seven. Hoping to get his job back with a sensational story, Ike hounds the preparations for Maggie's upcoming fourth wedding, this time to the high school football coach, who is utilizing sports psychology to get her down the aisle and over her "problem."

Maggie and Ike fall in love. Maggie jilts the coach at the wedding rehearsal and she and Ike decide to get married the next day. After all, the church has already been booked. What is different this time—Maggie knows it, and her friends know it—is that she has finally found a man who knows her. But she doesn't know herself. Maggie lacks self-knowledge and, along with that, she lacks the knowledge and habits of love, the self-constructions that would keep the relationship from collapsing. She does have a fundamental sense of honesty, however, as evidenced by her inability to go through with weddings that don't feel right. But this honesty only breaks through like an alarm bell at the last minute because she has only played at being in love through infatuation and enthusiasm for the appearances of love. In her self-deception and deception of others, she represents a secularized and romanticized version of what Jonathan Edwards would have called hypocrisy.[1]

Ike would fall into Edwards's other major category of damnation, that of melancholy. Like Maggie, he too has been driven by self-interest and lived without a real sense of love to others, not to mention to being-in-general. But he has rational knowledge about love. He knows what love ought to be, not only between marriage partners but also among family and friends. So he challenges the way they treat Maggie as a laughing stock and he challenges Maggie for being self-centered and manipulative. This truth-telling begins to free Maggie from her deceptions. At the same time, Ike begins to feel that love might be more than a distant country or insubstantial fiction.

But the wedding is a mistake. With Ike replacing the groom of the previous day, it is a rushed and hasty affair. Nevertheless, there is a sense of hopeful anticipation in the air as assembled family, friends, and news reporters gather in the church for the wedding ceremony and stand up together as Maggie makes her way down the aisle. She hesitates partway, but eye contact with Ike prompts her forward again. As she closes in on the altar, a camera flash disrupts the connection. Maggie backs off, shakes her head, turns, and runs away.

Some of the religious elements in the film are explicit, and others are more implicit and indirect. At the obvious level, Maggie's various weddings are sacred events, at least in external design. Some occur inside churches and, in this case, inside a church of New England Congregational style. If Maggie's handling of this wedding is reckless, her inability to go through with it reflects her sense that marriage involves some kind of sacred truth or ultimate reality that she is not ready to enter.

In a more indirect way, the romantic images of weddings that appear throughout the film point to a traditional concept of marriage as a loving, even mystical union between husband and wife. Marriage has long been associated with biblical and mystical imagery and with the idea that God's love for the saint is like a bridegroom's love for his bride. As a type of divine love, marriage has served as an emotional base for feelings and ideas about God and as a religious framework for constructing gender roles.

In American culture, this bridal mysticism has been redefined in the context of a market economy and its increasingly sophisticated commodification of sex and sentiment. As a number of scholars have argued, middle-class women and liberal Protestant ministers in the nineteenth century forged a cultural alliance marked by interpreting Christian values in terms of an idealization of domestic life.[2] Descriptions of the home as a sanctuary for marriage and childrearing fostered a profound connection between romantic sentiment and a market economy in which men were supposed to be breadwinners and women were supposed to be consumers. At the same time, the infusion of Christian values brought emotional depth into this process of constructing American middle-class culture. In reworking an older mystical paradigm of marriage, divine love became more down-to-earth, more explicitly linked to human feeling and psychology. It became more open to manipulation and marketing. It also became more open to analysis as a means to human development and happiness.

Prior to this market revolution and its attendant psychologizing of religion and marriage, divine love was more fixed and remote. The influential thirteenth-century Dominican friar Thomas Aquinas insisted upon a sharp distinction between substance and matter, which meant that qualities of being existing perfectly in God were essentially different from analogous but disproportionate qualities existing in God's creatures. As Aquinas argued, "since the act of existence proper to one thing cannot be communicated to another, it is impossible for a creature ever to attain the possession of something in the same manner in which God has it, just as it is impossible for it to attain the same being as that which God has."[3]

Deepening this distinction between substance and matter is an older dualism of spirit and flesh that can be traced back to Platonic and gnostic elements in Christian thought. In the fifth century, Augustine of Hippo developed this dualism in a way that helped to shape church teachings for centuries. On one hand, Augustine identified concupiscence, or disordered desire, as the root of all evil, and often associated concupiscence with sex. Sex epitomized the life of the flesh, and was thus inherently inferior, and dangerous, to the life of the spirit. On the other hand, Augustine formulated the concept of marriage as a spiritual companionship between the sexes that reflected appreciation of the comforts of a shared pilgrimage through life. But Augustine affirmed sexuality only as means to reproduction and never imagined that sexual intimacy between husband and wife could have anything to do with this companionship. In the shadow of this antipathy to human flesh, which colored Christian thinking for centuries, sexual union functioned as much as an antitype of divine love as a straightforward analogy. While medieval mystics called Christ a spouse and used sexual imagery to portray their love for him, their erotic religious language was expressed in the context of vows of sexual chastity that underscored belief in the opposition between spiritual and physical desire. In his sermons on the Song of Songs, the twelfth-century French mystic Bernard of Clairvaux wrote that "the affection between the word, Christ, and the Soul cannot be more sweetly expressed than by calling them bridegroom and bride."

But the monastic context of this writing assumed understanding that Christian love was a spiritual vocation not to be confused with ordinary matrimony.[4]

In the twelfth and thirteenth centuries, Peter Abelard and other church reformers softened the dualism implicit in Christian theology by celebrating companionate marriage as an appropriate context for religious life. But it was not until Martin Luther and other Protestant Reformers in the sixteenth-century that the longstanding opposition between sexuality and spiritual purity were directly challenged. These Reformers criticized celibacy, suppressed monasteries, and located religious virtue squarely in the context of marriage and domestic life. Luther gave up his vocation as a monk and married the former nun Katherina von Bora on the basis of his theological investment in marriage as well as his personal feeling for his bride. As the historian Steven Ozment observed, the early Protestant Reformers were "the first to set the family unequivocally above the celibate ideal and to praise the husband and the housewife over the monk and the nun in principle."[5]

With regard to the notion that marriage was a moral contract between two persons, English reformers before Luther were interested in the analogy between the heartfelt commitment of a loving marriage and a similar kind of commitment in grace. The fourteenth-century English church reformer John Wycliffe defined marriage in terms of an intentional commitment that ought to exist between husband and wife, rejecting the idea that the ecclesiastical ceremony of marriage had any binding power of its own. He challenged the doctrine of transubstantiation on similar grounds, arguing that the presence of Christ in the sacraments was a function of the believer's attitude and not of the sacraments themselves. With regard to the Eucharist, he explained, "the bodily etyng ne profites nouth to soule but in als mykul as the soule is fedde with charite."[6]

Among the foremost leaders of early English Protestantism, the sixteenth-century Bible translator William Tyndale extended Wycliffe's emphasis on right intention in a decidedly moralistic direction by defining faith as a means of acting righteously. In addition, he yoked the emphasis on right intention to a firm commitment to biblical authority and thus to belief in the conformity between right intention and biblical precepts. Puritans built on this moralistic tradition established by Tyndale and other early English Protestants, emphasizing the importance of the family as a center for Bible study, prayer, and moral armament in their efforts to make family government the principal agent of both social reform and social stability. As William Gouge explained in his manual of domestic order, "a family is a little Church, and a little Commonwealth."

It was also "a schoole wherein the first principle and grounds of government and subjection are learned: whereby men are fitted to greater matters in Church or Common-wealth."⁷

In New England, Puritans emphasized the family's importance as the building block of Christian society. They also moved with increasing ease between the language of theology and the language of human feeling, especially in their conceptualization of betrothal as a type of grace. In his famous address delivered on board the *Arbella* en route to New England in 1630, John Winthrop claimed that "to love and live beloved is the soul's paradise, both here and in heaven." He emphasized that "love among Christians is a real thing, not imaginary," and pointed to "the state of wedlock" as the closest thing on earth to heaven. Wedlock had its troubles, he acknowledged, but in its "exercise of mutual love," it contained an incomparable "sweetness" analogous to grace. In a similar vein, Winthrop's younger contemporary Anne Bradstreet nurtured the hope that Christ was her heavenly bridegroom while at the same time imagining divine love in terms of what she felt for her husband. "If ever two were one, then surely we," she wrote in her poem "To My Dear and Loving Husband," "Then while we live, in love lets so persever, / That when we live no more, we may live ever." A century later, Jonathan Edwards tilled similar ground in *The Nature of True Virtue* when he described marital love as being of "the same denomination" as religious affection and in his deathbed note to his wife when he referred to their marriage as an "uncommon union" whose "nature," he believed, was "spiritual."⁸

In their focus on the communication of divine grace to the individual human heart, and in their emphasis on the family as the building block of society, Protestant Reformers and English Puritans had interpreted the bridal mysticism of Christianity in a more humanistic way than it had been interpreted before. Making less of the distinction between essential substance and accidental matter than Aquinas, they allowed divine qualities and human feelings to intermingle more. Making less of the *literal* distinction between spirit and flesh, they focused more on the distinction between spiritual and fleshly *intention*. Jonathan Edwards advanced these changes further by describing the way in which the vital principle of grace completely reoriented the will, transforming all of a person's thoughts and actions. By subjecting the feelings involved in religious experience to systematic, rational analysis, he humanized the nature and activity of grace even as he insisted that its source lay beyond human control. Edwards's systematic analysis of the religious affections had the effect of modernizing Calvinist thought, and of opening the way for the study of religion as a universal, psychological phenomenon, as Mark Valeri suggested in his assessment of Edwards as a transitional figure straddling the divide between the authoritarian values of communal culture and universalist values of market culture.[9]

With regard to human love and happiness—the principal topics of this essay—Edwards also stands as a transitional figure who remained committed to the traditional understanding of Christian life as transcending ordinary human life while anticipating a more modern interpretation of religion as an ultimate concern at the heart of individual life. Pushing forward the longstanding Christian concept of love as an expression of grace, Edwards moved the idea of spiritual union in a more humanistic direction by emphasizing that genuine love for another person was a sign of grace. At the same time, by defining grace as an awakening to the larger reality of being-in-general, he resisted the tendency to simply equate religion with human feeling.

Belief in the relationship between love and happiness is deeply rooted in American culture. No less deeply rooted is the concept of marriage as a privileged union in which spiritual companionship and mutual happiness should coexist. In these respects, the world of Puritan theology is not altogether different from the world of Gary Marshall's romantic comedy.

The similarity goes further. In both the film and in Puritan literature, the *inability* to find love and happiness commands at least as much attention as the nature of love and happiness itself.

In both the film and in Puritan literature, recognizing dishonesty in love is a means of clarifying the nature of genuine love. *The Runaway Bride* uses Maggie's fickleness as a means of constructing a story about love as it ought to be. Similarly, Edwards's predecessors Thomas Shepard and Thomas Hooker used examples of the insufficiencies of womanly love as a foil that illumined the true wifely affection analogous to genuine love to Christ. In Shepard's *Parable of the Ten Virgins,* from which Edwards quoted extensively in his *Treatise Concerning Religious Affections,* the failures and insufficiencies of womanly love exemplified the very nature of religious hypocrisy. In probing the nature of their feelings for Christ, Shepard asked his followers, "Do you rejoyce more in . . . what you receive from him, than in what there is in him? It argues a whorish heart." Even more subtly, the hypocrite who focused more on his own sin than on the beauty of Christ was like the woman who called one man her husband but really loved another. As Shepard argued, "If a man complains more or chiefly for want of grace or righteousness, to remove sin and not so much for want of Jesus Christ: Then in this case 'tis as it is with a woman, that man for whose absence she mourns most, that is her husband: She saith the other is, no but he is not.[10]

Along with other Puritan divines who emphasized the importance of preparation for grace, Shepard focused on the problem of religious hypocrisy because he considered it a frequent danger fraught with negative consequence. He also thought that some of his colleagues overlooked the problem of hypocrisy, and even fell into its whorish promiscuities, in their desire for religious assurance. Among the minority of Puritan divines who downplayed the need for all the cautions and humilities attendant on preparation for grace, John Cotton was most influential. He celebrated the "sealing of the Spirit" as a "conjugal communion" beyond conversion—the full enjoyment of grace that brought assurance of salvation.[11]

At one important level, the debate between preparationists and proponents of religious assurance was really a debate about the qualities and privileges of love. Conversion only brought promises of Christ's love, Cotton complained, but the true Christian was never satisfied with promises alone, just as "there is little love in that woman to her absent husband, that is quieted with his letters of his purpose to returne; and longs not the more from the receiving of them, to see and enjoy himselfe."[12] In the *Religious Affections,* Edwards quoted extensively from Shepard in denouncing demands for assurance based on negative signs, such as visions or high emotion. For Edwards, that sort of demand for assurance ran counter to the quality of hopeful dependence on faith that true love entailed and to its meek spirit of humility.

In his own discussion of the "seal of the Spirit," Edwards maintained that a new impression on the heart changed a person's outlook and behavior. But this was not "an inward immediate suggestion, as though God inwardly spoke . . . by a kind of secret voice." As he explained, " 'Tis not prophecy, nor tongues, nor knowledge, but that more excellent divine thing, charity that never faileth, which is a prelibation and beginning of the light, sweetness, and blessedness of heaven, that world of love and charity."[13] As Ava Chamberlain has demonstrated, Edwards was much concerned about counterfeit piety, and he believed the devil often lured hypocrites into counterfeit piety through visions, voices, and other impressions that bolstered false confidence of grace. He focused on self-deception as the most common and pernicious form of religious hypocrisy and cautioned against the false confidence that intense feelings could sometimes generate.[14] Pointing to a reorientation of the will that awakened a person's capacity to love something larger than self, Edwards defined true virtue as an assent to being-in-general. This assent was not to be equated with proclamations of love or with sheer intensity of feeling, which might or might not be involved, and might or might not be rooted in being-in-general. Edwards believed that assent to being-in-general enabled feelings of genuine love for others and led inevitably to sincerity and gratitude. It also exposed desires for explicit assurance to be demanding, self-oriented, and hypocritical.

Nevertheless, Edwards did not condemn the intense feelings and altered states of consciousness that sometimes accompanied assent to being-in-general. He saw these as natural phenomena that easily could get mixed up with feelings of genuine love. Although the devil sometimes used them to confirm people in self-deception, natural phenomena might also accompany an awakening to God. They were not distinguishing marks of grace, but neither were they evidence of the absence of grace.

As Edwards indicated in *The Nature of True Virtue,* the reorientation of the will toward love to being-in-general inevitably reoriented one's relationships with other people. In countering the utilitarian argument that "all love comes from self-love," Edwards readily admitted that love to others often did boil down to self-love—"a man's love to those who love him, is no more than a certain expression or effect of self-love." But that was not the same thing as being united with another person in love, or being able to extend oneself to enjoy another's happiness. In these instances, it was not "a love to our own happiness" that caused us to love another person and to take delight in that person's happiness. Instead, Edwards explained, "the truth plainly is, that our love to the person is the cause of our delighting, or being happy in his happiness." Rather than drawing others into the orbit of our self-interest and essentially exploiting them for our own purposes, genuine love to the other expanded our capacity for pleasure beyond the narrow confines of self-love and thus opened the way for real happiness. Edwards defined happiness in terms of delight in, and identification with, the happiness of the other. And he traced the capacity for happiness to a prior inclination to love more than oneself. "Men who have benevolence to others have pleasure when they see others' happiness," Edwards explained, "because seeing their happiness gratifies some inclination that was in their hearts before."[15]

Edwards's understanding of the power of love to the other is part of a larger stream of American thought manifest in a wide range of cultural expression. The distinction he helped to define, between self-love and love to something more, can be found in a variety of places, many of which would not ordinarily be associated with Edwards or with Calvinist theology. Mark Twain's classic American novel *The Adventures of Huckleberry Finn* offers a good example. In wrestling with the moral dilemma of whether or not to make amends for helping the slave Jim escape from his mistress, Huck feared the implications of Calvinist preaching, especially with regard to his own future. Sensing "the plain hand of Providence slapping me in the face and letting me know my wickedness was being watched all the time from up there in heaven, whilst I was stealing a poor old woman's nigger," Huck believed he would escape hell only if he renounced his lying about Jim's whereabouts and helped return Jim to his rightful owner. Determined to inform Miss Watson where to find her property, Huck "felt good and all washed clean of sin" after writing a note to her that conveyed the crucial information. But after writing and resolving to send the note, Jim's face and friendship kept haunting Huck and made it impossible for him to sleep. So he picked up the paper, held his breath, and said, "'All right, then, I'll *go* to hell'—and tore it up."[16]

This great passage in American literature reflects the very distinction between self-love and love to the other that Edwards did so much to define— Twain's animus against Calvinism and its tendency to degenerate into harsh rationalism notwithstanding. Ironically, Twain used the distinction to discredit the system of Calvinist thought that commanded Edwards's loyalty. But Twain's depiction of Huck's resolution in behalf of his friend is reminiscent of something Sarah Edwards said to her neighbors during a particularly intense episode of religious experience in 1742. Responding to fears that she would die before her husband returned from preaching to another congregation, "I told those who were present," she wrote in her personal narrative, "that I chose to die in the way that was most agreeable to God's will, and that I should be willing to die in darkness and horror, if it was most for the glory of God."[17] While Sarah was willing to go to hell if it pleased God, Twain's Huck was willing to go to hell to save his friend. In addition to reflecting Twain's wicked sense of humor, this shift from God to friend reflects a larger movement in the direction of religious humanism to which Edwards himself contributed.

In the arena of religious psychology, a good deal of attention came to be directed to those high emotions, extreme behaviors, and occult phenomena that Edwards defined as not being distinguishing signs of grace. While for Edwards love to the other and delight in the other's happiness was a positive sign of grace, the distinction he observed between grace and self-love was sometimes lost in the abundance and confusion of religious expression associated with nineteenth-century revivalism and the proliferation of new religious movements. Discussions of human relationships were similarly complicated. While expressions of matrimonial love, maternal nature, and filial devotion have abounded since Edwards's time, the glorification of feeling as an end in itself often engulfed awareness of any distinction between self-interested love and love to the other for its own sake. Nonetheless, some of America's most gifted writers have specialized in describing the limitations of self-interested love, including Henry James and Edith Wharton. Others have specialized in describing love to the other for its own sake, including Emerson and Thoreau, Ernest Hemingway, and J. D. Salinger, to name but a few.

With regard to religious psychology, as Ann Taves recently showed, John Wesley's embrace of visions, voices, fits, and trances as part of genuine religious experience led to increased cultivation and study of these extraordinary states. Methodism's acceptance of extraordinary states helped to create and sustain the tradition of revivalism that is such a distinguishing feature of American religious history. This acceptance led to Pentecostalism and, as Taves explained, also fueled interest in mesmerism, Theosophy, and Spiritualism.[18] Some of these new religious movements laid the groundwork for "New Age" religions and contributed to the widespread interest in spirituality that dramatically affected American religious life in the late twentieth century.

Edwards would have been open to this enthusiasm for spirituality, much as he was open to the enthusiasm of the Great Awakening. At the same time, he would have distinguished its feverish aspects from true happiness. From the perspective of his thought, the intuitions, extrasensory perceptions, and oceanic feelings associated with many forms of New Age spirituality would not be distinguishing signs of grace. But neither would they be evidence of the absence of grace.

In his *Treatise Concerning Religious Affections*, Edwards differentiated the affections of religious virtue, which he equated with true happiness, from the unvirtuous affections of self-love, which he associated with sin, suffering, hell, and unhappiness. He also differentiated the affections that defined happiness from those that might accompany either happiness or unhappiness without being tied necessarily to one or the other. In this endeavor of systematization, Edwards pressed further than anyone before him toward a rational analysis of happiness. At the same time, he resisted the idea that rational analysis could produce happiness. Happiness, for Edwards, was a state of love, an affair of the heart. Rational analysis might assist in preparing for happiness by exposing self-deception and pride but could not produce it alone. The heart had to be touched by a being larger and more beautiful than itself to be freed of the suffering and unhappiness that Edwards associated with the natural state of humanity. In his insistence on the head's subservience to the heart, Edwards belongs to a tradition of American religious thought that is aesthetic and responsivist rather than rationalist and manipulative. In this respect, nature spirituality and romantic love better reflect Edwards's understanding of the importance of the affections than rationalist religions like Scientology on the one hand or biblical fundamentalism on the other. At the same time, however, Edwards believed that grace was entirely supernatural—nothing "natural" about it—and thus would have resisted equating it with nature spirituality or romantic love.

With regard to the self-help literature that overlaps with so much of both religious and humanistic psychology today, Edwards would have resisted the tendency prevalent in a good deal of this literature to describe happiness as the result of educated self-interest. Nevertheless, important continuities exist between an Edwardsian understanding of happiness in love to the other and current ideas about emotional well-being. To be sure, Edwards's belief in the supernatural context and transcendent meaning of true happiness is not reflected in humanistic psychology. Nor is his strict adherence to eighteenth-century Anglo Protestant interpretations of the Bible. But his interest in freedom from self-deception and his insight into its connection with happiness, love, and general emotional well-being do resonate with psychological insights in our own time. His equation of virtue and happiness remains supremely relevant, as does his understanding that sincerity and humility are essential to that equation. Indeed, Edwards's articulation of these principles played an important role in shaping an understanding of happiness that persists into our own time even as it has been advanced and elaborated upon in interesting new ways. In the context of current psychological insight, Edwards's insistence on supernatural intervention might be seen as an older way of thinking about profound psychological change and the difficultly of breaking free of deeply entrenched habits. Similarly, his insistence on conformity to Scripture might be read as a means of respecting, and taking direction from, received cultural wisdom.

In reconceptualizing original sin as a psychological reality, the Edwardsian tradition takes seriously the terrible power of *unhappiness* and the difficulties involved in finding the will to overcome it. In this regard, William James is a particularly important developer of Edwardsian psychology. In his discussion of the sick soul, James combined sensitive descriptions of melancholy with analysis of that condition as both a constitutional and spiritual problem. This problem could be expressed in somewhat different ways, but always boiled down to self-defeat. Whether by dwelling on "the vanity of moral things," or being preoccupied by the intractable sinfulness of one's own nature, or finding oneself overwhelmed with dread in response to the terrible insecurity of life, James believed that "in one or other of these three ways it always is that man's original optimism and self-satisfaction get leveled with the dust." By examining first-person accounts of extreme cases of melancholy, James reached the conclusion that unhappiness was "the real core of the religious problem." In the extreme and, to James, most revealing cases, there was "desperation absolute and complete, the whole universe coagulating about the sufferer into a material of overwhelming horror, surrounding him without opening or end. Not the conception or intellectual perception of evil," James reported, "but the grisly blood-freezing heart-palsying sensation of it close upon one, and no other conception or sensation able to live for a moment in its presence."[19]

James's vivid description of the sick soul harks back to Edwards's best-known piece of writing, "Sinners in the Hands of an Angry God." "You hang by a slender thread," Edwards warned his congregation, "with the flames of divine wrath flashing about it, and ready every moment to sing it, and burn it asunder." With "nothing to lay hold of to save yourself," he went on, there is "nothing to keep off the flames of wrath, nothing of your own, nothing that you ever have done, nothing that you can do, to induce God to spare you one moment."[20] Edwards urged men, women, and children to reflect on the desperate nature of their plight, and he focused a good deal of effort on exposing the hypocritical self-deception that kept people from awakening to the truth of their unhappy situation. Anticipating James a century and a half later, who pressed the issue much further, Edwards believed that religion was about happiness, and about relief from the desperate unhappiness of self-absorption that held so many in thrall. Like James, Edwards perceived that happiness came relatively easily to some people while others seemed unable to do anything to attain it. Edwards and James agreed that unhappiness was an inescapable predicament unless a new orientation of the will changed a person's outlook and established a new set of habits.

In his analysis of such similarities between Edwards and James, the historian William Clebsch argued that both men were devoted to understanding human experience and that both men associated the good aspects of it with a sense being at home in the universe. "In spite of Edwards's fealty to his inherited worldview," Clebsch argued, "his attention had focused on human experience when he made the religious question to be, How do men and women and children find God lovable?" In important respects, James "drew out the implications" of asking this question. For James, "no answers to the questions he framed about religion could be final." Religion "awaited what people made of themselves and their deities and their worlds." While James made religion's contingency on human experience completely explicit by translating Calvinist theology into psychological terms, Edwards established a trajectory and momentum that led to James. If Edwards was, as Clebsch asserted, "the last major American religious thinker who fully espoused an orthodox Christian worldview in all he thought and did," he was also a seminally transitional figure who carved out a psychology of happiness (and unhappiness) that has contributed profoundly to American thought. While Wesley's influence reaches into the present through revivalism into Pentecostalism on the one hand and mesmerism, Theosophy, and New Thought on the other, Edwards's interest in being at home in the universe reaches us through William James and others concerned with understanding unhappiness as humanity's core religious problem.[21] (Of course, neither Wesley nor Edwards would have been happy with all the results of their influence—this essay included.)

In its openness to the marketing of religious and psychological goods, our culture has been hospitable to the aesthetic, responsivist approach to life to which both Edwards and James contributed, and there are lots of examples of it both outside and inside of Christian churches. Like Edwards, many proponents of happiness today attempt to merge empirical understanding of human feeling with corresponding expressions of spiritual wisdom. But today's references to spiritual wisdom are as likely to come from the sayings of a venerable rabbi or from the teachings of the Buddha as from the New Testament. What counts as religious wisdom today is more diverse and inclusive than what Edwards understood it to be. However, it is also true, as Gerald McDermott argues, that Edwards did as much as anyone to lay the groundwork for understanding religion as a universal phenomenon.[22]

The Dalai Lama's 1999 best-seller, *The Art of Happiness,* is a good illustration of the way in which non-Christian texts on the market today contribute to a tradition of American religious thought in which Edwardsian psychology played an earlier, defining role. Along with a number of other recent books that reframe Buddhist psychology in light of American spirituality, the Dalai Lama's *Art of Happiness* has more in common with the ideas of Jonathan Edwards than with conceptions of religious life, whether Buddhist or Christian, that associate virtue with the resignation of happiness or with privileged forms of knowledge or special feelings about election, enlightenment, or rebirth. Unlike the traditional emphasis on mastery of occult powers characteristic of Tibetan Buddhism and the extinction of desire characteristic of many different forms of Buddhist monasticism, the Dalai Lama's book focuses on psychological insight and the deliberate integration of thought, feeling, and action. And unlike the emphasis popular in many Christian circles of proclaiming one's own new birth as a brand of identity in a pluralistic world, the book focuses on the search for release from suffering believed to underlie all religions and on the human capacity for compassion as the universal key to that release.

Like other books that combine Buddhist and Western psychology, *The Art of Happiness* is concerned with analyzing feelings and training the mind. This concern for mental discipline draws upon a Buddhist understanding of the need for release from selfhood that, in turn, is predicated on the idea that selfhood is an illusion. Although Buddhism is a heterogeneous tradition involving a variety of different schools of thought and practice, its proponents agree that human beings do not have egos or souls that persist through change and death. Instead, Buddhists believe, persons are comprised of *skandas*, or bundles of sensation, perception, and consciousness joined together as a result of the sequencing and combining of discernible causes. But human beings invest in the illusion of selfhood in an attempt to hold onto something permanent. The illusion of selfhood, along with other attempts to hold onto something permanent, causes suffering.

As a descriptor of human experience, this basic Buddhist principle of *anatman*, or no self, is similar in important respects to Edwards's view that self-love is based on the illusion of the self's autonomy with respect to being-in-general. In both cases, the illusion of independent selfhood is the cause of suffering and unhappiness. As Edwards argued in the *Religious Affections*, "false affections begin with self." Many people claim to love God, and many people experience intense feelings for God, Edwards believed. But in some of those people, the claim to love God is "consequential and dependent" on self-love. By contrast, Edwards argued, "the saint's affections begin with God; and self-love has a hand in these affections consequentially, and secondarily only."[23]

While Edwards wrote much about God, his theology was not theistic.[24] God was not a person existing separately from the world for Edwards, but being-in-general, the source, manifestation, and end of all existence. In addition to emphasizing the singularity of Christ, Edwards understood him to be the awakened presence of being-in-general in the world, the Son of God who transcended the short-sightedness common to humanity and realized that his own being rested in God. Like other Christian theologians, Edwards thought of reality in terms of being, defined God as the fullness of being, and evil as the absence of being. In contrast, much of Buddhist philosophy emphasizes the nonduality of being and nonbeing and traces suffering to the desire to escape impermanence, which leads to the reification of being over against nonbeing. While this difference is highly significant, the similarities between Edwardsian and Buddhist understandings of the nature of and need for spiritual awakening are no less so. With respect to the idea that Christ represents the human awakening to God as well as God's awakened presence in human form, Edwards's view of Christ resembles Buddhist ideas about the Buddha and the Buddha Mind. Saints, for Jonathan Edwards, were Christ-lits, little Christs, like his wife Sarah, who on more than one occasion felt "swallowed up with light and love" and "swam in the rays of Christ's love, like a little mote swimming in the beams of the sun."[25] In its sense of participation in an encompassing reality that incorporates her own impermanent and contingent being, this description of spiritual awakening is similar to Buddhist descriptions of enlightenment, even though Buddhists maintain the self's nonexistence in a way most Christians do not. Take, for example, the death poem of Eihei Dogen, the thirteenth-century founder of the Soto school of Zen Buddhism, which might be compared to Sarah Edwards's sense of being swallowed up with light and love:

> Fifty-four years lighting up the sky.
> A quivering leap smashes a billion worlds.
> Hah!
> Entire body looks for nothing.
> Living I plunge into Yellow Springs.[26]

As the best-known Buddhist in the United States, the fourteenth Dalai Lama Tenzin Gyatso has presented Buddhism as an antidote for the emotional pain from which he perceives many Americans suffer.[27] Inspired partly by the inroads into American psychotherapy made by students of the *vipassana* (or insight) school of Theravada Buddhism, the Dalai Lama incorporates Buddhist ideas into American psychology by utilizing the strong Tibetan emphasis on compassion as a means of distinguishing between useful and deleterious ideas about love prevalent in Western culture. Written in conjunction with the psychiatrist Howard Cutler, *The Art of Happiness* argues that happiness is found through open and honest relationships with other people and that compassion is the key to building those relationships. While human beings are naturally capable of compassion, the Dalai Lama believes, the desire for permanence stimulates harmful desires, like greed and lust, which override natural tendencies to compassion and mire people in illusions of selfhood. By disciplining their minds, the Dalai Lama explains, people can begin to practice the patience, tolerance, and forgiveness that will free them from the desires and illusions that cause unhappiness. In his own spiritual practice, the Dalai Lama recites a prayer by the eleventh-century Tibetan saint Langri Thangpa that asks "Whenever I associate with someone, may I think myself the lowest among all and hold the other supreme in the depth of my heart!" And "When I see beings of wicked nature, pressed by violent sin and affliction, may I hold these rare ones dear as if I had found a precious treasure."[28]

While treasuring persons who are difficult to love, the Dalai Lama criticized American culture's exaltation of romantic love because of its idealization of relationships and people. Insofar as it is essentially "a fantasy, unattainable," romantic love "may be a source of frustration," he argued, that "cannot be seen as a positive thing." On the other hand, this celibate monk praised the commitment "to build a truly satisfying relationship" in which knowledge of another and "genuine compassion" played an important role. While downplaying the spiritual significance of sexuality, he emphasized the intimacy and "sense of responsibility and commitment" in marriage.[29]

Such Buddhist contributions to American religious thought do not dovetail perfectly with the bridal mysticism so important to Puritan spirituality and its legacies in American culture and religious thought. Indeed, they carry American religious thought in directions Edwards could not have anticipated. Nevertheless, the Buddhist contributions work to further humanize the approach to happiness that Edwards carried forward from Thomas Shepard, and that subsequent writers carried forward from Edwards. Belief in the importance of care for the other is essential to this understanding of happiness, because this care is connected to freedom from the illusion of autonomous selfhood. As the Dalai Lama's book asserts, happiness is an art that involves disciplined efforts to attain patience, tolerance, and forgiveness. While he would disagree with Edwards about the necessity of supernatural intervention, the depravity of humanity's original nature, the centrality of the family in religious life, and the analogy between spiritual and sexual union, he would find much to agree with in Edwards's understanding of self-discernment, sincerity, humility, and benevolence as interconnecting habits of spiritual practice. Indeed, in its interpretation of the wisdom practices of Tibetan Buddhism for an American audience, the Dalai Lama's *Art of Happiness* feeds into a stream of American thought that Edwards helped to define.

In this regard, *The Runaway Bride* offers a good illustration of the confluence of Buddhist ideas about practice and American ideas about love that developed out of Puritanism. The male lead in the film, Richard Gere, is an actor famous for representing the transformation from cynicism to love. And he is probably the best-known Buddhist in the United States after the Dalai Lama. Gere credits the visualization techniques involved in Tibetan Buddhist practice with some of his success as an actor.[30] There is an explicit reference to Buddhism in the miniature Zen rock garden that Ike's editor (and former wife) plays with before firing him. More important, Buddhism lurks in the film through Gere himself and through the interplay of ideas about practice, visualization, and selfhood. In the context of this popular film, a message about the nature of love echoes important themes in both Buddhist and Judeo-Christian philosophy. This message underlies the film's thematic focus on betrothal and its relation to the problem of hypocrisy and the need for preparation. As an American romance, the film clearly celebrates the heart's power over the head and the need for sincere response. Within this responsivist context, the film explores the roots of hypocrisy in lack of self-knowledge and fear, and suggests that this unhappy state may be overcome by a combination of salvation and preparation. Ike can be Maggie's savior, but not until she is prepared to be saved. And this preparation involves visualizing the part and working systematically through the requirements of the role.

A pair of scenes from *The Runaway Bride* suggests how Buddhist ideas about practice advance the Puritan concept of preparation for grace and the Edwardsian belief in love as a sign of grace. In the first of this pair of scenes, Maggie is still betrothed to the football coach. Ike has been criticizing her for recklessly diving into relationships with little regard for the feelings of others. Like Thomas Shepard's arch hypocrite—the "foolish virgin unprepared for Christ"—Maggie has little understanding of the unity of grace and preparation that genuine love entails. For his part, Ike lacks a real sense of love. But he does know the proper script upon which to base a betrothal. In a scene that begins with Maggie showing off her most recent engagement ring, Ike is suspicious of the sincerity involved in Bob's presenting the ring at an Oriole's game.

"Wait, wait, don't tell me," Ike interrupts Maggie's account of how Bob proposed, "the scoreboard lit up with the words, 'MARRY ME MAGGIE.' . . ."

"It was one of the most wonderful moments," Maggie responds, somewhat unconvincingly, "of my life. . . ."

"Highly suspect, highly suspect," Ike rejoins, "If you've got to dress it up like that, it just doesn't ring true. I think the most anyone can say is," he goes on, explaining what would constitute a sincere and proper petition of marriage, "I guarantee there will be tough times. I guarantee that one or both of us, at some point, are going to want out. But I also guarantee that if I don't ask you to marry me I'll regret it the rest of my life because I know in my heart, you're the only one for me."

Several months after this explanation of right betrothal, Maggie and Ike have fallen in love and then fallen apart. Maggie discovers that she really does love Ike and she works through a process of knowing herself better. She also works out some of the preparations and practices of love. After not seeing Ike for some time, she finds his apartment and gets the doorman to let her in. She has come to understand the roots of her own dishonesty, which she admits. Then she presents Ike with a gift—a box with a pair of shoes inside.

"I'm turning in my running shoes to you," Maggie says.

"This is serious," Ike replies.

Maggie asks Ike to marry her. He is moved, but he tells Maggie he will have to think about it. She has prepared something more to tell him:

"I guarantee that we'll have tough times. And I guarantee that, at some point, one or both of us are going to want out. But I also guarantee that if I don't ask you to be mine I'll regret it for the rest of my life because I know in my heart, you're the only one for me."

There is no claim to or demand for assurance of love here. Instead, there is what might be called humbled but entreating love on Maggie's part—a forceful, honest, hopeful, unpretentious effort to win Ike's hand. At the heart of the film, this scene represents an understanding of love that has persisted for centuries and helped to define American ideas about marriage. It is an old understanding, rooted in Jewish and Christian literature about divine love and revitalized here in a romantic comedy influenced by Buddhist ideas about action as a form of spiritual practice. In the long historical development of this tradition of understanding love and happiness, Edwards's analysis of the religious affections stands as a major landmark. His understanding of the links between love, happiness, and sincerity contributed to the development of an important tradition in American thought whose branches are still sprouting.

In summary, *The Runaway Bride* can be interpreted in light of the problem of hypocrisy that concerned Edwards and in light of his understanding of the inherent connection between virtue and happiness and the need for both preparation and love. This essay has interpreted the film's focus on betrothal in terms of the Puritan preoccupation with love as a type of grace, and in terms of its coming down to earth in the context of increasingly consumerist and psychological approaches to sex and sentiment. The essay has also pointed to the concern for sincerity persisting through this process of historical change and suggested that it has come to be advanced by contact with American Buddhist ideas of selfless practice. In lifting up this line of thought and tracing it through these permutations, the essay points to expressions of feeling in American popular culture that some followers of Edwards might call spiritual.

NOTES

1. For discussion of the role of self-deception in Edwards's understanding of hypocrisy, see Ava Chamberlain, "Jonathan Edwards and the Relation between Hypocrisy and the Religious Life," in *Perspectives on American Religion and Culture,* ed. Peter Williams (Malden, Mass.: Blackwell Publishers, 1999), 336–52.

2. Ann Douglas, in *The Feminization of American Culture* (New York: Avon Books, 1977), was the first to make the argument. For additional discussion, see Amanda Porterfield, *Feminine Spirituality in America: From Sarah Edwards to Martha Graham* (Philadelphia: Temple Univ. Press, 1980).

3. Quoted in Thomas Aquinas, *Disputed Questions on Truth,* trans. R. W. Mulligan, J. V. McGlynn, and R. W. Schmidt (Chicago: Regnery, 1952), 1:112–13.

4. Bernard of Clairvaux, *Commentary and Homilies on the Song of Songs,* trans. R. P. Lawson (Westminster: Newman Press, 1957), quoted and discussed in Joan M. Ferrante, *Woman as Image in Medieval Literature: From the Twelfth Century to Dante* (1975; reprint, Durham: Labyribth Press, 1985), 27–28.

5. Steven Ozment, *When Fathers Ruled: Family Life in Reformation Europe* (Cambridge: Harvard Univ. Press, 1983), 7.

6. "Wyclif's Confessions on the Eucharist," *English Wycliffite Writings,* ed. Anne Hudson (Cambridge: Cambridge Univ. Press, 1978), 17.

7. William Gouge, *Of Domesticall Duties* (London: 1622, 1626, and 1634), 16–17.

8. John Winthrop, "A Model of Christian Charity Written on Board the Arbella on the Atlantic Ocean," reprinted in *The Puritans in America: A Narrative Anthology,* ed. Alan Heimert and Andrew Delbanco (Cambridge: Harvard Univ. Press, 1985), 88; Anne Bradstreet, *The Complete Works of Anne Bradstreet,* ed. Joseph R. McElrath Jr. and Allan P. Robb (Boston: Twayne Publishers, 1981), 180; Jonathan Edwards, *The Nature of True Virtue,* ed. William Frankena (Ann Arbor: Univ. of Michigan Press, 1960), 61; Jonathan Edwards, quoted in Samuel Hopkins, "The Life and Character of the Late Reverend Mr. Jonathan Edwards," in *Jonathan Edwards: A Profile,* ed. David Levin (New York: Hill and Wang, 1969), 80. For further discussion of the interplay between Puritan religious and marital imagery, see Amanda Porterfield, *Female Piety in Puritan New England: The Emergence of Religious Humanism* (New York: Oxford Univ. Press, 1992), 21–39 and 106–12.

9. Mark Valeri, "Religion and the Culture of the Market in Early New England," in *Perspectives on American Religion and Culture,* ed. Peter W. Williams (Malden, Mass: Blackwell Publishers, 1999), 92–104.

10. Thomas Shepard, *The Parable of the Ten Virgins,* ed. Jonathan Mitchell and Thomas Shepard Jr. (London: J. Hayes, 1660), 19. Similarly, in his *Poor Doubting Christian Drawn Unto Christ* (London, 1629), Thomas Hooker explained the sinner's claim not be worthy of Christ as like a wife's refusal to accept her husband's love.

11. John Cotton, *A brief exposition with practical observations upon the whole book of Canticles* (London: Printed by T. R. and E. M. for Ralph Smith, 1655), 10.

12. John Cotton, quoted in "Thomas Shepard to John Cotton," *The Antinomian Controversy: A Documentary History,* ed. David D. Hall (Middletown: Wesleyan Univ. Press, 1968), 26.

13. Jonathan Edwards, *A Treatise Concerning Religious Affections,* ed. John E. Smith, *The Works of Jonathan Edwards,* vol. 2 (New Haven: Yale Univ. Press, 1959 [1746]), 231, 236.

14. Edwards, *Works,* 2:222–23n. 7. Also see Chamberlain, "Jonathan Edwards."

15. Edwards, *Nature of True Virtue,* 44, 48.

16. Mark Twain, *The Adventures of Huckleberry Finn* (orig. 1885) in *The Unabridged Mark Twain,* ed. Lawrence Teacher (Philadelphia: Running Press, 1976), 899–900.

17. Sereno Edwards Dwight, "Memoirs of Jonathan Edwards," *The Works of Jonathan Edwards, A.M.,* ed. Sereno Edwards Dwight (2 vols.; London, 1840), quotation from Sarah Edwards in 1:cvii–cviii.

18. Ann Taves, *Fits, Trances, and Visions: Experiencing Religion and Explaining Experience from Wesley to James* (Princeton: Princeton Univ. Press, 1999).

19. William James, *Varieties of Religious Experience: A Study in Human Nature, Being the Gifford Lectures on Natural Religion Delivered at Edinburgh in 1901–1902* (New York: New American Library, 1958), 136–37.

20. Jonathan Edwards, "Sinners in the Hands of an Angry God" (orig. 1741), in *Selected Writings of Jonathan Edwards,* ed. Harold P. Simonson (1970; reprint, Prospect Heights, Ill.: Waveland Press, 1992), 107.

21. William A. Clebsch, *American Religious Thought: A History* (Chicago: Univ. of Chicago Press, 1973), 171–73.

22. In *The Nature of True Virtue,* Edwards described the affections and virtues of religion in a way that was largely free of any specific reference to Christian revelation or Scripture. As Gerald R. McDermott argues, Edwards's work with Native Americans in Stockbridge pushed him to reformulate the limits of grace beyond Christian parameters. See Gerald R. McDermott, *Jonathan Edwards Confronts the Gods* (New York: Oxford Univ. Press, 2000).

23. Edwards, *Works*, 2:246.

24. See for example, Roland Andre Delattre, *Beauty and Sensibility in the Thought of Jonathan Edwards: An Essay in Aesthetics and Theological Ethics* (New Haven: Yale Univ. Press, 1968).

25. Jonathan Edwards, quoting from his wife's written account, in *Some Thoughts Concerning the Present Revival of Religion in New England* (1742) in *The Great Awakening*, ed. C. C. Goen, *The Works of Jonathan Edwards*, vol. 4 (New Haven: Yale Univ. Press, 1972), 331–32. For discussion of Edwards's use of his wife's narrative, see Porterfield, *Feminine Spirituality in America*, 20–23 and 43–48.

26. Eihei Dogen, "Death Poem," in *Moon in a Dewdrop: Writings of Zen Master Dogen*, ed. Kazuaki Tanahashi, trans. Philip Whalen and Kazuaki Tanahashi (San Francisco: North Point Press, 1985), 219.

27. The introduction of Zen Buddhism into American culture owes much to the philosopher and translator Daisetz Teitaro Suzuki, who focused especially on the Rinzai school of Zen. In the United States, D. T. Suzuki worked effectively to dislodge Zen from the reactionary military culture of Japan with which it is was closely associated and to introduce it to Americans as a viable approach to life and an antidote to many of their own existential needs and dilemmas. Suzuki was familiar with Emerson, Kant, Kierkegaard, Heidegger, and Tillich and interpreted Buddhism in their light. Much as the Americanization of Zen owes much to D. T. Suzuki, in a similar way, the introduction of Tibetan Buddhism into American culture owes much to the fourteenth Dalai Lama Tenzin Gyatso. As a result of his own interest in Western culture and intellectual thought, the Dalai Lama dislodged Tibetan Buddhism from its feudal context and association with shamanism and popular magic and presented it to Americans as an antidote for psychological suffering that resonated with concerns for emotional suffering and interests in self-development.

28. Dalai Lama and Howard C. Cutler, *The Art of Happiness: A Handbook for Living* (New York: Riverhead Books, 1998). Other books along this line that might be mentioned include Bernard Glassman and Rick Fields's *Instructions to the Cook: A Zen Master's Lessons in Living a Life that Matters* (Boston: Shambala Publications audio imprint, 1996); Sylvia Bornstein's *It's Easier Than You Think: The Buddhist Way to Happiness* (San Francisco: Harper SanFrancisco, 1995); Mark Epstein's *Thoughts Without a Thinker: Psychotherapy from a Buddhist Perspective* (New York: Basic Books, 1995); and Daniel Goleman's *Emotional Intelligence: Why It Can Matter More than IQ* (New York: Bantam Books, 1995).

29. Dalai Lama and Cutler, *Art of Happiness*, 103–4.

30. See the "Interview with Richard Gere" in *Tricycle: The Buddhist Review* 19 (spring 1996).

Part Three

Edwards around the World

Remembered around the World

The International Scope of Edwards's Legacy

David W. Bebbington

"If the Spirit of God should be immediately poured out," mused Jonathan Edwards in his *Humble Attempt* of 1747, ". . . there must be an amazing and unparalleled progress of the work." The gospel would make enormous strides in future decades. Over the first fifty years, that is, by around 1800, vital religion might conquer "the Protestant world." Over the next fifty, by 1850, "the popish world" might submit to the truth. Over the succeeding fifty, by 1900, "the greater part of the Mahometan world, and . . . Jewish nation" might be brought into the gospel fold. And over the ensuing century "the whole heathen world" might be converted to the Christian faith. The year 2000 would in that case inaugurate "the happy state of the millennium."[1] Perhaps the New England Congregationalist was a truer prophet than he is usually supposed to have been in predicting a happy millennium for the year 2000. He was, of course, thinking in round numbers; and his version of the millennium was not the frenzied bout of self-congratulatory celebration that marked 1 January 2000 but a period of "holy rest." Yet he rightly envisaged that the gospel in the revivalist mode that he endorsed would advance steadily around the globe over the two and a half centuries after his time. Evangelicalism has indeed grown from its origins in Edwards's day to become a potent sector of world Christianity. Partly as a by-product, Edwards's own reputation has extended to girdle the earth. The process of evangelical growth, however, has not been as orderly as the theologian hypothesized; and the development of Edwards's reputation has been even less a matter of regular stages over time. The appreciation of Edwards has decayed as well as grown, and it has been disproportionately restricted to certain parts of the world. This paper aims to sketch the vicissitudes of Edwards's legacy outside America over the last two hundred and fifty years. It points to several distinct phases, suggesting that, notwithstanding times of downturn in his celebrity, at certain periods and places the theologian exercised an extremely powerful influence.

The first phase of Edwards's reputation was among contemporaries who continued to value his works after his death. In England his writings circulated widely because so many were published in London and elsewhere. The *Faithful Narrative* (1737) was actually issued, with a preface by the hymn-writer Isaac Watts and his fellow Congregational minister John Guyse, in England before it appeared in America. On the grounds of affinity with Edwards as a Congregationalist, the more intellectual members of the denomination in England tended to take a particular interest in his works. Four years after Edwards's death, for instance, in 1762, another Congregational minister, William Gordon, published in London an abridged edition of the New Englander's *Religious Affections*. Gordon, who was then minister of Gravel Lane Meeting in Southwark, seems to have imbibed a fascination for America because in 1770 he immigrated to Massachusetts, where he was to rise to become secretary to George Washington before, in the end, returning to the obscurity of a provincial pastorate at St. Neots, Huntingdonshire, in 1789.[2] Edwards's fame, however, was not confined to his fellow Dissenters. Members of the Church of England who were caught up in the Evangelical Revival admired a man who shared their gospel principles. John Newton, the slave ship captain turned clergyman, declared in 1762 that Edwards was "my favorite author."[3] Yet Anglican evangelicals increasingly tended to be wary of Edwards as too much a Calvinist and too much a metaphysician. Their exposed position as a small embattled minority within the established church made most of them reluctant to avow a Reformed theology, at least in public, and induced them to invoke the Bible alone rather than philosophy to defend their teaching. By 1779 Newton himself was criticizing what he called the "Scheme, System, & Notion" of American divinity, by which he meant the writings of Edwards and his followers, and fifteen years later he expressed regret that he had been in the habit of referring others to the *Freedom of the Will*.[4] Nevertheless even when Anglican evangelicals doubted the value of Edwards's philosophical theology, they honored his spirituality. William Wilberforce, the politician who led the agitation against the slave trade, praised the *Religious Affections* for its "close searching into the heart."[5] Edwards the champion of revival Christianity held a powerful attraction for the promoters of the gospel cause in England.

To one Englishman in particular, however, Edwards posed a dilemma. John Wesley, the founder of Methodism, was at the forefront of the evangelical movement, and therefore greatly valued Edwards's accounts of revival in the New World, where Wesley himself had served before his conversion. At the third annual Methodist conference in 1746, the *Faithful Narrative* and *Distinguishing*

Marks were read by the assembled preachers.[6] Yet Wesley was a militant Arminian who believed Calvinism to be a sinister threat to morality. If human beings were in any sense determined in their actions, he held, they were not responsible for their behavior. Hence his attitude to Edwards's writings was ambiguous. Wesley described the *Religious Affections,* for instance, as a "dangerous heap, wherein much wholesome food is mixed with much deadly poison."[7] So eager was Wesley to make the food available that he took upon himself the elimination of the poison. He drastically revised several of the more revival-orientated works for publication. Taking William Gordon's abridgement of the *Religious Affections,* which included roughly two-thirds of the original, Wesley cut out so much more that his version contained only about one-sixth of the original.[8] Having purged Edwards of his noxious errors, Wesley set about the propagation of the abridged work with characteristic energy. Four such Edwards abridgments—the *Faithful Narrative, Distinguishing Marks, Some Thoughts,* and *Religious Affections*—were included in the "Christian Library" that Wesley directed all his preachers to possess and sell. The Methodists continued the task of making known Edwards's revival writings into the following century. The standard nineteenth-century edition of the *Life of Brainerd,* cheap and pocket-sized, for example, was a version issued in 1808 that had been adapted from Wesley's abridgement.[9] The dissemination of Edwards's more practical writings in England owed much to John Wesley.

In Calvinist Scotland, Wesley's theological reservations did not exist among those identified with the evangelical cause. The circle of Presbyterians around William McCulloch, minister of the parish of Cambuslang, where revival broke out in 1742, saw their movement as being part and parcel of the Great Awakening that had begun at Northampton, Massachusetts. McCulloch and his friends corresponded across the Atlantic with Edwards, first suggesting the concert for prayer that is the subject of the *Humble Attempt*. One of them, John MacLaurin, so admired Edwards that he tried to obtain the New Englander's portrait during his lifetime.[10] Even the philosophers of Scotland took note of the Calvinist metaphysician. David Hume seems to have read Edwards, and Lord Kames tried to recruit the theologian in support of his version of fatalism, an attempt that Edwards rebutted in a letter that from 1768 was standardly printed in editions of the *Freedom of the Will*.[11]

The recipient of the rebuttal, John Erskine, was the most regular Scottish correspondent of Edwards during his lifetime and his most ardent champion after his death. Erskine was an urbane intellectual figure from an old landed family in Angus, who rose to become, as joint minister of Old Greyfriars, Edinburgh, the leader of the evangelicals in the Church of Scotland. It is true that he did not endorse every line of Edwards. The Scottish minister took issue, for example, with Edwards's sermons on justification.[12] Yet Erskine saw Edwards as the foremost advocate of evangelical Calvinism, and so determined to extend the New Englander's influence. Securing transcriptions of the manuscripts from Jonathan Edwards Jr., Erskine worked up a set of sermons into the *History of the Work of Redemption,* which was first published in Edinburgh in 1774. Its notices were by no means entirely favorable: the *Monthly Review* in London dismissed it as "merely an attempt to revive the old mystical divinity that distracted the last age with pious conundrums: and which, having, long ago, emigrated to America, we have no reason to wish should ever be imported back again."[13] Such contemptuous treatment may well have discouraged Erskine from continuing the publication of the manuscripts at that point, but in 1788, 1793, and 1796 he issued some sermons and two volumes of theological observations by Edwards, again for the first time.[14] Erskine was committed not only to the honoring of Edwards's name but also to the spread of his theology.

The revival enthusiasm that gripped Wesley and the Scottish ministers during Edwards's lifetime also extended to parts of Germany. The network of those eager for the revitalization of the Protestant cause included J. A. Steinmetz, superintendent of Magdeburg in Prussia. As the editor and biographer of Philip Spener, Steinmetz was deep in the pietist tradition. As early as 1738, the year immediately after its publication in London, Steinmetz became aware of Edwards's *Faithful Narrative.* Translating it into German himself, he added an account of soul-saving in German lands and New England. Perhaps, he surmised, "the Lord might finally remove his candlestick from ungrateful Europe and give the glory of Lebanon to the American wilderness."[15] His prophecy may have contained a grain of truth: the book fell on stony ground in his own land, creating no discernible effect. No other work by Edwards was translated into German during the eighteenth century.

Steinmetz's edition, however, did travel over the border into the Netherlands. A copy was obtained by Isaac Le Long, an avid book collector in Amsterdam who, because he enjoyed independent means, could usually secure titles he wanted, whether old or new. Le Long came from a Flemish Calvinist family, but had been brought up in Germany. When Count Zinzendorf's revivalistic Moravians arrived in Amsterdam in about 1733, Le Long was one of the first to give them his support.[16] Edwards's account of revival in the New World was bound to excite him. In 1740 Le Long published a translation not of the English-language original but of Steinmetz's German version. It achieved more success than its German equivalent, for it went into a second edition ten years later. In 1756, furthermore, the *Life of Brainerd* was translated into Dutch, this time directly from English and by another hand. News of the spread of the gospel was clearly attractive in the Netherlands, winning Edwards an audience even during his lifetime.

If the early interest of the Dutch was in Edwards the advocate of revival, that predominantly Reformed land began in the 1770s to gain an appreciation of Edwards the theologian. In 1774 the *Freedom of the Will* was translated into Dutch. Although there is no certain evidence, that development may have been on the initiative of John Erskine, the Edinburgh minister who had taken charge of Edwards's posthumous reputation. Certainly Erskine was starting to establish links with the Netherlands. Through David Thomson, minister of the Scots Kirk in Amsterdam, he made contact with Gijsbert Bonnet, professor of divinity at Utrecht.[17] Bonnet's stance, confessional but enlightened, appealed immensely to Erskine, who learned Dutch from scratch in his fifties in order to able to correspond with him.[18] Erskine no doubt recommended Edwards to Bonnet as the ablest protagonist of the same doctrinal perspective. In 1776 the *History of the Work of Redemption* appeared in Dutch, introduced by Erskine and with the formal approval of the classis of Utrecht, no doubt arranged by Bonnet.[19] The same translator was responsible for the life of Edwards published at Utrecht in 1791. Others in the Netherlands, however, also recognized in Edwards a bulwark of the twofold cause of vital piety and sound doctrine. Marinus Van Werkhoven, who had previously translated a range of English theologians, published a Dutch version of the *Religious Affections* in 1779 and went on to issue *Two Dissertations* in 1788 and *Original Sin* in 1790. The last was introduced by a veteran preacher, J. C. Appelius, who had previously defended orthodoxy against rationalist teaching.[20] The Reformed network linking Scotland with the Netherlands had successfully injected Edwards into the Dutch bloodstream.

In the first phase of remembering Edwards, therefore, the period when his reputation was sustained by his contemporaries, the world beyond America was more active in the task than America itself. The publication history of his writings down to 1775 confirms that verdict. Of Edwards's works relating to revival, twelve items were issued in America. The equivalent figure for England alone was twelve and for Scotland ten. Of his works relating to theology, seven items were published in America. The equivalent figure for England was six and for Scotland five. Only in the field of sermons was America far ahead, with twenty titles compared to one each for England and Scotland.[21] Britain, no doubt in part because of its vastly greater population, was well ahead in the publication of Edwards's treatises as opposed to his sermons. His fame extended to

Germany and, more substantially, to the Netherlands, where Scottish influence ensured that he took root in the late eighteenth century. Hungary, however, containing the next largest Reformed community, remained immune, never publishing a title by Edwards in the eighteenth century or, indeed, at any time afterward.[22] So Britain played a major part in the dissemination of Edwardsian influence. Perhaps that was to be expected when we recall that Edwards had recognized the solidarity of "all within the British dominions."[23]

In the second phase, lasting from the 1770s until long into the nineteenth century, Edwards shaped the shapers of opinion. The process is perceptible far beyond the religious sphere. In political thought following the French Revolution, when the world seemed to totter on its axis, Edwards's legacy was keenly contested in England. William Godwin is perhaps best known now as the husband of the early feminist Mary Wollstonecraft, but he was also one of the most radical thinkers in the wake of the revolution. In 1793 he published *An Enquiry Concerning Political Justice* praising liberty, equality, and fraternity. He explicitly appeals to Edwards on two scores: to establish the impossibility of free will and to dismiss the legitimacy of gratitude, the giving of preference to one person over another on grounds other than intrinsic worth—the second argument deriving from Edwards's *Nature of True Virtue*.[24] The debt is not surprising since Godwin had commenced a career as a Dissenting minister and had been trained by a tutor, Joseph Fawcett, who was a follower of Edwards.[25]

The implications of Godwin's two arguments, however, were alarming to defenders of the existing order in Britain. From the doctrine of necessity he drew, in the spirit of the secular Enlightenment, the inference that human beings are not truly responsible for their vices. "The ideas," he declared, "of guilt, crime, desert and accountableness have no place."[26] Likewise, from the rejection of gratitude he inferred that individuals have no obligations to their social superiors for benefits conferred. To his readers, the legitimacy of punishment and the very bonds of society seemed under threat, apparently as a result of Edwards's contentions. Accordingly Samuel Parr, a clerical schoolteacher and himself a very advanced Whig, but nevertheless a defender of the established social order, felt it essential to preach a sermon explaining that Godwin had misapplied Edwards. The New England theologian, though notable for "metaphysical acuteness" and "fervent piety," did not, according to Parr, have to be followed over free will; and, though gratitude was not a part of true virtue in Edwards's restricted meaning of the term, the New Englander did not deny that gratitude is an element in justice. Edwards, Parr concluded, could not be treated as an authority for revolutionary principles.[27]

In philosophy Edwards similarly made a mark. Sir James Mackintosh, the leading Whig ethicist of the turn of the nineteenth century, considered Edwards's powers of subtle argument "unsurpassed among men" and admired his moral theory because it took him far along the road toward Plato.[28] Likewise Dugald Stewart, the chief disseminator of Scottish common sense philosophy in the same generation, praised the ability of Edwards's case against free will and tried to assimilate him to the common sense school.[29] The New England theologian was recognized as a force to be reckoned with far beyond his own main department of knowledge.

In the theological sphere, naturally, Edwards's standing was even higher. His influence can be illustrated from the case of the English Baptists. They were troubled in the late eighteenth century by what had come to be called "the modern question" among orthodox Dissenters. Did Calvinism, with its confidence in the effectual calling of the elect, dictate that preachers must not make a free offer of the gospel? They would like to summon sinners to repentance, but did a consistent theology prohibit the practice? Jonathan Edwards's distinction between natural and moral inability provided a solution to the conundrum. Sinners possessed a natural ability to respond to the gospel, according to Edwards, even though their actions were part of a chain of causation. Their failure to repent and believe, however, was a case of moral inability, a willful refusal that rendered them guilty before the Almighty. Hence human beings had an obligation to believe; and hence, in turn, ministers of the gospel had to challenge them to believe.

Here was a potential resolution of the difficulty of the English Baptists. Caleb Evans, the principal of their Bristol Academy, was teaching this distinction between natural and moral inability by 1772,[30] but the idea only gradually dawned on others in the denomination. In about 1775 it was reading Edwards's *Freedom of the Will* that gave light on the subject to John Ryland, who was later to succeed Evans as principal at Bristol and so to pass on this view to several generations of Baptist ministers.[31] Ryland became an Edwards enthusiast: in 1780 he published the theologian's sermon on "The Excellency of Christ" as a tract at the low price of four pence each "or 3 shillings per Dozen to those who give them away"; he even called his sons "David Brainerd Ryland" and "Jonathan Edwards Ryland."[32] The circle of Ryland's friends in and around Northamptonshire eagerly obtained more of Edwards's writings from other sources. In 1784, for instance, John Erskine, the Scottish promoter of Edwards, sent Ryland a copy of the *Humble Attempt*. The Baptists reissued the book, which declared on its title page that it was published at "Northampton, in Old

England." The result was a series of monthly prayer meetings for revival that helped quicken the pace of denominational growth.

Probably most important in the reception of Edwards by the English Baptists was the impact on Andrew Fuller, minister at Soham in Cambridgeshire and later at Kettering. Fuller was personally refreshed by the *Religious Affections,* was struck that David Brainerd had no inhibitions about preaching to American Indians, and embraced Edwards's distinction between natural and moral inability.[33] As a result, Fuller, in his *Gospel Worthy of All Acceptation* (1781), urged ministers to proclaim the obligation of their hearers to receive the gospel, the principle of "duty faith." Fuller became the outstanding theologian of evangelical Dissent at the turn of the nineteenth century. His teaching was to remain the touchstone of orthodoxy for several generations. In 1872 the secretary of the Baptist Union of Great Britain and Ireland was still pointing to Fuller as the paramount authority in theology.[34] And Fuller was basing himself on the premises supplied by Edwards.

Another case study can be made of the Welsh Independents. Although they were of the same denomination as Edwards, "Independents" being the equivalent of "Congregationalists," the members of this Welsh body were largely ignorant of Edwards's reputation for much of the eighteenth century because of the language barrier. Most of their congregations, and even their ministers, used only Welsh. Edwards was known in Wales to the English-speaking revivalist Howell Harris in the 1740s through contact with Scotland, but Harris belonged to the Calvinistic Methodists who remained associated with the Church of England and so distant from the Independents.[35]

The breakthrough of Edwards into the denomination in the Welsh-speaking world was achieved by Edward Williams, who was principal of the Independent academies at Oswestry and then at Rotherham. Williams, who was bilingual in Welsh and English, eventually corresponded with Edwards's circle in America, and it may well have been through them that he originally became aware of the New Englander's stature.[36] It was Williams who brought out the first collected works of Edwards to appear anywhere in the world, the Leeds edition of 1806–1811. While engaged on this project, Williams published his *Essay on the Equity of the Divine Government* (1809), which propagated the Edwardsian approach to theology among the Independents of England as well as those of Wales.

In Williams's native country, however, there was a particular stirring of interest. John Roberts, Independent minister at Llanbrynmair, Montgomeryshire, who had briefly been under training by Williams, took up the cudgels for his mentor's position in the Welsh language. In 1807 Roberts issued a *Friendly*

Address to Arminians, urging them to recognize the distinction between natural and moral inability and so to turn to moderate Calvinism.[37] Two years later he issued a series of extracts from Edwards's *Religious Affections,* and in 1814 published, in opposition to higher Calvinists, the significantly titled *Humble Attempt* in order to resolve the question of the extent of the atonement.[38] Roberts was a militant exponent of what was called in Wales the "New System," opposed to the beliefs of Wesleyan Arminians and Calvinistic Methodists alike. This ideology was the motor of denominational expansion, Roberts's own area becoming the "cradle of early Independency in Wales."[39] As others adopted his Edwardsian principles, the denomination emerged as a major force in the north of the principality. Edwards inevitably became sought after by Welsh readers. In 1827 there was a translation of the *History of Redemption* and in 1833 one of the *Religious Affections. Freedom of the Will* followed later, in 1865, together with *Two Dissertations* at about the same time and *Original Sin* in 1870, all translated by Independent ministers. The whole Welsh denomination was invigorated by a commitment to the Edwardsian framework of belief.

Almost the same can be said of Scottish Presbyterianism. Erskine's efforts in the eighteenth century created awareness of Edwards, but it was in the following century, through Thomas Chalmers, the evangelical leader in the Church of Scotland, that the New England theologian made his greatest impact. Chalmers was trained at St. Andrews, where the professor of divinity, George Hill, though not aligned with the evangelicals, acknowledged a heavy debt to Edwards as an able defender of Calvinism, and especially of the doctrine of original sin.[40] Although Chalmers learned from Hill to respect Edwards, it was only after his own subsequent conversion to evangelical religion that he became a disciple of the American. In an 1821 work, Chalmers lauded Edwards as the man who, when David Hume was undermining religion and morality, had most powerfully defended the Christian faith.[41] As professor of divinity at Edinburgh from 1828 to 1843 and for four years afterward as the prophet of the Free Church of Scotland that he led out of the established church, Chalmers instilled the worth of the New Englander into his receptive students. Edwards, he claimed, was the most incontrovertible writer on necessity and the origin of sin, superior to Leibniz on both topics.[42] "My Theology," he remarked at the end of his life, "is that of Jonathan Edwards."[43] The supreme achievement of the American, according to Chalmers, was to demonstrate that religion was for "men of cultivated minds."[44]

In Scotland, however, Edwards was revered not only for his intellectual capacity but also for his other qualities. Horatius Bonar, the Free Church hymn writer, published extracts from the *Faithful Narrative* in 1845 and, six years later, the *Life of Brainerd*, which soon ran to a third edition. Edwards the promoter of revival was warmly admired. So, furthermore, was Edwards the man of personal piety. The most popular Edwards title in the homes of Victorian Scotland, according to the theologian James Orr, was the *Religious Affections*.[45] The New Englander enjoyed a secure place in the hearts of nineteenth-century Scottish Presbyterians because of his great versatility.

Edwards was also known beyond Great Britain. One of the chief agencies for the dissemination of his works was the missionary movement, in which during the nineteenth century Britain took the lead. William Carey, the pioneer Baptist missionary to India, came from the group of Northamptonshire ministers whose zeal for spreading the gospel had been rekindled by Edwards. To Carey the *Life of Brainerd* was "almost a second Bible."[46] As a result of the planting of a Baptist mission in India, there was printed at Calcutta in 1859 a reissue of Edwards's prayer call from the *Humble Attempt*.[47] Other missionary societies also found Edwards's writings an inspiration. The predominantly Congregational organization called at first simply the Missionary Society sponsored another edition of the *Humble Attempt* in 1814.[48] The Church Missionary Society, an evangelical Anglican body, published an abridgement of the *Life of Brainerd* in its periodical, subsequently reissued in book form in 1834.[49]

Awareness of Edwards extended to the continent. In Paris, perhaps as a result of the work of the British agents of the Continental Society, the *Humble Attempt* was translated into French in 1823. The *History of Redemption* followed it into the French language in 1854. In Switzerland, the *Life of Brainerd* appeared in French in 1838 and in German thirteen years later. Perhaps the most striking instance of the international penetration of the New Englander's writings is a translation into Arabic, at Beirut in 1868, of the *History of Redemption*, quaintly described as being written by "the Learned Chief Jonathan Edwards." There was a real global interest in Edwards during the nineteenth century; but the interest, it will be noticed, was only in certain works: *Humble Attempt*, *Life of Brainerd*, and *History of Redemption*. In missionary endeavor, inevitably, the books relating most directly to mission, human and divine, were the ones that attracted attention.

Yet in Britain itself what had been erected on the foundations of Edwards's thought during the second phase of the theologian's reputation was an elaborate doctrinal structure. There were, of course, reservations about points in his system and modifications of aspects of his legacy even among the most favorably disposed. Andrew Fuller, Edward Williams, and Thomas Chalmers all accepted the governmental theory of the atonement, drawing on Joseph Bellamy as their source rather than on Bellamy's master, Edwards. It would be fairer to claim them as exponents of the New England theology than of simple Edwardsianism. By the 1830s, furthermore, it was becoming common, even among Edwards's admirers, to censure him for not being empirical enough in his methods.[50] Despite his unstinted praise for Edwards, Chalmers could dismiss the American's a priori reasoning on some topics as "execrable rubbish."[51] Nevertheless these were criticisms from within Edwards's system, suggestions for improvement rather than proposals for replacement. Edwards had created an intellectual framework within which his successors in the English-speaking (and Welsh-speaking) world did their thinking and their mission. The Almighty was the giver of the laws of determinism; these were compatible with human liberty; therefore the gospel could be preached in the twofold confidence that God was in charge of the world and that human beings were free to respond. This was the worldview of moderate evangelical Calvinism, and it exercised a profound sway.

It was, in fact, relatively more influential in Britain than in the United States. In America this synthesis was championed, as Joseph Conforti has shown, by Edwards A. Park of Andover, and it certainly achieved popularity.[52] Yet it was resisted as too innovative by the Old School Presbyterians of Princeton and regarded as too traditional by the Consistent Calvinists of New Haven. The mediating position was criticized by these higher and lower Calvinists alike. In Britain, by contrast, there was no contemporary school of high Calvinism that carried intellectual weight; nor was there an attempt to adopt a system similar to Consistent Calvinism until the 1840s, when Charles Finney's popular theology was imported from America. Neither Princeton nor New Haven had an equivalent in Britain. Therefore, the theology deriving from Edwards reigned supreme in the denominations possessing a self-conscious Reformed heritage. His paradigm molded the evangelical Calvinist tradition in Britain until after the middle of the nineteenth century.

The third phase, overlapping with the previous one, was a period in which Edwards's reputation was challenged and declined. A new intellectual mood arose during the nineteenth century that was much less favorable to the theologian. Rooted in Romanticism, the rising temper of the age stressed the categories of growth, will, and emotion, looking askance at rule-governed models of the world. Its origins were in Germany, where there was little awareness of Edwards. Among the German philosophers of the Romantic age, it is true that he was known to J. G. Fichte, who praised "this solitary thinker of North America" for rising to "the deepest and loftiest ground which can underlie the principles of morals."⁵³ But German theologians in the age of Schleiermacher knew nothing of Edwards.⁵⁴ In the Netherlands, despite the earlier burst of interest in Edwards's works, he did not mold the Reformed mind as he did in Britain. There was no publication or republication of his writings in Dutch at all during the nineteenth century. Willem Bilderdijk, the celebrated pietist poet at the opening of the century, had works by the American in his library, but he and his associates in the Dutch Reveil movement were deeply swayed by the new stirrings of Romanticism and must have found both the style and the content of Edwards's books uncongenial. The New Englander might still be honored by some as a spiritual writer, but his weightier philosophical theology faded from the Dutch memory.⁵⁵

Likewise in England the Romantic poet Samuel Taylor Coleridge knew of Edwards, but thought his position superseded by idealist philosophy. "I greatly admire President Edwards's Works," he told John Ryland in 1807, "but am convinced that Kant in his Critique of Pure Reason has completely overthrown the edifice of Fatalism."⁵⁶ Failing to distinguish between an absolute fatalism and Edwards's determinism, Coleridge rejected what he called "the New England system."⁵⁷ Many of the next generation, swayed by Coleridge and other advocates of metaphysical liberty, were equally unable to draw the distinction. Among them was the young W. E. Gladstone, the future prime minister, who in 1839, while moving from his early evangelicalism to a form of High Church Anglicanism, spent some time each day for a whole month wrestling with Edwards. The texts he used survive, complete with their copious annotations. First he read the life of the theologian, finding much to admire in his spiritual dedication. Gladstone sprinkled the margins with marks of appreciation. Then, however, he passed on to the *Freedom of the Will*, and the signs of approval turned to crosses of dissent.⁵⁸ He could not accept the contrast between natural and moral inability, and so saw Edwards as a covert advocate of the slavery of the human will. The New Englander's book, he concluded, "proceeds upon unsound psychological assumptions, and confusions of things palpably distinct, and it has no ground either in Scripture or in metaphysics."⁵⁹ Edwards was ceasing to persuade minds affected by the fresh currents of thought coursing through the nineteenth century.

In theology the new temper of the age brought a reaction against Edwards's synthesis in its British heartland. Thomas Erskine, a nephew of Edwards enthusiast John Erskine and a Scottish Episcopal layman, gradually departed from his uncle's moderate Calvinism during the 1820s and 1830s. In 1837 Erskine's *Doctrine of Election* argued that Edwards's definition of freedom reduced human beings to the level of animals, depriving them of their proper moral dignity, and that Edwards's restriction of the Almighty's love to the elect denied the great doctrine of the Fatherhood of God.[60] Erskine's contemporary John McLeod Campbell, expelled from the Church of Scotland ministry in 1831 for abandoning received orthodoxy, reached his mature views, as he explained in *The Nature of the Atonement* (1856), through mental debate with Edwards and his Calvinist successors. Edwards was to be preferred to later theologians in the same tradition, according to McLeod Campbell, because he came closer to the truth as he saw it of divine pardon for the whole of humanity through a universal atonement. Yet McLeod Campbell felt that the New Englander's legal language handicapped him, keeping him away from the right conception intellectually, "though I do not think spiritually."[61] This generation of theologians, affected by the milder and more sentimental opinions of the day, wanted to stress love rather than justice, God as Father rather than God as lawgiver. The standard evangelical Calvinist framework was the target of their complaints. As these thinkers rejected the paradigm, they turned away from Edwards.

The shift is clear in F. D. Maurice, the trendsetter in Broad Church Anglican opinion in the middle years of the century. In 1862 he praised the *Freedom of the Will* as the "most original" product of colonial America, rightly meeting opponents on metaphysical grounds. Yet Edwards, according to Maurice, was tainted by the eighteenth century's exaltation of happiness, being too much a disciple of Locke, and limited by a deterministic universe, so that human beings were the victims of their motives. The New Englander, Maurice concluded, undervalued freedom and the compassion of the incarnate God.[62] Edwards could be no mentor in theology to the Victorian world. By the end of the century, not least through the influence of Maurice, a law-governed cosmos with the atonement at its center was being replaced among theologians by a world under the care of a benign Father with the incarnation at its heart. The Edwardsian mold had been broken.

A few resisted the trend. In the Scottish Highlands, where a stern theology had put down roots, the older synthesis survived. Edwards's *Sinners in the Hands of an Angry God* was translated into Gaelic for Highland use in 1848 and again in 1876. John Kennedy, the doughty Free Church of Scotland minister of Dingwall, denounced the new teaching that the Almighty was Father of all because that would restrict the free exercise of his sovereignty.[63] Kennedy's friend C. H. Spurgeon, pastor of the Metropolitan Tabernacle in London, held a similar position. At Spurgeon's training college for Baptist pastors, the principal from 1881 to 1893, David Gracey, still praised the New Englander's theological method, quoted him with approval, and expressed a preference for Edwards over Charles Hodge on the imputation of sin.[64] Their fellow Baptist Joseph Angus, the principal of Regent's Park College, London, was commending the joint convictions of Edwards and Bellamy on tests of regeneration as late as 1895.[65] In general, the reputation of Edwards was greenest among conservative Presbyterians and Baptists. Yet, there were certain Calvinistic Anglicans who appreciated the New England theologian. J. C. Ryle, Bishop of Liverpool from 1880 to 1900, for instance, highly valued his *Religious Affections*.[66] Furthermore, at least in Wales, there were Congregationalists who maintained esteem for their co-religionist. Robert Thomas, who had translated the *Freedom of the Will* into Welsh in 1865, continued to teach an Edwardsian moderate Calvinism at Bala College down to his death in 1880.[67] Many of his former students must still have been serving in the chapels when the Welsh Revival descended in 1904, and may have been convinced of its authenticity by Edwards's tests. The theological legacy of Edwards persisted, though only within attenuated groups, into the twentieth century.

Even late Victorian liberal theologians and freethinkers sometimes took notice of the New Englander, and, despite dismissing his views, paid him at least a grudging tribute. James Martineau, the leading English Unitarian theologian of the Victorian age, treated Edwards in 1888 as one of the modern necessitarians he wished to refute. He did so by the simple device of claiming that Edwards's argument for divine foreknowledge rested only on a body of scriptural texts, which nobody now accepted as decisive. "But," he admits, "the proof that the Scriptures contain Edwards's view is unanswerable."[68] W. E. H. Lecky, the freethinking historian of rationalism, also felt constrained to acknowledge Edwards's massive ability and "great ingenuity" even while condemning his *Original Sin* as "one of the most revolting books that have ever proceeded from the pen of man."[69] John Stuart Mill, the great Liberal philosopher and another freethinker, believed that Edwards argued the determinist case "as keenly as any modern."[70] Perhaps most intriguing is the appreciation in 1876 by Leslie Stephen, the agnostic intellectual who was the descendant of an evangelical family and the father of novelist Virginia Woolf. Edwards, according to Stephen, with Benjamin Franklin, represented the genuine Yankee, combining "an element of shrewd mother-wit and an element of transcendental enthusiasm." Stephen detested the doctrine of election as an "appalling dogma" and found much else to reject. Yet he was entranced by the New Englander's acute reasoning, lofty morality, and tendencies toward a Spinozan pantheism.

Edwards, he suggested, was "formed by nature to be a German professor, and accidentally dropped into the American forests."[71] Even those who were miles apart from Edwards in their religious convictions found something to impress when they looked into his pages.

What did not happen, however, during the late nineteenth century in Britain was a cultural revival of Edwards. At the time when America was turning the theologian into a national icon, there were equivalent native Puritans for Britain to heroize: Oliver Cromwell in England and the Covenanters in Scotland. Consequently Edwards was superfluous. There were nevertheless a few symptoms of the tendency to treat Edwards as an artifact from the past rather than as a man with a message for today. As early as the 1850s, Alexander Grosart, a young minister of the United Presbyterian Church of Scotland, traveled to meet Tryon Edwards in Connecticut in order to explore the possibility of printing some of his ancestor's unpublished manuscripts. Grosart was an admirer of Edwards's Christian thought, but his enterprise also had an antiquarian flavor. He was delighted to discover a manuscript on grace "carefully placed within folds of thick paper, and tied up with silk ribbon," perhaps by the hand of Edwards himself.[72] Grosart took the materials back to Scotland, and in 1865 privately printed a selection of the manuscripts, with a facsimile, but never took the project further.

One or two others in Britain developed a similar interest in Edwards as a historical figure. While visiting America in 1881, A. A. Bonar, like his brother Horatius a Free Church of Scotland minister, made a pilgrimage to Northampton as "a place of sacred memories."[73] The most obvious instance, however, was when, on the erection in 1889 of Mansfield College as a Congregational foundation in the University of Oxford, one among the sixty doctors of the church depicted in the stained glass windows of the chapel was Jonathan Edwards.[74] A handful of Congregationalists still regarded Edwards as theirs; but to most people in Britain who were aware of his name, he was, as Grosart put it in the title of his book, "Jonathan Edwards of America." The absence of a cultural revival confirms that the standing of the theologian was in decay.

The fourth phase in the vicissitudes of Edwards's reputation came in the twentieth century. It consisted in an Edwards revival, or rather in a series of Edwards revivals. The first was in the Netherlands in the early years of the century, but proved abortive. The Reformed confessional movement led by Abraham Kuyper saw in Edwards a potential ally. Kuyper himself shows no familiarity with Edwards, but the theologian Herman Bavinck refers several times to the American in his *Reformed Dogmatics* (1895–1901).[75] The young minister Jan Ridderbos, later professor at Kampen Theological University, received his doctorate in 1907 for a thesis on "The Theology of Jonathan Edwards." The dissertation reveals an ambiguous attitude toward Edwards. There is praise for Edwards's resistance to Arminianism, for his clear thinking, and for his warm heart; but there is also trenchant criticism, because, according to Ridderbos, Edwards allowed his theology to be polluted by the philosophy of the day. Therefore, as a pure system of Reformed doctrine, Edwards's work is judged to be "useless."[76] Although Ridderbos published an appreciative article on Edwards in 1957, at the end of his life, it is clear that he could not recommend him wholeheartedly.[77] Edwards was not Calvinistic enough for the taste of the early twentieth-century Re-reformed Church of the Netherlands.

A longer lived revival started in Wales. In 1929 Martyn Lloyd-Jones, a former physician who had entered the ministry of the Calvinistic Methodists, bought a two-volume set of the 1834 edition of Edwards's works in a Cardiff secondhand bookshop. The tight reasoning suited Lloyd-Jones's deductive cast of mind. He became absorbed by Edwards, who effectively turned a commonplace evangelical into a Calvinist zealot. Lloyd-Jones would relax on holiday by reading the New Englander, calling excitedly from the kitchen, "Listen to what Jonathan Edwards has to say on this." The Welsh preacher came to appreciate the Puritans as a whole, but at the end of his career he still ranked Edwards above John Owen—or even John Calvin.[78] From 1955, gathered round Lloyd-Jones, there was an Evangelical Movement of Wales in whose circles Edwards was highly rated. The impulse, however, spread far beyond Wales. From 1939 Lloyd-Jones was minister of Westminster Chapel in central London, exercising a potent influence in the evangelical world. During the 1950s and 1960s he presided over an annual Puritan Conference that attracted hundreds to the Reformed cause. It encompassed J. I. Packer and other young men from Oxford, together with Iain Murray and other young men from Durham. Together they challenged the reigning conservative evangelical theology of the day, a compound of Keswick holiness teaching, pre-millennial adventism, and, in many quarters, a suspicion of the mind. Edwards provided a sovereign antidote. When Murray set up a publishing agency, the Banner of Truth Trust, the *Select Works of Jonathan Edwards* was, in 1958, the fourth title to appear under its imprint. Later, in 1987, Murray published the American's biography. As Banner of Truth books circulated around the world, to Australia, South Africa, and elsewhere, so a fresh awareness of Edwards was kindled. The New Englander was rediscovered as a champion of a thoughtful but vibrant Calvinism.

Pockets of interest in Edwards continued to exist independently. Theologians of the small continuing Free Church of Scotland had not ceased to respect his writings, and there were occasional outcrops such as the appearance in Switzerland in 1960 of a German translation of *Sinners in the Hands of an Angry God*. But it was charismatic renewal, a gathering global force from the 1960s, that did the most to bring Edwards to a new audience, primarily as an analyst of revival. In 1989, for example, an English study of renewal called *Delusion or Dynamic?* included an afterword by J. I. Packer using Edwards's criteria for distinguishing a genuine spiritual movement.[79] The bursting forth in the mid-1990s of the Toronto Blessing, a new phase of renewal exhibiting prostrations and animal noises, elicited a fresh spate of books and articles appealing to Edwards for a verdict either for or against its authenticity. Guy Chevreau, one of the leadership team at the Toronto Airport Vineyard Fellowship where the phenomenon originated, wrote a book in its defense that reached a worldwide audience, soon being translated into German. Fully one-third of its text is a discussion of Edwards.[80] Here was widespread popular interest not in Edwards the Reformed theologian but in Edwards the advocate of true spiritual renewal.

The final type of revival was the upsurge of academic attention to Edwards. It started in the late 1950s, the same time as the appearance of the first volume in the Yale edition of the theologian's works, and was no doubt stimulated by the new series. This revival, which can be studied chiefly through the admirable bibliographies compiled by Max Lesser, was threefold: literary, philosophical, and theological. The spread of interest in Edwards as a *littérateur*, a master of rhetoric and imagery, can be traced from the first dates of publication in that field in particular counties: Germany in 1963, England in 1966, Ireland in 1979, and Russia in 1981. Steadily fresh language barriers were surmounted. All these instances, however, are European. There was an isolated article published in an African journal in 1965, but it was written by an author with an English surname and so no doubt represents a surviving outpost of empire. The real exception to the European monopoly of literary attention to Edwards therefore came from Argentina. J. L. Borges, the polymathic national librarian in Buenos Aires, published in 1967 an appreciation of Edwards in a handbook to the literature of North America. Two years later he followed it up with a poem on Edwards in Spanish, treating the theologian as a Calvinistic curiosity: Edwards's world is a "Vessel of wrath," his deity a "prisoner, God, the Spider."[81] Edwards clearly appealed to the taste for the bizarre of this most metaphysical of twentieth-century authors. Yet Borges was self-consciously European in his cultural orientation; the great breakthrough to global concern for Edwards the writer did not come until 1992, with an article in Japanese by a Japanese author in a Japanese periodical.[82] At last Edwards had attained fully international status in literary studies.

The scholarly interest in Edwards the philosopher followed a similar pattern. The first works in this field appeared in Italy in 1966, in a neoscholastic journal, and in Germany in 1972, specifically on the New Englander's political thought. Although an English philosopher published an edition of some theological writings of Edwards in 1971, England did not pay attention to the strictly philosophical side of Edwards until 1985, when he was included, though with a speaker from abroad, in a series of Royal Institute of Philosophy Lectures on American themes. Canadian studies of Edwards's philosophy, an outgrowth from the United States, began in 1973. The chief interest in this area, however, came from France, reflecting the national penchant for the discipline. A century before, in 1888, there had in fact been a chapter on Edwards's immaterialism in a book by Georges Lyon published in Paris. From 1979 there was a series of articles in French periodicals by Miklós Vetö, culminating in a masterly book on Edwards's thought that appeared eight years later. That in turn led to a batch of reviews in French, including one from the Ivory Coast. Outside Europe there was little else, except that in 1983 a set of lectures in English by Richard R. Niebuhr was issued in Kyoto. So attention to Edwards the philosopher outside America was primarily a European phenomenon, though by the 1980s it was just starting to extend beyond that continent.

In Edwards's theology, as was natural, there was an even greater degree of academic interest. German publications in this field date from 1958, Swiss (in German) from 1978, Canadian from 1976, and French from 1981. Italy forms a special case here as the base of the Roman Catholic Church. A Jesuit, though not an Italian, presented a doctoral dissertation at the Pontifical Gregorian University as early as 1967, a first fruit of the broadening of Catholic sympathies after the Second Vatican Council. Twelve years later an Italian submitted another on Edwards to the same institution. In both there was a sense of excitement that the distance of Edwards from the Catholic tradition was less than might have been imagined. The same ecumenical temper is exhibited in an article in Portuguese on Edwards the preacher published in Brazil in 1982. Book reviews in French and German of works about Edwards's theology multiplied from around 1980. By 1997 there were two significant landmarks: Edwards was discussed, apparently for the first time, in a Czech work; and excerpts from Edwards on revival were actually translated into Italian in a scholarly collection of Protestant texts.[83] Asian scholars studying in America were also becoming fascinated by Edwards, and so his fame reached Korea and Japan. So again there was a spread of interest in Edwards's theology beyond the United States and Europe. Toward the end of the fourth phase of Edwards's legacy, respect for the New Englander was being globalized.

Edwards's reputation outside America, we may therefore conclude, has passed through four phases. In the earliest, when the theologian's works were first becoming known, non-Americans, and especially John Erskine, played a major part in their dissemination. Edwards's fame, however, was largely confined to the English-speaking world, together with the Netherlands. In the next phase, Edwards's writings constituted the foundation of the New England theology that shaped the dominant version of Calvinism in England, Wales, and Scotland. Edwards's legacy molded the evangelical intellectual hegemony in Britain and gave dynamism to the missionary impulse abroad. Spreading Romantic assumptions, however, gradually eroded that synthesis, Calvinism fell into decay (except in the Netherlands), and outside America there was little interest in Edwards as a cultural icon. Consequently the third phase of Edwards's reputation represented a decline, so that in the first half of the twentieth century he was decidedly out of fashion. A series of revivals, however, buoyed his fame in the later twentieth century, both at a popular and at an academic level. In the final phase he reached a far wider geographical constituency than ever before. Edwards hoped, as he put it, that by the year 2000 "the whole . . . world should be enlightened."[84] His celebrity, like that of the gospel he preached, is still far from universal. Yet his legacy has played a crucial role internationally, not least in the spread of the evangelical movement. And there is no doubt that in the year 2000 his global fame is again on the increase.

NOTES

1. Jonathan Edwards, *Apocalyptic Writings,* ed. Stephen J. Stein, *The Works of Jonathan Edwards,* vol. 5 (New Haven: Yale Univ. Press, 1977), 411.

2. "William Gordon," *Dictionary of National Biography* (Oxford: Oxford Univ. Press, 1959–1960).

3. D. Bruce Hindmarsh, *John Newton and the English Evangelical Tradition between the Conversions of Wesley and Wilberforce* (Oxford: Clarendon Press, 1996), 167.

4. Ibid., 154.

5. R. I. and Samuel Wilberforce, *The Life of William Wilberforce,* 5 vols., 2nd ed. (London: John Murray, 1839), 3:66.

6. Albert C. Outler, ed., *John Wesley* (New York: Oxford Univ. Press, 1964), 156.

7. Ibid., 473.

8. R. E. Brantley, "The Common Ground of Wesley and Edwards," *Harvard Theological Review* 83 (1990): 276.

9. Joseph A. Conforti, *Jonathan Edwards, Religious Tradition, and American Culture* (Chapel Hill: Univ. of North Carolina Press, 1995), 69.

10. W. H. Goold, ed., *The Works of the Rev. John MacLaurin* (Edinburgh: John Maclaren, 1860), xlviii.

11. Christopher W. Mitchell, "Jonathan Edwards's Scottish Connection and the Eighteenth-Century Evangelical Revival, 1735–1750" (Ph.D. diss., St. Andrews University, 1998), 11n.; Jonathan Edwards, *Letters and Personal Writings*, ed. George S. Cleghorn, *The Works of Jonathan Edwards*, vol. 16 (New Haven: Yale Univ. Press, 1998), 705–18.

12. John R. McIntosh, *Church and Theology in Enlightenment Scotland: The Popular Party, 1740–1800* (East Linton, East Lothian: Tuckwell Press, 1998), 167.

13. Jonathan Edwards, *A History of the Work of Redemption*, ed. John F. Wilson, *The Works of Jonathan Edwards*, vol. 9 (New Haven: Yale Univ. Press, 1989), 86.

14. Jonathan Edwards, *Practical Sermons* (Edinburgh: for M. Gray, 1788); Jonathan Edwards, *Miscellaneous Observations* (Edinburgh: for M. Gray, 1793); Jonathan Edwards, *Remarks on Important Theological Controversies* (Edinburgh: for J. Galbraith and Archibald Constable, 1796). The second of these items contains a preface by Erskine.

15. W. R. Ward, *The Protestant Evangelical Awakening* (Cambridge: Cambridge Univ. Press, 1992), 91.

16. *Biografisch Lexicon voor de Geschiedenis van het Nederlandse Protestantisme*, ed. D. Nauta, 3 vols. (Kampen: J. H. Kok, 1978–1990), 1:255–56. I am grateful to Jan Oosthoek of the University of Stirling for obtaining and translating this and other items from Dutch; and to Roel Kuiper of the Erasmus University for further invaluable help with Dutch sources.

17. A. L. Drummond, *The Kirk and the Continent* (Edinburgh: Saint Andrew Press, 1956), 157.

18. Sir Henry Moncreiff Wellwood, *Account of the Life and Writings of John Erskine, D.D., Late One of the Ministers of Edinburgh* (Edinburgh: for Archibald Constable and Co., 1818), 315–16; *Biografisch Lexicon*, ed. Nauta, 2:78–80.

19. The classis approval is noted in the copy of Edwards's translated *History of the Work of Redemption* in the library of the Free University of Amsterdam.

20. *Biografisch Lexicon*, ed. Nauta, 1:32–34.

21. From tables created by Mark A. Noll, to whom, and to whose research assistant, I am grateful for this and for much other generous help. The basis for the tables is Thomas H. Johnson, *The Printed Works of Jonathan Edwards, 1703–1758: A Bibliography* (Princeton: Princeton Univ. Press, 1940), which has also provided most of the otherwise unattributed bibliographical information in this paper.

22. I am grateful to Janos Pasztor of the Reformed Academy at Debrecen for this point.

23. Edwards, *Works*, 16:204.

24. William Godwin, *An Enquiry Concerning Political Justice,* 2 vols. (London: for G. G. J. and J. Robinson, 1793), 1:302, 84.

25. William Godwin, *Enquiry Concerning Political Justice and its Influence on Morals and Happiness,* ed. F. E. L. Priestley, 3 vols. (Toronto: Univ. of Toronto Press, 1946), 3:18n.

26. Godwin, *Enquiry* (1793), 1:314.

27. Samuel Parr, "A Spital Sermon, preached at Christ Church," in *The Works of Samuel Parr, LL.D.,* ed. J. Johnstone, 8 vols. (London: Longman, Rees, Orme, Brown and Green, 1828), 2:488–93.

28. Sir James Mackintosh, *Dissertation on the Progress of Ethical Philosophy* (Edinburgh: Adam and Charles Black, 1836), 182.

29. Dugald Stewart, *Dissertation: exhibiting the Progress of Metaphysical, Ethical and Political Philosophy, since the Revival of Letters in Europe* (Edinburgh: Thomas Constable and Co., 1854), 307, 424, 573.

30. Roger Hayden, "Evangelical Calvinism among Eighteenth-Century British Baptists, with particular reference to Bernard Foskett, Hugh and Caleb Evans and the Bristol Baptist Academy, 1690–1791" (Ph.D. diss., Keele, 1992), 217.

31. John Ryland, *Pastoral Memorials,* 2 vols. (London: B. J. Holdsworth, 1826–1828), 1:15.

32. Johnson, *Printed Works,* 95; Conforti, *Jonathan Edwards, Religious Tradition, and American Culture,* 69n.

33. Andrew Fuller, "The Gospel Worthy of All Acceptation," *The Complete Works of the Rev. Andrew Fuller,* ed. A. G. Fuller, 6 vols. (London: Holdsworth and Ball, 1832), 2:1–3.

34. Edward Steane, *The Doctrine of Christ Developed by the Apostles* (Edinburgh: Edmonston and Douglas, 1872), ix.

35. G. M. Roberts, *Selected Trevecka Letters (1742–1747)* (Caernarvon: Calvinistic Methodist Bookroom, 1956), 119.

36. Joseph Gilbert, *Memoir of the Life and Writings of the Late Rev. Edward Williams, D.D.* (London: for Francis Westley, 1825), 419.

37. William Evans, *An Outline of the History of Welsh Theology* (London: James Nisbet and Co., 1900), 126.

38. John Roberts, *Cyfarwyddiadau ac Anogaethau I Gredinwyr . . . a Gasglwyd yn Benaf Allan o Waith Jonathan Edwards* (Bala: R. Sanderson, 1809). I am grateful to Densil Morgan of the University of Wales, Bangor, for this and other Welsh references. Evans, *Welsh Theology,* 131–32.

39. "John Roberts," *The Dictionary of Welsh Biography down to 1940* (London: Honourable Society of Cymmrodorion, 1959), 866.

40. George Hill, *Lectures in Divinity*, 3 vols. (Edinburgh: for Waugh and Innes, 1821), 2:372, 3:101.

41. Thomas Chalmers, *The Christian and Civic Economy of Large Towns*, 3 vols. in 1 (Glasgow: for William Collins, n.d.), 1:318.

42. Thomas Chalmers, *Prelections on Butler's Analogy, Paley's Evidences of Christianity and Hill's Lectures in Divinity* (Edinburgh: Sutherland and Knox, 1849), 131. Thomas Chalmers, *Institutes of Theology*, 2 vols. (Edinburgh: Sutherland and Knox, 1849), 2:386.

43. G. D. Henderson, "Jonathan Edwards and Scotland," *The Burning Bush* (Edinburgh: Saint Andrew Press, 1957), 159.

44. [Thomas Chalmers], "Edwards's Inquiry, with Introductory Essay," *The Presbyterian Review* 2 (1831): 238. The authorship of this article is identified by Henry Rogers, "An Essay on the Genius and Writings of Jonathan Edwards," in *The Works of Jonathan Edwards, A.M.* [1834], 12th ed. (London: William Tegg and Co., 1879), xxxi n.

45. *The Congregationalist and Christian World*, 3 October 1903, 467.

46. Conforti, *Jonathan Edwards, Religious Tradition, and American Culture*, 69n.

47. *Extracts from the Call to Extraordinary Prayer published in 1748 by President Edwards* (Calcutta: for Calcutta Christian Tract and Book Society, 1859).

48. J. A. De Jong, *As the Waters Cover the Sea: Millennial Expectations in the Rise of Anglo-American Missions* (Kampen: J. H. Kok, 1970), 182.

49. Josiah Pratt, *The Life of the Rev. David Brainerd* (London: R. B. Seeley and W. Burnside, 1834), vii.

50. E.g. Henry Rogers, "An Essay on the Genius and Writings of Jonathan Edwards," in *The Works of Jonathan Edwards, A.M.* [1834], 12th ed. (London: William Tegg and Co., 1879), iii, v, xliv.

51. [Chalmers], "Edwards's Inquiry," 249.

52. Conforti, *Jonathan Edwards, Religious Tradition, and American Culture*, chap. 5.

53. J. G. Fichte, *System der Ethik*, vol. 1, pp. 544–55, par. 225, quoted by Mattoon M. Curtis, "Kantean Elements in Jonathan Edwards" in *Philosophische Abhandlungen: Max Heinz zum 70. Geburtstage* (Berlin: Ernst Siegfried Mittler, 1906). I am grateful to Dan Holder of Muhen, Switzerland, for this reference and for other help with German sources.

54. Later on Edwards was still virtually unknown to German theologians. In K. R. Hagenbach's *History of Christian Dogmatics*, the section on Protestant church doctrine outside Germany merely notes his existence as the author of *Freedom of the Will* and *Original Sin* (Edinburgh: T. and T. Clark, 1881), 3:283.

55. I owe this estimate to Roel Kuiper.

56. Earl Leslie Griggs, ed., *Collected Letters of Samuel Taylor Coleridge*, 6 vols. (Oxford: Clarendon Press, 1955–1971), 3:35.

57. S. T. Coleridge, *Aids to Reflection*, ed. John Beer (Princeton: Princeton Univ. Press, 1993), 157.

58. The marked copy is at St. Deiniol's Library, Hawarden, Flintshire.

59. Gladstone Papers, British Library, Add. MS 44728, f.303v.

60. Thomas Erskine, *The Doctrine of Election,* 2nd ed. (Edinburgh: David Douglas, 1873), 333–47.

61. John McLeod Campbell, *The Nature of the Atonement* (London: James Clarke and Co., 1959), chap. 4 , quoted at p. 101. The doctrine of vicarious repentance, often thought to have been derived from Edwards by McLeod Campbell, was not in fact so: Michael Jinkins, *A Comparative Study in the Theology of Atonement in Jonathan Edwards and John McLeod Campbell* (San Francisco: Mellen Research Univ. Press, 1993), 354n.

62. F. D. Maurice, *Modern Philosophy* (London: Grifffin, Bohn and Co., 1862), 469–75.

63. John Kennedy, *Man's Relations to God* (Edinburgh: John Maclaren, 1869), 21–38.

64. David Gracey, *Sin and the Unfolding of Salvation* (London: Passmore and Alabaster, 1894), 28, 118, 109.

65. Joseph Angus, *Six Lectures on Regeneration* (London: Alexander and Shepheard, 1897), 68.

66. J. C. Ryle, *Holiness,* 3rd ed. (London: William Hunt and Co., 1887), vi.

67. "Robert Thomas," *Dictionary of Welsh Biography,* 963.

68. James Martineau, *A Study of Religion,* 2 vols. (Oxford: Clarendon Press, 1888), 2:277.

69. W. E. H. Lecky, *History of the Rise and Influence of the Spirit of Rationalism in Europe,* 2 vols. (London: Longman, Green, Longman, Roberts and Green, 1865), 1:403–4 n.

70. As reported by John Morley: Asa Briggs, ed., *Gladstone's Boswell: Late Victorian Conversations* (Brighton: Harvester Press, 1984), 203.

71. Leslie Stephen, *Hours in a Library (Second Series)* (London: Smith, Elder and Co., 1876), 44, 50, 105.

72. Alexander B. Grosart, *Selections from the Unpublished Writings of Jonathan Edwards of America* (N.p.: Printed for private circulation, 1865), 12.

73. Marjory Bonar, ed., *Andrew A. Bonar, D.D.: Diary and Letters* (London: Hodder and Stoughton, n.d.), 268.

74. Dale A. Johnson, *The Changing Shape of English Nonconformity, 1825–1925* (New York: Oxford Univ. Press, 1999), 176.

75. I owe this point to Roel Kuiper.

76. Jan Ridderbos, *De Theologie van Jonathan Edwards* ('s-Gravenhage: Johan A. Nederbragt, 1907), 316.

77. *Christelijke Encyclopedee* (Kampen: J. H. Kok, 1957), 544–45.

78. Iain H. Murray, *D. Martyn Lloyd-Jones,* 2 vols. (Edinburgh: Banner of Truth Trust, 1982–1990), 1:253–54; 2:375, 421.

79. Gervais Angel, *Delusion or Dynamic? Reflections on a Quarter-Century of Charismatic Renewal* (Eastbourne: MARC, 1989).

80. Guy Chevreau, *Catch the Fire: The Toronto Blessing* (London: Marshall Pickering, 1994).

81. M. X. Lesser, *Jonathan Edwards: A Reference Guide* (Boston: G. K. Hall, 1981), 282.

82. M. X. Lesser, *Jonathan Edwards: An Annotated Bibliography, 1979–1993* (Westport, Conn.: Greenwood Press, 1994), 147.

83. Josef Smolik, *Kristus a jeho Lid* (Prague: Oikumene, 1997), 143–47; Emidio Campi and Massimo Rubboli, ed., *Protestantesimo nei Secoli: Fonti e Documenti* (Turin: Claudiana, 1997), 2:290–307. I owe these references to Josef Smolik of Prague and Eugenio Biagini of Robinson College, Cambridge.

84. Edwards, *Works,* 5:411.

The Reception of Jonathan Edwards by Early Evangelicals in England

D. Bruce Hindmarsh

It may be hard for us to realize, as we leaf through the handsome critical editions produced by the editors of *The Works of Jonathan Edwards* for Yale University Press, that there was a time when the Edwards manuscripts languished for lack of interest and the will to see them through publication. It was not until seven years after Edwards's death that his disciple Samuel Hopkins (1721–1803) managed to get his *Life and Character of Edwards,* together with eighteen of Edwards's sermons, printed in Boston. The *Two Dissertations* followed shortly afterward. Hopkins was disappointed with the response and gave up the idea of preparing any more of Edwards's manuscripts for the press. His *Life of Edwards* would not be reprinted for nearly forty years.

Two men in England, however, were more than pleased with Hopkins's work. The Particular Baptist minister John Collett Ryland (1723–1792) and his son John Ryland Jr. (1753–1825) cherished their copy of the first volume. It belonged to the senior Ryland, then was passed on to his son in 1773, and then finally the son bought another copy and gave the original back to his father. The book is now in the possession of Bristol Baptist College, and it is heavily annotated. The flyleaf is inscribed,

> John Ryland, jun^r
> 1773—
> his Book—and an inestimable
> one it is. The Life of the greatest, wisest, humblest & holyest
> of uninspired Men! And 18
> of his Sermons.
> If ever I lend it I desire the utmost
> Care must be taken of it.

Then below this, in another hand, his father wrote,

> J. R. j. having bo't a new
> one for himself for 2/6^d
> re-turned this to his Father
> October 1786
> J. Ryland sen^{rl}

By this inscription hangs a tale—almost, I am inclined to say, a tale of two cities—since by a wonderful coincidence the Rylands were closely associated with the town of Northampton in England, just as Edwards was with the town of Northampton in New England.

The Rylands also shared a copy of Edwards's *Life of Brainerd* (1765) that was published in Edinburgh the same year as Hopkins's *Life of Edwards.* The book is heavily annotated in two hands, father and son. On page 279, a note in the son's hand reads, "J. R. j. read thro this a second time 16.1.1776. O God give me the like Spirit." In his father's hand, in different ink, is written a bold, "Amen, Amen, Amen!" On the flyleaf of this volume, John Ryland Jr. wrote that this was his book, "which he prizes above almost all others."[2]

The annotations also tell another story, however, for the father meticulously and furiously noted all the places in this unexpurgated edition where John Wesley had bowdlerized Edwards in his edition of *Life of Brainerd.* Against passages where Edwards had included a Calvinist gloss to Brainerd's experience, Ryland wrote marginalia such as, "Shamefully omitted of Wesley all these pages which spake much against his principles—" or, again, "All this is studiously omitted as making against Mr. Wesley's Notion of Faith."[3] Wesley was the first to reprint the *Life of Brainerd* (1768) in England, and it was an abridgement, like his earlier reprints of Edwards's works on revival. And like these other works, it was a highly edited popularization which, in the words of Luke Tyerman, aimed "to separate the rich ore of evangelical truth from the base alloy of Pelagian and Calvinian error."[4]

The Rylands and Wesley both figure largely in the story that follows, since both represent ways in which Edwards's influence was felt in England. My aim is to analyze the reception of Jonathan Edwards in England by the early evangelical communities, such as those represented by these men. By surveying Edwards's influence upon Methodists, Baptists, Congregationalists, and Anglican evangelicals, I hope to demonstrate the variety of ways in which Edwards was interpreted and put to use. Despite this variety, however, all of the early English evangelicals found that Edwards's writings gave them hope—hope that they might see revival, too. And all were helped in the task of revising evangelical theology in modern terms. Moreover, and perhaps ironically, the writings of Edwards persuaded large numbers of evangelicals to accept a larger role for human agency in evangelism and salvation. If we are careful to put the term in quotation marks, we could even say that Edwards moved English evangelicals in an "Arminian" direction.

The Reception of Edwards among English Methodists

The first writings of Edwards to cross the Atlantic were not his *Freedom of Will, Original Sin,* or *Nature of True Virtue*. These sinewy works of high doctrine, moral theology, and philosophical reflection would have their influence in England in due course, in the 1760s and afterward, but the first Edwards that England knew was the Edwards who wrote about revival and reflected on the nature of true Christian experience.

The tangled publishing history of Edwards's *Faithful Narrative* has been rehearsed elsewhere, but it was, of course, the London edition of 1737 that brought Edwards and Northampton to the attention of the world.[5] Several scholars have pointed out that Edwards's account of revival in Northampton was received as an *exemplary* narrative.[6] What began as a private provincial correspondence became significant internationally because it answered the hopes of ministers across the North Atlantic world. As his narrative of revival was read aloud to congregations, as it was serialized in revival magazines in London and Glasgow, it inspired ministers to expect that such an experience could be replicated among their own people. Consequently, the narratives from the revivals at Cambuslang and Kilsyth, and elsewhere, very much followed the pattern laid down by Edwards. James Robe resorted to the same "strange-but-true" formula as Edwards even in the title of his *Faithful Narrative of the Extraordinary Work . . . at Kilsyth* (1742, 1789).[7]

This new spirit that Edwards inspired in the early evangelicals was a spirit of optimism and possibility, very different from the acquiescent piety of merely "going to church and sacrament" that was so much in evidence in Augustan England. As David Bebbington has argued, these early evangelicals were forward-looking, expectant *activists*.[8] Edwards's *Faithful Narrative*—a runaway best-seller—did much to stimulate this religious climate. It was the first sign that his influence would be to move all English evangelicals toward more ebullient views of human agency in evangelism and salvation. For Edwards it was, of course, an unintended consequence of writing a familiar letter to another minister to explain how he preached down Arminianism and saw local revival. But Edwards's narrative was taken out of his hands and thrown to the larger winds of North Atlantic culture, so that his story was reified in the contemporary revolution in print media, consumer culture, communication, and transportation—in all of which the early evangelicals were so implicated.[9] In modern parlance, the Connecticut Valley revival became a media event. As Charles Goen shrewdly observes, "During the awakening of 1734–35 Edwards faithfully pursued his pastoral work with reverent wonder, for . . . his surprise was genuine. But when he gave his narrative to the world, the simple fact is that no revival could ever be a surprise again."[10]

In England, Isaac Watts and John Guyse epitomized the tradition of Old Dissent. Though they sponsored the first edition of Edwards's narrative, their own views about revival, when they saw it in the flesh in the likes of George Whitefield, was more ambivalent—more like the socially conservative Old Calvinists of New England.[11] In contrast, Edwards's narrative hit at the right psychological moment for Methodism, right around the time of the Aldersgate experience of John Wesley and the Pentecostal joy of his brother Charles in 1738, while Methodism was still in its infancy. John Wesley read the *Faithful Narrative* while traveling between London and Oxford, and his response was one of amazement: "This is the Lord's doing, and it is marvellous in our eyes."[12] Wesley made extracts from Edwards's narrative, and published his own abridgement in about 1744. He later revised and reprinted four other works by Edwards. To analyze the reception of Jonathan Edwards in England in the 1740s and '50s, we must therefore turn to John Wesley.

Here it is important to emphasize that Wesley's editions of *The Faithful Narrative* ca. 1744), *The Distinguishing Marks* (1744), *Some Thoughts Concerning the Present Revival* (1745), *The Life of David Brainerd* (1768), and the *Treatise on Religious Affections* (1773) did much to *popularize* a certain version of Edwards for large numbers of English evangelicals.[13] Wesley's editions of Edwards were not calf-bound, gilt folios that sat high on a gentleman's bookshelf or adorned a well-beneficed clergyman's study. In this, as in so much else, Wesley had a shrewd eye for economy and for the ordinary person. His first two abridgements of Edwards were calculated to come out at exactly forty-eight pages duodecimo; that is, enough text to make up two sheets of paper each, printed twelve pages per side, folded four times, trimmed and sewn. The result was a cheap, unbound paperback that sold for eight pence, and that you could stick in your coat pocket. Wesley's editions got Edwards out to the people.[14] But they also popularized an Edwards who was shorn of his Calvinism.

That Wesley was opposed to the Calvinism of Edwards is beyond question. During the Calvinistic Minutes controversy of the 1770s, Wesley wrote a tract entitled *Thoughts upon Necessity* (1774) in which he describes Edwards as the one person who "connects together and confirms" all the worst historical examples of Stoicism and Calvinism. In short, Edwards was a fatalist.[15] Consequently, many of Wesley's elisions to Edwards's writings were unabashedly anti-Calvinistic. This was what raised the ire of John Ryland Sr. as he pored over Wesley's version of the *Life of Brainerd*. Wesley left out the more stroppy bits of Edwards's Calvinism in his other reprints as well. In his edition of *Some Thoughts Concerning the Present Revival of Religion*, for example, he was not about to include lines such as, "And I would now beseech those that have hitherto been something inclining to Arminian principles, seriously to weigh the matter . . . ," or, "Now is a good time for Arminians to change their principles." These lines were the climax of Edwards's appeal, and Wesley silently omitted them, so that Edwards's argument was considerably blunted and appeared only an exhortation for the enemies of revival to cease their opposition. Wesley's evangelical Arminianism was worlds apart from the rational Arminianism of Charles Chauncy that Edwards had in view, but it still provided an editorial principle for Wesley's selection, omission, and emendation of Edwards's writings.

In the preface to Wesley's edition of the *Religious Affections*, he was more explicit about his editorial concerns. He complained about Edwards's "curious, subtle, metaphysical distinctions" that troubled plain men and women. Wesley thought Edwards was trying to argue that backslidden converts had never been true believers in the first place. According to Wesley, Edwards should simply have admitted that a true believer can make shipwreck of his faith. Consequently, Wesley took a high hand with Edwards's treatise: "Out of this dangerous heap, wherein much wholesome food is mixt with much deadly poison, I have selected many remarks and admonitions which may be of great use to the children of God."[16] Needless to say, intellectual property rights were in their infancy in 1773. When Wesley's Edwards appeared in print, he was not much of a Calvinist.

Much of what came under Wesley's blue pencil in the *Religious Affections* was in fact in the category of "subtle, metaphysical distinctions." For example, Wesley elided Edwards's emphasis upon disinterested love for God in his second and third signs—that affections are grounded in the transcendent excellency of divine things in themselves. It is hard to imagine an idea more central to Edwards than this, and as Norman Fiering and others have shown, Edwards's ethic of disinterested virtue and his contemplative religious aesthetic was a profound response to eighteenth-century moral thought.[17] Wesley's audience, however, was not a tightly nucleated community of freeholders, but the working poor of London and Bristol and Newcastle, and the colliers of

Kingswood and Cornwall, and the lay preachers who would speak to them all. Wesley was not much interested in engaging these plain men and women in a debate about eighteenth-century benevolism or setting them on the path to a Neoplatonic appreciation of pure being. So he simply struck that part of Edwards. But even here, one can see a subtle anti-Calvinist concern on Wesley's part. By quietly omitting an emphasis upon the origin of religious affections in God's essential nature, an origin that is without reference to self-interest, Wesley was perhaps trying to avoid any possible implication of quietism, an issue over which he had earlier separated from the Moravians.[18]

These were Wesley's sins of omission. He could also use Edwards more positively to heighten human effort in evangelism and salvation, or to defend revival. When one woman wrote to complain about how several persons fell down, cried out, and were violently affected under Methodist preaching, John Wesley responded with a rhetorical question, "Have you never read . . . Dr. Edwards's *Narrative*?"[19] Another example comes from the *Large Minutes*, Wesley's authoritative summary of Methodist conference proceedings from 1744 to 1753. In question fifty-six, Wesley asked what could be done to revive the Methodist work where it had decayed. His answer: "Let every Preacher read carefully over the *Life of David Brainerd*. Let us be followers of him as he was of Christ, in absolute self-devotion."[20] To the lay preacher Thomas Rankin, Wesley wrote likewise, "Read David Brainerd again, and see your pattern! He was a good soldier of Jesus. Ah! But he first suffered, and then saw the fruit of his labour. Go and do likewise!"[21] This was not an exhortation to wait quietly upon God in the means of grace. This was an exhortation for his preachers to redouble their efforts.

To sum up, Wesley selected only Edwards's writings on revival (not his serious doctrinal works), he purged even these of much of their Calvinism and anti-Arminian polemic, and he turned Edwards's descriptive narratives into active hortatory counsel for his followers. This served the cause of Wesley's evangelical Arminianism. All five of Wesley's abridgements of Edwards were included in the first edition of his collected *Works* (1771–1774), and four were reprinted by Thomas Jackson in 1827. The *Faithful Narrative* and *Some Thoughts* were reissued in 1842. Wesley's version of the *Life of Brainerd* alone ran into seven editions between 1768 and 1825.[22] For at least a hundred years, from roughly the mid–eighteenth to the mid–nineteenth century, Wesley's interpretation of Edwards exerted a steady influence upon English Methodists.

The Reception of Edwards among the Particular Baptists and Congregationalists

John Collett Ryland and John Ryland Jr., who inscribed their early copies of Edwards's works so lovingly, represent a second significant community in eighteenth-century England for whom the influence of Edwards would be decisive: the Particular (or Calvinistic) Baptists. At the time when Wesley was first reading Edwards's *Faithful Narrative,* a large number of Dissenters in or near Northamptonshire were preoccupied with a theological and practical question that came out of the logic of high Calvinism. It was the so-called modern question of whether it was properly the duty of the unconverted to believe the gospel. For if Christ died only for the elect, then none but the elect have the power to believe the gospel. How then could it possibly be the duty of the unconverted to believe, if they had not the power to do so? In practical terms, this meant that many preachers felt restrained in the appeal they could make to a mixed congregation to repent and believe.[23] John Collett Ryland was one of those who held that he should not *offer* the gospel indiscriminately from the pulpit, but should only *declare* a general warrant or provision of salvation in the work of Christ.[24] It is hard to imagine a theological milieu more removed from that of Wesley and his followers. Yet Edwards's influence among a younger generation of Baptists who came to maturity in the 1760s and '70s, including the younger Ryland, was decisive in moving them out of this high Calvinism.

Chief among those who challenged the high Calvinist hegemony in Baptist theology were a group of pastors from the Northamptonshire and Midlands region, many of whom had links to Bristol Baptist Academy. These include Andrew Fuller of Kettering, Robert Hall Jr. of Arnesby, John Sutcliff of Olney, and John Ryland Jr. of Northampton. Fuller's *Gospel Worthy of all Acceptation* (1785) gave expression to a more evangelical Calvinism that injected new life into the denomination and stimulated a burst of activity in education, associational life, prayer for the unconverted, and foreign missions. This new outlook was key to the foundation of the Particular Baptist Society for Propagating the Gospel among the Heathen (1792) and the missionary career of William Carey, which in turn inspired similar growth in missionary society activity on the part of other denominations at the end of the century. The theology of Fuller ("Fullerism") was the fulcrum upon which several Calvinistic Baptist congregations turned from being inward-looking, exclusive sects to becoming part of an expansive and confident denomination.[25]

What was the role of Edwards's writings in all of this? Although the Baptist minister Benjamin Beddome (1717–1795) had already inscribed his name on his copy of Edwards's *Faithful Narrative* in 1742, and the principal of Bristol Baptist Academy, Caleb Evans (1737–91), was also acquainted with the works of Edwards from an early date, it was in the 1760s and especially in the 1770s that Ryland, Sutcliff, and Fuller began to read Edwards carefully for themselves and to see the revolutionary implications of his writings.[26] In his funeral sermon for Sutcliff, Fuller remarked, "I cannot say when he first became acquainted with the writings of President Edwards, and other New England Divines; but, having read them, he drank deeply into them. . . . The consequence was that while he increased in his attachment to the Calvinistic doctrines of human depravity, and of salvation by sovereign and efficacious grace, he rejected, as unscriptural, the high, or rather hyper, Calvinistic notions of the Gospel, which went to set aside the obligations of sinners to every thing spiritually good, and the invitations of the Gospel as being addressed to them."[27] It was in about the late 1770s that Sutcliff, Fuller, and Ryland began to read Edwards's *Inquiry into Freedom of Will*. Edwards's exposition of the distinction between moral and natural inability, though by no means a new idea, was the key that unlocked the question of duty faith for these men. In 1776 the Anglican clergyman John Newton of Olney also introduced this circle to the writings of John Smalley (1734–1820), a disciple of Edwards and Bellamy. Ryland writes, "In 1776, I borrowed of Mr. Newton, of Olney, two sermons on this subject [i.e., the distinction between moral and natural inability], by Mr. Smalley, which Brother Sutcliff afterwards reprinted from the copy which I transcribed. I well remember lending them to Mr. Hall of Arnsby, to whom I remarked, that I was ready to suspect that this distinction, well considered, would lead us to see, that the affirmative side of the Modern Question was fully consistent with the strictest Calvinism."[28] Hall was at first doubtful but, soon after, was fully satisfied that Ryland was correct. The book which Newton loaned to Ryland was *The Consistency of the Sinner's Inability to comply with the Gospel; with his inexcusable guilt in not complying with it, illustrated and confirmed in two Discourses, on John VIth, 44th* (1769), written by John Smalley of New Britain, a Yale College graduate and ardent New Divinity man.[29] To Ryland the distinction between moral and natural inability meant that sinners could be freely invited to respond to the gospel because they were under no natural inability to comply with its terms. It was precisely this argument that unhinged the high Calvinism of Ryland and his circle. Moreover, it led to activism in mission. William Carey said to Andrew Fuller, "If it be the duty of men when the Gospel comes to believe unto salvation, then it is the duty of those who are entrusted with the Gospel to endeavour to make it known among all nations for the obedience of faith."[30]

It remains a question *why* Edwards's argument about natural and moral inability should have had so revolutionary an impact on these men, when it did not on others. The elder Ryland is a complex figure, and the epithet "gruff hyper-Calvinism" does not do him justice. He was an open-communion Baptist with a wide range of close friendships with Anglican evangelicals. His preaching was energetic and he added 323 members to his church over the course of his ministry. As we have already seen, he read Edwards enthusiastically. But theologically, he was a follower of John Gill, John Brine, and Joseph Hussey—high predestinarians all of them—and he did not seem to find Edwards particularly revolutionary. He remained a high Calvinist who rejected duty faith, even while understanding and recommending Edwards on moral and natural inability. One of his students compiled a theological dictionary from his papers, and it includes the entry: "*Impotence,* natural and moral. Natural inability arises from some obstacle extrinsic to the will, and is not the proper subject of praise or blame. Moral inability consists in the opposition or want of inclination of will, and may be either commendable or blameable.— See President *Edwards* on Original Sin."[31] When the younger generation began to dig deep into Edwards on the subject, the senior Ryland responded with characteristic drollery about it all. He remarked, "The devil threw out an empty barrel for them to roll about, while they ought to have been drinking the wine of the kingdom. That old dog, lying in the dark, has drawn off many good men to whip syllabub, and to sift quiddities, under pretence of zeal for the truth."[32] Ironically, he thought the younger Baptist generation were preoccupied with minute points of doctrine to the harm of vital spiritual life. The difference between the two Rylands is nicely symbolized by the fact that J. C. Ryland named one of his sons Herman Witsius Ryland, after a Dutch confessional Calvinist, but John Ryland Jr. named one of his sons Jonathan Edwards Ryland.

The reception of Edwards among the Particular Baptists was crucial for the younger generation. Beginning in 1780 the circular letters of the Northamptonshire Baptists regularly recommended the works of Edwards, including *Some Thoughts Concerning Revival,* the *Treatise on the Religious Affections,* and ("especially to our younger brethren in the ministry") *The Life of David Brainerd.* These general pastoral letters were read aloud at church meetings, and all of the rank-and-file Baptists in the association would have been aware of the books recommended. Incidentally, an extended footnote in the circular letter for 1781 bears all the marks of the elder Ryland. It is a withering attack on Wesley for "his most *partial* and *mutilated* abridgement of *President Edwards's Account of the life of David Brainerd;* the original of which we warmly recommended in our last letter."[33] There was no way Ryland was going to have the Baptist faithful hoodwinked by Wesley.

There were abundant signs elsewhere too of the influence of Edwards among the Baptists. At the Rylands' church at Northampton they had a long wooden table under the pulpit where church members from outlying villages could eat their dinner between services on Sundays. The table had built-in shelves stocked with books "for the use of the country people." Whatever their lunch, their theological diet would be substantial. John Ryland Sr. donated several works by John Gill for the use of the people. But his son gave an octavo edition of the *Life of Edwards,* bound up with his posthumous *Eighteen Select Sermons* (Glasgow, 1785). It was inscribed as his gift to the church, "always to be kept in the Table Pew or the Vestry."[34]

Sutcliff was so indebted to Edwards that some accused him of preaching more of Edwards than of Christ.[35] He wrote a catechism for children in 1783 that included five questions and answers probing the child's knowledge of moral and natural inability, and calling for examples of each. Question forty-seven is even nicely rounded off with a learned footnote.[36] In 1784 Sutcliff received from John Erskine (1721–1803) in Scotland Edwards's *Humble Attempt to Promote Explicit Agreement and Visible Union of God's People in Extraordinary Prayer,* and he immediately presented a proposal to the Baptist Association for monthly prayer meetings for revival. This plan was soon adopted by other associations and denominations, and raised the consciousness of large numbers of Baptists of the need for evangelism and mission.[37] The eager reception of the *Life of Brainerd* also helped to stimulate this concern for mission that climaxed in the founding of the Baptist Missionary Society. When William Carey left for India, he took a copy of the *Life of Brainerd,* and he considered it "almost a second bible."[38] The writings of Edwards were an important part of the chain of events that led to early modern missionary endeavour.

Thus, Edwards's works on revival stimulated the Baptists, as they did Wesley, but whereas Wesley rejected Edwards's Calvinism outright, the Baptists probed deeply into the Edwards of *Freedom of Will.* Far from finding it full of overly subtle distinctions and metaphysical digressions, they made it the ideological foundation of a whole program of new initiatives in mission. Roger Hayden sums up Edwards's influence among the English Baptists:

Jonathan Edwards's impact on eighteenth century Baptists in Britain is almost incapable of exaggeration. Out of his experience of revival and through his theological and narrative writing he produced evidence for a vital evangelical Calvinism which could stand side by side with the vitality of the Wesleyan movement. He produced theological keys which unlocked the closed doors of hyper-Calvinism with absolutely no concessions to Arminianism or antinomianism. He fired the English Particular Baptist imagination with his own involvement with revival and his description of the remarkable missionary endeavours of David Brainerd among the American Indians. What English Baptists yearned for, as the Association letters testify so often, Edwards was able to demonstrate as the true heart of the old Puritan Gospel—an evangelical Calvinism which could legitimately reach out into all the world with the Gospel of Christ.[39]

The Baptists started out with a much more pessimistic view of human capacity than Wesley, but they too were moved to higher views of human agency in evangelism and salvation by the writings of Edwards.

Among the Congregationalists or Independents a similar story could be told. While Watts and Doddridge might have had an arms-length relationship to the Evangelical Revival, there were younger ministers, indebted to Methodism, who would draw upon Edwards to reconstruct Calvinism in a more evangelical mode. William Gordon (1728–1807) was famous and infamous for his political sympathies with the American patriots in the revolutionary period, but earlier, in 1762, he published an abridgement of the *Religious Affections*.[40] In his preface, Gordon remarked that he had earlier been impressed by some theological ideas in a controversial work by Robert Sandeman, *Letters on Theron and Aspasio,* notwithstanding the antagonistic and extravagant elements of that book. He later found that the most important insights in Sandeman's book were original with Edwards. Indeed, he sent someone to find out if Sandeman had read Edwards, and upon learning that he had, he accused him of plagiarism.[41] Gordon offered his abridgement of Edwards's *Religious Affections* as a more pure and less rancorous presentation of the differences between substantial and circumstantial evidence of genuine piety.

Of greater importance, however, was the influence of Edwards upon Edward Williams (1750–1813), whom R. Tudur Jones describes as "the leading Congregational theologian of his generation."[42] Williams was raised in the Established Church, came under the influence of the Methodists, and joined an Independent church as a young man. Ordained in 1776, he was involved in most of the major developments in evangelical Dissent in the last quarter of the century. He was a pioneer of Sunday schools, one of the first editors of the *Evangelical Magazine,* a prime mover in the London Missionary Society, and an early advocate of Congregational Union. In 1795 he moved to Rotherham to preside over the Dissenting academy there. In the last decade of his life he made his most significant theological contribution. He edited works by John Owen, Matthias Maurice, Jonathan Edwards, Isaac Watts, and Philip Doddridge, and he wrote his major works, *An Essay on the Equity of Divine Government and the Sovereignty of Divine Grace* (1809) and *A Defence of Modern Calvinism* (1812). As a theologian, he played the same role within Congregationalism that Fuller played among the Particular Baptists. He was the architect of a reconstructed Calvinism—"an attempt to restate Calvinism in a way which would provide a viable ideological background to the evangelical activity of the late eighteenth century."[43]

While there were many sources for Williams's evangelical Calvinism, he had clearly read Edwards carefully, and the influence of Edwards is everywhere apparent. Not only does Williams draw upon the Edwardsian distinction between natural and moral inability in *Freedom of Will,* but he also makes much use of *Religious Affections* and *End of Creation*.[44] His position within the denomination, alongside David Bogue (1750–1825) and others involved in the sending and training missionaries, allowed him to transmit a modernized Calvinism, influenced by Edwards, to a whole generation. The effect, as with the Particular Baptists, was to provide a revised Calvinistic framework that would accommodate higher views of human agency and mission activity.

The Reception of Edwards among Evangelicals in the Church of England

The third group of early evangelicals in England who read Edwards were the evangelical clergy within the Church of England. In the eighteenth century Anglican evangelicals were not a tightly organized party with their own magazines, conferences, religious societies, and patronage trusts. These elements of partisan identity would develop in the late eighteenth century and early nineteenth century. Yet large numbers of evangelical clergy were bound together by ties of friendship, churchmanship, and spiritual concern. With a few exceptions, most were also moderate Calvinists. As such, they often felt a particular need to defend their theological position at a time when Calvinism was unfashionable in the Established Church. Their favorite appeal was to the Thirty-Nine Articles, but in developing and defending their theology, they often made appeal to Jonathan Edwards also.

There are three clergyman who illustrate this use of Edwards particularly well. John Newton (1725–1807) was a converted slave trader who entered Anglican orders and became widely known as a spiritual director and hymn writer. When he began reading Edwards is not certain, but he was well read enough in Edwards to be able to counsel John Ryland Jr. in the finer points of Edwards's theology in his own spiritual pilgrimage.[45] Newton was also a theological mentor to two Anglican ministers, also indebted to Edwards, who would themselves be held in high regard as writers by nineteenth-century evangelicals. Thomas Scott (1747–1821) told the story of his intellectual path from Socinianism to evangelical faith in his autobiography, *The Force of Truth* (1779); in the nineteenth century, he would be known to evangelicals as "the commentator" for his massive commentary on the whole Bible. Joseph Milner (1744–1797) was an influential schoolmaster and clergyman at Hull who wrote a multi-volume *Church History* that did service for evangelicals for several generations. Newton was the key link, as a good friend and correspondent of both Scott and Milner, and he helped to shape their theological views. All three men were influential, shaping evangelicalism in the Church of England well into the nineteenth century. And each of them had a high regard for Edwards, though they expressed some reservation about particular elements in his thought.

Newton was clearly impressed by Edwards from an early date. In 1762 he claimed Edwards was "my favourite author." In 1778 he gave him "the laurel for divinity in this century."[46] Newton himself had neither the disposition nor the inclination for writing sustained, discursive theology. He liked instead to write letters. This meant that, on any given day, he had to do what theology he did in the space of a quarto sheet. So, like a good general practitioner, he referred difficult theological cases—often to Edwards. In 1767 he wrote to a theological student who had met with some Calvinists who objected to the way Newton exhorted sinners in his sermons. In response, Newton explained that such an address to sinners was perfectly consistent with Calvinism, and he excused himself from arguing the point further by referring his correspondent to Edwards's *Freedom of Will* (published in England five years previously).[47]

Newton realized that Edwards's complex argumentation was unfashionable, but this did not keep Newton from extolling his works. He was never as enamored with Edwards, though, as some of the Baptists. And he was ambivalent about the Edwardsians. He wrote to John Ryland Jr. during the American war: "I long as earnestly as you for an end to the Unhappy war—not so much for the sake of American Divinity. For I think so far as Scheme, System, &

Notion are concerned, we have as tolerable stock at home."[48] By 1794, however, Newton had significantly changed his view of Edwards as a theologian. In fact, he repented altogether of ever having recommended books such as *Freedom of Will:* "I was younger then than I am now. I do not now recommend it.... Mr. E. was an excellent man, but some of his writings are too metaphysical, and particularly that book. If I understand it, I think it rather establishes fatalism and necessity, than Calvinism in the sober sense."[49] This was an important turnaround. Newton's version of Calvinism was never very metaphysical, and he became even more unsystematic in his old age. William Jay recalled the old Newton saying once, "I am more of a Calvinist than anything else; but I use my Calvinism in my writings and my preaching as I use this sugar." Newton then took a lump and, putting it into his teacup and stirring it, added, "I do not give it alone, and whole; but mixed and diluted."[50]

Thomas Scott, on the other hand, was a much more serious theologian than Newton. Indeed, Newton once introduced Scott to a group of local Baptists as "the man who, he hoped, would prove the Jonathan Edwards of Old England."[51] He had won every theological conviction he had by dint of hard intellectual work as he climbed out of heterodoxy in the 1770s. He claimed an early acquaintance with Edwards, Brainerd, and the New England divines. Indeed, in a sermon before the London Missionary Society in 1804, Scott acknowledged that these writers had instilled in him a concern for the unevangelized several years before there were any organized missionary societies.[52] As to New England theology, Scott gave his overall assessment in 1793: "In general I accord with the American divines: and yet, in some things, I rather dissent from them; especially in that, as I think, they rather consider what true religion is in the abstract, than as it subsists in the mind of such poor creatures as we are, with all our infirmities.... They seem sometimes to give too little encouragement to inquirers: and in that they would have self-love almost excluded from religion; whereas it seems to me, that it is a part of our nature as God made us, not as sin hath made us."[53] Scott was, however, always more ready to excuse Edwards on this account, than he was Hopkins or Bellamy. To John Ryland Jr. he also confided his opinion about how Old and New England compared theologically: "Much of the religion of Old England seems to me to renounce or confound the most important scriptural distinctions, and all depth of study and investigation whatever: much of that... of New England, &c. to run into unscriptural disquisitions and refinements."[54] Scott left more of a place for disciplined theological reflection than Newton, but like Newton he worried that Edwardsian Calvinism tended to become too academic.

Joseph Milner was also a moderate Calvinist, and his appreciation for Edwards was evident in his essay "Scriptural Proof of the Influence of the Holy Spirit on the Understanding" (1789), where he closely paraphrased Edwards for two pages, drawing at times verbatim from the *Religious Affections* on the new sense or "principle of nature" that operates in the spiritual person.[55] Milner likewise used Edwards's sensationalist epistemology of religion to oppose the rationalism and scepticism of Hume and Gibbon.[56] Like the other evangelicals, he was aware of Edwards's distinction between moral and natural inability, and how it could be used to defend Calvinism against the charge of arbitrariness. In volume 2 of his *History of the Church of Christ,* Milner devotes a good deal of space to his favorite, Augustine. He tangles with the eminent German historian Mosheim in a footnote over Augustine's alleged inconsistencies, and calls in Edwards for help, saying, "I shall only here refer the reader to Edwards's masterly treatise on Free-will, which I think has not yet been answered. Had Mosheim better understood the grounds of the subject of human liberty, he would not so rashly have charged Augustine with inconsistency."[57] The poor man had not read Edwards.[58]

Like Newton, though, Milner had little concern about absolute rational consistency in his Calvinism, describing himself as "partly siding with Methodists in opinion, and partly with those called Calvinists," and appealing to the constitution of the Church of England, the Scripture, and the importance of the main "things" of repentance, faith, and love, over against mere words.[59] This appeal to *res non verba* was common among Anglican evangelicals when Calvinism became complicated.

Scott, Newton, and Milner illustrate the way that moderate Calvinists in the Church of England read Edwards.[60] Edwards's theological writings shored up their faith. They knew they could always turn to him for intellectual heft when they needed it. But while they clearly admired the rigor of Edwards and New England divinity, they also critiqued it from the perspective of biblical and pastoral theology, and experience. Scott in particular shared some of Wesley's concerns that Edwards's preoccupation with pure disinterested love might well intimidate the beginner in the faith. All three were concerned to maintain a more kerygmatic approach to theology than they observed in the speculative theology of New England.

Here then are three groups of early evangelicals ranging from evangelical Arminian Methodists, to moderate Calvinist Anglicans, to strict and even high Calvinist Baptists with their Congregationalist counterparts. How did they receive Edwards? To state it baldly, the Baptists championed Edwards, the Anglican evangelicals were ambivalent, and Wesley simply corrected him. But in all three cases, the writings of Edwards worked to encourage English evangelicals that their faith and experience could be expressed and defended in the modern world. For this reason, Edwards's empiricism and sensationalist psychology consistently appealed to all these groups of early English evangelicals.[61]

I have also argued that Edwards's example and his writing moved all these English evangelicals to affirm a larger role for human agency in evangelism and salvation. That was the direction in which so many developments in the early modern world were pointing, in any case. But it is possible today to give so much weight to large cultural forces such as the consumer revolution, democratization, and pre-romanticism that we fail to recall the important role still played by individuals and by religious ideas within history. At the level of high theology, Edwards's distinction between innocent natural inability and culpable moral inability gave English Calvinists permission to be consistent with their own beliefs while appealing to sinners. By demonstrating how faith could properly be the duty of all people, Edwards also gave them permission to make evangelism and mission their own duty—to use means. And, finally, by offering all these groups an exemplary narrative of revival and of consecrated missionary service, Edwards inspired English evangelicals to apply the same principles and work for similar results in their own lives. The consequences of that in the nineteenth century would be far reaching, indeed. It was the beginning of Edwards's substantial legacy within English evangelicalism.

NOTES

1. The Rylands' autograph inscription is on the flyleaf of Jonathan Edwards, *Sermons on Various Important Subjects. Being some of the Remains of the late Reverend and Learned Mr. Jonathan Edwards* . . . (Boston: Printed and Sold by S. Kneeland, 1765), to which is prefixed *The Life of the late reverend, learned and pious Mr. Jonathan Edwards* . . . [by Samuel Hopkins] (Boston: Printed and Sold by S. Kneeland, 1765). The Rylands' copy of the book is in the possession of Bristol Baptist College, Bristol, England.

2. Jonathan Edwards, *An Account of the Life of the late Reverend Mr David Brainerd, Minister of the Gospel, Missionary to the Indians . . . chiefly taken from his own diary, and other private writings, written for his own Use; and now published by Jonathan Edwards . . . to which is annexed I. Mr Brainerd's Journal while among the Indians. II. Mr Pemberton's Sermon at his Ordination* . . . , 8vo ed. (Edinburgh: Printed by John Gray and Gavin Alston, 1765). Ryland's copy is in the possession of Bristol Baptist College, Bristol, England.

3. Ibid., 231.

4. L. Tyerman, *The Life and Times of the Rev. John Wesley*, 3rd ed., 3 vols. (London: James Sangster and Co., 1876), 2:65

5. C. C. Goen, introduction to Jonathan Edwards, *The Great Awakening*, ed. C. C. Goen, *The Works of Jonathan Edwards*, vol. 4 (New Haven: Yale Univ. Press, 1972), 32–46.

6. John Walsh, "'Methodism' and the Origins of English-Speaking Evangelicalism," in *Evangelicalism: Comparative Studies of Popular Protestantism in North America, the British Isles, and Beyond, 1700–1990*, ed. Mark Noll, George Rawlyk, and David Bebbington (New York: Oxford Univ. Press, 1994), 21–22; Susan O'Brien, "A Transatlantic Community of Saints: The Great Awakening and the First Evangelical Network, 1735–55," *American Historical Review* 91 (1986): 811–32; Susan O'Brien, "Eighteenth-Century Publishing Networks in the First Years of Transatlantic Evangelicalism," in *Evangelicalism*, ed. Noll, Bebbington, and Rawlyk, 38–57; W. R. Ward, *The Protestant Evangelical Awakening* (Cambridge: Cambridge Univ. Press, 1992), 285–86.

7. Likewise, Howell Harris read Edwards's *Faithful Narrative* very early, and when he saw revival in Wales, he remarked, "Sure the time here now is like New England." Ward, *The Protestant Evangelical Awakening*, 322.

8. D. W. Bebbington, *Evangelicalism in Modern Britain: A History From the 1730s to the 1980s* (London: Unwin Hyman Ltd., 1989), 10–12.

9. See, e.g., Frank Lambert, *"Pedlar in Divinity": George Whitefield and the Transatlantic Revivals* (Princeton: Princeton Univ. Press, 1994).

10. Goen, introduction to Edwards, *Works*, 4:27.

11. Walsh, "'Methodism' and English-Speaking Evangelicalism," 22.

12. *The Journal of the Rev. John Wesley*, ed. Nehemiah Curnock, and John Telford, 8 vols. (London: R. Culley, 1909), 2:84. Cf. Richard B. Steele, *"Gracious Affection" and "True Virtue" According to Jonathan Edwards and John Wesley* (Metuchen, N.J.: Scarecrow Press, 1994), 131–34; Albert Outler, introduction to *John Wesley* (New York: Oxford Univ. Press, 1964), 15.

13. In each case the parenthetical dates are those of the first edition of Wesley's abridgement. For an analysis of the publishing history of each of these editions, see the introductions in *The Works of Jonathan Edwards* (Yale edition), vols. 2, 4, and 7. See also Steele, *"Gracious Affection" and "True Virtue,"* 182–267; Gregory S. Clapper, "'True Religion' and the Affections: A Study of John Wesley's Abridgement of Jonathan Edwards's *Treatise on Religious Affections*," *Wesleyan Theological Journal* 19 (1984): 77–89; Thomas Walter Herbert, *John Wesley as Editor and Author* (Princeton: Princeton Univ. Press, 1940).

14. Cf. Herbert, *Wesley as Editor and Author*, 121.

15. John Wesley, *The Works of John Wesley*, ed. Thomas Jackson, reprinted from the 1872 edition, 14 vols. (Grand Rapids, Mich.: Baker, 1978), 10:463–67.

16. John Wesley, *The Works of Rev. John Wesley*, ed. John Emory (New York: Carlton and Porter, n.d.), 7:557–58, cf. 7:525.

17. Norman Fiering, *Jonathan Edwards's Moral Thought and Its British Context* (Chapel Hill: Univ. of North Carolina Press, 1981).

18. For a further analysis of Wesley and Edwards with regard to eighteenth-century theological ethics and philosophy, see Richard E. Brantley, "The Common Ground of Wesley and Edwards," *Harvard Theological Review* 83, no. 3 (1990): 271–303; Henry H. Knight III, "The Relation of Love to Gratitude in the Theologies of Edwards and Wesley," *Evangelical Journal* 6 (1988): 3–12; Robert D. Smith, "John Wesley and Jonathan Edwards on Religious Experience: A Comparative Analysis," *Wesleyan Theological Journal* 25, no. 1 (1990): 130–46; C. A. Robers, "John Wesley and Jonathan Edwards," *Duke Divinity School Bulletin* 31 (1966): 20–38; Richard B. Steele, "John Wesley's Synthesis of the Revival Practices of Jonathan Edwards, George Whitefield, and Nicholas von Zinzendorf," *Wesleyan Theological Journal* 30, no. 1 (1995): 154–72.

19. John Wesley, *The Letters of John Wesley*, ed. John Telford, 8 vols. (London: Epworth Press, 1931): 7:207.

20. Isabel Rivers, "'Strangers and Pilgrims': Sources and Patterns of Methodist Narrative," in *Augustan Worlds*, ed. J. D. Hilson, M. M. B. Jones, and J. R. Watson (Leicester: Leicester Univ. Press, 1978), 189–203, 195–96.

21. Wesley, *Letters of John Wesley*, ed. Telford, 7:57.

22. Joseph Conforti, "Jonathan Edwards's Most Popular Work: 'The Life of David Brainerd' and Nineteenth Century Evangelical Culture," *Church History* 54 (1985): 188–201.

23. Geoffrey F. Nuttall, "Northamptonshire and *The Modern Question:* A Turning-Point in Eighteenth-Century Dissent," *Journal of Theological Studies*, n.s., 16 (1965): 259–74.

24. William Newman, *Rylandiana: Reminiscences Relating to the Rev. John Ryland, A.M. of Northampton* (London: George Wightman, 1835), 50.

25. L. G. Champion, "Evangelical Calvinism and the Structures of Baptist Church Life," *Baptist Quarterly* 28 (1978): 196–208; Raymond Brown, *The English Baptists of the Eighteenth Century* (London: Baptist Historical Society, 1986); Olin C. Robison, "The Particular Baptists in England, 1760–1820" (Ph.D diss., Oxford Univ., 1963); E. F. Clipsham, "Andrew Fuller and Fullerism: A Study in Evangelical Calvinism," *Baptist Quarterly* 20 (1963–1964): 99–114, 146–54, 214–55, 268–76.

26. Roger Hayden, "Evangelical Calvinism among Eighteenth-Century British Baptists with Particular Reference to Bernard Foskett, Hugh and Caleb Evans and the Bristol Baptist Academy, 1690–1791" (Ph.D. diss., University of Keele, 1991), 341.

27. Andrew Fuller, *The principles and prospect of a servant of Christ: a funeral sermon for the Rev. J. Sutcliff with a memoir* (Kettering, 1814), 46, quoted in Hayden, "Evangelical Calvinism," 348.

28. John Ryland Jr., *The Life and Death of the Reverend Andrew Fuller* (London: Button and Son, 1816), 9 n. Ryland also recommended Edwards and Smalley on this subject in his sermon *God's Experimental Probation of Intelligent Agents. A Sermon Preached at a Meeting of Ministers at Kettering, in Northamptonshire, October 3, 1780* (Northampton: Printed for the Author by Thomas Dicey, 1780). He refers to Smalley as well in an article in *The Theological Miscellany* 3 (1786): 604.

29. William Allen, *An American Biographical and Historical Dictionary*, 2nd ed. (Boston: W. Hyde, 1832), s.v. "Smalley, John"; Sydney E. Ahlstrom, *A Religious History of the American People* (New Haven and London: Yale Univ. Press, 1972), 410–11.

30. James Culross, *The Three Rylands: A Hundred Years of Various Christian Service* (London: Elliot Stock, 1897), 79.

31. Newman, *Rylandiana*, 53.

32. Ibid., 78; cf. Culross, *Three Rylands*, 63.

33. Hayden, "Evangelical Calvinism," 138–40; Thornton Elwyn, "Particular Baptists of the Northamptonshire Baptist Association as Reflected in the Circular Letters, 1765–1820," *Baptist Quarterly* 36 (1996): 368–81.

34. John Taylor, *Early History of College Lane Chapel* (Northampton: Taylor and Son, 1870), 35–36; Ernest A. Payne, *College Street Church, Northampton, 1697–1947* (London: Kingsgate Press, 1947), 19–20.

35. Hayden, "Evangelical Calvinism," vii.

36. John Sutcliff, *The First Principles of the Oracles of God, Represented in a Plain and Familiar Catechism for the Use of Children,* [revised by Joseph Belcher] (Whitchurch, Salop: R. B. Jones, 1820), questions 43–47.

37. Michael Haykin, "'A Habitation of God, Through the Spirit': John Sutcliff (1752–1814) and the Revitalization of the Calvinistic Baptists in the Late Eighteenth Century," *Baptist Quarterly* 34 (1992): 304–19; Michael Haykin, *One Heart and One Soul: John Sutcliff of Olney, His Friends and His Times* (Durham: Evangelical Press, 1994).

38. Conforti, "Edwards's Most Popular Work," 193.

39. Hayden, "Evangelical Calvinism," 344.

40. Jonathan Edwards, *A Treatise Concerning the Religious Affections . . . By the late Rev. Jonathan Edwards . . . Abridged by William Gordon,* ed. William Gordon (London: Printed for T. Field, 1762).

41. Ibid., x. Sandeman's *Letters* were part of a war of pamphlets and books that arose in response to the florid defense of Calvinism and imputed righteousness mounted by the evangelical clergyman James Hervey in a series of mock-classical dialogues, *Theron and Aspasio; or, A series of dialogues and letters, upon the most important and interesting*

subjects (Printed by C. Rivington for J. and J. Rivington, 1755). Sandeman responded with *Letters on Theron and Aspasio. Addressed to the author,* 2nd ed., 2 vols. (Edinburgh: Printed by Sands Murray Donaldson and Cochran, 1759). The controversy widened to involve debate about "Sandemanianism," and before it was concluded it involved a large number of the leading evangelicals of the eighteenth century in England, Scotland, and New England, including John Wesley, Andrew Fuller, Anne Dutton, John Erskine, and the Edwardsian Joseph Bellamy, who published, *Theron, Paulinus, and Aspasio: or, letters and dialogues, upon the nature of love to God, faith in Christ, assurance of a title to eternal life: Containing some remarks on the sentiments of the Revd. Messieurs Hervey and Marshal [sic], on these subjects: Published at the request of many* (Boston: Printed by S. Kneeland, 1759).

42. R. Tudur Jones, *Congregationalism in England, 1662–1962* (London: Independent Press, 1962), 170.

43. Ibid., 171.

44. See further the cross references to Edwards in Williams's *Essay on the Equity of Divine Government and the Sovereignty of Divine Grace* in Evan Davies, ed., *The Works of the Rev. Edward Williams,* 4 vols. (London: James Nisbet and Co., 1862), 1:145, 157, 196–97, 354, 382, 423–24.

45. Bruce Hindmarsh, *John Newton and the English Evangelical Tradition* (Oxford: Oxford Univ. Press, 1996), 142–59.

46. *Private Journals and Literary Remains of John Byrom,* ed. Richard Parkinson, 2 vols. (Manchester: Printed for the Chetham Society, 1854–1857), 2:638; *The Original Letters of the Reverend John Newton to the Rev. W. Barlass* (London, 1819), 60; cf. *The Works of the Rev. John Newton,* 6 vols. (London, 1808–1809), 2:52, 102.

47. *Works of Newton,* 2:52.

48. Newton to John Ryland Jr., 26 July 1779, manuscript letter, Lambeth Palace Library, London.

49. John Newton, *Sixty-Eight Letters from the Rev. John Newton to a Clergyman* [James Coffin] *and his Family* (London: Simpkin, Marshall, 1845), 91.

50. *Autobiography of William Jay,* ed. George Redford and John Angell James (1854; reprint, Edinburgh: Banner of Truth, 1974), 272.

51. John Ryland Jr., "Remarks on the *Quarterly Review,* for April 1824, Relative to the Memoirs of Scott and Newton," in *Pastoral Memorials of the Rev. John Ryland* (London: B. J. Holdworth, 1826–1828), 2:352.

52. John Scott, *The Life of the Rev. Thomas Scott,* 6th ed. (London: L. B. Seeley and Son, 1824), 654.

53. Ibid., 255. In another letter this same year he equates Samuel Hopkins with those who held the negative view of the modern question in England (ibid., 313, cf. 336–38, 643).

54. John Scott, *Letters and Papers of the Late Rev. Thomas Scott* (London: L. B. Seeley, 1824), 135, cf. 131, 139–42.

55. Joseph Milner, *Essays on several religious subjects, chiefly tending to illustrate the Scripture-doctrine of the influence of the Holy Spirit* (York: Printed by Ward and Peacock, 1789), 248–49; cf. Jonathan Edwards, *Religious Affections*, ed. John E. Smith, *The Works of Jonathan Edwards,* vol. 2 (New Haven: Yale Univ. Press, 1959), 206.

56. Joseph Milner, *Gibbon's account of Christianity considered: together with some strictures on Hume's dialogues concerning natural religion* (York: Printed by A. Ward, 1781), 126.

57. Joseph Milner, *The History of the Church of Christ*, ed. Isaac Milner, 5 vols. (London: Luke Hansard and Sons for T. Cadell, 1827), 2:386n.

58. See also ibid., 2:412, 417.

59. See his letter to Mr. D. H——e, 21 December 1780, printed in the *Evangelical Magazine*, n.s., 1 (1823), 232.

60. Another evangelical in the Church of England to read and publish Edwards was Charles De Coetlogon, editor of the *Theological Miscellany*. See further, Jonathan Edwards, *The Eternity of Hell Torments, by the late Rev. Jonathan Edwards . . . revised and corrected by the Rev. C. E. De Coetlogon*, ed. Charles E. De Coetlogon (London: Printed by W. Justins for R. Thomson, 1808). See also the references to Edwards in the *Theological Miscellany* (1784), 1:xii, and (1787), 4:604. The issue of the free offer of the gospel and duty faith was fully canvassed in the *Theological Miscellany* in 1785 and 1786. John Sutcliff's children's catechism was reviewed in (1784), 1:364.

61. See further the thorough discussion in David Bebbington, *Evangelicalism in Modern Britain: A History from the 1730s to the 1980s* (London: Unwin Hyman, 1989), 47–50; cf. Frederick Dreyer, "Faith and Experience in the Thought of John Wesley," *American Historical Review* 87 (1983): 12–30.

Jonathan Edwards's Scottish Connection

Christopher W. Mitchell

According to Susan O'Brien, one of the most impressive and historically influential developments created by the mid-eighteenth-century English-speaking revivals was the network of correspondence that developed between Scottish revivalists and their American counterparts. Among the ten ministers O'Brien cites as forming the core of this eighteenth-century evangelical letter-writing connection were Jonathan Edwards and four of the most prominent evangelical ministers of the Church of Scotland: John MacLaurin of Glasgow, William McCulloch of Cambuslang, James Robe of Kilsyth, and John Erskine of Edinburgh.[1] In addition to the four ministers O'Brien cites, John Willison of Dundee and Thomas Gillespie of Carnock also figured prominently in Edwards's relationship with Scotland.[2] Although O'Brien's study is primarily concerned with the role Edwards and his Scottish correspondents played in the larger transatlantic network, the formative role she gives to the Edwards-Scotland connection goes a long way in substantiating two centuries of testimony concerning the importance of Edwards's Scottish connection.[3]

At the heart of Edwards's connection with these Scottish ministers was a spiritual quest that consisted of their mutual pursuit and practice of what they routinely referred to as true religion,[4] and their efforts to reestablish the integrity of its Calvinist and evangelical character within their respective religious communities and beyond. The catalyst for the connection was the revivals. By 1742, MacLaurin and company were well enough acquainted with Edwards's published commentary and analysis of the American revivals to be convinced that he was a Calvinist divine of superior rank and genius and unquestionable evangelical piety, and one who could argue their case against the hostile intellectual forces of their day with unequal command and in a way that was "well-adapted" to the Scottish context.[5] As we know, Edwards went on to produce the most enlightened, most articulate and influential presentation and defense of revivalism and evangelical Calvinism published in the eighteenth century. It is not at all surprising, therefore, to find that these Scottish ministers initiated the relationship, actively promoted his work, sought his counsel, and enlisted his help. In fact, due to their efforts, Edwards became one of the chief advocates of Scottish evangelical Calvinism in the eighteenth century without ever crossing the Atlantic.[6] Having said this, let me hasten to add that what Edwards received in return from his Scottish correspondents proved equally significant. In fact, during his lifetime he was to find no better friends than the Scottish ministers with whom he had the pleasure to correspond. Yet, as significant as this connection was for Edwards, it has not, as far as I know, been given any attention. This essay is an attempt to redress this situation.

Although this work deals primarily with the impact of the Scots on Edwards, with their general contribution to his ministry, it is worth pausing to note how much influence moved the other way, from Edwards in America to his fellow Calvinists in Scotland. Edwards spearheaded the theological defense and management of the revivals in Scotland. Two early works, both published in Scotland, provided the theological foundation. The first, *A Faithful Narrative* (Edinburgh, 1737), propelled Edwards into the forefront of Scottish revivalism and set the paradigm by which the Scottish revivalists conducted and interpreted the work within their own country. In the second, *The Distinguishing Marks of a Work of the Spirit of God* (Edinburgh and Glasgow, 1742), Edwards laid out a comprehensive and enlightened defense of the revivals by delineating the distinguishing marks of true piety overagainst counterfeit notions. Believing the work represented the most scriptural and well-reasoned presentation on experimental religion available, these Scottish Revivalists freely appropriated its teaching to defend the revivals against their detractors and to safely guide the subjects of the revivals through the experience of conversion. Following the revivals, these same ministers relied heavily on Edwards's *Distinguishing Marks, Some Thoughts Concerning the Present Revival of Religion* (Edinburgh, 1743), and later *Religious Affections* (1746) to work through the problems of sanctification for those who had "to appearances" been converted. In this context Edwards began to impress his particular religious ideals and values upon Scottish evangelicalism. In the end, his efforts helped his Scottish friends redefine Scottish evangelical Calvinism by adapting it from its old didactic/catechizing function within a godly commonwealth, to a more mission-oriented role where the faith of the individual became prominent and the pursuit of sanctification, not salvation, defined the Christian's life. One of the most far-reaching results of this shift was the growth of Scottish missions.[7]

Although the initiative for the Edwards/Scotland connection came from the Scottish side, Edwards looked on the prospect of corresponding with these Scots ministers as a gift and a privilege. By 1743, he had already received sufficient reports about the Scottish revivals for him to have gained a sense of the spiritual orientation and theological caliber of the men wanting to write him, and he was genuinely honored. "I esteem my correspondence with you and my other correspondents in Scotland," he wrote in 1745, "a great honor and privilege; and hope that it may be improved for God's glory, and my profit."[8] When speaking of the profit to himself that he hoped to gain, no doubt Edwards had in mind a thought he expressed in a diary entry twenty years earlier.[9] I am "more convinced than ever," he wrote on 6 February 1724, "of the usefulness of free religious conversation. I find by conversing . . . , I gain knowledge abundantly faster, and see the reasons of things much clearer, than in private study. Wherefore earnestly to seek at all times for religious conversation; for those that I can with profit and delight and freedom so converse with."[10] Edwards had learned early the personal benefits of the kind of informed dialogue these Scottish ministers could offer him, and he was eager to use this opportunity to its full advantage. The actual benefits Edwards derived from his correspondents were to exceed even his expectations. In fact, as I intend to demonstrate, he stood to benefit from the connection, at least on a personal level, more than his Scottish counterparts.

The outstanding benefit Edwards experienced from his Scottish correspondents was their remarkable capacity for helping him overcome the social, intellectual, and spiritual liabilities his living situation placed upon him. Geographically Edwards spent the first twenty-three years of his ministerial career in the provincial town of Northampton, located on the edge of the New England wilderness, and he spent the last seven years of his life in the wilderness on its western frontier at his missionary station at Stockbridge, Massachusetts. The effect of such isolation on the intellectual life was twofold. The first result was the limitation of opportunities for intellectually and spiritually stimulating conversation. When, in February 1724, Edwards recorded in his diary his thoughts on the usefulness of social conversation as a means of learning, he was then enjoying one of the rare times in his life in which his living situation afforded him such an environment. Unlike Yale, Northampton did not hold the same social and intellectual stimulation for Edwards. Much of what New England had to offer him in this way lay far to the east, in the vicinity of Boston. The best outlet in Northampton for the kind of conversation he desired came through the students he tutored who attended the informal theological school he had set up. Two of the students, Joseph Bellamy and Samuel Hopkins, became intimate, lifelong friends and ardent followers.[11] The other possible source of the kind of social discourse that Edwards hungered for came by way of visitors. Individuals en route to some place other than Northampton would often stop for the evening. However, with the exception of the years 1740 to 1743, such visits were somewhat infrequent.

The second effect was the lack of access to libraries and opportunities for securing books. Books were difficult to obtain in frontier towns, and public libraries were few and far between. Private libraries were even rarer. Before 1730 there were hardly more than half a dozen private libraries of any importance in the colonies.[12] Although the decade following would see a sharp improvement in the availability of books, most of what was available reflected popular tastes. During the same decade a number of new libraries were established as well, but none were accessible to Edwards. Typically, frontier ministers borrowed and swapped amongst themselves to secure suitable books.[13]

In addition to the liabilities of his geographical location, Edwards's social isolation was compounded by a growing alienation between himself and his congregation that began to surface not long after his Scottish correspondence commenced in late 1742 or early 1743. Tensions steadily increased during the years following the revivals, until, in 1749, he publicly announced that he could no longer in good conscience open the communion table to any but those who could make a sound profession of faith evidenced by an experiential work of grace. This brought Edwards into open conflict with his people. A year and a half later the Northampton congregation dismissed him from his charge.[14]

If during the years of Edwards's Scottish correspondence Northampton increasingly offered him much less of the kind of learned discourse he expressed a desire for in his diary that February day in 1724, his move to Stockbridge in 1751 served to exaggerate even more his social and intellectual isolation. Still, he was constantly driven by the desire for the exchange of ideas and the hunger for news of the learned world. His own attempts to rise above the liabilities his location imposed upon him included attendance at commencements at Yale and Princeton, the trips he took to Boston, his presence at a ministers' convention, and most importantly his continued association with Bellamy and Hopkins and his association with the students who attended his theological school.[15] Yet as helpful as these occasions and contacts may have been, with the exception of his students at Northampton and Hopkins during Edwards's Stockbridge years, they were relatively infrequent. Furthermore, they were often limited to provincial concerns, and lacked the intimacy of friendship.

The exchange of letters between Edwards and his Scottish correspondents, on the other hand, were generally frequent, filled with local, regional, and international religious and political news, and characterized by an intimacy unique to much of the corpus of Edwards's correspondence. Edwards's abiding interest in news of the work of God in the world was routinely stimulated as well as satisfied by these transatlantic missives. "When the day is so dark here in New England," he remarked, "it is exceeding refreshing and reviving to hear, by your and other letters, and Mr. Robe's history, of religion's being to such a degree upheld in the power and practice of it, in those parts of Scotland, that have been favored with the late revival."[16] Communication took place as often as their circumstances allowed. Delays could not always be avoided, however, and on occasion they produced concern over the state of their friendship. This occurred twice in the case of Edwards and William McCulloch. On each occasion, however, they reaffirmed their esteem for each other and commented on how "pleasant and profitable" they viewed their correspondence.[17] A letter written by William Cooper to John MacLaurin in June 1743, just as Edwards's epistolary connection with Scotland was beginning, provides a poignant illustration of the qualitative difference between Edwards's Scottish connection and many of his associations at home. Responding to MacLaurin's request for information about Edwards's ministry, Cooper admitted he had little to offer, that he had yet to pay Edwards a visit because of the great distance between Boston and Northampton, and that his Scottish correspondent probably knew more about matters pertaining to Northampton than he did anyway because of the particular accounts Edwards had been giving him.[18] The point is that Edwards's isolation was real, and the spiritual and intellectual camaraderie offered by his Scottish correspondents was viewed by him not as a luxury, but rather as the means of meeting a fundamental need in his life and ministry.

In contrast to the kind of isolation Edwards suffered, his Scottish correspondents were generally well connected and often enjoyed the kind of spiritual discourse he lacked. Even so, they recognized in Edwards a kindred spirit of uncommon ability.[19] Each one of his correspondents shared a common conviction that God had uniquely gifted and appointed Edwards to bring light and understanding in their day on some of the most important subjects pertaining to true religion. They were especially desirous to see his abilities enlisted on behalf of Scotland, confident from what they had already seen that his thinking would continue to be well adapted to their particular situation.[20] Consequently, each one found ways of encouraging Edwards's thinking, writing, and publishing, and each one used his position to promote the reading of the New Englander's works.

It took approximately three years before Edwards's Scottish epistolary network was complete. With one exception, the initiative in each case came from the Scottish side. John MacLaurin was the catalyst.[21] He initiated the epistolary connection and was the main instrument in bringing his fellow Scots into the network. Although none of the early correspondence between Edwards and MacLaurin has survived, Edwards's first letter to James Robe, dated 12 May 1743, suggests that MacLaurin's first letter must have been written no later than the early spring of that same year, and most likely before.[22] Parish minister of Ramshorn, Glasgow, MacLaurin was ten years Edwards's senior. He took an M.A. from the University of Glasgow in 1712 and spent a period of study in Leyden. He was ordained in 1719 and was translated to the Glasgow parish of Ramshorn in 1723, where he remained until his death in 1754.[23] As a theologian, he competed with William Leechman for the chair of Divinity at Glasgow, and though the overwhelming favorite, he was edged out through the influence of a powerful minority.[24]

It is not at all surprising that MacLaurin initiated the correspondence. By 1743 he had read enough of Edwards's work to recognize that he shared with Edwards a common theological vision and articulated it in a similar manner. He was nearer Edwards's equal than any of the others, and shared the same passion for the advancement of true religion in the world.[25] Like Edwards, he functioned theologically on a level above most of his contemporaries, and displayed the same ability as his New England counterpart to use Enlightenment conceptions for the purpose of explicating and defending orthodox and evangelical Calvinism.[26] Similarly, he recognized that the old formulations of doctrine and the categories of thought used to express them were rapidly becoming either obsolete or no longer relevant in light of the new complex of ideas and questions posed by the Enlightenment.[27] Moreover, he recognized that the new learning was not necessarily hostile to Christianity, and in fact could be used to philosophically ground evangelical Calvinism more firmly and articulate it much more effectively. As with Edwards, the alliance was made in order to harness the new thinking for the service of true religion; what was needed were "new wineskins," not new wine. The two also held as central concerns the reassertion of a divine centrality to the universe, the defense of the doctrines of grace, and the promotion of the free, unrestricted preaching of the word. Both men combined in an unusual way for the time the strains of evangelist and apologist. "In both of them," observed John MacLeod, "massive intellect went hand in hand with heart godliness of the most pervasive, controlling and winsome character."[28] What has been said of Edwards equally applied to MacLaurin: he was first and last a religionist who knew well "how to make all his reading subservient to religion."[29]

The only surviving piece of correspondence between Edwards and MacLaurin that is verifiable is an extract of a letter from Edwards dated 10 August 1743, published in the Boston-based periodical *Christian History*.[30] However, it is clear from the many references to their correspondence in the letters between Edwards and his other Scottish correspondents that the exchanges between them were not only frequent but extensive, and indicate a deep and mutual respect for one another. Part of MacLaurin's design for Edwards's letters was to distribute them to other interested parties. Consequently, a large number of the letters Edwards wrote to MacLaurin were written with a wider distribution in mind.[31] Through their long and extensive correspondence MacLaurin stimulated, challenged, and sharpened Edwards's thinking through a constant stream of news and ideas, and like his fellow Scots revivalists, MacLaurin defended Edwards's interpretation of the revivals, both against attacks brought against it in Scotland and in New England.[32]

MacLaurin's earnestness to help facilitate the propagation of Edwards's thinking is illustrated in a letter addressed to Mr. William Hogg. The letter concerns their plan to raise funds and other financial support in Scotland to assist Edwards and his family following his dismissal from Northampton. Speaking of the need, MacLaurin pointed out that such aid was deserving of one whose past works had been so greatly used of God and who holds such wonderful prospects for the future.[33] It was MacLaurin's deep conviction that the friends of true religion should do all they could to encourage the work of one as gifted as Edwards. In this context, it is interesting to notice that when MacLaurin penned the letter to Hogg some of the most important works of Edwards were yet to be written. Among them would be Edwards's celebrated treatises *Freedom of the Will* (1754) and *Original Sin* (1758). With respect to the former, the printing was actually postponed in Boston due to MacLaurin and John Erskine's offer to circulate subscription proposals in Scotland. As a result of their efforts, forty-five subscriptions were procured and eighty-eight copies were ordered.[34]

Soon after MacLaurin began writing Edwards, he encouraged James Robe, of Kilsyth, to do the same. Born in 1688, educated at Glasgow, and ordained to the ministry at Kilsyth in 1713, Robe posted his first letter to Edwards during the spring of 1743.[35] By the time he took up his pen, he was well acquainted with the heart of Edwards's religious convictions. He was one of the earliest in Scotland to endorse Edwards's *Faithful Narrative*, and drew from it both the inspiration and the pattern he used to structure his own revival histories: *A Short Narrative of the Work at Cambuslang* and *A Faithful Narrative of the Work of the Spirit of God at Kilsyth*. He was also the first Scot publicly to hail Edwards's *Distinguishing Marks of a Work of the Spirit of God* as a definitive justification of the revivals as a genuine work of the Spirit of God, and he spilled more ink in defense of Edwards's understanding of the revivals than any of his other fellow revivalists. His promotion of Edwards's ideas included the reprinting of letters from Edwards and excerpts from the *Faithful Narrative* in his monthly religious periodical, *Christian Monthly History*. Robe also succeeded in giving widespread distribution to Edwards's ideas by utilizing Edwards's morphology of conversion and principles of experimental religion set forth in his revival works to manage the revival at Kilsyth and to construct his own revival histories. Finally, Robe's industrious and methodical temperament richly served Edwards's hunger for religious news, as he sent report after report to him on Scottish and English religious events, first to Northampton and later to Stockbridge.

William McCulloch, of Cambuslang, was the third link in the epistolary chain. Ordained in 1731, McCulloch's influential ministry at Cambuslang spanned a half century.[36] He first heard of Edwards and the Northampton revival in the early part of 1735. Soon after he entered the ministry, McCulloch began to suffer from periods of doubt about his own conversion and his fitness for the ministry. A preaching series on the nature of conversion delivered during his first year helped to precipitate the crisis. The more he preached, he said, the less sure he became about his own spiritual experience.[37] News of the powerful outpouring of God's grace in the conversion of so many in Northampton in 1735 through the preaching of the doctrines of grace, however, succeeded in lifting McCulloch's spirits and inspired him to press on in hope that God might do the same at Cambuslang. Seven years later his hope was realized. With the coming of the Cambuslang Wark and the need to instruct and guide his people into an authentic saving encounter with Christ, McCulloch's appreciation of and reliance upon the New England minister's understanding of the nature and progress of conversion reached new heights. McCulloch was convinced that God had united Cambuslang and Northampton through a common work of the Spirit, and he was now eager and ready to further that connection through correspondence.

MacLaurin had informed Edwards that McCulloch had intended to send a letter to him with his and Robe's, but for some reason was prevented from doing so. Hearing this, Edwards promptly took the initiative himself and penned a letter to McCulloch on 12 May 1743: "Mr. MacLaurin of Glasgow, in a letter he has lately sent me, informs me of your proposing to write a letter to me, and being prevented by the failing of the expected opportunity: I thank you, Rev. Sir, that you had such a thing in your heart."[38] McCulloch was one of the first ministers of Scotland to take parts of Edwards's *Faithful Narrative* into the pulpit to read to his congregation. In addition he published extracts from Edwards's published works and letters in his religious periodical, the *Glasgow-Weekly-History*. Through his correspondence he gave Edwards opportunity to expand his thinking, especially concerning the relationship between present events and the apocalyptic events depicted in the Scriptures.

Edwards's coterie of epistolary friends also included John Willison.[39] Willison was the senior member of the group and one of the most respected and influential evangelical ministers of the Church of Scotland in the first half of the eighteenth century. He was born in 1680 and ordained in 1703, the year of Edwards's birth. In 1716 he took up the parish of Dundee South, where he remained until his death in 1750.[40] He published several influential works of devotion and publicly endorsed the revivals on both sides of the Atlantic, which in the case of the Scottish revivals was taken by many as an indication of their orthodoxy. As a part of his promotion of Edwards's work and thinking, Willison wrote the prefaces for the Scottish publications of Edwards's treatise *Distinguishing Marks of the Work of the Spirit of God* (Glasgow, 1742) and his sermon *Sinners in the Hands of an Angry God* (Edinburgh, 1745). His enthusiastic commendation of the former did much to establish Edwards's reputation as a champion of true religion.

> The ensuing Treatise, by the Reverend Mr. *Edwards* at *Northampton* in *New-England*, concerning the Work and Operations of the Holy Spirit upon Men's Consciences, is, in my humble Opinion, a most excellent, solid, judicious, and scriptural Performance, which, I hope, thro' the Divine Blessing, will prove most useful to the Church, for discerning a true and real Work of the Spirit of God, and for guarding against Delusions and Mistakes. It is certain a great Mercy to the Church, that this Subject hath been undertaken and handled by such an experienced well-furnish'd Scribe, that hath been long acquainted with the Spirit of God his Dealings with the Souls of Men, in his own Congregation, and Country where he lives. And seeing the extraordinary Work there at present . . . is of the same Kind with that at *Cambuslang*, and other Places about, and meets with the same Opposition; the Author doth, with great Judgment, answer the common Objections which are made against the Work, both here and there, so that scarce any Thing further needs be added.[41]

In 1743, Willison stepped forward and defended Edwards against James Fisher's vitriolic critique of *Distinguishing Marks*. Fisher (1697–1775), one of the founders of the Secession Church, painted Edwards as disillusioned, heretical, and an enemy of the lovers of true religion.[42] No doubt Willison also did what he could to promote Edwards's *Humble Attempt*, which he greatly admired and wished were spread throughout the world. His sentiments about the book seem to suggest, at least in part, the reason behind Edwards's favorable reputation among Scottish evangelicals. Speaking of the *Humble Attempt*, he states, "I both love and admire the performance upon subjects so uncommon."[43] Whatever subject Edwards treated, his Scottish friends came to expect from him a fresh and well-reasoned approach.

Thomas Gillespie opened the epistolary channel to Edwards with a letter written on 24 November 1746. Gillespie took his first degree at the University of Edinburgh and then attended the theological Academy at Northampton, where he came under the instruction of Philip Doddridge. He received his ordination in England, but afterward returned to Scotland, where he received a call to the parish at Carnock in Fife in the spring of 1741. He was deposed from his charge in 1752 by decision of the General Assembly and subsequently cofounded the Relief Church in 1761. He was a close friend of James Robe and on several occasions assisted him with the revival at Kilsyth.[44]

Like the others, Gillespie had carefully read Edwards's published works and found himself in essential agreement with him. He had especially benefited from Edwards's *Some Thoughts Concerning the Revival*, and had already perused Edwards's most recent work, *A Treatise Concerning Religious Affections*, by the time he wrote his first letter to the New Englander. With regard to the latter, he was particularly eager to solicit more from Edwards on the subject. Yet he delayed writing him. Apparently, being five years Edwards's junior, Gillespie was hesitant to impose himself on the celebrated minister.

> I have ever honored you for your works' sake, and what the great Shepherd made you the instrument of.... This much I think myself bound to say. I have many a time, for some years, designed to claim humbly the privilege of correspondence with you. What had made me defer doing it so long, when some of my brethren and good acquaintances have been favored with it, for a considerable time, it is needless now to mention. I shall only say, I have blamed myself for neglect in that matter. I do now earnestly desire a room in your prayers and friendship, and a letter from you sometimes, when you have occasion to write to Scotland; and I shall wish to be regular as I can, in making a return. With your permissions, I propose to trouble you now and

then with the proposal of doubts and difficulties that I meet with, and am exercised by; as for other reasons, so because some solutions in the two mentioned performances [*Distinguishing Marks* and *Some Thoughts*] were peculiarly agreeable to me, ... All the apology I make for using such freedom, though altogether unacquainted, is that you will find from the short attestation in Mr. Robe's Narrative, I am no enemy to you, or to the work you have been engaged in, and which you have defended in a way I could not but much approve of.[45]

Gillespie, as much as anyone, believed Edwards was uniquely gifted and called by God to write on the most pressing religious issues of the day. In his first letter to Edwards, he strongly encouraged him to write more fully on the subject of *supposed immediate revelations of facts and future events* which he had touched on first in *The Faithful Narrative*, treated at more length in *Distinguishing Marks* and *Some Thoughts*, and most fully in *Religious Affections*: "I humbly think the Lord calls you, dear Sir, to consider every part of that point in the most critical manner, and to represent fully the consequences resulting from the several principles in that matter.... And as (if I don't mistake) Providence has already put that in your hand as a part of your generation-work, so it will give me, as well as the others, vast satisfaction to find more said on the subject by you."[46] Gillespie's motive for wanting Edwards to explore the subject more thoroughly was that he was convinced that a complete discussion of the subject by Edwards would be "one of the most seasonable and effectual services done the church of Christ, and interest of vital religion through the world."[47]

Gillespie, like Edwards's other Scottish correspondents, believed Edwards was uniquely equipped to bring forth truth and understanding on the most critical matters pertaining to true religion. Consequently, in addition to his advocacy for Edwards's publishing enterprise, Gillespie also successfully drew Edwards into discussions that pushed him to develop and further clarify his thinking on issues of vital interest to Scotland. Gillespie's first question to Edwards, relating to his book *Religious Affections*, is a case in point. Gillespie perceived that Edwards's argument that confident believing and trusting in God is impossible "without spiritual light or sight" was open to misrepresentation, not only by his Scottish "friends," but more importantly by his Scottish detractors: "I expect a mighty clamor," he remarked, "if the book shall fall into their hands."[48] Consequently, he pressed Edwards on two different occasions to clarify his thinking on the subject.

John Erskine was the last to join the circle of Scottish ministers with whom Edwards corresponded on a regular basis. From the account provided us by

Erskine's biographer, Sir Henry Moncrieff Wellwood, it appears that Erskine first contacted Edwards near the end of 1746.[49] Erskine began his ministerial career at Kirkintilloch (1744–1753), moved to Culross (1753–1758), was translated to New Greyfriars in Edinburgh in 1758, and then to Old Greyfriars in 1767, where he ministered until his death in 1803. He was one of the leaders of the evangelical party in the Church of Scotland in the second half of the eighteenth century and was instrumental in its rise in influence at the beginning of the nineteenth century.[50] As a student at the University of Edinburgh, he had zealously defended the revivals.[51] In 1745, he published three sermons under the title *The People of God Considered as All Righteous,* with a preface in which he acknowledged his indebtedness to Jonathan Edwards's *Discourses on Important Subjects,* published in Boston in 1738. The impression made by this collection of sermons, especially Edwards's "Justification by Faith Alone," was the beginning of the New Englander's theological influence on Erskine.[52] Throughout the remaining years of his life Erskine would expend time, money, and much energy promoting and even publishing Edwards's works.

Although the youngest of all of Edwards's correspondents, none labored longer or more diligently on his behalf than Erskine. Erskine identified most fully with Edwards's writing and publishing enterprise, and embodied the expanded international evangelical perspective evident among his Scottish counterparts perhaps more thoroughly than the rest.[53] Almost from the moment he began corresponding with Edwards, Erskine sought to enhance, encourage, and stimulate the growth and impact of Edwards's writing and publishing ministry. This is nowhere more evident than in the flow of books, pamphlets, and sermons he sent to Northampton. Although the exchange of published materials was something that went on between Edwards and his other Scottish correspondents, the total contributions of the other five pale in comparison to what Erskine sent Edwards's way. Like the others, Erskine believed that it was part of the "generation-work" of Edwards to write on the most pressing theological questions of the day, and one of the ways he demonstrated this conviction was his habit of sending Edwards whatever books and pamphlets he thought useful. In just fourteen surviving letters between them, Edwards acknowledged receiving no less than fifty-four separate titles, and at least fourteen other books not specified, numerous sermons and pamphlets, and three entire packets of books and pamphlets that he failed to itemize. How many more books and pamphlets in addition to these Erskine may have sent we are unable to determine. But it seems certain that there were more.

In his first letter to Erskine, Edwards mentioned his plan to write a comprehensive refutation of Arminianism. With Erskine's next letter Edwards received several of the best books written in Britain in support of the Arminian position.[54] Among them were John Taylor's *Scripture-Doctrine of Original Sin, A Key to the Apostolic Writings,* and his *Paraphrase with Notes on the Epistle to the Romans.*[55] Edwards was particularly grateful for the paraphrase, which he had not heard of. He remarked that had he known of it, he would "not have been easy" until he had seen it.[56] The paraphrase would supply Edwards with the scriptural arguments behind Taylor's position which he later used in his work on the subjects of freedom of the will and original sin.

On 7 July 1752, Edwards wrote to Erskine, "I wish I could see a *History of Enthusiasm,* through all ages, written by some good hand, a hearty friend of vital religion, a person of accurate judgment, and a large acquaintance with ecclesiastical history. Such a history, well written, might doubtless be exceedingly useful and instructive, and a great benefit to the Church of God: especially, if there were united with it a proper account and history of true religion."[57] Soon after, Erskine sent Edwards two batches of pamphlets on the subject.[58] Then, in the spring of 1755, Edwards received another packet of books and pamphlets with the following titles among them: *Casaubon on Enthusiasm,* Warburton's *Principles of Natural and Revealed Religion,* Campbell's *Apostles No Enthusiasts, Discourse on the Prevailing Evils of the Present Time, Remarks on Apostles No Enthusiasts,* Moncrief's *Review and Examination of some Principles in Campbell's Apostles No Enthusiasts.* None of these fit the description of what Edwards was looking for, but it may have been that Erskine had it in mind to supply Edwards with the needed resources so that he could write the desired work on Enthusiasm himself.[59] Edwards did fit his own description of the sort of person to do it, with the possible exception of "well acquainted with ecclesiastical history."[60]

What Erskine's contribution meant to Edwards becomes even more apparent when comparing it with the total contents of Edwards's personal library. We know that by 1753 (just five years before his death) Edwards possessed 300 volumes and 536 pamphlets, which, according to the standards of the day, was unusually large for a personal library.[61] Given what we do know Erskine sent, and the fact that this very likely does not represent everything, it is possible that Erskine's contribution may have accounted for nearly a third of Edwards's library.[62] The importance of Erskine's contribution was that it allowed Edwards to bring to his thinking and writing a thoroughness of research, a depth of historical and contemporary understanding, and an international perspective almost unheard of among New England clergy. Edwards's literary acquaintance, concluded Thomas Johnson, would have been "unusual for any colonial minister; it was phenomenal for a provincial one."⁶³ What is obvious, though possibly not until now truly appreciated, is that behind the reality of this tribute lies Edwards's Scottish connection, and most prominently John Erskine.

Erskine's efforts were not limited to the sending of books. He also possessed a wealth of religious and intellectual knowledge that Edwards greatly desired. A facility in Latin, Greek, Hebrew, French, and later in Dutch and German opened for Erskine numerous avenues of information otherwise closed to the vast majority of evangelical ministers. He maintained literary correspondence with men in Holland and Germany, read foreign literary journals, and kept abreast of books published abroad. Few in the Church of Scotland were better acquainted with the state of learning, religion, and morals on the Continent, and whatever he thought was useful he passed on through private correspondence.⁶⁴ Edwards's connection with such a man was nothing less than an intellectual windfall, and he immediately recognized it to be the case and was anxious to receive as much as Erskine was prepared to share. In his letter of 14 October 1748, Edwards expressed his heartfelt thanks for the books and sermons sent, and then went on to say,

> I hope, dear Sir, you will continue still to give me particular information of things that appear, relative to the state of Zion and the interests of religion, in Great Britain or other parts of Europe. In so doing, you will not only inform me, but I shall industriously communicate any important informations of that kind, and spread them amongst God's people in this part of the world; and shall endeavour to my utmost to make such an use of them, as shall tend most to promote the interest of religion. And among other things I should be glad to be informed of any books that come out, remarkably tending either to the illustration or defence of that truth, or the promoting the power of godliness, or in any respect peculiarly tending to advance true religion.⁶⁵

In addition to feeding Edwards's mind, Erskine also actively sought to promote his works among his fellow Scots. For example, as observed earlier, with the aid of MacLaurin he procured forty-five Scottish subscriptions for eighty-eight copies of the first edition of Edwards's *Freedom of the Will*, published in Boston in 1754. But Erskine's esteem for Edwards inspired him to even greater efforts. Writing to McCulloch a few months after Edwards's death in 1758, he confessed, "I do not think our age has produced a divine of equal genius or judgment."⁶⁶ The real significance of this statement is revealed in Erskine's tireless engineering of the publication of hitherto unpublished manuscripts of

Edwards following his death. This he did through the cooperation of Edwards's son, the Rev. Dr. Jonathan Edwards Jr. The result was the publication in Edinburgh in 1774 of the series of sermons that Edwards had preached at Northampton in 1739, entitled by Erskine *A History of the Work of Redemption*. There followed in 1793 the *Miscellaneous Observations on Important Theological Subjects*, and in 1796 *Remarks on Important Theological Controversies*. These were some of the most important works of Edwards published posthumously, and it was Erskine that saw them through the press.[67]

Like the others, Erskine offered Edwards friendship as well. In these six Scottish ministers, Edwards found the intimacy, encouragement, comfort, trust, and loyalty that was all too rare in New England. The well-worn idea of "kindred spirits" seems to describe Edwards's Scottish epistolary connection particularly well. Never was this more evident than during the period of Edwards's dismissal from Northampton in the summer of 1750. At the time he had ten children and no prospects of resettlement. Nearly a year went by before he settled in Stockbridge, an Indian mission station located on the western frontier of Massachusetts. During the interim Edwards and his family were kept afloat through some preaching he was able to secure and through the generous gifts and efforts of their friends, not the least of which were those in Scotland.

The initial response from Edwards's Scottish correspondents to the news of his dismissal was an outpouring of comfort. Letters of sympathy and encouragement were sent by each one of his correspondents with the exception of Willison, who had died two months before. Gillespie's reaction is particularly noteworthy. Writing in reply to Gillespie's letter, Edwards began by acknowledging Gillespie's "most kind, affectionate, comfortable and profitable letter of Feb. 2, 1751. I thank you, Sir, for your sympathy with me under my troubles, so amply testified, and the many suitable and proper considerations you suggest to me for my comfort and improvement. May God enable me to make a right improvement of them."[68] Gillespie was well acquainted with the experience of spiritual conflict and temptation, and had recently written on the subject.[69] His capacity to empathize with Edwards is well attested to by Edwards's grateful and thoughtful response. Little did Gillespie know at the time that within a year the tables would be turned, that by a decision of the General Assembly he would be deposed and like his New England counterpart left without a charge.[70]

Edwards's friends in Scotland responded not only with sympathy and timely counsel, but also with money. W. H. Goold, in his edition of *The Works of John MacLaurin,* records a series of letters from MacLaurin to Mr. William Hogg, a merchant from Edinburgh and an admirer of Edwards, concerning donations arranged by MacLaurin and others for the aid of the Edwards family. In these letters, MacLaurin gives a running account of the reception of funds earmarked for Edwards's family, noting the amounts received and their origin.[71] Reference is also made concerning a collection of goods already underway that were to be shipped to Boston to be sold, the proceeds designated for the care of Mr. Edwards and family.[72] The following brief account of MacLaurin's attempt to secure the best possible return for the store of goods further underscores the sense of responsibility he had assumed.

> [. . .] as to providential Advantages by meeting with one thus allied to Mr. Edwards: one is, that instead of directing the Cargo to be sold by any of Mr. Edwards's friends to merchants at Boston, he shewed that if all were sent up the river of Connecticut, on which it seems Northampton stands, to Mrs. Edwards, she, by her fitness to dispose of such things in places near her, might make possibly about 15 per cent more than would be got by selling to Merchants at Boston.[73]

Mentioned as well is an attempt to secure a "Painter and Engraver" in Boston to draw a picture of Edwards to be printed on copper plates. These were to be shipped back to Scotland to be sold for the aid of Mr. Edwards.[74] While it is true that Edwards also received help from New England, it pales before the unusual and most extraordinary effort and expense freely expended on his behalf by his Scottish friends. It really is quite remarkable what these ministers of the Kirk were willing to do for a New England minister located on the edge of the Massachusetts wilderness; and it stands as a glowing tribute of their affection for him and the great esteem in which they held him.

However, the most revealing overture from Scotland came in a letter Erskine sent, interestingly enough, before Edwards's dismissal. Erskine had been aware of the escalation of difficulties between Edwards and his people for some time, and was writing to invite him to move his family to Scotland, volunteering at the same time to help negotiate clerical employment for him in the Church of Scotland. Erskine's letter has not survived, but Edwards's response has. His answer, written 5 July 1750 immediately following his dismissal, is particularly revealing and is quoted here in full.

> You are pleased, dear sir, very kindly to ask me, whether I could sign the Westminster Confession of Faith, and submit to the Presbyterian form of

Church Government; and to offer to use your influence to procure a call for me, to some congregation in Scotland. I should be very ungrateful, if I were not thankful for such kindness and friendship. As to my subscribing to the substance of the Westminster Confession, there would be no difficulty; and as to the Presbyterian Government, I have long been perfectly out of conceit of our unsettled, independent, confused way of church government in this land; and the Presbyterian way has ever appeared to me most agreeable to the word of God, and the reason and nature of things; though I cannot say that I think, that the Presbyterian government of the Church of Scotland is so perfect, that it cannot, in some respects, be mended. But as to my removing, with my numerous family, over the Atlantic, it is, I acknowledge, attended with many difficulties, that I shrink at. Among other things, this is very considerable, that it would be on uncertainties, whether my gifts and administration would suit any congregation, that should send for me without trial; and so great a thing, as such a removal, had need to be on some certainty as to that matter. If the expectations of a congregation were so great, and they were so confident of my qualifications, as to call at a venture, having never seen nor heard me; their disappointment might possibly be so much the greater, and they the more uneasy, after acquaintance and trial. My own country is not so dear to me, but that, if there were an evident prospect of being more serviceable to Zion's interests elsewhere, I could forsake it. And I think my wife is fully of this disposition.[75]

Edwards appears not to have considered the prospect of taking up a ministry in Scotland as disagreeable—daunting, yes: daunting at the thought of the journey across the Atlantic with his large family and the potential situation of being found unfit by a Scottish congregation. Theologically, there is reason to believe that he would have made the transition from a New England congregational minister to a minister of the Kirk relatively easily. His last sentiments would also indicate that with certain assurances he could possibly have been persuaded to undertake the arduous journey. At least it appears Erskine thought so, for by January of the following year he and MacLaurin had begun discussing a proposal, and in February met together to hammer out the fine details.[76] "I expect Mr. Erskine in town to-morrow," wrote MacLaurin to William Hogg, "and propose to concert with him as to laying before Mr. Edwards different overtures that have been thought of, as this, by Divine Blessing, may help to make a right choice and determination."[77] What became of this second proposal we do not know. None of the subsequent correspondence has survived. Although the prospect never materialized, one cannot resist asking the question, what if Edwards had taken up a ministry in the Scottish Kirk? It is a question that Erskine and MacLaurin pondered long in their willingness and eagerness to bring him to Scotland.[78]

The contributions to Edwards's thinking, writing, and spiritual well-being by his Scottish correspondents are difficult to overestimate. Many of the books that figured into Edwards's later works would have been extremely difficult, if not impossible, to acquire without the contributions particularly from Erskine. Further, given Edwards's location on the edge of the New England wilderness for much of his career, and in the wilderness the last several years of his life, the spiritual and intellectual fare his Scottish friends provided him kept his mind and heart healthy, fertile, lively, and on the cutting edge of the intellectual and religious currents of the day. Speaking of Edwards's isolation, Dwight observed that he was "with no libraries to explore, and with no men of eminence with whose minds his could come into daily contact."[79] How much more exaggerated would Edwards's isolation have been without the likes of Erskine and company?

Looking at Edwards's Scottish connection from the angle this paper has sought to provide, it is evident that the epistolary link opened a new chapter in Edwards's life, bringing unanticipated benefits that enhanced his ministry and intellect. Through their many exchanges these six Scottish ministers became some of Edwards's closest and most loyal friends, his most ardent supporters, and some of the most important contributors to the life of his mind during his remaining years. From them came a steady stream of books to expand his understanding and to sharpen his pen, and a loyalty that ultimately demonstrated itself in their willingness to make him a son of the Kirk.

NOTES

1. Susan O'Brien, "A Transatlantic Community of Saints: The Great Awakening and the First Evangelical Network, 1735–1755," *American Historical Review* 4 (October 1986): 819. O'Brien's work on the New England–Scotland revival connection represents the single most in-depth study of the subject available. See also, Susan Durden (O'Brien's maiden name), "A Study of the First Evangelical Magazines," *Journal of Ecclesiastical History* 27 (July 1976): 255–75, and Susan Durden, "Transatlantic Communications and Literature in the Religious Revivals, 1735–1745" (Ph.D. diss., University of Hull, 1978).

2. O'Brien, "Transatlantic Community of Saints," 819. Although Edwards did on occasion correspond with other Scottish ministers, for example Henry Davidson of

Galashiels and John Gillies, when he referred to his Scottish correspondents, he had these six primarily in mind.

3. Samuel Hopkins stated that Edwards had the "applause and admiration of America, Britain, Holland and Germany . . . , and has been honored above most others in the Christian world" in the eighteenth century (*The Life and Character of the Late Reverend Mr. Jonathan Edwards* [Boston: S. Kneeland, 1765], in David Levin, *Jonathan Edwards: A Profile* [New York: Hill and Wang, 1969], 22–23); Sereno E. Dwight, Edwards's great grandson, wrote in 1830 that Edwards's works "had gained him a reputation for powerful talents, both in Europe and America, which left him without a competitor, either in the colonies or the mother country" ("Memoirs," *The Works of Jonathan Edwards* [Edinburgh: Banner of Truth Trust, 1976 (reprint of the two-volume 1832 London edition)], 1:cxiv; hereafter cited as *Works of Edwards*). Of Edwards's transatlantic importance, both Hopkins and Dwight make the point that Edwards's ties with Scotland were by far the most significant. A. V. G. Allen, one of Edwards's nineteenth-century biographers, echoed this sentiment when he claimed that Scotland felt the influence of Edwards more than any other country (*Life and Writing of Jonathan Edwards* [Edinburgh: T and T Clark, 1889], 91). In 1903, for the bicentennial celebration of Edwards's birth, the renowned Scottish theologian James Orr spoke of Edwards's influence on Scotland as penetrating and "readily traceable" on a number of fronts ("Jonathan Edwards: His Influence in Scotland," *The Congregational and Christian World* 88 [1903]: 467); similarly, the Scottish historian G. D. Henderson stated that "there can be no doubt as to the importance of the influence he himself [i.e. Edwards] has exerted upon Scotland," and that "he undoubtedly left a permanent impression upon Scotland" (*The Burning Bush: Studies in Scottish Church History* [Edinburgh: Saint Andrew Press, 1957], 159, 162). In addition to the comments of Orr and Henderson, Sir James Mackintosh claimed that Edwards's "power of subtle argument was perhaps unmatched, certainly unsurpassed among men" (quoted in John Brown, ed., *Theological Tracts, Selected and Original* [London: A Fullerton and Co., 1853], 2:293–94). Similar tributes can be found in the writings of such prominent Scots as John Erskine, Dugald Stewart, Thomas Chalmers, and John MacLeod Campbell. More recently, American scholars of Edwards have initiated claims for Edwards's influence on Scotland: Paul Ramsey, commenting on Edwards's influence on Lord Kames's revisions to his *Essays on the Principles of Morality and Natural Religion* (1751), concluded that "these revisions clearly reflect the influence of Jonathan Edwards's ideas, and show, in one instance, what a force the theologian from the wilderness of America was in determining the currents of intellectual life in Scotland in the mid-eighteenth century" (Jonathan Edwards, *Freedom of the Will*, ed. Paul Ramsey, *The Works of Jonathan Edwards*, vol. 1 [New Haven: Yale Univ. Press, 1957], 444; hereafter cited as *Works*). John E. Smith, in his assessment of the correspondence that passed between Edwards and the

Scottish minister Thomas Gillespie, remarked that the "extent of Edwards's influence upon the religious situation in Scotland was considerable and it seems not to be generally known" (Jonathan Edwards, *Religious Affections,* ed. John E. Smith, *The Works of Jonathan Edwards,* vol. 2 [New Haven: Yale Univ. Press, 1959], 467).

4. The terms "vital," "real," and "serious" were also used at times to convey the idea behind "true" religion. The only treatment of the subject pertaining to the eighteenth century that I have been able to discover is found in Jaroslav Pelikan's *Christian Doctrine and Modern Culture (since 1700), The Christian Tradition: A History of the Development of Doctrine* (Chicago: Univ. of Chicago Press, 1991), 5:101–17.

5. In summary, the dramatically shifting intellectual atmosphere of eighteenth-century Europe that encouraged the role of reason, encouraged the belief in a law-governed universe, increased man's own sense of potential for moral and social good, and effectively overthrew Calvinism in England posed a serious threat to the doctrinal standards of Scotland and New England. See G. R. Cragg, *From Puritanism to the Age of Reason* (Cambridge: Cambridge Univ. Press, 1966), 13, chap. 2 passim.

6. For a full treatment of the subject, see Christopher W. Mitchell, "Jonathan Edwards's Scottish Connection and the Eighteenth-Century Scottish Revival, 1735–1750" (Ph.D. diss., University of St. Andrews, 1998).

7. Ibid.

8. *Apocalyptic Writings,* ed. Stephen J. Stein, *The Works of Jonathan Edwards,* vol. 5 (New Haven: Yale Univ. Press, 1977), 444. Although the recipient of the letter, dated 20 November 1745, is not given, it was most likely John MacLaurin.

9. Edwards made it a habit to regularly review the earlier resolutions he had made.

10. Hopkins, *Life and Character of the Late Reverend Edwards,* 21.

11. Bellamy took a ministry in Bethlehem, Connecticut, which at the time was on the northwestern outskirts of the colony, nearly seventy-five miles south of Northampton. For twenty-six years, beginning in December 1743, Hopkins served a Congregational church in Housatonic (later Great Barrington, Massachusetts), some forty miles southwest of Northampton but no more than ten miles from Stockbridge, which means that Edwards had the pleasure of more regular visits from Hopkins during the final years of his ministry.

12. Thomas H. Johnson, "Jonathan Edwards's Background Reading," *Publications of the Colonial Society of Massachusetts* 28 (Dec. 1931): 217.

13. Ibid., 218. "What literary background Edwards as a provincial minister could have," concluded Johnson in his study of Edwards's background of reading, he must have gotten "not by casually following the taste of the community, or by reading easily circulated books of the time, but rather only by an eager, patient, persistent effort of inquiry and intermittent reading." See ibid., 220–21.

14. An account of the events that led up to Edwards's dismissal and those that immediately followed is provided by Patricia Tracy, *Jonathan Edwards, Pastor: Religion and Society in Eighteenth Century Northampton* (New York: Hill and Wang, 1980), 147–94.

15. Johnson, "Jonathan Edwards's Background Reading," 221. In a letter to John Erskine, dated 5 July 1750, Edwards said of Bellamy: "he is one of the most intimate friends that I have in the world" (Jonathan Edwards, *Letters and Personal Writings*, ed. George S. Claghorn, *The Works of Jonathan Edwards*, vol. 16 [New Haven: Yale Univ. Press, 1998], 348).

16. Edwards, *Works*, 5:444.

17. See Edwards's letters of 21 January 1747, 7 October 1748, and 6 July 1750 to McCulloch in *The Works of President Edwards* (New York: Converse, 1829), 1:230, 261–62, 413.

18. *Christian Monthly History: or an Account of the Revival and Progress of Religion, Abroad and at Home*, 4 February 1744 (Edinburgh: R. Fleming and A. Alison, 1743–45), 6; hereafter cited as *CMH*.

19. The source of their confidence was the considerable body of Edwards's published work available in Scotland in 1743, and the testimonies concerning Edwards received from New England and printed in Scotland. For examples of the latter, see the *Glasgow-Weekly-History Relating to the Late Progress of the Gospel at Home and Abroad* (Glasgow: Wm. Duncan, 1743) (hereafter cited *GWH*), 35:1–5, 36:1–8, 37:1–5; and *CMH* (1743), 2:12, and (1745), 4:93–100.

20. Edwards, *Works*, 2:470.

21. According to Sereno E. Dwight, Edwards's great-grandson, Edwards's Scottish connection was initiated by John MacLaurin ("Memoirs," *Works of Edwards*, 1:lxxii).

22. In his letter to Robe, Edwards was responding to Robe's first letter written to him, which most likely was written sometime in March or April. In the same letter Edwards acknowledged that he had received a letter from MacLaurin the same day he received Robe's. If MacLaurin's letter was his second to Edwards, and a response to Edwards's reply to his first, it is reasonable to assume that MacLaurin would have initiated his first letter no later than February. However, we have no way of knowing for certain that these letters represent the beginning of their correspondence.

23. *Fasti Ecclesiae Scoticanae: The Succession of Ministers in the Church of Scotland*, ed. Hew Scott, 8 vols. (Edinburgh: Oliver and Boyd, 1915), 3:439. Hereafter cited as *FES*.

24. Burleigh attributes MacLaurin's defeat to Francis Hutcheson's "judicious wire pulling" that secured "against much opposition" Leechman's appointment (J. H. S. Burleigh, *A Church History of Scotland* (London: Oxford Univ. Press, 1960) 295–96.

25. John Gillies, "Memoir," in John MacLaurin, *The Works of John MacLaurin*, ed. W. H. Goold (Edinburgh: John MacLaren, 1860), 1:xvi, xix, xxiii.

26. James Walker, *Theology and Theologians of Scotland, 1560–1750* (Edinburgh: John Knox Press, 1982), 33–35; John MacLeod, *Scottish Theology: In Relation to Church History* (Edinburgh: Banner of Truth Trust, 1974), 189–97.

27. See Ian D. L. Clark, "Moderatism and the Moderate Party in the Church of Scotland" (Ph.D. diss., University of Cambridge, 1963), viii–ix.

28. MacLeod, *Scottish Theology*, 191.

29. Gillies, "Memoir," 1:xiv. For examples of MacLaurin's use of the new learning, see *Prejudices Against the Gospel*, 269–313, and *On the Scripture Doctrine of Divine Grace*, esp. sections 4–6, in MacLaurin, *Works of MacLaurin*, 1:402–85; and *Philosophical Inquiry into the Nature of Happiness*, in MacLaurin, *Works of MacLaurin*, 2:479–501.

30. *Christian History, containing Accounts of the Revival and Propagation of Religion in Great Britain and America*, ed. Thomas Prince, vols. 44–45 (Boston: Dec. 1743–Jan. 1744): 352–53. The missing correspondence between Edwards and MacLaurin is one of the most unfortunate dimensions of Edwards's Scottish connection. Two extant letters from Edwards to unnamed correspondents in Scotland (20 November 1745, in *CMH* 8 [Nov. 1745]: 234–54, and 12 May 1746, in *CMH* 10 [Jan. 1746]: 296–99) are thought to be addressed to MacLaurin.

31. MacLaurin, *Works of MacLaurin*, 1:xvi–xvii. Edwards regularly refers his other Scottish correspondents to his letters to MacLaurin.

32. For example, see *GWH*, 35:1–5; 36:1–8; 37:1–5.

33. MacLaurin, *Works of MacLaurin*, 1:xlviii.

34. Dwight, "Memoirs," *Works of Edwards*, 1:clxi. The figures were gathered from the subscriber list published with the 1754 Boston edition of Edwards's *Freedom of the Will*. The most important subscriber in terms of Edwards's association with Scotland was the celebrated minister of the Moderate Party, Hugh Blair, who ordered six copies.

35. *FES*, 3:479.

36. Ibid., 3:237–38. For a full account of McCulloch, I recommend Arthur Fawcett, *Cambuslang Revival: The Scottish Evangelical Revival of the Eighteenth Century* (London: Banner of Truth Trust, 1971). There is also an informative manuscript profile of McCulloch written by one who knew him, bound together at the beginning of vol. 1 of the Cambuslang manuscript testimonies, "Examination of Persons under Scriptural Concern at Cambuslang," at New College, Edinburgh.

37. Fawcett, *Cambuslang*, 43.

38. Edwards, *Works*, 16:105–7.

39. Unfortunately, we have no way of determining when the correspondence between Edwards and Willison began. We do know that Willison had been exchanging letters with Benjamin Colman since the 1730s, and with the Boston Presbyterian minister John Moorehead since the early 1740s. We also know that in 1743 he began

corresponding with Boston's influential Congregational minister Thomas Prince, who edited the religious periodical *Christian History*. The earliest extant evidence of a letter between Edwards and Willison is from Willison, dated 10 May 1748. It may be safe to assume that Willison's epistolary connection with Edwards began sometime between 1742, the year he wrote the preface for the Scottish edition of *Distinguishing Marks,* and 1745, when he wrote the preface to Edwards's sermon *Sinners in the Hands of an Angry God.* Cf. *GWH,* 42:1–3; Edwards, *Works,* 5:271.

40. *FES,* 5:320–22; See also, W. M. Hetherington, "An Essay on His Life and Times," in *The Practical Works of the Rev. John Willison* (Glasgow: Blackie and Son, 1844).

41. Willison, "Preface," 23 June 1742, *Distinguishing Marks* (Glasgow: R. Smith, 1742).

42. James Fisher, *Review of the Preface to the Kilsyth Narrative* (Glasgow: Patrick Bryce, 1742).

43. Letter from Willison to Edwards, 17 March 1749, *Works of President Edwards* (New York: Converse, 1829), 1:272.

44. *FES,* 5:10–11; see also *The Life and Times of the Rev. Thomas Gillespie, father and Founder of the Relief Church,* in William Lindsay's *Lives of Ebenezer Erskine, William Wilson, and Thomas Gillespie, Fathers of the United Presbyterian Church* (Edinburgh: A. Fullerton and Co., 1849), 217–306.

45. Letter to Edwards, 24 November 1746, Edwards, *Works,* 2:470–71.

46. Ibid., 2:471.

47. Ibid. Gillespie's interest in the subject of immediate revelations was longstanding, and he eventually published a small treatise on the topic entitled *An Essay on The continuance of immediate revelations of facts and future events in the Christian church* (Edinburgh: A. Murray and J. Cochran, 1771). Although it was not published until 1771, William Lindsay judges that it was probably written sometime during the year 1747, soon after Gillespie began his correspondence with Edwards (Lindsay, *Life and Times of Thomas Gillespie,* 253).

48. Edwards, *Works,* 2:473, 474. The argument Gillespie is referring to is found on pp. 175–76.

49. Wellwood indicates that Edwards responded to Erskine's first letter in 1747. In the postscript to his letter, Edwards mentioned he was including a copy of his book *Religious Affections,* which had recently been published. *Religious Affections* was published in Boston in 1746, and Gillespie had access to it by November of the same year. This would seem to indicate that Edwards's letter must have been penned early in 1747, if Wellwood is correct. This in turn would suggest that Erskine's initial letter was likely written near the end of 1746. See Sir Henry Moncrieff Wellwood, *Account of the Life and Writings of John Erskine, D.D. Late one of the Ministers of Edinburgh* (Edinburgh: George Ramsay and Company, 1818), 195–97.

50. *FES,* 1:47–48. See also Thomas Davidson, *A Sketch of the Character of Dr. John Erskine, one of the Ministers of the Old Gray Friars Church of Edinburgh,* . . . *being the concluding part of a Sermon delivered in that Church, on the Lord's Day immediately after his Funeral* (Edinburgh: H. Inglis, 1803); and Rev. John Inglis, *The Memory of the Righteous; A Sermon, Preached in the Old Gray Friar's Church, Edinburgh, on 30th January 1803, Being the first Sabbath After the Funeral of the Rev. John Erskine* (Edinburgh: James Ballantyne, 1803).

51. Richard B. Sher, *Church and University in the Scottish Enlightenment: The Moderate Literati of Edinburgh* (Princeton: Princeton Univ. Press, 1990), 31–32. Erskine published his thoughts on the Scottish revival while a student at the University of Edinburgh in an essay entitled *Sign of the Times consider'd: or, The High Probability, that the present Appearances in New-England and the West of Scotland, are a Prelude of the Glorious Things promised to the Church in the latter Ages* (Edinburgh: T. Lumisden and J. Robertson, 1742).

52. Henderson, *The Burning Bush,* 154.

53. Ned Landsman makes out a similar case for Erskine in "John Witherspoon and the Problem of Provincial Identity in Scottish Evangelical Culture," *Scotland and America in the Age of Enlightenment,* ed. Richard B. Sher and Jeffrey R. Smitten (Princeton: Princeton Univ. Press, 1990), 34.

54. Wellwood, *Life and Writings of Erskine,* 199–201.

55. John Taylor (1694–1761) was minister at Norwich from 1733 until 1757, when he took a post of divinity tutor at Warrington Academy. The influence of Samuel Clarke's *Scripture-Doctrine of the Trinity* caused Taylor by 1737 to formally give up his Trinitarian belief, and in 1740 he made explicit his Arminian convictions in his work on original sin.

56. Letter to Erskine, 31 August 1748, in Edwards, *Works,* 16:248.

57. Edwards, *Works,* 16:490.

58. Edwards to Erskine, 23 November 1752, in Edwards, *Works,* 16:537. Among the books received was a French edition of a treatise *Against Fanaticism,* which Edwards admitted he could not use because he could not read French.

59. Edwards to Erskine, 15 April 1755, in Edwards, *Works,* 16:661.

60. Edwards preached a series of sermons in 1739 on the subject of Redemption from a historical perspective that demonstrates a fair measure of conversancy in the area of the history of the Church. See Jonathan Edwards, *A History of the Work of Redemption,* ed. John F. Wilson, *The Works of Jonathan Edwards,* vol. 9 (New Haven: Yale Univ. Press, 1989).

61. The figures come from a will that Edwards made in 1753 cited in Johnson, "Jonathan Edwards's Background Reading," 199.

62. Although Erskine was better settled financially than most ministers of his time, the flow of books and pamphlets he sent to Edwards was primarily the result of a naturally generous spirit and his desire to provide others with the same advantages he himself possessed, among whom Edwards was chief (Davidson, *A Sketch of the Character of Dr. Erskine,* 12–13). Erskine makes clear his estimate of the importance of Edwards to the church in the eighteenth century in a letter to McCulloch on 8 August 1758: lamenting the untimely death of Edwards, he states, "The loss sustained by his death, not only by the College of New Jersey, but the church in general is irreparable. I do not think our age has produced a divine of equal genius or judgment" (Wellwood, *Life and Writings of Erskine,* 224).

63. Ibid., 221.

64. Davidson, *A Sketch of the Character of Dr. Erskine,* 12–13. Although Erskine's acquaintance with German and Dutch came too late for Edwards to benefit, the fact remains that Erskine was, along with MacLaurin, a primary source of international religious news.

65. Edwards, *Works,* 16:260.

66. Wellwood, *Life and Writings of Erskine,* 224.

67. It is worth mentioning that Erskine's edition of the *Work of Redemption* was only superseded in 1989 with John Wilson's definitive edition (see Edwards, *Works,* vol. 9), and only with the completion of the Yale edition of Edwards's "Miscellanies" will the material contained in Erskine's editions of *Observations* and *Remarks* be superseded. If Erskine had not collected and printed these works, very likely they would have remained unpublished.

68. Letter to Gillespie, 1 July 1751, in Edwards, *Works,* 16:380.

69. Thomas Gillespie, *A Treatise on Temptation* (Edinburgh, 1774). Although, it was not published until 1774, Gillespie composed it sometime in 1744 (Lindsay, *Life and Times of Thomas Gillespie,* 240.).

70. On the deposition of Gillespie, see Gavin Struthers, *The History of the Rise of the Relief Church* (Edinburgh, 1848), 219–23; Hugh Watt, "Thomas Gillespie," *Records of the Scottish Church History Society* 15 (1966): 89–101; and Kenneth B. E. Roxburgh, *Thomas Gillespie and the Origins of the Relief Church in Eighteenth-Century Scotland* (Bern, New York: Peter Lang, 1999). For a view taken from the Moderate side of the controversy, see Sher, *Church and University in the Scottish Enlightenment,* 54–55, 68.

71. MacLaurin, *Works of MacLaurin,* 1:xlvii–liii.

72. Ibid., xlvii, xlix–liii.

73. Ibid., li–lii.

74. Ibid., xlviii.

75. Edwards, *Works,* 16:355–56.

76. MacLaurin, *Works of MacLaurin,* 1:l, lii.

77. Ibid., 1:lii. The letter is dated 11 February 1751.

78. See Wellwood's discussion of this proposal in *Life and Writings of Erskine,* 514–15n. X.

79. Dwight, "Memoirs," *Works of Edwards,* 1:clxxxvii.

Missions and Historical Memory
Jonathan Edwards and David Brainerd

Andrew F. Walls

The Missionary Movement and Western Christianity

The missionary movement was a result of the shock impact upon Europe of the worlds beyond the West; in the religious sphere it was the most important outcome of that impact, not least because it occurred at the high point of the Europeanization of Christianity. Over the centuries in which Christianity was being honed to the conditions of Europe, and taking a distinctively Western form, the once buoyant and expansive forms of Christianity that had been characteristic of much of Asia and parts of Africa were going into eclipse. The form of Christianity that Europeans knew, and seemed to them normative, was territorial in expression. Conceptually, Christendom consisted of contiguous territory ruled according to the law of Christ by Christian princes subject to the King of kings, with no public place for idolatry, or blasphemy, or heresy.

When Europe emerged in the late fifteenth century from its long insulation into a much wider world, the first instinct of Western Christians was to seek to incorporate the lands they now came upon into Christendom. For this purpose the already established model of crusade was adapted. In the Spanish Americas and some other places conversion followed conquest and the boundaries of Christendom were thereby enlarged. A few places—the Congo kingdom of Soyo, for instance—entered Christendom voluntarily. But in most of the new world now open to the West, especially in the great Asian land mass, conversion was at best a distant dream, and conquest an impossibility.

This reality produced differing reactions among European Christians. Economic and political considerations now tied the Western powers—first Spain and Portugal, then the powers of northern Europe—to ongoing involvement in the non-Western world; but the concept of the maintenance and extension of Christendom, originally integral to the enterprise, gradually receded from view. The public policy of the states of Christendom no longer actively pursued it as a goal desirable in itself. Europeans settled or working in the non-Western world could ring-fence their own Christian profession, and get on with the business of war, or settlement, or simply making money, without much concern about the religious systems of the host societies.

It was radical Christians, what one might call totalitarian Christians, those for whom the religious imperatives overcame the economic and political, who found this state of disengagement unacceptable. And it was among the radical Christians that the missionary movements, first Catholic and then Protestant, arose. The missionary principle differed from the crusading principle in that it was based on demonstration and persuasion rather than coercion. It did not in itself extend Christendom (though for a long time, many, perhaps most, missionaries hoped that it eventually would do so). It operated outside the sphere of Christian law and beyond the concept of a Christian civil society.

Relations with the non-Western world, and the colonial relationship in particular, helped to undermine the Christendom principle in Europe.[1] At the same time, largely through the agency of the missionary movement, new Christian communities developed in the non-Western world, communities which did not embody the territorial Christendom principle. The missionary movement was rarely a primary concern of the official Western church, and usually involved the energies of only a minority among those in Europe who professed and called themselves Christians, but it did much to change the demographic and cultural composition of the Christian church. What began as an attempt to extend Christendom ended by superseding Christendom.

The extent of the revolution effected through the missionary movement was not visible until the second half of the twentieth century. Since European minds were shaped by the experience of centuries of Christendom, Western missionaries held to Christendom concepts even when the logic of their activities and of the situation pointed in other directions. For a long time after the beginnings of the movement the only instruments, intellectual or logistical, that missionaries and their sponsors had were instruments that had been forged in Christendom. The very concept of a missionary had to be built from European patterns of Christian ministry; and those patterns were conditioned by territorial concepts, such as the parish. (It was fortunate that there were additional structures available in Western Christianity—Catholic orders and societies, Protestant voluntary societies, Methodist itinerancy—that had arisen where parochial and other territorial models had manifestly failed). The message that the missionary was expected to proclaim, the duties which he (inevitably "he," since the foundation on which the missionary concept was raised was that of the male territorial ministry within Christendom) was expected to carry out, were in all essentials those thoroughly tested by experience in Europe. The responses to be expected to the missionary's message and the result of his activities were similarly shaped by the experience of Christendom. Radical Christians, who sought reformation and renewal and were dissatisfied with the normal standards of attainment in Christendom, had particularly clear expectations about the forms of response, both positive and negative, that would follow faithful proclamation of the Christian message. Missionaries began by doing what they had always done, usually in the way they had always done it, expecting the patterns of response that had emerged in the experience of Christendom. They entered upon the great learning experience of Western Christianity when, as representative Western Christians, they discovered the limitations of the confident encyclopedia of knowledge, theology, and practice that had been built up over the centuries of Christian interaction with European cultures, and sought to expand or transcend it. In the process they found themselves cultural and theological brokers between two worlds.

The Historical Memory of the Missionary Movement

The missionary movement had its own historical memory and a highly developed sense of pedigree. As it was a product largely of peripheral forces within Western Christianity, few of the central, norm-setting figures of church history figure prominently in it. Its main dynamic always came from radical Christians, and among radical Protestants the Reformation and the Evangelical Revival always held a high symbolic place in the memory. But attempts to detect a serious concern for mission in the non-Western world in Luther or Calvin have never looked convincing, and it might be argued that John Wesley (despite meanings imported into his famous phrase "The world is my parish") did as much to restrain Methodists from activity outside the Western world as to promote world mission.

Jonathan Edwards was in this respect rather unusual, a central, norm-setting figure whose place in the historical memory of the missionary movement is secure. He can, like John Wesley, be held to have been personally a participant in missions, even if largely by default, through his Stockbridge exile. More significantly, he was an important theological influence on early Protestant missionaries from the English-speaking world. A stream of thinking passed from Edwards through Hopkins and watered the soils in which the early American missionary recruits grew and flourished. Edwards's theological principles on the freedom of the will and the religious affections also helped to liberate English (and perhaps Scottish) Calvinism and to make a dynamic theology of mission possible for Calvinists.[2] The greater number of the English-speaking missionaries whose service began in the last decade of the eighteenth century and the first three decades of the nineteenth had their background in that liberated Calvinism.

A good representative of Edwards's indirect influence is David Bogue,[3] a Scot who influenced a whole generation of missionaries. The Missionary Society, as the body later known as the London Missionary Society was originally called, initially demanded no theological education of its would-be missionaries. The assumption was that most candidates would come from the shop or the forge, rather than from the usual sources of supply of the ministry, and that the manual skills of such people would fully compensate for any inadequacy in the dead languages which underlay conventional theological education.[4] There were enough unmitigated disasters among missionaries recruited on this principle to persuade the Missionary Society otherwise, and from 1800 until his death in 1825 the Society entrusted the theological education of missionaries to Bogue. Candidates continued to come from the shop or the forge, but they were put through a demanding course of study. Bogue did not lecture; he wrote an outline of a topic, leaving several inches of space under each heading, and gave a reading list. Students were expected to copy the outline, fill in the intervening spaces, and enter into oral dialogue with Bogue on the results. The readings were from books in his own library, and Edwards is prominent in the lists. That the system was judged effective by those who went through it is shown by the fact that a group of his students conspired to publish the outlines (without the intervening spaces) after his death, and by the appearance of an American edition immediately thereafter.[5] When a college was established in the 1840s in Raratonga for the training of Polynesian evangelists for service in the Pacific, the resident missionary, Aaron Buzacott, took the students through Bogue's lectures, and eventually translated them into the vernacular and printed them.[6] Under such circumstances a somewhat diluted version of Edwards's teachings was spreading in the South Pacific long after his death.

But great as his direct and indirect influence undoubtedly was, Edwards the theologian, with one well-known exception, does not figure greatly in the historical memory of the missionary movement. Individual missionaries, as Stuart Piggin has shown,[7] read him avidly, but not all missionaries were avid theological readers. And the mentor that a generation of LMS missionaries remembered was not Edwards, but Bogue.

The exception, the one element in the Edwardsian theological inheritance that entered into the collective missionary memory is, of course, the *Humble Attempt to Promote Explicit Agreement and Visible Union of God's People in Extraordinary Prayer*.[8] More than forty years after its composition, this tract helped to inspire the Baptist circle to which William Carey belonged, and was thus instrumental in the founding of the Baptist Missionary Society,[9] despite the fact that the book's eschatological scheme was by then demonstrably flawed. One of the circle, John Sutcliff, produced a cheap new edition,[10] and Carey himself cited the work in his *Enquiry into the Obligations of Christians to Use Means for the Conversion of the Heathens*.[11]

The story, involving as it does contact and interaction between Congregationalists in New England, Presbyterians in Scotland, and Baptists in the English Midlands, illustrates the informal networks that linked practitioners of evangelical religion across barriers of geography and confession.[12] It also offers a study in the application of ideas. The *Humble Attempt* is not a book about missions; it is a book about prayer. It became a book about missions because the group of people who were reading it already had the germ of the idea of an overseas missionary enterprise. Edwards's expansive ideas of the sovereignty of Christ and the post-millennial eschatology which these latter day Puritans inherited served to enrich, inform, and confirm an enterprise already conceived.

The Life of Brainerd and the Missionary Movement

Despite legend, the work of Carey does not mark the beginning of the Protestant missionary movement, only the significant entrance of British Christians into it. The movement had begun almost a century earlier in Germany and central Europe.[13] But in one sense it had begun earlier still. The missionary movement as it developed was essentially maritime in its thinking; Christendom and the non-Christian world were divided by oceans. But in North America Protestant Christians for the first time lived side by side with a non-Christian people. As happened elsewhere, the initial desire to bring these peoples into the Christian fold, while never abandoned, receded before temporal considerations. Theological principle—the Redeemer's throne set up in America where Satan had once ruled—sat uneasily with the practical realities of daily relations between Western Christians and Native Americans. The latter were not a distant people to be evangelized by specially devised means; they were the neighbors, and neighbors with whom relations were, to say the least, ambivalent. It is from this borderland of Christendom, a mission field without the maritime element that came to be an essential ingredient in Western thought about missions, that Edwards's greatest impact on the historical memory of the missionary movement was made.

Incomparably the fullest and most direct influence of Edwards on the later missionary movement lay in his making available the journal of David Brainerd, missionary to the Native Americans of the Society in Scotland for Promoting Christian Knowledge.[14] Many hundreds of missionaries and prospective missionaries read the book in some shape or form, and many were stirred by it. By the early nineteenth century Brainerd had become the Protestant icon of the missionary, its ideal type, as a result of the published journal. Every new missionary—typically, a man in his twenties, was taught thereby to see this young man as the pattern for what his own life ought to be.

Brainerd's status as the icon of the Protestant missionary was perhaps attained by only one other figure, the English clergyman Henry Martyn, who ironically was not in the technical sense a missionary but a chaplain of the East India Company.[15] Martyn was himself deeply influenced by Edwards's presentation of Brainerd's journal. And Martyn's story had much in common with Brainerd's—young, cultured, articulate, consumptive, depressive men, marriage unfulfilled for the gospel's sake, burning themselves out in the work. The portraits elided; Martyn was Brainerd for a new generation.[16]

Martyn felt Brainerd coming alive from the page, so that he entered into a sort of conversation with him. He confides, "I feel my heart knit to that dear man, and really rejoice to think of meeting him in heaven."[17] On another occasion he says, "That dear saint of God David Brainerd is truly a man after my own heart. Although I cannot go half way with his spirituality and devotion, I cordially unite with him in such holy breathings as I have attained unto."[18] When his ship put into Cape Town en route for India, and he made the acquaintance of James Read of the London Missionary Society, his mind again went to the book: "I was so charmed with his company that I fancied myself in company with David Brainerd."[19] For Martyn, born more than thirty years after Brainerd's death, Brainerd had become a contemporary.

And at the end of the nineteenth century, the high peak of the missionary movement, Brainerd's life was still being set before missionary recruits. Eugene Stock, the historian of the (Anglican) Church Missionary Society, writing in the 1890s after referring to the great Native American in-gathering at Crossweeksung in response to Brainerd's preaching, goes on: "But Brainerd did less in his lifetime than his biography, by President Edwards, did after he was gone. In its pages is presented the picture of a man of God such as is rarely seen. No book has, directly or indirectly, borne richer fruit."[20]

The spiritual fathers of late Victorian times who pointed new missionaries toward Brainerd recognized that we know Brainerd only because of Edwards. When Sereno Edwards Dwight produced an enlarged edition of the Brainerd journals in 1822, he described Brainerd as the person "who would probably be selected by all denominations of Christians as the holiest *missionary*, if not the holiest *man* of modern times," and he suggested that the time was near when Brainerd would be better known all over the world than Alexander, Julius Caesar, or Napoleon.[21] Nevertheless he did not include the book in his collected works of Jonathan Edwards, his reason being that so little of the work was by Edwards himself.[22] The fact remains that the book owed its origin and its shape to Edwards, and it probably had a more profound effect on a wider range of people than did many of the master's weightier treatises.

But there was a dash of gall mixed into this spiritual elixir, and every reader could taste it. It is impossible to disguise the depressive strain in Brainerd's journals, and Edwards does not attempt to do so. He reproduces sections where the writer is "filled with sorrow and confusion,"[23] "distressed by a sense of spiritual pollution,"[24] and so confused by inward anguish that he lost the track of his sermon.[25]

Edwards actually warns the reader against this "melancholy," which he did not regard as a necessary ingredient of proper self-examination. He reflected that it might have been contained had Brainerd gone with a companion; after all, the Lord sent his disciples in pairs. He also identified a physical element and thought Brainerd willfully reckless in putting his life into danger.[26] Martyn, with depressive tendencies himself, takes up the hint. He concludes it was improper for Brainerd to attempt what he did at a time when he should have been in medical care—was Brainerd perhaps overanxious to obtain his own good opinion?[27] The editor of an early short version advises the reader to discount the melancholy as "purely animal,"[28] that is, arising from Brainerd's distressing physical condition. Others found its origin in the theological and pastoral inadequacies of Calvinism. "How much of his sorrow and pain had been prevented" cries Wesley, "if he had understood the doctrine of Christian perfection!"[29] For the spiritual mentors of the Student Volunteers, deeply influenced by the doctrines and experiences of the Keswick Convention, Brainerd's melancholy was a theological puzzle. "I know nothing more resembling Pentecost than the scenes following [Brainerd's] preaching at Crossweeksung," says A. J. Gordon of Boston,[30] but how did someone who manifestly displayed the indwelling of the Holy Spirit not know the exultant spiritual liberty that was part of the Keswick message and a regular ingredient of much contemporary evangelical teaching?

Brainerd—Missionary or Minister?

For a period at the beginning of the nineteenth century, Edwards's presentation of Brainerd had another place in the historical memory of the missionary movement. Not only did *Life of Brainerd* provide the icon of the missionary as regards motivation and inner life; it was also one of the very few accessible accounts in English of the day-to-day work of a missionary in contact with people of another language and culture—one of the very few works that reflected on what a preacher so circumstanced should say and how he should communicate it.

When the group of Anglican clergymen who formed the Church Missionary Society in 1799 set up their first library, "Brainerd's Life" was the first of the titles they selected. There were only thirteen titles in all, and five of these were current periodicals. Apart from Edwards's presentation of Brainerd's journals, the committee could find only a few continental works in translation describing the work of Moravian missions and that of the Danish Lutheran Hans Egede in Greenland[31] to provide firsthand accounts of modern Protestant endeavors to present the gospel across a cultural divide.

It is something of a shock to realize that this is not how Edwards viewed Brainerd's work. The founders of the Church Missionary Society who compiled this library had the maritime consciousness characteristic of the developing missionary movement—mission lay overseas. Edwards was looking out at the New England that he knew, with its diverse layers of population.

The chapter that Edwards appended to *Life of Brainerd*,[32] in which he assesses the significance of Brainerd, is instructive. The first and longest section focuses not on the Indians' conversion, but on Brainerd's own. It analyzes the marks of authenticity in his experience that were missing from the testimonies of many who claimed the same experience of conversion to God. The second section distinguishes between the genuine and the spurious in religious affections as displayed in times of revival, rebutting the idea that Brainerd's work at Crossweeksung was of the same kind as some recent revivals among white settlers. Edwards's point, however, is not that the Crossweeksung movement took place in a Native American community, but that (unlike some contemporary movements among the settlers where the response was spectacular, but transient) it effected a lasting transformation. The third section argues that Brainerd's life displays the sharp difference between experimental religion and mere emotional imaginations. The fourth seeks to demonstrate that Brainerd's ministry proves the efficacy of the doctrines of grace, in opposition to Arminian objections. The fifth displays Brainerd as an exemplar for candidates for the ministry, and the sixth as an exemplar for religious practice, notably with regard to fasting. Only with the seventh reflection, a short one, do we reach what one might call the specifically missionary dimension of Brainerd's career; how it encourages God's people to prayer and endeavors for the advancement and enlargement of the kingdom of Christ in the world, and in particular for the conversion of the Indians "on this continent." Edwards pauses to consider how Crossweeksung might be the forerunner of something much more glorious and extensive of that kind. But the visionary pause is brief; he quickly passes to practical matters like sending missionaries in pairs (we have already seen that he believed this might have kept Brainerd's depressive tendencies in check) and to a consideration of the special providences attending Brainerd's last illness and death.[33]

For people building up a library for an infant mission agency, the life of Brainerd was a rare example of Christian preaching among people of another language and culture, or, as they would have said, other manners and customs. For Edwards, who made that life known to the world, it was primarily a demonstration of the true character, authentic experience, and proper doctrine of a Christian minister. An almost contemporary throwaway remark by John Wesley suggests a similar conclusion. Wesley believed that "even so good a man" as Brainerd overestimated his own work. "The work among the Indians, great as it was, was not to be compared to that at Cambuslang, Kilsyth, or Northampton."[34] For Wesley, who made the first of the hosts of popular abridgements of the memoir, it was valuable not because it would call people to the mission field, but because it would teach them devotion and acceptance of harsh conditions in their service in England.[35] For Wesley and Edwards alike, what we would call the cross-cultural aspect of Brainerd's work was coincidental. For them, Crossweeksung is of one kind with Cambuslang and Northampton. A generation later, in the historical memory of a missionary movement that saw its task as the establishment of the Church of Christ among non-Western and hitherto non-Christian peoples, Brainerd, as presented by Edwards, was reconceived as the missionary par excellence.

Evangelical Preaching, Christendom, and the Missionary Movement

The missionary movement, with its requirement to live on terms set by the life of a society other than one's own, marked a breach with the centuries-old idea of Christendom. This posited a civil society in nominal allegiance to Christ, and a pastoral duty of the Church to bring that civil society into true harmony with its Christian profession. There is very little sense of such a breach in Edwards, very little to indicate that he saw any particular significance in the missionary office that was not already present in the ministerial.

Edwards and Brainerd—and for that matter Wesley—are transitional figures in the history of the missionary movement. They operated before the movement emerged in the English-speaking world as a distinct element in Protestant consciousness. They thought in terms of Christendom and the traditional responsibility of the Christian ministry within it. But they thought as evangelicals, that is, as radical, "totalitarian" Christians.

Evangelical consciousness saw all humanity as one in sin, misery, and loss, one in redemption and holiness in Christ. There was thus a single message for the moneymaking merchant in Massachusetts and those whom merchant and minister alike might describe as "rude savages." Brainerd refers to "white heathens" being affected during the movement among the native peoples at Crossweeksung.[36] Heathenism was not a religion but a state of mind, and it had nothing to do with race.

Evangelical religion was a product of Christendom. It assumed a civil society that nominally accepted Christian symbols and Christian norms, but which fell drastically short of those norms in reality. Evangelicalism was thus about "real Christianity" over against the formal and the nominal profession of it, about the inward religion of the heart turned toward God. Evangelicalism was by its nature protest religion, a protest movement against a society that claimed to be Christian but denied that claim in its practice. Classical evangelicalism required nominal Christianity in order to define itself, and assumed the presence of a Christian (even if defectively Christian) civil society.

The Native Americans that Brainerd and Edwards knew lived on the margins of Christendom. These damaged, dislocated, partially demoralized, and perennially alcoholic communities had lost the integrity of traditional life. Their whole existence was a marginal one, on the fringes of white society. Brainerd calls them "poor pagans," but his own journals reveal that they were not *mere* pagans. A whole spectrum of attitudes toward Christianity can be discerned in what he says about them. Brainerd's interpreter, Moses Tinda, though at first "a stranger to experimental religion" was nevertheless very desirous that his people should "renounce heathenish notions and practices and conform to the customs of the Christian world."[37] These are very much the principles on which Christendom operated. Among those converted in the movement at Crossweeksung were people whom Brainerd describes as "secure and self-righteous," which suggests that they were at least regular church attenders. Among these was a man who claimed to have been a Christian for ten years.[38]

Brainerd was clearly not working in entirely virgin territory but among people where gradual and uneven accommodation to white society had produced at least a degree of Christian profession and absorption of Christian ideas and practice. The native community was also well aware that there were "white heathens" who paid little or no heed to the religious norms of white society. Brainerd was working in a frontier district of Christendom, and that district responded to the radical, totalitarian evangelical preaching of Brainerd in a way similar to that in which contemporary white society in other parts of Protestant Christendom responded to similar preaching. Crossweeksung saw the mourning for sin and the testimonies to personal experience of the love of Christ that characterized revivals in the nominally Christian areas of old Christendom, according to the recognized evangelical paradigm of conversion. Brainerd the missionary is thus seen by Edwards as the model of a young minister, working under conditions of exceptional hardship.

Not surprisingly, the early Protestant movement, which was principally evangelical in character, initially brought to the non-Western world the same message and the same methods that it brought to the nominally Christian world which produced evangelical radicalism. And it expected the responses (and evangelicals had plenty of experience within Christendom of hostile or indifferent response) to be along the same lines.

This had an important and often overlooked outcome. It meant that the early missionary movement was not racist, however "culturist" it might be. Evangelical conviction about the solidarity of humanity in sin and in grace meant that even those viewed as "rude savages" or "poor pagans" were open to the highest operations of divine grace, just as "white heathens," not to mention "secure, self-righteous" churchgoers, were open to the same condemnation as the "savage heathens."

Brainerd was as "culturist" as his contemporaries in general. He had little sympathy for Native American ways of life and was puzzled that the unregenerate actually preferred these ways as superior to the unremitting busy-ness of white society. Even the regenerate were not eager to start cultivation and the more laborious lifestyle that would accompany it. When one group refused to abandon a noisy dance despite the presence close by of a very sick man, Brainerd attributed the decision to the callous inhumanity of the heathen heart. But justice immediately forced him to add, "Although they seem somewhat kind in their way,"[39] even if it was a different way.

No doubt Brainerd took for granted that regeneration would dispose converted Native Americans to adopt "civilized" ways. He was engaged in moving his converted people to conditions where this would be easier when he was overtaken by his last illness. But he was in no danger of identifying regeneration and civilization.

Pastoral experience within Christendom suggested that there was a recognizable pattern of authentic response to the gospel, a paradigm of genuine religious experience. It also recognized certain common deformations of that experience, and some blind alleys that prevented its attainment. Neither Edwards nor Brainerd had any reason to doubt that the paradigm was universal, and Crossweeksung appeared to prove the point.

If the Native American community there was already reflecting a fair degree of acculturation, the high degree of conformity to the paradigm established among whites is not altogether surprising. A substantial section of the Native American community may have had sufficient knowledge of and nominal adherence to Christianity to be shatteringly convicted of their deficiencies and delightedly responsive to the hope of "an interest in Christ."

Moses Tinda

Brainerd does reflect a degree of puzzlement about how the paradigm worked within his Delaware society in at least one instance. We have already seen that his interpreter, Moses Tinda Tautamy (or Tattamy), was, even before he met Brainerd, strongly in favor of "civilized" ways and wanted his people to renounce idolatry. Presumably this was at least part of the reason that Brainerd offered him the post, and that Tinda accepted it. Nevertheless, Brainerd believed him to be without experimental knowledge of the gospel. Already distressed to find that the language had no words for the staple terms of evangelical preaching—salvation, grace, justification—and disposed like some later missionaries to blame the language for this, Brainerd was thus further frustrated by an interpreter who showed no fervency. All this changed a short time before the striking events at Crossweeksung. The interpreter, who had already shown signs of genuine concern for his soul, fell seriously ill. Brainerd recognized the signs of conviction of sin, and the evidence of the changed life that followed his recovery. Tinda's style of interpretation also changed; he conveyed Brainerd's fervor as he became fervent himself. He became so committed to spreading the gospel that he hardly knew when to stop. Brainerd found that when he himself had left a place, Tinda would stay behind to explain or reinforce what the missionary had said. The Crossweeksung movement with its flood of conversions, baptisms, and communions followed Tinda's transformation.

And yet Brainerd was never entirely satisfied about Tinda's personal experience. It was clear that he had known awakening, conviction of sin had been evident—his conduct was exemplary, his fervor unbounded, and no one could have been more devoted to the work of the gospel. It was through his effectiveness that the missionary had become effective. But Brainerd felt unhappy that

Tinda could not give distinct views of Christ, nor a clear account of his soul's acceptance "which," concludes Brainerd sadly, "makes his experience the more doubtful."[40]

It is fair to assume that Tinda played a critical role in the movement that led to the ingathering at Crossweeksung. Yet his own experience conformed only in part to the paradigm of conversion that had emerged from evangelical preaching in Protestant Christendom.

The Later Missionary Movement and the Paradigm of Conversion

Such mismatches with expectations increased as missionaries crossed the seas and proclaimed their message in settings where there was no trace of the Christian civil society that was characteristic of Christendom.

The evangelical paradigm of conversion was shaped by the distinction between real and nominal Christianity. Missionaries, converted people themselves and true to their evangelical heritage, declared a single gospel for all humanity without distinction of race or religious profession. They continued to recognize conversion as a requirement for all. But attitudes to indigenous culture softened as acquaintance deepened. A key factor in deepening acquaintance was language. Brainerd did his best, but he never mastered the Delaware vernacular; hence the crucial position of his interpreter.[41] Beyond the boundaries of Christendom the only way of proceeding was by agonizingly, and for a long time inexpertly, struggling with someone else's language. At first language seemed, as it had to Brainerd, to be simply a barrier to be overcome in order to communicate the gospel. Gradually language was seen to be the outer gate to an inner world in which the gospel must take root if meaningful conversion was to take place. Sometimes that conversion did not follow the paradigm, yet appeared to missionaries to be the work of God. Beyond Christendom people might respond to the gospel without responding to the missionaries' experience of the gospel. And this was sometimes particularly evident where the communication took place through indigenous people—through the likes of Moses Tinda, in fact.

In the Pacific, for instance, Calvinistic evangelical missionaries of the London Missionary Society who had learned Edwardsian theology through study under Bogue saw mass movements to the faith in Tahiti and Raratonga. In the latter case, indigenous preachers had been particularly important in bringing the movement about. Kings and chiefs sought baptism, multitudes threw their cult objects into bonfires, whole villages crowded into church and school and demanded to be taught the Christian way. What was happening appeared to match the New Testament phrase "turned from idols to serve the living and true God."⁴² No missionary could fail to rejoice at such events, yet elements of the paradigm of conversion were missing. Sometimes there was little sign of conviction of sin, despite an obvious break with idolatry; and frequently what Brainerd called "views of Christ" were vague, even though there might be signs of conviction of sin. What was undeniable in Pacific Christianity was the renunciation of traditional cult and public allegiance to Jehovah.

In Tahiti the perplexed missionaries waited six years after the first professions of faith—when the names of those who declared their faith were written down—before baptizing anyone. During that time they studied all the theological authorities available to them, and they concluded that none of the theological works they could find envisaged the circumstances of Tahiti. They worked out a position for themselves, distinguishing between church members, who had renounced idolatry and declared their allegiance to Jehovah, and communicants, who showed the marks of regeneration.⁴³

Protestant missionaries were beginning to discover what their Catholic predecessors had found two centuries earlier; that a theology, however comprehensive, which had been shaped by the experience of Christendom was not extensive enough or flexible enough to cover the unprecedented situations that arose from the preaching of Christ in the worlds beyond the West. That David Brainerd himself perhaps had some inkling of this is suggested by one curious incident.

Brainerd had no doubt that Satan ruled in the howling wilderness, with complete sway over the Native Americans in their natural state. He speaks of their religious practices as foolish, puerile, and depraved, and of their notions of the divine as confused and indistinct. One day he encountered that religion in its full Satanic horror: a shaman advancing toward him, in colored mask with hideous mien, dancing with calabash rattle in hand. "Of all the sights I ever saw, none appeared so frightful, so near akin to what is imagined of 'infernal powers.'"⁴⁴

Involuntarily, he shrank away, even though it was broad daylight and he knew the identity of the person behind the mask. But sitting down with the same shaman, he found in him a reforming prophet who believed he had been called by God and claimed that he had come to know God. His task was to summon his people to repentance. Those people were sinking into alcoholic demoralization because they were forsaking God and the old ways under white influence. Brainerd went through with him some of the themes of Christian teaching; "Now that I like," or "So God has taught me," was the shaman's response on several occasions. Their main item of difference was not over the work of redemption but over the existence of the devil. This, the shaman said, was not to be found in traditional cosmology; he evidently had less difficulty over the work of Christ. "Some of his sentiments seemed very just," Brainerd notes, and he adds, "There was something in his temper and disposition which looked more like true religion than anything I have ever discovered among other heathens."[45]

One senses a strange fellow-feeling between reforming shaman and evangelical missionary, both seeking to turn a people to God, both converted men after their respective fashions, both assured of their divine calling, both outsiders ("precise Zealots," as Brainerd puts it) in their own communities.

Brainerd had lived long enough among the Native Americans to qualify some easy assumptions about the nature and results of the devil's role in the wilderness. He knew that the Native Americans had suffered robbery, dispossession, and exploitation at the hands of his own kinfolk, though his vivid apprehension of the transitoriness of early life and the transcendence of the eternal may have blinded him to the depth of the consequent trauma. He could see that the experience of mistreatment by whites was a serious obstacle to conversion, and he sought to explain the matter in evangelical terms—such deeds were the work of nominal, not real Christians. After his initial frustrations at having no words for the standard themes of preaching, and despite his not acquiring competence in the vernacular himself, he began to break down such abstractions as grace and justification into translatable language, a first step beyond Christendom, a first movement toward living intellectually and theologically on terms set by others.

Here again we see Brainerd's and Edwards's transitional status in the Protestant missionary movement. They stand within the bounds of Christendom and work as agents in Christendom's revival. Brainerd stretches these bounds to the limit as his preaching embraces the most marginal people in Christendom.

The movement as it developed was to go much farther. Its historical memory acknowledged its debt to Edwards. The debt to Edwards the theologian, indeed, was scarcely remembered, for it was an inheritance shared with evangelical theology as a whole, and largely mediated to the mission field through others. What the historical memory retained was the impression of the life, work, and death of young David Brainerd, as Edwards had presented him from his journals. Brainerd was not remembered in the movement as Edwards remembered him, the model of a Christian minister whose ministerial charge happened to be among Native Americans; he was reinterpreted for the new century, a model missionary pioneer of the maritime age of missions.

The resetting of the image is not illegitimate. Brainerd is a transitional figure linking the revival in Christendom with the evangelization of the non-Western world and showing early traces of the way the missionary movement became the learning experience of Western Christianity.

NOTES

1. This is argued in Andrew F. Walls, *The Cross-Cultural Process in Christian History* (Maryknoll, N.Y.: Orbis, 2002), 27–48.

2. See J. van den Berg, *Constrained by Jesus' Love. An Enquiry into the Motives of the Missionary Awakening in Great Britain in the Period between 1698 and 1815* (Kampen: Kok, 1956); Sidney H. Rooy, *The Theology of Mission in the Puritan Tradition* (Grand Rapids, Mich.: Eerdmans, 1965).

3. On Bogue (1750–1825), see James Bennett, *Memoirs of the Life of the Rev David Bogue D.D.* (London: F. Westley and A. H. Davis, 1827); John Morison, *Fathers and Founders of the London Missionary Society* (London: Fisher, 1844).

4. See Andrew F. Walls, *The Missionary Movement in Christian History,* (Maryknoll, N.Y.: Orbis, 1996), 160–72.

5. Joseph Samuel C. F. Frey, *Theological Lectures by the Rev. David Bogue* (New York: L. Colby, 1849).

6. J. P. Sutherland, *Mission Life in Islands of the Pacific, being an account of the life and labours of the Rev. Aaron Buzacott* (London: Snow, 1866).

7. See Stuart Piggin, "The Expanding Knowledge of God: Jonathan Edwards's Influence on Missionary Thinking and Promotion," in *Jonathan Edwards at Home and Abroad: Historical Memories, Cultural Movements, Global Horizons,* ed. David W. Kling and Douglas A. Sweeney (Columbia: Univ. of South Carolina Press, 2003).

8. Jonathan Edwards, *Humble Attempt to Promote Explicit Agreement and Visible Union of God's People in Extraordinary Prayer* (Boston: D. Henchman, 1747).

9. See, for example, Arthur Fawcett, *The Cambuslang Revival* (London: Banner of Truth Trust, 1971).

10. On Sutcliff, see Ernest A. Payne, *The First Generation, Early Leaders of the Baptist Missionary Society in England and India* (London: Carey Press, 1937), 38–45.

11. William Carey, *Enquiry into the Obligations of Christians to Use Means for the Conversion of the Heathens* (Leicester: Ann Ireland, 1792).

12. See, for example, Susan O'Brien, "Eighteenth-Century Publishing Networks in the First Years of Transatlantic Evangelicalism," in *Evangelicalism: Comparative Studies of Popular Protestantism in North America, the British Isles and Beyond, 1700–1990,* ed. Mark A. Noll, David W. Bebbington, and George A. Rawlyk (New York: Oxford Univ. Press, 1994), 38–57.

13. See Walls, *Cross-Cultural Movement,* 194–214.

14. Jonathan Edwards, *An Account of the Life of the Reverend Mr. David Brainerd, Minister of the Gospel, Missionary to the Indians, by Jonathan Edwards, A. M.* (Boston, 1749). References in this article are to: Jonathan Edwards, *The Life of David Brainerd,* ed. Norman Pettit, *The Works of Jonathan Edwards,* vol. 7 (New Haven: Yale Univ. Press, 1985). Edwards indicates the work is "chiefly taken from [Brainerd's] own diary and other private writings, written for his own use." William Bradford had already published parts of the diary in two parts as *Mirabilia Dei inter Indicos,* and *Divine Grace Displayed or the continuance and progress of a remarkable work of grace among some of the Indians* (both Edinburgh, 1746). Edwards omitted the parts already printed (what he calls "the public journal"), though many later editions conflate the texts. For the publishing history of both *Journal* and *Life of Brainerd,* see Edwards, *Works,* 7:71–85.

15. The influence of Martyn on different generations of missionaries is reflected in his biographies, each going through several editions. See John Sargent, *Memoir of the Rev. Henry Martyn* (London: Seeley, 1816); Samuel Wilberforce, ed., *Journal and Letters of the Rev. Henry Martyn* (London: R. B. Seeley and W. Burnside, 1837; New York: Dodd, 1867); George Smith, *Henry Martyn: Saint and Scholar, first modern missionary to the Mohammedans, 1781–1812* (London: Religious Tract Society, 1892); Constance E. Padwick, *Henry Martyn, Confessor of the Faith* (London: SCM, 1922; revised edition, IVF, 1953).

16. The Congregational divine R. F. Horton, addressing student volunteers on "The Spiritual Preparation of the Missionary," says "so far as I know the history of missionaries, whether I read the life of Henry Martyn who learned the secret from David Brainerd, or the life of Mackay who learned the secret from Henry Martyn . . . their success and that power and their Christlikeness in service are all accurately measured by their powers and Christlikeness in prayer" (*Students and the Missionary Problem: Addresses Delivered at the International Student Missionary Conference* [London: Student Volunteer Missionary Union, 1900], 181). At the same conference a High Church Anglican, Leonard Dawson, remarked of Martyn's life, "Although there is a certain melancholy tone about that life, yet personally, I found in it my first inspiration as a missionary" (ibid., 533).

17. Wilberforce, *Journal and Letters of the Rev. Henry Martyn* (New York: Dodd, 1867), 80.

18. Ibid., 200.

19. Ibid., 133.

20. Eugene Stock, *The History of the Church Missionary Society* (London: Church Missionary Society, 1899), 1:27. Stock links Brainerd with Martyn, as well as with a more recent missionary hero, James Hannington.

21. Sereno Edwards Dwight, *Memoirs of the Rev. David Brainerd, Missionary to the Indians . . . by Rev. Jonathan Edwards . . . including his Journal, now for the first time incorporated with the rest of his diary in a regular chronological sequence* (New Haven: S. Converse, 1822), 9.

22. Ibid.
23. Edwards, *Works,* 7:272.
24. Ibid., 7:278.
25. Ibid., 7:284.
26. Ibid., 7:95.
27. Wilberforce, *Journals and Letters of Martyn,* 204.
28. *An Account of the Life of the Rev. David Brainerd* (Newark, N.J.: J. A. Crane, 1811), preface.
29. John Wesley, *Letters of the Rev. John Wesley, A. M.,* ed. John Telford (London: Epworth Press, 1931), 5:95.
30. A. J. Gordon, *The Holy Spirit in Missions* (London: Hodder and Stoughton, 1893), 207.
31. Charles Hole, *The Early History of the Church Missionary Society for Africa and the East to the End of AD 1814* (London: Church Missionary Society, 1896), 48.
32. Edwards, *Works,* 7:500–541.
33. Ibid., 7:531–34.
34. John Wesley, *Journal of the Rev. John Wesley, A. M.,* ed. Nehemiah Curnock (London: Charles H. Kelly, n.d.), 3:449.
35. Wesley, *Letters,* 5:282.
36. Cf. Edwards, *Works,* 7:309. He found one group of whites "behaved more indecently" during his preaching "than any Indians I ever addressed" (318).
37. Dwight, *Memoirs of the Rev. David Brainerd,* 218.
38. Ibid., 210.
39. Brainerd had particular difficulty with a group influenced by Quakers, who seemed to him to be trusting in sobriety and sincerity for salvation (Edwards, *Works,* 7:346).
40. See Dwight, *Memoirs of the Rev. David Brainerd,* 210–11, 213. Edwards preserves few of the references to Moses Tinda Tautamy in his version, though he refers to the interpreter's awakening (Edwards, *Works,* 7:277) and to his being "amazingly assisted and I doubt not but the Spirit of God was upon him, (though I had no reason to think he had any true and saving grace, but was only under conviction of his lost state)" (Edwards, *Works,* 7:279). On Tinda, see also Edwards, *Works,* 7:254 and note.
41. Brainerd refers to the frustrations of having only a pagan interpreter in a place (Juniata Island) where the traditional religion was intact (Edwards, *Works,* 7:326).
42. 1 Thessalonians 1:9.
43. William Ellis, *Polynesian Researches during a residence of nearly eight years in the Society and Sandwich Islands* (London: Fisher and Jackson, 1831), vol. 2, chap. 2. On Raratonga, see Sutherland, *Mission Life in Islands of the Pacific.*
44. Edwards, *Works,* 7:329.
45. Ibid., 7:330.

The Expanding Knowledge of God

Jonathan Edwards's Influence on Missionary Thinking and Promotion

Stuart Piggin

Jonathan Edwards was massively constitutive of modern Protestant missions. The main reasons for that, however, can only be understood from a perspective of greater height and distance than most missionaries have had the opportunity to attain. He lived too long before William Carey[1] and too far away from London, destined to become the missionary-sending center of the universe, and he had too many non-missionary-specific thoughts to be a candidate in historical memory for the honored position of father of modern missions.[2] But those apparent handicaps combined to give him potent leverage on the movement.

First, Edwards's life span occupied an interlude in missionary history, "an interlude between one great cycle of missionary activity and another,"[3] leaving the New Englander with space to construct a new paradigm for missions. Behind him lay the great age of Catholic missions, and the foundations of Anglican and Moravian missions were laid without his aid. But a half century farther on Anglo American evangelical Protestant foreign missions would be born, a child whose appearance and personality point to the paternity of Edwards. Admittedly, the length of the pregnancy and the nature of the birth demand explanation:[4] obstetric historians would label it a transverse deep arrest. Second, Edwards lived on the periphery of the Protestant world. But God, being a fringe-dweller, seemed happiest to live there too, and, in the awakenings, Edwards shared and analyzed the power of the gospel to transform the lives of colonial whites, enslaved blacks, and indigenous reds. He concluded that it could do the same for all the races of humankind. And conscious as he was of being at one end of the earth, Edwards saw more clearly than his British contemporaries that God wanted his kingdom to come to all the ends of the earth: Edwards's longings to see the expansion of the kingdom of Christ were as sweet and virile as any of his desires in adolescence.[5] Third, Edwards polished his multifaceted thought into a beautiful diamond, perhaps the most efficient paradigm of missions yet designed. But few since have had eyes for all the facets of the missionary diamond. Most have been mesmerized by the beauty of one or two facets only.

These three factors of time, place, and intellectual and spiritual power (history, geography, and genius) explain the formative magnitude of Edwards's influence on missions. They also account for the extensive and rhapsodical,[6] but ultimately inadequate, reflections on this influence to be found in the recorded historical memory of the missionary movement. We shall here review that historical record with particular reference to Edwards's impact on the British[7] missionary movement to India[8] and conclude by exploring the implications of Edwards's thought for the nineteenth-century perception of Hinduism by missionaries. But it is by looking into the diamond that we will begin to understand the full dimensions of Edwards's missionary legacy. The historian of ideas can trace explicitly the impact of Edwards's ideas in a few areas, but almost certainly his influence was more pervasive as the sap of his thinking was drawn up into the tree of evangelicalism, of which the missionary movement was a major branch.

Edwards's Missionary Paradigm

Edwards's missionary diamond has at least seven facets: theology, history, philosophy, pragmatics, practice, spirituality, and aesthetics. The theology facet flashed with many inducements to mission. Since the ultimate end of creatures is to glorify God, who is love and whose love, in Edwards's thought, is expressed in the communication of himself in his holiness and happiness to intelligent beings, they best demonstrate their intelligence by sharing in that work of communication, which is missionary work. The work of making intelligent beings themselves holy and happy is the work of redemption, which includes preaching the gospel, the main missionary task. Divine sovereignty combined with human accountability and optimistic postmillennial eschatology produces missionary effort with confidence. Justification by faith, the core of the gospel, is the divine instrument for the renovation of all humankind.

From the history facet emanated not only the well-known understanding of the role of providence in history and the recurring interest in the conversion of the Jews,[9] but also Edwards's depiction of redemption as progressive, the knowledge of God as expanding,[10] and the experience of God as enlargement.[11] Edwards identified missions and revivals as the means by which God achieved this redemption progressively.[12] Lots of new lights sparkled from that hitherto largely unexplored facet, the absence of a history of missions themselves being its only flaw.[13]

From the much explored facet of philosophy, Edwards's brilliance shone more brightly than that of his contemporaries. Natural ability and moral inability came to be seen as the key to the issue of free will, making all responsible for their response to the offer of the gospel. The nature of true virtue as disinterested general benevolence was personified by missionary David Brainerd,[14] and humanitarianism, philanthropy, and social action were its outworking both in Western societies and on the mission field. Lockean and Newtonian philosophies, as adapted by Edwards, justified a view of conversion as felt or sensate experience.[15]

Flashing on the pragmatics plane are the use of "means," which became integral to Protestant missionary strategy. The means included prayer, as expounded in the *Humble Attempt* (1748), and the example of individual converts such as Abigail Hutchinson and little Phebe Bartlet in *Faithful Narrative* (1736), his own wife in *Some Thoughts Concerning the Revival* (1742), and Brainerd in *True Virtue* (published posthumously in 1765). Theological colleges (Yale and especially New Jersey) were looked to by Edwards as potent instruments of Christian extension.

On the practice facet we observe the value attached to duty and the evidencing of conversion by fruit (rather than by profession). The latter resulted in caution on the mission field. The value attached to education justified commitment to that activity on the mission field, while the insistence that civilization was not a prerequisite to conversion proved liberating. And by his own precept and example at Stockbridge, Edwards demonstrated the importance of missionary work.[16]

The spirituality facet was exceptionally brilliant: religious affections as critical to true religion; steering between rationalism and enthusiasm; the preference of the true saint for godly habit over spiritual ecstasy; the concern to foster exertion rather than experiences; the urgency to save from hell, understood as the horrific opposite to the unimaginable glory of heaven.

But it was on the aesthetics plane that the most enchanting lights played: nature enthusiasm and sensibility tantalizingly adumbrative of Romanticism;[17] the new language making abstractions tangible and reality felt; the predilection for identifying beauty with holiness; and the appreciation of God's design, his schema, his plan. Perhaps his missionary heirs gazed least upon this facet, and that might explain why they did not often see the diamond as a whole. It was post-Romantic John Henry Newman who said "I believe in design because I believe in God; not in a God because I see design."[18] Edwards had a multi-faceted vision of God and therefore a belief in an intricate, comprehensive design that focused on fostering mission for the supreme end of glorifying God.

This vision had the power, as we shall see, to set evangelicalism on a decidedly missionary course. But it must also be acknowledged that the vision was diluted and polluted the further it flowed from its source and the more instrumentally it was used for the purpose of driving missions. One of the few who came close to grasping Edwards's holistic missionary vision was Thomas Chalmers, leader of the evangelical party in the Church of Scotland during the high noon of its missionary contribution.[19] As a student at St. Andrews in 1795–1796, not content with Professor Hill's clinical analysis of Calvinism "upon the scheme of Jonathan Edwards," Chalmers embarked on the study of Edwards's *Freedom of the Will* for himself. It left him, as it left me at Yale in 1985, "in a sort of mental elysium" as his enraptured soul fixated on the "one idea" of the "magnificence of the Godhead, and the universal subordination of all things to the one great purpose for which He evolved and was supporting creation." His own reflection on this experience a quarter of a century later itself sounds rather Edwardsian: "O that He possessed me with a sense of His holiness and His love, as He at one time possessed me with a sense of His greatness and His power, and His pervading agency."[20]

It might be expected that Chalmers's most celebrated missionary student, Alexander Duff, would have imbibed his professor's understanding of and enthusiasm for Edwards.[21] But I cannot establish that Duff went through the same mental and spiritual exercises over Edwards. Duff almost certainly read some of Edwards, particularly *Life of Brainerd*, but I have not been able to establish that he did. He is not reported anywhere to have read any Edwards, and he did not borrow any Edwards work from the library at St. Andrews University. He would have borrowed from the University Missionary Association's Library at St. Andrews, but that collection held only *Life of Brainerd*.[22] While Duff shared with both Chalmers and Edwards a capacity for ecstasy and a similar vocabulary of piety, he seemed (to put it crudely and judgmentally to make the point) to be more interested in the glory of missions than the glory of God. He came to think of Chalmers as "the leading missionary spirit of Christendom,"[23] he habitually characterized God as "the God of Missions," and he insisted that missions were the chief end for which God created the Church.[24] For such a programmatic purpose the purple poetry of Highland Scotland came more readily to mind than the sharp, clear light from Edwards's diamond. The more self-contained and self-perpetuating the missionary movement became, the less aware it became of the many-angled light which Edwards's diamond had focused on it.[25]

From the Great Awakening to the Birth of the Modern Missionary Movement

The assertion made above, that the 1740s experience in revival of the conversion of blacks and pagan Indians was the soil out of which modern Protestant missions grew in the 1790s, invites analysis. It was not the conversion of pagans alone that led to this outcome. They had been converted a century earlier under the legendary John Eliot, but those conversions had only been "prized as evidence of the spiritual virility of New England, of the fact that the Lord had not abandoned his Zion, rather than as an experimental laboratory to an ongoing missionary obligation."[26] The obligation on Christians to use means for the conversion of the heathens resulted not only from this contact which Western Christians had with real heathens for the first time in about a millennium, but also from the fact that the conversion of these heathens was accompanied by revival, a sure sign of divine endorsement. Contemporaneously, the same (apparently accidental) juxtaposition of revival and paganism was experienced in Estonia and Livonia, where revived Moravians met with "one of the last pagan populations of Europe," resulting in the Baltic revivals of the 1730s.[27] In their displaced populations, Moravians already had a missionary force, whereas the British and the Americans had to build one—hence the half century of delay before the forces of evangelicalism were readied for overseas service.

That half century is threaded through with many cords connecting Edwards with the founders of modern Protestant missions. On 9 and 10 October 1738, about four months after he had his heart "strangely warmed" at Aldersgate Street in London, John Wesley, "walking from London to Oxford," read Edwards's account of the revival in Northampton, Massachusetts, and was inflamed thereby.[28] "The crisis which followed," claims Outler, "ranks with Aldersgate in importance if not in drama."[29] Wesley continued to fluctuate in his assurance after Aldersgate, and the *Faithful Narrative* raised for him acutely yet again the problem of those, including himself, who are "weak in faith." This led him after his arrival at Oxford to reflect on 2 Corinthians 13:5, "Examine yourselves, whether ye be in the faith." The episode was one of the key experiences to his evolution as a revival preacher. It is not surprising, therefore, that when in March 1745 James Erskine, Lord Grange, a member of parliament and friend of Whitefield, wrote to John Wesley including James Robe's invitation to participate in a Concert of Prayer for revival and world mission, Wesley warmly accepted the invitation and suggested that "the concurrence of Mr Edwards in New England"[30] might also be sought.[31]

The historical significance of this exchange of letters is not that Edwards thereby learned about the Concert of Prayer, so seminal in the birth of Anglo American missions. He had already been invited to lend it his support by John MacLaurin from Glasgow. The invitation to Wesley and his enthusiasm for the prayer concert and for Edwards's involvement in it are important early signs of the ecumenism that was to become a characteristic of evangelical missions.[32] While Wesley excised (admittedly, with surgical precision) all the metaphysical subtlety attributable to Edwards's Calvinism in his abridgements of the New Englander's works, the fact that he was eager to publish and republish so many of Edwards's writings raises the interesting question of how much of Edwards's paradigm had to be dismantled before it would no longer fly. Wesley clearly believed it was a Boeing 747 and could fly on fewer than all four of its engines. Given Wesley's critical, opinionated mind, it is striking that he let Edwards take off at all, but he did not believe in breaking with other Christians over opinions, just over essential doctrines and practices.[33]

Edwards, whom Wesley accused of holding to his opinions too rigorously, actually had a similar strategy, resisting the "domino theory" of the orthodox that the slightest concession on doctrinal purity would contaminate the whole, with the contention that this applied neither to nonfundamental doctrines nor even to "secondary elements of fundamental doctrines."[34] Zeal for the truth, contended Edwards, is an expression of divine love, but only if "it is against *things,* and not *persons.*"[35] The wisdom of such distinctions is foundational to the ecumenical achievements of evangelical missions; the difficulty of putting those distinctions into practice, no doubt, helps to account for the many failings of ecumenism in missionary history. For his part, Wesley sometimes broadcast his critical opinions. At least one such opinion suggests why it was Edwards, whose life was foreshortened compared with Wesley, who made the more decisive contribution to the development of missions. In December 1749 Wesley read an extract of *Life of Brainerd* and commented, "I could not but grieve at this: that even so good a man as Mr Brainerd should . . . [magnify] his own work, above that which God wrought in Scotland, or among the English in New England: whereas in truth, the work among the Indians, great as it was, was not to be compared to that at Cambuslang, Kilsyth, or Northampton."[36] Except, one might observe that the Indians were genuine pagans.

So there is much to be learned even from Wesley's cavils, but his main view was that both Brainerd and Edwards were combustible sources of divine fire and that therefore their writings were essential reading. Wesley's eagerness to publish and republish edited versions of Edwards's writings made him one of the chief eighteenth-century propagators of Edwards's thought.[37] It is of some significance to establish this because extant primary sources do not allow us to recover the reading done by Wesleyan missionaries as do those for the Anglicans, Congregationalists, and Baptists. It is also true that the Wesleyans were more given to reading their own material than members of other evangelical movements and might not have read much of Edwards had Wesley not published him. That Wesley did put so much of Edwards into circulation and that the Methodist leaders Francis Asbury and Thomas Coke[38] were as influenced as any by Edwards's *Life of Brainerd* (1749) suggests that Edwards may have been as major a shaper of Wesleyan missions as he was of other evangelical missions.

Edwards, invited to join the prayer concert by a Calvinist and an Arminian, was inspired by the whole idea, as was David Brainerd, who lay dying of tuberculosis in Edwards's house, and who was always inspired by whatever inspired Edwards. In another providential juxtaposition of a kind that always seems to present itself to the great, making them great, Edwards was able to publish nearly contemporaneously *Life of Brainerd* (1749) and (in the previous year) his sermons on the Concert of Prayer proposal, the *Humble Attempt*.[39] The latter is a study of the relationship between revival, prayer, prophecy, and missions. The idea caught on and spread throughout North America, Britain, and the continent of Europe. One of the original Scottish ministers who had approached Edwards over the prayer concert was John Erskine. Almost forty years later, in 1784, the same Erskine sent the *Humble Attempt* to John Ryland, co-pastor of College Lane Baptist Church, Northampton, who shared it with a group of English Baptist ministers, including John Sutcliff of Olney and Andrew Fuller of Kettering.[40] Fuller wrote in his diary: "July 9 [1784]. Read to our friends, this evening, a part of Mr Edwards's Attempt to Promote Prayer for the Revival of Religion, to excite them to the like practice. Felt my heart profited and much solemnised by what I read. July 19. Read some more of Edwards on prayer, as I did also last Monday night, with sweet satisfaction."[41]

The group issued a call to concerted prayer, agreeing to meet on the first Monday of each month to pray for the spread of the gospel, and the prayer movement spread both rapidly and extensively.[42] Having created the demand, in 1789 Sutcliff wrote a preface to a new edition of the *Humble Attempt*. That modern missions were born of a movement for extraordinary and united prayer suggests that it was the product of Edwards's piety as much as any revolutionary theological thinking,[43] but the *Humble Attempt* did get the faithful thinking as well as praying. Neither Sutcliff nor presumably his Baptist brethren endorsed the precise dates of Edwards's eschatological calendar,[44] but they did embrace his notion of the progressive unfolding of the plan of redemption in fulfillment of prophecy. As to the timing of the beginning of the end, they were excited by his question based on Psalm 102, "Who knows but that the generation here spoken of may be this present generation?"[45] In 1785, having wrestled with Edwards's *Freedom of the Will*,[46] Fuller published *The Gospel Worthy of All Acceptation*, in which he demonstrated that there was no contradiction between God's sovereignty in election and the universal obligation on all who hear the gospel to believe in Christ. Hence they now had an incentive to pray for missions and to believe theologically in the obligation to world mission. Now they needed a plan. This was set out in Carey's *Enquiry*.

It was this group of Baptist ministers who in 1792 formed the Baptist Missionary Society (BMS), the first of the great Protestant missionary societies, and sent William Carey, the "Father of modern missions," to India. Carey had used the *Humble Attempt* in his *Enquiry* to discount the contention that certain prophecies had to be fulfilled before the heathen could be converted.[47] He also repeatedly cited Brainerd's experience among the Indians as an example of the power of the gospel to convert the heathen before they were civilized.[48] The *Humble Attempt* also caught the imagination of the founders in 1795 of the London Missionary Society (LMS), who published yet another edition of it, and in 1796 it was old John Erskine himself who was the chief instrument in the formation of the Scottish Missionary Society (SMS).[49]

The direct line from Edwards to Carey via Erskine has been often observed.[50] What is not so well known is that the Baptist love affair with Edwards in the 1780s coincided with the publication of a large number of Edwards's works.[51] Many of them were edited or recommended by the London-based Calvinist divine Charles Edward de Coetlogon (1746–1820), who must be ranked as one of Edwards's most devoted disciples in this period. Coetlogon had brought out an edition of *The Justice of God in the Damnation of Sinners* in 1774. Then in 1788 he brought out editions of both *The Eternity of Hell Torments*[52] and *God's Last End in the Creation of the World*, and in 1789 *Original Sin*. Meanwhile, editions of the *Religious Affections* (1746) were brought out in 1787 and 1789; Erskine's version of *History of the Work of Redemption*, first published in 1774, came out again in 1786, 1788,[53] and 1791; and *Freedom of the Will* (1754) was republished in 1790. Between 1788 and 1796 sermons and theological essays of Edwards never before published also appeared.

So the BMS, LMS, and SMS were born in a world awash with Edwards. And following Edwards's trajectory, Fuller and, after him, the Congregationalist Edward Williams tweaked Calvinism into a missionary theology *par excellence*. Indeed, the founders and fathers of BMS, LMS, and the Church Missionary Society (CMS), and the great pastors who sent out many missionaries, such as Joseph Fletcher and John Angell James[54] among the Congregationalists, John Ryland and John Sutcliff among the Baptists, Charles Simeon and John Buckworth among the Anglicans, and the most celebrated of all Scottish evangelical leaders, Thomas Chalmers, were all professed adherents of Edwards's system, as were the clerical supporters of the Irish Presbyterian Mission and the Welsh Calvinistic Methodists.[55] Among the tutors who taught prospective missionaries, Thomas Scott, David Bogue, and Thomas Chalmers again were greatly indebted to Edwards. In his theological lectures, Bogue referred his students to over three hundred works, but some are far more frequently cited than others, and among them Edwards is the most preferred. Bogue's Gosport Theological Academy and Missionary Seminary must be seen as a major center of Edwardsian acculturation.[56] Edwards's dominance over the ideology of the missionary movement in the first half of the nineteenth century, then, is demonstrable. It was probably eroded by progressive challenges to his "strict" if "evangelical" Calvinism,[57] but a resurgence in his significance for missions is found in the recent revival of prayer concerts,[58] and in the expansion of that branch of Pentecostalism associated with the "Toronto Blessing" that engendered a debate on the nature of true religion in which Edwards is the third speaker or whip on both sides.[59]

Edwards's Impact on Missionaries to India, 1790 to 1860

BMS, LMS, and CMS records refer to some of the books read by some British missionary candidates before or during their training in this period. These reading patterns reveal something of the extent and nature of Edwards's influence not only on future missionaries, but also on their ministers and tutors, and the directors of those societies. No surprises—just a close look at how Edwards was used to oil the machinery of missions.

Four books were very commonly read by missionaries in this period: William Paley's *View of the Evidences of Christianity* (1794), Joseph Butler's *The Analogy of Religion* (1736), John Sargent's *Memoir of the Rev. Henry Martyn* (1817), and Jonathan Edwards's *Life of Brainerd* (1749). All four were read far more frequently than a fifth, Philip Doddridge's *Rise and Progress of Religion in the Soul* (1745). We do not find extensive reflections on Paley or Butler in the primary sources, but on Martyn and especially Brainerd prospective missionaries waxed lyrical. Biographies were then the most popular genre among the Christian reading public. In 1856 a writer in the *Quarterly Review* wrote that it was "a most hopeful sign of the times" that religious biographies "invariably command a larger circulation than any other species of literature."[60] In the century after Edwards, the generality of the Christian public looked to biographies for paradigms of piety rather than to systematic theologies for paradigms of precision. In preparing what has been called the first full missionary biography ever published, Edwards was fully aware that he was editing a manuscript of paradigmatic value.[61] *Life of Brainerd* was chiefly paradigmatic of the tough piety essential to the missionary's survival in his arduous work.[62] William Carey, according to Ryland, so devoured Brainerd that it became "almost a second Bible to him."[63] *Life of Brainerd* was reputedly read by the mission group of which he was part three times a year. "Let us often look at Brainerd in the woods of America, pouring out his very soul before God. Prayer, secret, fervent, expectant, lies at the root of all personal godliness."[64] William Miller, a Scot, applying to LMS, commented at some length on *Life of Brainerd*: "Brainerd was indeed an eminently pious, disinterested, and devoted servant of Christ. As a Missionary to the heathen he was remarkably zealous, faithful, self denied and indefatigable in the discharge of his arduous duties. . . . May I be favored with a portion of the spirit which he breathed! The ardent love and compassion which he manifested toward those who were ignorant and far from God—the jealousy he constantly exercised over his own heart—the exquisite tenderness of conscience and deep abhorrence of sin, which he uniformly displayed, and the frequent acts of self-dedication to God his Savior in which he engaged, surely present a model for the imitation of Christian Missionaries."[65]

Brainerd was also a paradigm of missionary motivation. John Sugden, after reporting to the LMS directors that he had read Brainerd and Martyn, professed to be motivated by the desire to "honor God in the spread of the Gospel of his Son, and a desire to promote the happiness of my fellow men by seeking the conversion of their hearts and the illumination of their understandings."[66] It would be interesting to know the extent to which the stereotypical use of the word "happiness" in such a context[67] was owing to Edward's penchant for the word. John MacDonald (who went to India in 1837 with the Church of Scotland Mission) wrote of his missionary calling thus: Soon after it pleased God, of his great grace, "to reveal his Son in me," as in most, if not in all such cases, I was filled with a vehement desire to make known the salvation of Christ to *all* men: and having a door thrown open to me just then in my immediate neighborhood for the doing of good, I was enabled to embrace the opening. In pursuing one department, the formation of a Sabbath School Library, I was most unexpectedly led to the perusal of certain missionary biographies, and amongst the rest of Martyn and Brainerd. I was immediately smitten like Saul to the ground; and under the oppression of what was mightier than any human hand, I was led for many weeks to cry day and night, "Lord, what wilt Thou have me to do?"[68]

MacDonald, possibly because he was older than most on application, was one of very few critical of Brainerd, sharing Edwards's own reservations about Brainerd's excessively introspective piety. There was a danger, MacDonald observed, in making feelings the arbiter of whether or not one had faith rather than looking at the objective work of Christ and having an understanding of the unconditional freeness of the gospel and its suitability for human need. "In many cases," he wrote, "that error becomes at last a morbid mental disease, which eats into the soul so as to consume its spiritual vigour; and not a few, like Haliburton, for example, and Brainerd have hung down the head like a bulrush for many restless years . . . instead of finding rest, [the soul] can find only labour and sorrow."[69]

No doubt for many future missionaries much of their theology was imbibed from Brainerd as well as their piety. Joseph Benjamin Coles, who gave fifty years' service to LMS in India, having read the lives of Brainerd and Martyn, expressed the view that the missionary spirit was characterized by "an earnest desire for the increase of Messiah's kingdom, and a firm belief in the prophecies relating to that event."[70]

Life of Brainerd was even a paradigm of missionary strategy. Joshua Rowe (BMS) feared that his interest in missions might have arisen only from an indiscrete zeal that would soon evaporate when faced with the harsh reality of missionary life. So he read *Life of Brainerd* and two other works on missions and "by this means . . . attained a greater knowledge of the nature of Missionary service."[71] From America, Samuel Hopkins wrote to Andrew Fuller, then BMS secretary, that he was "pleased to hear that Edwardean principles are gaining ground" and that William Carey had "imbibed these principles."[72] And if celibacy may be construed as a strategy, it may have been the example of Brainerd which helped Henry Martyn, tormented by his longings for his "beloved Lydia," to persevere with his celibacy: "When I think of Brainerd, how he lived among the Indians, travelling freely from place to place, can I conceive he would have been so useful had he been married? . . . Voluntary celibacy seems so much more noble and glorious, and so much more beneficial in the way of example, that I am loath to relinquish the idea of it."[73]

Brainerd was more than a paradigm, however. He was the missionary as saint with whom some missionaries longed to identify in a union of almost mystical intensity. "Read Brainerd," wrote Martyn. "I feel my heart knit to this dear man, and really rejoice to think of meeting him in heaven."[74]

William Beynon, who spent fifty years in India and died there, wrote of Brainerd when he applied to LMS: "In viewing the sincere and decided piety of this holy Missionary—his indefatigable zeal—his incessant and toilsome labours in the propagation of the gospel among the Indians; I verily thought that it was the greatest presumption in me to think of devoting myself as a Missionary to the heathen, but the more I perused—the more I read and studied of the life of this pious man, the more, methought, I imbibed of his spirit, and was ready to say with zealous Henry Martyn 'that my very soul cleaved unto him.'"[75] John Chamberlain (BMS) found Brainerd equally attractive: "October 12th [1800]. Rose a little after three; was very dull; could not pray, was so wandering. Read dear Brainerd's Life, especially part of the 8th of his diary: experienced an alteration in my mind; perceived my hardness departing, and soon became much affected. I long to be like him. Surely, if ever I arrive at the heavenly world, I shall be eagerly desirous of seeing him."[76]

Edwards's writings were sometimes demonstrably formative, not only of the missionary, but also of basic theological and spiritual orientation. Robert Nesbit (SMS) had read Brainerd and Martyn before applying to be a missionary.[77] Before this, reading Edwards had done for him what it did for Wesley on the road to Oxford in 1738: it reinforced his habit of self-scrutiny and self-doubt. He had entered upon his theological studies at St. Andrews in 1820. In his diary of 9 September 1825 he wrote: "About half a year ago I was almost satisfied that I was in a safe state. But since reading Edwards's sermons on Justification, Pressing into the Kingdom, &c,[78] I begin to entertain doubts of my state. Is the Lord punishing me for my late sins as a father doth his child whom he loves? Or is he striving with me by His Spirit, to bring me to a Saviour in whom I have not yet trusted?"[79]

We know that MacDonald read a lot of Edwards and was confirmed in a spirituality appropriate to Calvinism by him. After reading Paley's *Natural Theology* (1802), MacDonald was tempted to conclude that no one could be an atheist after reading that, but then said to himself, "Ah! Yes: I am afraid that a *perverted will* can hold out against a convinced understanding."[80] This insight he owed apparently not so much to *Freedom of the Will* as to "exact discriminations" and "searching analysis" of *The Religious Affections*, about which he enthused in his diary on 11 January 1826:

What a masterly production it is! I never read a religious book before which, I may say, made me reluctant to go to bed but it. I pray God it may practically change my views of things, as I think it has speculatively in some degree. Never before had I such a view of the state of the human heart; and never had I such a view of Christian experience, and the difficulty of attaining to it. 'Tis in the Christian, beyond all others, that the wickedness and deceitfulness of the human heart are most exhibited. Even after he has undergone a thorough change—after new dispositions, desires, and affections, have been implanted in his heart—still, through the agency of Satan, these very exercises of his heart may be turned into instruments of deceit and pride, so that the Christian can never, for a moment, be off his guard, nor lay the very slightest stress on these holy exercises.[81]

No wonder evangelical missionaries were suspicious of the heathen heart even after conversion; they were so suspicious of their own. The evangelical missionary nervousness about mass movements of Hindus into Christianity and the more general reluctance to baptize heathen who professed conversion was based on this suspicion. Any doubts MacDonald might have had on the implications of this were quieted by his reading further in Edwards: "April 8 [1828]—I am now engaged in reading 'Edwards on Original Sin,' a work in which I feel much interested, and which peculiarly satisfies my turn of mind. The subject is one on which I formerly felt at a loss, particularly with regard to the imputation of Adam's sin to his posterity of our being all born into the world sinful. This doctrine I have fully *believed* from Scripture, because it is made plain there; but I was not fully convinced regarding its consistency with the attributes of God, and human notices of justice. From what I have read of Edwards's my cavils have been silenced."[82]

Imbibing the thinking of Jonathan Edwards was not left up to chance. If a candidate had not worked out for himself that he should read *Life of Brainerd* in particular and Edwards in general, then he might easily be told to do just that by his minister. William Miller (LMS), when he had expressed concern for the salvation of others, was directed by his minister, A. Ewing of Thurso, to read *Life of Brainerd*, Henry Martyn's *Memoirs*, and "the Missionary Reports." If he still had not read Brainerd by the time he was examined before the society, he would be required so to do by the Committee of Examination, who took the exercise to be a further guide to the suitability of the applicant. William Crow (LMS), for example, when he was brought before the LMS Committee of Examination, was found to have respectable abilities, decided piety, theological knowledge "upon the whole, correct," and a good disposition. So he was presented with a copy of *Life of Brainerd* for his perusal and given one month to write an essay on "Your Views of the character, difficulties, and privations of a Christian Missionary." This was well received, so he was sent to Gosport.[83] So many CMS applicants in the 1820s said that they had read both Brainerd and Martyn that it is obvious that they had been asked if they had done just that. The conjoint effect of the two famous biographies must have been highly formative, especially since both expressed their spiritual power in exemplary faithfulness rather than in multitudes of converts.[84] Then, if they managed to get through their missionary training and had still not read Edwards, future missionaries were given a book allowance out of which they were expected to buy certain books, including "Edwards's Works,"[85] and thus we know, incidentally, that Edwards's "Works" were taken to India. George Gogerly (LMS), for example, went to India as a printer in 1819. In 1823 he applied to be appointed as a catechist. The LMS Committee agreed and resolved to send him ten books as the foundation for his theological library. Three of them were written by Edwards: *The Religious Affections, Original Sin,* and *History of the Work of Redemption.*[86]

Edwards's Influence on Missionary Thinking on Heathenism, Especially Hinduism

Having reviewed the possible influence of Edwards's writings on missionaries to India, it is reasonable to ask what impact they might have had on their understanding of Hinduism. Edwards was surprisingly interested in non-Christian religions. The recent masterful work of Gerald R. McDermott[87] helps us to understand why. The deists had raised the question of the eternal fate of the heathen so acutely that Edwards felt Christian apologetics could no longer avoid the challenge.[88] Deism he believed to be the most dangerous enemy of Christianity, and he took seriously its argument that, since only a fraction of the world's population had any chance of hearing the gospel, God would be quite unjust to require obedience to it from the majority of humankind. All that God could require justly of humans was their sincere obedience to the dictates of reason, understood as "the light of nature" available to all.[89] Edwards vigorously countered these deist doctrines, contending that only the light of revelation could save, and that revelation had been far more accessible to all humankind than the deists allowed. He agreed with the deist argument that there was a surprising amount which the world's religions had in common, even conceding what the deists would not allow, that many of the doctrines of grace were found surprisingly numerously in other religions. But he argued that this was not due to the light of nature which all had in common. It was due to what McDermott has identified as three other factors which, when combined, amounted to a thorough vindication of the justice of God in demanding obedience to revealed truths.[90] The first was the influence of Jewish thought, that repository of divine revelation, which had been extensively adopted and adapted and, admittedly, polluted by other nations. Edwards proposed, secondly, the omnipresence of revelation in a world that is thoroughly typological (all creation and all history are revelatory, including the history of religions). Third, Edwards suggested that there were some outside the Christian fold who were disposed to respond with humility to their awareness that God was a holy god who required holiness from his creatures.

To establish these three propositions, Edwards studied non-Christian religions with the remarkable thoroughness that marked all his intellectual pursuits. For the most part he was not impressed with what he found, and the overwhelming impression on non-Christian religions which Edwards gives is one of negativity. Nineteenth-century missionaries would have had their own already-negative views of Hinduism strengthened by their reading of Edwards. Their understanding of Edwards's perspective on the heathen came primarily from their reading of his *History of the Work of Redemption* and *Humble Attempt*, both of which deal with heathenism extensively, but with unrelenting negativity. For the most part Edwards's miscellanies and more typological writings, on which McDermott bases his case for an Edwards intrigued by the extent of the truth to be found in non-Christian religions,[91] were not yet published. Edwards's view, for example, that revelation was universally accessible in a thoroughly typological world was not one shared by the early Protestant missionaries.[92] It was not that they disagreed with it; it was just that they had never heard of it. Typological thinking was very rare among nineteenth-century evangelicals.

So while accepting gratefully the valuable light thrown by McDermott on our principal concern here, namely what the missionary understanding of Hinduism might have been, we should acknowledge that his purpose is not the same as ours. His twin concerns are to demonstrate how comprehensive is Edwards's response to deism, and how potentially valuable that response is in today's world of religious pluralism. McDermott focuses on Chinese religion rather than Hinduism, as the chief expression of contemporary heathenism,[93] and he is not concerned with the history of missionary thought.[94] Our purpose here is to document the largely negative assessment of Hinduism which Edwards bequeathed to the early missionaries, and then to conclude with an acknowledgment that Edwards's thought did contain the seeds of a new, more positive approach to Hinduism.

Edwards did not speak of "Hinduism"[95]—no one did for a further half century after Edwards,[96] who accepted the current taxonomy of world religions as Christianity, Roman Catholicism, Judaism, Islam, then most commonly labeled Mahometanism,[97] and Heathenism (or paganism, or superstition, or idolatry). The word "Hinduism" is used in this section, admittedly unsatisfactorily, because occasionally it is clear from the context that Edwards specifically had in mind the pagan religions of the East Indies.

As to what Edwards might have known about Hinduism, Europeans had been attempting to interpret Hinduism for a century and a half by the time Edwards wrote.[98] They had already distinguished between "popular" and "philosophical" Hinduism. They had settled into almost universal criticism and condemnation of it at the popular level, but occasionally conceded that its metaphysics and ethics were not entirely dissimilar from those of the West, although this may have been due to their inability to perceive such things in anything other than Western terms. By Edwards's day there was already a tradition of depicting Hinduism as vile and ridiculous, coupled with the opinion that its very occasional resemblance to Christian truth were due to the dictates of God-given reason, and to the fact that Hindus were descendants of the one human race scattered at the tower of Babel.[99] Edwards was not unsympathetic to either of these opinions. He did not concede, however, that reason, unaided by the "new sense," could discover the truths of revelation by which alone we can be saved. And while he believed that all religious notions were degenerations from a once universally revealed truth,[100] they were always so degenerate in heathenism as to make recovery of the original truth impossible. Revelation was essential,[101] for, without the light of the gospel, no other types, images, or shadows of the truth could be seen in their true light. That made the agents of gospel light—missionaries—mandatory.

How much did Edwards really know about Hinduism? He was aware of the recent history of Western mercantile endeavor in India and of the progress of the Danish mission in procuring converts there.[102] He had read Chevalier Ramsay, who argued that a mediator who suffers vicariously for others is found in the Hindu Vedas.[103] But his view of Hinduism was determined primarily by biblical data on heathenism interpreted in the light of the need to refute deism. In the last decade of his life, his experience of the only heathen he knew firsthand,[104] the Indians at Stockbridge, also influenced his thinking on the heathen.

Edwards first acknowledged that heathenism was the commonest form of non-Christian religion, prevailing over most of the world for most of its history. There were more heathens in the world than Jews, Muslims, and Christians put together. The preponderance of heathen and the relative smallness of Christian adherents (one-sixth of the world's population at the most) was foundational to the deist argument that the Christian God was not just to require people to be responsible for their disobedience to a revelation of which they were unaware.[105] Unlike most of the Reformed orthodox, Edwards did not deny that this argument was a serious challenge to the truth of the Christian faith. He responded, not only by arguing that the true light had shone more universally than deists would allow. He also called the church to its missionary obligation to increase the proportion of its adherents throughout the world.

Second, Edwards repeatedly asserted that heathenism was idolatrous, and idolatry was "stupid": "The Scriptures are abundant in representing the idolatry of the heathen world as their exceeding wickedness, and their most brutish stupidity. They that worship and trust in idols, are said themselves to be like the lifeless statues they worship, like mere senseless stocks and stones (Ps.115:4–8, 135:15–18)."[106] Edwards reinforced this biblical view of idolatry as senseless with his experience of the idolatry of the North American Indian, whom the devil had had in his exclusive possession since the Deluge.[107] Those parts of the globe where the light of the gospel had not penetrated—South and North America, Africa, and Asia—manifested the dismal deformity of "the most stupid paganism."[108] In "Notes on the Apocalypse" and in *History of the Work of Redemption* he saw heathenism and idolatry symbolized by the dragon, Mahometanism by the false prophet, and false Christianity by the beast (Revelation 16:13). The power of each was the devils and unclean spirits that came from their mouths.[109]

Edwards did show qualified respect for the "wise heathen,"[110] those few heathen who had written the Greek and Roman classics integral to the construction of European civilization. But his experience of the American Indians gave him no grounds to revise his assessment of heathenism as essentially "stupid" and "devilish." It is significant for the understanding of missions, however, to realize that if he saw no good in their religion, he saw plenty of potential in the Indians themselves. The revivals which Brainerd had reported among them were signs of the future and imminent extension of Christ's kingdom to the heathen all over the world. Their "inclination" to hear the gospel was evidence that the Holy Spirit was at work in them. Their responsiveness to the preaching of the gospel encouraged him both to defend the role of missionaries and to champion the rights of Indians against whites who dismissed them spiritually and sought to liquidate them physically.[111] These gospel and social priorities were to become integral to the missionary movement in the next century.

The widespread admiration of *Life of Brainerd* by missionaries would have contributed significantly to that.

The justification that Edwards gave for Christian missions was typically comprehensive. First, with his historical view of God's plan of redemption, Edwards was able to explain why heathenish darkness had prevailed and still prevailed over the great majority of humankind. It was so that from "long experience" the heathen might recognize the "remedilessness of their disease" without Christ.[112] Edwards further insisted that any sincerity that the heathen might possess could not save them[113] without the holiness that comes from the work of this divine grace in the soul. The heathen needed to hear about Christ and his grace, and that meant they needed to hear from missionaries.

Second, the idolatry of heathenism necessitated Christian missionaries, those messengers of grace, through whose agency all the idols would be abolished "agreeable to Is. 2.18."[114] The darkness of idolatry necessitated the light of the gospel. Only the message of the deliverance that comes from divine grace could bring light to the heathen.[115] Not "the light of nature," but a divine and supernatural light was required for the salvation of the heathen as of everyone else.[116] The light of nature could not be extinguished—Romans 1:19, 20 said so—not even by atheism, leaving the conscience fearful of punishment by a supreme governor, but that fear was not of itself sufficient to motivate the will to grasp truths above sense.[117] That there is only one true God is "plainly agreeable to the light of nature" and reason, but only after the gospel has revealed it,[118] making evident what the "wisest" heathen have failed to see through unaided, speculative reason.[119] The chief task of the missionary, then, was to be a teacher of "the knowledge of the truths of divinity," for there could be "no spiritual knowledge of that of which there is not first a rational knowledge."[120]

Third, that heathenism was of the devil meant it was destined to put up a fight against Christianity, which it would lose at the hands of missionaries who were the agents of the Spirit as the millennium dawned. God had promised that heathenism would be destroyed, including in India, that "great and populous part of the world . . . that are now mostly worshippers of the devil."[121] "There will be a wonderful spirit of pity towards them," Edwards prophesied, "and zeal for their instruction and conversion put into multitudes, and many shall go forth and carry the gospel unto them."[122] This meant that there was bound to be a struggle[123] against Christianity in the East Indies,[124] where Satan was worshipped by priests who carried round serpents in brazen vessels, charming them with music and verse.[125] But it would be an unequal struggle, because the sixth angel was pouring out its vile against the anti-Christian forces (Revelation 16:12), preparing the way for the coming of Christ (Revelation 16:15). Missionary work in the East Indies then would be accompanied by a great pouring out of the Spirit of God, and indeed, were there not already signs that this latter-day revival had begun? The forces of the French East India Company were being quelled—if not always by force of arms, then by the powers of nature, as gales sent French shipping to the bottom—and the increasing wealth of Protestant merchants would be holiness to the Lord in fulfillment of Isaiah 23:18.[126] All this spelled out in the *Humble Attempt* must have appeared even more propitious in the decades following Edwards's death, as Warren Hastings strengthened the hold of the British East India Company and displaced the Catholic powers in India.

A fourth justification for missions may have been the most persuasive, even if it operated at a subliminal level and was rarely made explicit. It may have been Edwards's response to the insistence of the deists that only a fraction of the world's population had any opportunity to hear the gospel, and that therefore God could not make its acceptance a condition of salvation, which galvanized Protestants into ensuring through great missionary exertion that the gospel was more comprehensively global in its reach.

With his predominantly negative view of heathenism, and his comprehensive apology for the necessity Christian missionaries, Edwards's impact on missionary understandings of Hinduism at first ran along predictable lines. For most of the nineteenth century the great majority of missionaries propagated an unequivocally hostile attitude toward Hinduism.[127] Indeed, in the early decades of the century, Protestant missions became demonstrably more hostile as more missionaries were actually exposed to "popular" or epiphenomenal Hinduism.[128] To give but one example, Joseph Fletcher, an English Congregationalist minister influenced by Edwards who sent missionaries to India from his congregation, in a sermon preached for the BMS, thundered: "you know, brethren, that idolatry is now just what it was eighteen centuries ago. It is contemptible, monstrous, disgusting, whether it be seen in a classical or savage form, whether among civilized or barbarous nations. It is 'earthly, sensual, and devilish.' It debases the female character; it casts infants out to perish; it forces widows on to the funeral pile; it crushes its victims beneath the wheels of its car. Superstition lives in tortures and in flames: she issues her mandates without control. She maddens her victims with sensuality, and converts a charnel house into a temple. Her joy is the joy of fiends: 'Hell is naked before her, and destruction hath no covering.'"[129]

But if it is easy to see in Edwards's thought one of the roots of hostility toward Hinduism, we also find tiny seeds of the more tolerant view that developed a century and a half down the track, and which McDermott claims is capable of much further development to reduce the defensiveness of Christianity in a religiously pluralistic world.[130] In his more speculative moments, Edwards relaxed just a little his unequivocal condemnation of heathenism. He thought it was not as bad as the Papal Antichrist, just as lifeless, filthy matter is not as loathsome as living slime.[131] Romanists and Muslims were more inexcusable in their errors because they had been given greater light.[132] Further, he conceded, the world is so miserable and "sottish" without the appearance of Jesus that it was "proper that some of the wise heathen expected it"[133]; and since all the world was a typological world, he believed that some heathen perceived "a shadow of the truth" when they contended that the world was created in love.[134] Some even had "obscure notions about a future judgment," even if "the light of nature or mere unassisted reason was not sufficient to instruct the world of fallen men in this doctrine."[135] Every feeble glimpse of saving truth evinced by the heathen was evidence to Edwards that God was just, since it signified that knowledge for all of God as redeemer was possible as well as knowledge of God as creator.[136]

In the broad context of historical missiology, then, how might we assess the impact of Edwards's thinking on Hinduism? Edwards shared (and articulated better than anyone) that worldview which fashioned the way Hinduism was perceived by the West. For a start, Edwards shared an Enlightenment view of science that objectified religion. This made the identification and labeling of Hinduism, in parallel with Christianity and Islam, a possibility. Before the end of the eighteenth century, to repeat, the label "Hinduism" was not used, the less specific "paganism" and "heathenism" being preferred.[137] Missionary activity is justified by the difference between religions, and there predominated in Edwards's thought lines of reasoning that he shared with others in the West that emphasized the difference between Christianity and Hinduism.[138] This resulted in the initial condemnation of Hinduism, but upon reflection (by the end of the nineteenth century) led to less categorical castigation and a revised understanding of mission based on continuity and shared values. Indeed, Andrew Walls has demonstrated that this tradition of continuity, like the tradition of discontinuity, is as old as the New Testament, reflecting in particular the divergent possibilities of Paul's letter to the Romans, chapter one.[139]

At the birth of modern Protestant missions, the tradition of discontinuity was in the ascendancy. Hinduism was typically criticized first for not being rational, second for being idolatrous, and third for being mythical. Edwards, with some other evangelicals such as Wesley, was a champion of reason and rationality, if not of rationalism, and joined with the deists in attributing heathenism and popery to blindness,[140] and so Hinduism was condemned on the grounds of reason. But Christianity was also engaged in the enterprise of defending its special revelation against the deists. In missionary apologetics, then, reason was a two-edged sword—as it was for Christianity in other areas. Edwards had to resort to distinguishing between "regenerate" reason, which operated in conjunction with the divine light of the new sense, by which alone saving knowledge could be discerned, and "unregenerate" reason, the unaided, speculative reason of the light of nature, which was blind to saving truth.[141] Most missionaries would have believed that they were following Edwards's belief that not many Hindus were blessed with "regenerate" reason. It took time for the implication to sink in of the fact that some Hindus were disposed to shaping their conduct in the light of the holiness of God.

Second, as may be seen in the theological lectures given to prospective missionaries by David Bogue, Edwards identified idolatry as a principal justification for missionary activity because of its blindness and devilishness.[142] But idolatry was also recognized not as a substitute for the real God, but as a distorted representation of the true God, even as degeneration from "a universal primitive monotheism."[143] That other religions should promote the worship of natural images is something that Edwards readily explained, thanks to his typological thinking: "It being so much God's manner from the beginning of the world to represent divine things by types, hence it probably came to pass that typical representations were looked upon by the ancient nations—the Egyptians in particular—as sacred things, and therefore called 'hieroglyphics,' which is a word that signifies as much as 'sacred images,' or 'representations.' And animals being very much made use of in the ancient types of the church of God, so they were very much used in the Egyptian hieroglyphics, which probably led the way to their worship of all manner of living creatures."[144] So idolatry was sometimes recognized as a degeneration from the real thing, allowing those who enjoyed discomforting Christians to suggest that, in the remote past, Hinduism may have possessed as much truth as Christianity. Edwards was prepared to court the risk that the deists would make that claim, since it was more important for him to use the degeneration argument to defend the justice of a God who communicated saving truth generously to all people. Again the first reasonable response to Edwards's teaching was to insist that missionaries must take the gospel to the benighted heathen. The contention that Hinduism was not impenetrable darkness sank in to missionary thinking only with time.

Similarly, third, the prevailing view that Hinduism was a congeries of mythological fables also contained the possibility of ancient verity, and of dispensations, which made it not incompatible with Edwards's understanding of history as a series of dispensations and a gradual enlargement of the knowledge of God in which everything, including Hinduism, would have its place.[145] The initial response was to seek to displace the mythological fables with divine truths through the proclamation of the gospel by missionaries. It took a more considered response to concede that God's providential purposes were also served by adherence to Hinduism by a large portion of the human race. So if Edwards's multi-faceted missionary paradigm justified and empowered a century-long assault on the bastion of Hinduism, it also contained elements that later minds were to work into a different paradigm.

NOTES

1. M. X. Lesser, *Jonathan Edwards, A Reference Guide* (Boston, Mass.: G. K. Hall, [1981]), 179, says Edwards was the principal architect of missions, not John Wesley or George Whitefield.

2. There is no chapter on Edwards, for example, in *Mission Legacies: Biographical Studies of Leaders of the Modern Missionary Movement*, ed. G. H. Anderson, R. T. Coote, N. A. Horner, and J. M. Phillips (Maryknoll, N.Y.: Orbis, 1995). That work contains only two passing references to his impact on William Carey and Henry Martyn. The chapters in *Mission Legacies* are taken from the missionary legacies articles in the *International Bulletin of Missionary Research*. Since the book's publication in 1995, an article on Edwards has appeared in the journal: Ronald E. Davies, "Jonathan Edwards: Missionary Biographer, Theologian, Strategist, Administrator, Advocate—and Missionary," *International Bulletin of Missionary Research* 21, no. 2 (April 1997): 60–67. Davies writes: "It is past time to recognise Edwards's influence on the development of the modern Protestant missionary movement. William Carey is often spoken of as the father of modern missions, and a similar epithet is sometimes used of Samuel Hopkins in the American scene. In that case, Jonathan Edwards deserves the title 'grandfather of modern Protestant missions,' on both sides of the Atlantic" (60).

3. W. R. Ward, "Missions in their Global Context in the Eighteenth Century," in *A Global Faith, Essays on Evangelicalism and Globalisation*, ed. M. Hutchinson and O. Kalu (Sydney: CSAC, 1998), 110.

4. One stimulating suggestion is found in Joris van Eijnatten, "Civilizing the Kingdom: Missionary Objectives and the Dutch Public Sphere around 1800," in *Missions and Missionaries*, ed. Pieter N. Holtrop and Hugh McLeod. Studies in Church History, Subsidia 13 (Woodbridge, Suffolk, and Rochester, N.Y.: Boydell Press for the Ecclesiastical History Society, 2000), 65–80.

5. "My heart has been much on the advancement of Christ's kingdom in the world. The histories of the past advancement of Christ's kingdom have been sweet to me.

When I read histories of past ages, the pleasantest thing in all my reading has been, to read of the kingdom of Christ being promoted." "Personal Narrative," in Jonathan Edwards, *Letters and Personal Writings*, ed. George S. Claghorn, *The Works of Jonathan Edwards*, vol. 16 (New Haven: Yale Univ. Press, 1998), 800. One history of past advancement which Edwards appears to have read shortly after publication was Robert Millar, *The History of the Propagation of Christianity and Overthrow of Paganism*, 2 vols. (Edinburgh: Thomas Ruddiman, 1723). He owned a copy of the third edition (1731), but appears to have read it before then. See R. E. Davies, "Robert Millar: An Eighteenth-Century Scottish Latourette," *Evangelical Quarterly* 62, no. 2 (1990): 143–56; John Foster, "A Scottish Contributor to the Missionary Awakening: Robert Millar of Paisley," *International Review of Missions* 37 (1948): 138–45; A. Fawcett, *The Cambuslang Revival* (Edinburgh: Banner of Truth Trust, 1971), 213–15.

6. For example: "His is far the highest name which the New World has to boast of. . . . Never was there a happier combination of great power with great piety. . . . I would hold it as the brightest eulogy both on the character and genius of any clergyman, that he copied the virtues and had imbibed the theology of Edwards." Thomas Chalmers, cited in Mark A. Noll, "Thomas Chalmers (1780–1847) in North America (ca. 1830–1917)," *Church History* 66, no. 4 (December 1997): 763.

7. For the impact of Edwards on American missions, see the works cited in David W. Kling, "The New Divinity and Williams College, 1793–1836," *Religion and American Culture* 9, no. 2 (summer 1996): 215n. 2, and in Kling, "The New Divinity and the Origins of the American Board of Commissioners for Foreign Missions," *Church History* 72, no. 4 (Dec. 2003), endnote 1, in press.

8. Focusing on India reflects my own research interests, but it is not without more general justification. Yale, where Edwards studied, was named after Elihu Yale, governor of Madras and later a director of the East India Company. Yale's foundation purpose was to "propagate in this wilderness the blessed Reformed Protestant Religion" to whites and to the "barbarous natives" (O. G. Myklebust, *The Study of Missions in Theological Education* [Oslo: Egede Instituttet, 1955], 65).

9. Jonathan Edwards, *Apocalyptic Writings*, ed. Stephen J. Stein, *The Works of Jonathan Edwards*, vol. 5 (New Haven: Yale Univ. Press, 1977), 19.

10. Janice Knight, "Learning the Language of God: Jonathan Edwards and the Typology of Nature," *William and Mary Quarterly*, 3rd ser., 48 (1991): 533, 541. Edwards knew well Robert Millar's *History of the Propagation of Christianity and Overthrow of Paganism;* see also Jonathan Edwards, *A History of the Work of Redemption*, ed. John F. Wilson, *The Works of Jonathan Edwards*, vol. 9 (New Haven: Yale Univ. Press, 1989), 408n. 2.

11. Edwards, *Works*, 5:39.

12. Ibid., 9:433–37.

13. It may be significant that in the development of the Baptist Missionary Society, while Edwards's writings were predominant, the remarkable history of missions, written by Robert Millar of Paisley in Scotland and published as early as 1723, namely *The History of the Propagation of Christianity and Overthrow of Paganism*, did make a marked impact on Andrew Fuller (see Fawcett, *The Cambuslang Revival*, 214, 229). See note 5 above.

14. Kling, "The New Divinity and Williams College, 1793–1836," 195.

15. John McCaffrey, "The Life of Thomas Chalmers," in *The Practical and the Pious: Essays on Thomas Chalmers*, ed. A. C. Cheyne (Edinburgh: Saint Andrew Press, 1985), 37.

16. Thomas A. Schafer, "The Role of Jonathan Edwards in American Religious History," *Encounter* 30 (1969): 213–23.

17. Stuart Piggin and Dianne Cook, "The 'Eternal Language' in the Aesthetics of Jonathan Edwards and S. T. Coleridge" (paper delivered at the Christian Poetics Conference, Robert Menzies College, Sydney, 1999).

18. J. H. Newman to W. R. Brownlow, 13 April 1870, in John Henry Newman, *The Letters and Diaries of John Henry Newman*, ed. C. S. Dessain et al. (London: T. Nelson, 1984), 25:97.

19. For Edwards's impact on Chalmers, see Noll, "Thomas Chalmers (1780–1847) in North America," 762–77.

20. William Hanna, *Memoirs of the Life and Writings of Thomas Chalmers* (Edinburgh: Sutherland and Knox, 1850): 1:17.

21. For Chalmers's impact on Duff, see Stuart Piggin and John Roxborogh, *The St. Andrews Seven* (Edinburgh: Banner of Truth, 1985).

22. There may have been two editions of *Life of Brainerd* in the library, one of them being that of the Wesleyan John Styles, who abridged Wesley's abridgement! Catalogue of Books belonging to the Students in the University of St. Andrews (1824), 44, 54.

23. George Smith, *The Life of Alexander Duff* (London: Hodder and Stoughton, 1900), 24.

24. A. Duff, *Missions the Chief End of the Christian Church* (Edinburgh, 1839).

25. Ian Maxwell, an authority on Duff, concurs with this interpretation. (Email from Ian Maxwell to Stuart Piggin, 2 March 2000).

26. Ward, "Missions in their Global Context," 114.

27. Ibid., 117.

28. John Wesley, *Journal of the Rev. John Wesley, A. M.*, ed. Nehemiah Curnock (London: Charles H. Kelly, n.d.), 2:83, 84; M. A. G. Haykin, "Jonathan Edwards (1703–58) and his Legacy," *Evangel* (autumn 1991): 18.

29. A. C. Outler, ed., *John Wesley* (New York: Oxford Univ. Press, 1964), 15.

30. Frank Baker, ed., *The Works of John Wesley,* vol. 26, Letters II, 1740–1755 (Oxford: Clarendon, 1982), 128.

31. Edwards, *Works,* 5:38n. 9; Fawcett, *The Cambuslang Revival,* 226, 227.

32. Stuart Piggin, "Sectarianism versus Ecumenism: The Impact on British Churches of the Missionary Movement to India, c. 1800–1860," *Journal of Ecclesiastical History* 27, no. 4 (1976): 387–402.

33. Wesley, *Journal,* ed. Curnock, 3:178 (29 May 1745).

34. Jaroslav Pelikan, *Christian Doctrine and Modern Culture since 1700* (Chicago: Univ. of Chicago Press, 1989), 57.

35. Jonathan Edwards, *Religious Affections,* ed. John E. Smith, *The Works of Jonathan Edwards,* vol. 2 (New Haven: Yale Univ. Press, 1959), 353.

36. Wesley, *Journal,* ed. Curnock, 3:449 (9 December 1749).

37. Wesley abbreviated and had published two editions of the *Faithful Narrative* in 1744(?) and 1755, with a third appearing in 1827; three editions of *The Distinguishing Marks* (1744, 1755, and 1790, then 1796 and 1827); and an edition of *Some Thoughts* in 1745, followed by editions in 1798 and 1827. He made an abridgement of *Religious Affections* in 1773, but it does not appear to have been published before 1801, and then again in 1827; his extracts of *Life of Brainerd* were published in 1768, 1771, 1772, 1792, 1815, 1825, and 1900.

38. Jonathan Edwards, *The Life of David Brainerd,* ed. Norman Pettit, *The Works of Jonathan Edwards,* vol. 7 (New Haven: Yale Univ. Press, 1985), 3.

39. Jonathan Edwards, *An Humble Attempt to promote explicit agreement and visible Union of God's people in extraordinary prayer for the Revival of Religion and the Advancement of Christ's Kingdom on Earth* (1748), vol. 5 of *Works.*

40. "The Prayer Call of 1784" is found in John Ryland Jr., *The Nature, Evidences, and Advantages of Humility* (Circular Letter of the Northamptonshire Association, 1784), British Library.

41. Andrew Fuller, *The Complete Works of the Rev. Andrew Fuller,* 3 vols. (Philadelphia: G. and J. Dyer, 1845), 1:35–47.

42. Brian Stanley, *The History of the Baptist Missionary Society, 1792–1992* (Edinburgh: T&T Clark, 1992), 5.

43. Brian Stanley, *The Bible and the Flag* (Leicester: Apollos, 1990), 60

44. Edwards, *Works,* 5:87, 88.

45. Ibid., 5:352; Timothy George, *Faithful Witness: The Life and Mission of William Carey* (Leicester: Inter-Varsity Press, 1991), 50.

46. Lesser, *Jonathan Edwards, A Reference Guide,* 24, cites Edwards as the "principal" theological influence on Andrew Fuller (1754–1851), and *Freedom of the Will* as the "most powerful" book to influence him apart from the Bible.

47. William Carey, *An Enquiry into the Obligations of Christians to use Means for the Conversion of the Heathens* (1792; reprint, London: Carey Kingsgate Press, 1961 edition), 12.

48. Carey, *Enquiry*, 36, 69–71.

49. Fawcett, *Cambuslang Revival*, 234.

50. E. A. Clipsham, "Andrew Fuller and Fullerism: A Study in Evangelical Calvinism," *Baptist Quarterly* 20 (July 1963): 99–114; G. D. Henderson, *The Burning Bush: Studies in Scottish Church History* (Edinburgh: Saint Andrew Press, 1957), 151–62; Earl R. MacCormac, "Jonathan Edwards and Missions," *Journal of the Presbyterian Historical Society* 39 (December 1961): 219–29; John Foster, "The Bicentenary of Jonathan Edwards's 'Humble Attempt,'" *The International Review of Missions* 37, no. 148 (1949): 375–81; David Kling on the impact of Edwards on American missions, note 7 above; K. S. Latourette, *A History of the Expansion of Christianity* (New York: Harper and Row, 1941), 4:78, 79; Ernest A. Payne, "The Evangelical Revival and the beginnings of the Modern Missionary Movement," *Congregational Quarterly* 21 (July 1943): 223–36; Ernest A. Payne, "From India's Coral Strand," *Christian Science Monitor* 25 (July 1942): 5, 12; Ernest A. Payne, *The Prayer Call of 1784* (London: Baptist Laymen's Missionary Movement, 1941), 4–11; W. T. Whitley, *Calvinism and Evangelism in England, especially in Baptist Circles* (London: Kingsgate Press, [1933]); Iain Murray, *The Puritan Hope* (London: Banner of Truth, 1971); S. H. Rooy, *The Theology of Missions in the Puritan Tradition* (Grand Rapids, Mich.: Eerdmans, 1965).

51. David Kling has documented his claim that between 1780 and 1800 Edwards's works were more frequently republished in America than in the twenty years following his death. See his *A Field of Divine Wonders: The New Divinity and Village Revivals in Northwestern Connecticut, 1792–1822* (University Park: Pennsylvania State Univ. Press, 1993), 80 n. 7, which reads as follows: *History of the Work of Redemption* (1786, 1792, 1793); "Sinners in the Hands..." (1786, 1796, 1797); *Thoughts on Revival* (1784); *Religious Affections* (1784, 1787, 1794); *Freedom of the Will* (1786, 1790); *Faithful Narrative* (1790); *True Grace* (1790, 1791, 1799); *Humble Attempt* (1789, 1794); *Divine and Supernatural Light* (1795); *The Justice of God in the Damnation of Sinners* (1799). In addition, nearly thirty separate editions or parts of Edwards's works were issued between 1800 and 1819.

52. This edition provoked replies from Elhanan Winchester and George Clark.

53. This edition has a dedication to a number of prominent evangelical Calvinists, many of whom were to be prominent in the foundation in 1795 of the London Missionary Society: "To the reverend Joseph Barber, Samuel Brewer, B. D., John Clayton, John Eyre, Rowland Hill, A. M., Torial Joss, J. A. Knight, John Martin, Samuel Medley, John Rippon, A. M., John Towers, Thomas Wills, A. M., The Recommenders of this edition of President Edwards's *History of Redemption*, it is most respectfully dedicated by their obliged humble servant, Thomas Pitcher, No. 44, Barbican."

54. He introduced the 1839 edition of "Edwards on Revivals" (*Faithful Narrative* and *Thoughts on the Revival* [London: J. Snow]).

55. Stuart Piggin, *Making Evangelical Missionaries, 1789–1858* (Oxford: Sutton Courtenay Press, 1984), 85–93.

56. Ibid., 175.

57. Murray, *The Puritan Hope,* 146.

58. In the last twenty years concerts of prayer have been revived again to encourage Christians to pray for revival and the spread of the gospel. Edwards's call for concerts of prayer has been taken up in recent years by David Bryant of the American Inter-Varsity Christian Fellowship and member of the Lausanne Committee for World Evangelization. His prayer gatherings for fullness (that is, revival) and fulfilment (that is, world evangelization) aim to reflect not only the earnestness implied in the adjective "concerted," but also the joyful celebration implied in the noun "concert." On Bryant, see Edward Roomer, ed., *Spiritual Power and Missions* (Pasadena: Carey Library, 1995), 143, 145; David Bryant, *Concerts of Prayer* (Venture, Calif.: Regal Books, 1988), 14.

59. For the use of Edwards to support the Toronto Blessing, see Guy Chevreau, *Catch the Fire* (London: HarperCollins, 1994); Patrick Dixon, *Signs of Revival* (Eastbourne: Kingsway, 1994). For the use of Edwards against the Toronto Blessing, see Stanley Porter and Philip Richter, eds., *The Toronto Blessing—Or Is It?* (London: Darton, Longman, and Todd, 1995).

60. *Quarterly Review* (March 1856): 383.

61. Timothy George, *Faithful Witness: The Life and Mission of William Carey* (Leicester: Inter-Varsity Press, 1991), 45.

62. For general studies of Brainerd's impact on missions, see Edwards, *Works*, vol. 7; Joseph Conforti, "David Brainerd and the Nineteenth-Century Missionary Movement," *Journal of the Early Republic* 5 (fall 1985): 309–29; Conforti, *Jonathan Edwards, Religious Tradition, and American Culture* (Chapel Hill: Univ. of North Carolina Press, 1995), chap. 3.

63. Payne, *Church Awakes,* 85.

64. John Thornbury, *David Brainerd* (Darlington: Evangelical Press, 1966), 298.

65. LMS, Candidates Papers, 20 August 1823, 8 December 1823.

66. LMS, Candidates Papers, 14 November 1844.

67. "Happiness" was, of course, the favorite term of the contemporary Utilitarians.

68. John MacDonald, *Statement of Reasons for accepting a Call to go to India as a Missionary, from the Committee of the General Assembly of the Church of Scotland for the Propagation of the Gospel in Foreign Parts* (Glasgow: David Bryce, 1839 edition), 23, 24.

69. W. K. Tweedie, *The Life of the Rev. John MacDonald,* 2nd ed. (Edinburgh: Johnstone and Hunter, 1849), 89.

70. LMS, Candidates Papers, 25 October 1837.

71. BMS, Correspondence, IN/23, 14 September 1803, "An account of the Life and experience of Joshua Rowe."

72. Cited by David Kling in "The New Divinity and the Origins of the American Board of Commissioners for Foreign Missions," endnote 14, from W. E. Lowe, "The First American Foreign Missionaries: The Students, 1810–1820" (Ph.D. diss., Brown University, 1962), 2.

73. G. Smith, *Henry Martyn* (London: Religious Tract Society, 1892), 60.

74. C. E. Padwick, *Henry Martyn, Confessor of the Faith* (London: Inter-Varsity Press, 1953), 49

75. LMS, Candidates Papers, 27 May 1824, 6 August 1824.

76. Yates, *Memoirs of Mr John Chamberlain,* 75.

77. J. Murray Mitchell, *Memoir of the Rev Robert Nesbit, Missionary of the Free Church of Scotland, Bombay* (London: James Nisbet and Co., 1858), 38.

78. Preached at the time of the 1734/1735 awakening at Northampton and published in 1738. See Jonathan Edwards, *Sermons and Discourses, 1734–1738,* ed. M. X. Lesser, *The Works of Jonathan Edwards,* vol. 19 (New Haven: Yale Univ. Press, 2001), 272–304.

79. Mitchell, *Memoir of the Rev Robert Nesbit,* 16.

80. Tweedie, *Life of MacDonald,* 65.

81. Ibid., 66.

82. Ibid., 84.

83. LMS, Minutes of the Committee of Examination, 28 September 1818, 26 October 1818.

84. Thornbury, *Brainerd,* 299.

85. LMS, Candidates Papers (Henry Crisp), 25 November 1826; (James Gordon), 13 September 1834; (William Porter), 9 April 1840.

86. LMS, Minutes of the Committee of Examination, 19 January 1824.

87. See Gerald R. McDermott, "A Possibility of Reconciliation: Jonathan Edwards and the Salvation of Non-Christians," in *Edwards in our Time: Jonathan Edwards and the Shaping of American Religion,* ed. Sang Hyun Lee and Allen C. Guelzo (Grand Rapids, Mich.: Eerdmans, 1999), 173–202, and also Gerald R. McDermott, *Jonathan Edwards Confronts the Gods* (New York: Oxford Univ. Press, 2000).

88. Jonathan Edwards, *Ecclesiastical Writings,* ed. David D. Hall, *The Works of Jonathan Edwards,* vol. 12 (New Haven: Yale Univ. Press, 1994), 157–59; McDermott, "A Possibility of Reconciliation," 174.

89. McDermott, *Jonathan Edwards Confronts the Gods,* 29.

90. McDermott in *Jonathan Edwards Confronts the Gods* systematizes the liberalizing elements in Edwards's view of other religions under three heads: *prisca theologia*

(which contended that fundamental Judaeo-Christian beliefs were originally revealed to all); typology (types of the divine are to be found not only in the Bible, but also in nature, history, and in the history of religions); and dispositional salvation (that some in all religions and cultures had dispositions to see the heinousness of sin and the holiness of God). See also McDermott, "Possibility of Reconciliation," 199.

91. McDermott, *Jonathan Edwards Confronts the Gods,* 206, 214, 216.

92. Ibid., 129.

93. Ibid., 42, 92, 207–16.

94. But see the suggestive discussion in ibid., 196–200.

95. I am indebted to Dr. Geoff Oddie, University of Sydney, for this and other observations on this section.

96. The word appears to have been coined first by William Ward in his diary on 28 February 1801. See Geoff Oddie, "William Ward and the Protestant Missionary Constructions of Hinduism: with special reference to the role of Indian Christian informants" (unpublished, 1995).

97. McDermott, *Jonathan Edwards Confronts the Gods,* 174.

98. McDermott, "A Possibility of Reconciliation," 176, speaks of "the flood of travelogues and other reports of heathen religions" in the seventeenth and early eighteenth centuries and refers to Donald F. Lach, *Asia in the Making of Europe* (Chicago: Univ. of Chicago Press, 1965), 3:549–97.

99. P. J. Marshall, ed., *The British Discovery of Hinduism in the Eighteenth Century* (Cambridge: Cambridge Univ. Press, 1970), 20–26.

100. Edwards maintained that heathen stories about gods were distortions of revelations originally made to the Hebrews, corrupted as they trickled down through the ages. Such polluted waters were purified by occasional fresh revelations in Jewish history so that those who maintained the errors were without excuse. McDermott, "A Possibility of Reconciliation," 181; McDermott, *Jonathan Edwards Confronts the Gods,* 44, 96.

101. McDermott, *Jonathan Edwards Confronts the Gods,* 38–45.

102. Edwards, *Works,* 9:435

103. McDermott, *Jonathan Edwards Confronts the Gods,* 94, 211–15.

104. Ibid., 195.

105. McDermott, "A Possibility of Reconciliation," 175; McDermott, *Jonathan Edwards Confronts the Gods,* 24, 25, 51, 92.

106. Jonathan Edwards, *Original Sin,* ed. Clyde A. Holbrook, *The Works of Jonathan Edwards,* vol. 3 (New Haven: Yale Univ. Press, 1970), 152, cf. 7:11.

107. Edwards did not deny that some apparently unconverted Indians were virtuous, but he still did not hold out much hope for them. McDermott, "A Possibility of Reconciliation," 191, 192, 199.

108. Edwards, *Works,* 3:151.

109. Ibid., 5:173; see also 9:463

110. McDermott, *Jonathan Edwards Confronts the Gods,* 182, 185, 188. The chief qualification in his respect for the "wise heathen" was his attraction to the idea that their discoveries of any saving truth were derived from the Hebrews, not the light of nature. McDermott, *Jonathan Edwards Confronts the Gods,* 177.

111. Ibid., 196–200.

112. Edwards, *Works,* 9:298.

113. Jonathan Edwards, *Freedom of the Will,* ed. Paul Ramsey, *The Works of Jonathan Edwards,* vol. 1 (New Haven: Yale Univ. Press, 1957), 319, 430; Jonathan Edwards, *Ethical Writings,* ed. Paul Ramsey, *The Works of Jonathan Edwards,* vol. 8 (New Haven: Yale Univ. Press, 1989), 181.

114. "Types of the Messiah," in Jonathan Edwards, *Typological Writings,* ed. Wallace E. Anderson, Mason L. Lowance with David H. Watters, *The Works of Jonathan Edwards,* vol. 11 (New Haven: Yale Univ. Press, 1993), 297; see also Edwards, *Works,* 9:251.

115. Edwards, *Works,* 3:147. This was also the doctrine of his early sermon "Christ the light of the World," in Jonathan Edwards, *Sermons and Discourses 1720–1723,* ed. Wilson H. Kimnack, *The Works of Jonathan Edwards,* vol. 10 (New Haven: Yale Univ. Press, 1992), 537.

116. This was clearly argued in the Robert Breck affair of 1735–1737. See Edwards, *Works,* 12:4–17, 91–163.

117. Jonathan Edwards, *Sermons and Discourses, 1730–1733,* ed. Mark Valeri, *The Works of Jonathan Edwards,* vol. 17 (New Haven: Yale Univ. Press, 1999), 50–52.

118. Edwards, *Works,* 9:398, 399.

119. Ibid., 17:74; 9:441.

120. J. Edwards, "The Importance and Advantage of a Thorough Knowledge of Divine Truth (1739)," in *The Sermons of Jonathan Edwards: A Reader,* ed. W. Kimnach, K. Minkema, and D. Sweeney (New Haven: Yale Univ. Press, 1999), 32.

121. Edwards, *Works,* 9:472.

122. Ibid., 9:471

123. The imagery of warfare prevailed. Hinduism would be replaced, not fulfilled, by Christianity.

124. Notes on the Apocalypse, Edwards, *Works,* 5:174.

125. Edwards, *Works,* 15:202.

126. Ibid., 5:423, 427.

127. K. A. Ballhatchet, "Some Aspects of Historical Writing on India by Protestant Christian Missionaries during the Nineteenth and Twentieth Centuries," in *Historians of India, Pakistan and Ceylon,* ed. C. H. Philips (Oxford: Oxford Univ. Press, 1961),

344–53. William Ward (BMS) depicted Hinduism as the "greatest piece of priestcraft, and the most formidable system of idolatry, that ever existed in the world" (quoted in Samuel Stennett, *Memoirs of the Life of the Rev William Ward* [London: Simpkin and Marshall, 1825], 146).

128. Piggin, *Making Evangelical Missionaries,* 117, 118.

129. "The Gospel the Great Want of the World," preached for BMS, 1827, *The Select Works and Memoirs of the Rev. Joseph Fletcher, edited by J. Fletcher, Junr* (London: n.p., 1846): 3:363, 364.

130. See note 90 above.

131. Jonathan Edwards, *The 'Miscellanies' (entry Nos a–z, aa–zz, and 1–500),* ed. by Thomas Schafer, *The Works of Jonathan Edwards,* vol. 13 (New Haven: Yale Univ. Press, 1994), 186; cf. Edwards, *Works,* 9:334, 489, 490; McDermott, "Possibility of Reconciliation," 193.

132. McDermott, *Jonathan Edwards Confronts the Gods,* 166, 167.

133. Edwards, *Works,* 13:289

134. Ibid., 13:303

135. Jonathan Edwards, *Sermons and Discourses 1723–1729,* ed. Kenneth P. Minkema, *The Works of Jonathan Edwards,* vol. 14 (New Haven: Yale Univ. Press, 1997), 514

136. McDermott, "A Possibility of Reconciliation," 182, 183, 195, 202.

137. John Stratton Hawley, "Naming Hinduism," *Wilson Quarterly* 15 (1991): 20–34.

138. I am indebted to Dr. Geoff Oddie for this observation.

139. Andrew F. Walls, *The Missionary Movement in Christian History* (Maryknoll, N.Y.: Orbis, 1996), 56.

140. Edwards, *Works,* 9:445

141. McDermott, *Jonathan Edwards Confronts the Gods,* 86.

142. Bogue, in number 6 of his 121 lectures on theology, "On the Spirituality of God," refers to the idolatry of modern pagans, adding, "This should induce us to help and send them the gospel," and among references has "Edwards" (available at the School of Oriental and African Studies, University of London).

143. Walls, *The Missionary Movement,* 57.

144. Edwards, *Works,* 11:202.

145. It was William Miller, missionary with the Free Church of Scotland, who in the 1890s wrote of the place of Hinduism in the history of the world and of Christ as the fulfillment of the aspirations of Hinduism and other religions. See Eric J. Sharpe, *Not to Destroy but to Fulfil* (Uppsala: Swedish Institute of Missionary Research, 1965), 85–88.

An Honor Too Great

Jonathan Edwards in Print Abroad

M. X. Lesser

"All modern American literature," Ernest Hemingway famously said, "comes from one book by Mark Twain called *Huckleberry Finn*"; what Hemingway didn't say was that his iconic text was first published abroad. And the first book of that most New Englandy of poets, Robert Frost, was first published in London. So it was with "America's theologian."[1] Although Jonathan Edwards had earlier published two pamphlets and a letter, his first book—it ran to 132 pages—was published in London in 1737, a year before it appeared in Boston. As displeased as he apparently was with its publication then, it nevertheless marked the beginning of his international renown. For all his provincial humility—"The world will expect more modesty," he had cautioned himself, "because of my circumstances—in America, young, etc."[2]—he surely must have welcomed the attention of so widespread an audience, a bearer now of glad tidings from the New World to the Old. Besides, he had already sought to broaden his ministry by revising a two-part lecture on justification to treatise length and gathering it and four other revised sermons for book publication as early as 1736.[3] By the turn of the century, his major works had found their way overseas as reprints and translations, although several titles were originally published in Edinburgh, and the collected works was published in Yorkshire two years before it was published in Massachusetts. By the end of the century he was translated into French and Swedish, Welsh and Gaelic, Arabic and Choctaw; by the end of the millennium, into Chinese and Korean, Italian and Spanish. Here, then, is a brief account of that foreign affair, and it begins, as such things often do, with letters of anguish and intrigue.

"In answer to your desire," Edwards wrote Benjamin Colman, minister of the Brattle Street Church, Boston, in late spring 1735, "I here send you a particular account of the present extraordinary circumstances of this town, and the neighboring towns with respect to religion"; four days later he added, "My

Uncle Hawley, the last Sabbath day morning, laid violent hands on himself, and put an end to his life, by cutting his own throat." Later that week, Edwards appointed a day of fasting in the town; later that month, he preached on Ps. 46:10, "Be still, and know that I am God."[4] So ended the "little awakening," barely five months along, and so began Edwards's progress abroad.

Both *God Glorified*, published in 1731, and *A Divine and Supernatural Light*, published three years later, were sermons preached before his Northampton congregation, expanded and revised for the press[5]; now, anticipating publication, he was urged to expand and revise his letter. Colman had sent extracts of it to John Guyse, who shared them with his London congregation and Isaac Watts, a fellow Dissenting minister. Their pleasure with the extracts, and Guyse's desire to publish them, persuaded Colman to ask Edwards—indirectly, through his uncle, the Rev. William Williams, of Hatfield—for a complete report. Colman received it in November of the following year, reduced it to eighteen pages, appended it to Williams's *The Duty and Interest of a People*, and had it on the streets in Boston and off to his correspondents in London by mid-December. In late February and again in early April 1737, Watts implored Colman to publish the whole of it—"we have not heard any thing like it since the Reformation," he wrote, "nor perhaps since the days of the apostles"—and pledged five pounds to its American subscription. But Boston publication proved impolitic, as Edwards explained to Colman in May: "You mention, Sir, my being displeased at the liberty taken in the extract at the end of my uncle Williams's sermons: certainly somebody has misrepresented the matter to you; I always looked upon it an honor too great for me, for you to be at the trouble to draw an extract of my letter to publish to the world, and that it should be annexed to my honored uncle Williams's sermons: and my main objection against it was that my uncle *Williams* himself never approved of its being put into his book."[6] By mid-October the text was at the London printers, edited, with a fourteen-page preface by Guyse and Watts, and a title of their own devising, *A Faithful Narrative of the Surprizing Work of God in the Conversion of Many Hundred Souls in Northampton, and the Neighbouring Towns and Villages of New-Hampshire in New-England*. It was published in London— "stitch'd 1s. Bound in Calf-Leather, 1s. 6d."—and shortly after in Edinburgh, and sold there and in Glasgow, the beginning of a relationship with Scottish Presbyterians that continues still. Within a year Edwards's first book was in its second edition.[7]

"With regard to the *letter* itself that I wrote, which you have sent to Dr. *Watts*, and Dr. *Guyse*," Edwards went on, "I willingly submit to their correction, if they think fit to publish it after they come to see it: I am sensible there are some things in it that would not be best published in *England*." Edwards never made clear what those things might be, but Watts and Guyse did. Near the end of their preface they questioned his "style" and "inferences" and the conversion narratives of a dying Abigail Hutchinson and an articulate four-year-old, Phebe Bartlet. When he came to see their correction, he was somewhat less willing to submit to it. He emended the title page, returning the revival to the county of Hampshire from the province of New Hampshire where they had put it, an error repeated far into the next century, even in, of all places, Exeter, New Hampshire. And he pored over the text from first page to last, much as he would any work he saw through the press, detailing errata. He recast the penultimate paragraph of the preface, in which Guyse and Watts referred to "defects" and "imperfection[s]," later substituting without comment his version for theirs in the American edition. "It must be noted," he wrote on the flyleaf of his copy, "that the Rev. publishers of the ensuing narrative by much abridging of it, and altering the phrase and manner of expression, and not strictly observing the words of the original, have through mistake, published some things diverse from fact, which is the reason some words are crossed out: and besides there are some mistakes in the preface, which are noted in the margins."[8] Although he would suffer and bear such alterations in later editions of his work, in 1738 he could do something about it: the first American issue, or third edition, of *Faithful Narrative* appeared without the Guyse and Watts preface. It had, instead, an unqualified recommendation by four Boston ministers, and, to attest to the events described in the account, a letter to Colman signed by six Hampshire ministers, first among them the venerable William Williams. Two issues of the narrative published later the same year restored the Guyse and Watts preface unremarked, while retaining the Boston recommendation and the Hampshire testimony.[9]

That year, 1738, *Faithful Narrative* was translated into German with an introduction by Johann Adam Steinmetz and published in Magdeburg, the only work of Edwards ever published in Germany. Two years later it was translated into Dutch, with the Steinmetz introduction, and reissued unchanged in 1742.[10] Extracts of the narrative appeared soon after in the *Glasgow-Weekly-History*, edited by William McCulloch, of Cambuslang, and in the Edinburgh *Christian Monthly History*, edited by James Robe, of Kilsyth, both correspondents of Edwards, both revivalists; sometime later a one-page extract appeared in a Dutch compilation.[11] About then, John Wesley reduced the text by more than a third and published it for four pence, the first of five texts he would later abridge and expurgate. He justified his editorial practice—"much wholesome food is mixt with much deadly poison," he wrote to readers of *Religious Affections*—but never attempted the works of the Stockbridge years—the "whole mistake," he said, of the "good and sensible" Edwards was his doctrine of necessity. In all, the five titles were published more than twenty times "throughout the kingdom," seven of them the *Life of Brainerd*.[12]

Within a year of its Boston publication, *Distinguishing Marks* was reprinted in Philadelphia—by Benjamin Franklin—and in London and Glasgow, the last bearing "an Epistle to the Scots Reader" by John Willison, of Dundee, another correspondent of Edwards, and an endorsement by George Whitefield: "'Tis the best Thing of its Kind I ever saw. You would think the Author had been at Cambuslang." And *Sinners in the Hands of an Angry God*, reprinted seven times here after its initial publication in Boston in 1741, was published abroad only once during the century, in Edinburgh in 1745.[13] With the single exception of a Dutch translation of *Life of Brainerd*, that would be the last year that any of Edwards would be published abroad until 1762, four years after his death. When publication resumed—spurred in part by Samuel Hopkins's *Life of Edwards*—more than half were published in Scotland; half of those were never issued elsewhere.[14]

In 1774, the same year as the Dutch publication of *Freedom of the Will* in Utrecht, John Erskine, a leading evangelical and frequent correspondent, edited and published *History of Redemption* in Edinburgh, the first appearance of the series of sermons Edwards preached thirty-five years before. A Dutch translation was published two years later—six years before its American issue—and was followed by translations of *Religious Affections, End of Creation, Original Sin,* and Hopkins's *Life of Edwards*.[15] Thus, by the end of the eighteenth century, there were about as many of Edwards's major works published on one side of the Channel as the other; by the end of the nineteenth century, the map had been considerably redrawn. Publication ceased in Amsterdam and Utrecht, began in Bala and Caernafon, and spread to Beirut, Paris, Stockholm, and Zürich.

In general, there was a consolidation of titles abroad, the work of the Northampton period translated more often in the century than any others: *Humble Attempt* appeared in French; *Life of Brainerd* in French, German, and Swedish; *Sinners in the Hands of an Angry God* in Gaelic and Arabic; *History of Redemption* in French and Arabic.[16] And, in something of a turnaround, the American Tract Society published *Life of Brainerd* and *Personal Narrative* in German and *History of Redemption* in Welsh for newly arrived Americans; and the Mission Press of the Cherokee Nation published *Sinners in the Hands of an Angry God* in Choctaw for native ones.[17] The exception to the shortened list of titles was Wales. In addition to translations of early texts like *Religious Affections* and *History of Redemption*, there were late ones like *Freedom of the Will*, *Original Sin*, and *End of Creation*.[18] Such a run of Welsh translations tallies with the Dutch of an earlier time, an index of Edwards's significance to Independent churches and Reformed. Even so, the Stockbridge treatises were never translated again and, other than in collected editions, were seldom published in English after mid-century.

All through these years publication of Edwards continued in Boston and Edinburgh, New York and London, but it went on elsewhere as well. The first volume of the first edition of the collected works, for example, was published in Leeds in 1806 for booksellers there and in Edinburgh, Glasgow, London, Northampton (Old England), Rotherham, York, and Philadelphia; two years later, the first five volumes of an eight-volume American edition was published and sold in Worcester.[19] Both first volumes borrowed Hopkins's memoir, the Leeds edition following it with *Freedom of the Will* and *End of Creation*, the Worcester with Edwards's farewell sermon, the result of the council that dismissed him, his revised qualifications for full church membership, and his defense of it. The Leeds situates Edwards in an unspecified, broadly theoretical context, the Worcester in a local, at best a regional, one. Later collected editions follow one order or the other, focusing at the outset on the early work or the late, the pastoral Edwards or the polemical.

The first four volumes of the Leeds were reprinted in London in 1817, and, under another imprint that year, *Religious Affections* was issued in a pared down version with a rather cranky preface.[20] Defending his abridgment, W. Ellerby argued that Edwards's style was so "ambiguous and verbose" that it left his ideas "feeble" and "obscure" amid a "monstrous profusion of words"; it was, he concluded, "the most remarkable specimen of bad writing" of the time. Text and preface were reprinted in Boston by James Loring in 1821, and again in 1824, and, beginning in 1833 the American Tract Society, undismayed, printed and sold seventy-five thousand copies of both. Other nineteenth-century editors shared the sentiments, if not the tone, of Ellerby, changing Edwards at will. Although Sereno E. Dwight is usually singled out for meddling with the texts of his ten-volume New York edition, Edward Hickman, the editor of a double-columned two-volume London collection five years later, was as intrusive. The Dwight was reissued only once, but the Hickman carried on its mischief through a dozen reprints into the 1970s and survives even now in facsimile. In fact, none of these editions, not the first English or first American nor the much used, and highly touted, revised Worcester of 1843, can be counted on to render a fair text, nor can any text such as *Sinners in the Hands of an Angry God Made Easier to Read,* published, alas, in 1996.[21]

Fair text or foul, there was a profound drop in publication following the revised Worcester, about half as many items over the eighty years after it as the forty years before it, four items between 1870 and 1879, none between 1910 and 1919. Although the pace quickened between the world wars, the publications of note were not by Edwards but about him, as scholars, approaching the tercentennial of both Massachusetts Bay and Harvard College, took renewed interest in American Puritanism and in Edwards, its intellectual exemplar. Of the more than sixty items published then—introductions, articles, parts of books, monographs, a biography, a bibliography, a dozen dissertations—all but a handful were American made. With the publication in 1949 of Perry Miller's *Jonathan Edwards*—not surprisingly, in the American Men of Letters series—came a dramatic shift to studies literary and cultural. Still, the transforming event of the academic recovery occurred eight years later when Yale University Press published *Freedom of the Will,* edited by Paul Ramsey, of Princeton, the first volume of *The Works of Jonathan Edwards,* then under the general editorship of Perry Miller, of Harvard, "a kind of intellectual ecumenicity in the Ivy League," as one reviewer put it.[22] The following year a countertext to the Yale appeared, calculated to advance the evangelical Edwards, but based, sadly, on a corrupted copy, an 1839 reprint of Hickman. The first volume of *The Select Works of Jonathan Edwards* included *Faithful Narrative, Distinguishing Marks,* and three sermons, "Natural Men in a Dreadful Condition," "Christ Exalted," and "God's Sovereignty in the Salvation of Men." It was edited by Iain H. Murray, who, twenty years later, would write *Jonathan Edwards: A New Biography* to confute the "anti-supernatural animus" of the old one. Both were published by Banner of Truth Trust.[23]

Almost from the start there were two venues for Edwards's work, commercial and religious houses, their eighteenth-century title pages like so many street directories. *Faithful Narrative,* for instance, was published and sold in London by John Oswald "at the Rose and Crown, in the Poultry, near Stocks-Market" and in Boston by Samuel Kneeland and Thomas Green, "over against the Prison in Queenstreet." The first edition of Wesley's abridgment was printed in Bristol by Felix Farley and "sold by him at his House in Castle-Green" and "at the several Societies in England"; the third edition, published in London, was "Printed for G. Whitfield, City-Road, and sold at the Methodist

Preaching-Houses in Town and Country." Publication in the nineteenth century kept to the practice, if not its directions, with religious houses as varied as commercial. By the twentieth century hardly any door was open to him; by century's end a good many were, but by then publication had become more nearly an American enterprise and, increasingly, an evangelical one.

Religious presses cropped up in towns across the land—in Delaware, Illinois, Indiana, Kentucky, Michigan, Minnesota, Ohio, Oregon, Pennsylvania, Tennessee—their imprints often as much message as form—Faith Publishers, The Inheritance of Our Fathers, Soli Deo Gloria Publications, Sovereign Grace Publishers, Sword of the Lord. Of the roughly fifty items issued in the last decade, about half were from Yale and Banner of Truth, either volumes in their collected editions or selections befitting their source, from Yale *A Jonathan Edwards Reader* (1995), from Banner of Truth *Jonathan Edwards on Knowing Christ* (1993). The other half were from other publishers and divided between selections with sermonic titles—*The Experience that Counts!, Experiencing God, The Wrath of Almighty God, Altogether Lovely, God's Passion for Glory*[24] —and separately published works, three times as many drawn from the Northampton years as from the Stockbridge, five times as many published in America as in England—cultural artifacts of the American century or, at least, half century, as were a spate of continental studies of Edwards.

Early remarks abroad were framed as prefaces and introductions to his work, at times narrowly so: a note justifying excisions in Edwards's preface to *Original Sin* "the better to adapt them to the European Reader."[25] Other, less parochial, evaluations followed, but they came a good deal later than those at home and were, for the most part, pious memorials, short reviews, and fugitive references in longer works. In the nineteenth century, while Americans fought over Edwards's theology and claimant rights to it, Europeans engaged him elsewhere: on free will in the first issue of the Edinburgh *Presbyterian Review;* on liberty and necessity in an essay by William Hazlitt; on the Northampton revival in a German history of New England Congregationalism; on his limitations in *Fraser's Magazine;* on his immaterialism in a French survey of English idealism; and, at greater length, on his idealism in a German dissertation.[26] Nor was there anything overseas like the celebrations and retrospectives that so occupied Americans in the early years of the twentieth century. And the restoration that unfolded between 1920 and 1940 was all but absent abroad. To be sure, there was a Dutch study of Edwards's theology early in the century and a few others later on,[27] but with the publication of the Yale and Banner of Truth editions came a rush of work—on his influence on missions, on his typology, and on his political thought in German; on his sermonic style in Italian; on the unity of his thought in French; on his importance to British evangelicals in Welsh; on his experimental theology in German.[28] And there was a small shelf of articles and reviews in French, German, Hungarian, Italian, Japanese, Korean, Portugese, Russian, and Spanish—American triumphalism indeed.[29]

Translations of his work were few, only seven in well over a hundred years, and once again, most from the Northampton years, all published since the collected editions. Two were in Chinese—a 425-page selection published in Hong Kong in 1960 and an abridged *Religious Affections* published in Taipei in 1994; one was in Korean, *Faithful Narrative* published in Seoul in 1997; two were translations of *Distinguishing Marks,* one in French, published in Chalon-sur-Saône in 1996, and the other in Italian published in Rome in 1998; and two were translations of *Sinners in the Hands of an Angry God,* one in Spanish published in Léon in 2000, and the other in German, published in Langenthal, *onhe Jahr,* undated[30]—yet another reminder, if any were needed, of the timelessness of Jonathan Edwards.

Bibliography

This list of Edwards's works published abroad is arranged alphabetically by title and within a title chronologically, approximate dates of publication in brackets; it includes only texts separately published. An asterisk preceding an entry marks an item published abroad before its first American issue, two asterisks for an item published only abroad. For a descriptive bibliography of Edwards's works published both in America and abroad, see my revision of Thomas H. Johnson, *The Printed Writings of Jonathan Edwards,* forthcoming.

An Account of the Conversion and Religious Experience of the Late Reverend and Learned Mr. Jonathan Edwards. London: J. Mathews, 1780.

An Account of the Life of Mr. David Brainerd. Edinburgh: J. Ogle, 1798.

An Account of the Life of Mr. David Brainerd. London: R. Ogle, 1798.

An Account of the Life of the Late Reverend Mr. David Brainerd. Edinburgh: William Gray, 1765.

Aidehauazi xuan ji. Xiangang: Jinling shen xue yuan tuo shi bu: Jidu jiao fu qiao chu ban she, 1960. [*Selected Writings* (Chinese).]

Yr Athrawiaeth Fawr Gristionogol o Bechod Gwreiddiol yn Cael ei Hamddiffyn. Caernarfon: H. Humphreys, [1900]. [*Original Sin* (Welsh).]

Een Bepaald en Nauwkeurif Onderzoek van de Thans Heerschende Denkbeelden over de Vryheid van den Wil. Utrecht: Gisbert Timon van Paddenburg, 1774. [*Freedom of the Will* (Dutch).]

A Careful and Strict Enquiry into the Modern Prevailing Notions of that Freedom of Will. London: Thomas Field, 1762.
A Careful and Strict Enquiry into the Modern Prevailing Notions of that Freedom of Will. Glasgow: James Duncan, 1790.
A Careful and Strict Enquiry into the Modern Prevailing Notions of that Freedom of Will. London: C. Dilly, 1790.
A Careful and Strict Enquiry into the Modern Prevailing Notions of that Freedom of Will. Edinburgh: Oliver and Boyd, 1818.
A Careful and Strict Enquiry into the Modern Prevailing Notions of that Freedom of Will. Edinburgh: Thomas Turnbull, 1818.
A Careful and Strict Enquiry into the Modern Prevailing Notions of that Freedom of Will. London: Richard Baynes, 1818.
A Careful and Strict Inquiry into the Modern Prevailing Notions of that Freedom of Will. 3rd ed. London: J. Johnson, 1768.
A Careful and Strict Inquiry into the Modern Prevailing Notions of that Freedom of Will. 4th ed. London: J. Johnson, 1775.
A Careful and Strict Inquiry into the Modern Prevailing Notions of that Freedom of Will. 5th ed. London: J. Murgatroyd, 1790.
A Careful and Strict Inquiry into the Modern Prevailing Notions of that Freedom of Will. London: T. Hamilton, 1816.
A Careful and Strict Inquiry into the Modern Prevailing Notions of that Freedom of Will. Edinburgh: Peter Brown, 1830.
Charity and Its Fruits. Edited by Tryon Edwards. London: James Nisbet and Co., 1852.
Charity and Its Fruits. Edited by Tryon Edwards. Edinburgh: Banner of Truth Trust, 1969. (Reprinted 1978, 1982, 1986, 1991, 1996, 1998.)
Cyfarwyddiadau ac Annogaethau I Gredinwyr. Edited by John Roberts. Bala: R. Saunderson, 1809. [*Religious Affections:* selections (Welsh).]
David Brainerd, His Message for Today. Edited by Oswald J. Smith. London: Marshall, Morgan, and Scott, 1949.
David Brainerd, Man of Prayer. Edited by Oswald J. Smith. London: Marshall, Morgan, and Scott, 1975.
David Brainerd, the Mighty Man of Prayer. Toronto: A. Sims, [1900].
The Diary of David Brainerd; The Journal of David Brainerd. 2 vols. London: Andrew Melrose, 1902.
*A Dissertation on God's Last End in the Creation of the World. Edited by C. De Coetlogon. London: H. Trapp, 1788.
The Distinguishing Marks of a Work of the Spirit of God. Edinburgh: T. Lumisden and J. Robertson, 1742.

The Distinguishing Marks of a Work of the Spirit of God. Glasgow: R. Smith, 1742.

The Distinguishing Marks of a Work of the Spirit of God. London: S. Mason, 1742.

The Distinguishing Marks of a Work of the Spirit of God. Edited by John Wesley. London: W. Strahan, 1744.

The Distinguishing Marks of a Work of the Spirit of God. Edited by John Wesley. 2nd ed. London: Henry Cock, 1755.

The Distinguishing Marks of a Work of the Spirit of God. Edited by John Wesley. 3rd ed. London: G. Paramore, 1795.

The Distinguishing Marks of a Work of the Spirit of God. Edited by John Wesley. 4th ed. Dublin: B. Dugdale, 1790.

The Distinguishing Marks of a Work of the Spirit of God. Edited by John Wesley. 4th ed. London: G. Story, 1803.

Y Dull y Dylid Ymofyn Iechydwriaeth yr Enaid. Llangollen: H. Jones, 1845. [*The Manner in which the Salvation of the Soul is to be Sought* (Welsh).] (Reprinted [1860].)

Dull y Farn Ddiweddaf. Abertawy: Howel Powel, [1830]. [*History of Redemption:* selection (Welsh).]

Edwards on Revivals. Edited by William Patton. London: John Snow, 1839.

*An Essay on the Nature of True Virtue. London: T. Payne and Son, 1778.

*The Eternity of Hell Torments. Edited by C. E. De Coetlogon. London: R. Thomson, 1788.

The Eternity of Hell Torments. Edited by C. E. De Coetlogon. 2nd ed. London: R. Thomson, 1789.

*The Excellency of Christ. Northampton [England]: Thomas Dicey, 1780.

The Excellency of Christ. 2nd ed. Northampton [England]: Thomas Dicey, 1780.

The Excellency Of Christ. London: Religious Tract Society, [1830].

The Experience That Counts! Edited by N. R. Needham. London: Grace Publications Trust, 1991.

The Experience That Counts. Edited by Phoebe Ma. Taipei: Jonathan Chao, 1994. [*Religious Affections* (Chinese).]

Experiencing God. Edited by Robert Backhouse. [London]: Marshall Pickering, 1995.

An Extract of the Life of the Late Rev. Mr. David Brainerd. Edited by John Wesley. Bristol: William Pine, 1768.

An Extract of the Life of the Late Rev. Mr. David Brainerd. Edited by John Wesley. 2nd ed. Bristol: William Pine, 1771.

An Extract of the Life of the Late Rev. Mr. David Brainerd. Edited by John Wesley. 3rd ed. London: G. Paramore, 1793.

An Extract of the Life of the Late Rev. Mr. David Brainerd. Edited by John Wesley. 4th ed. London: G. Story, 1800.

An Extract of the Life of the Late Rev. Mr. David Brainerd. Edited by John Wesley. 4th ed. Dublin: R. Napper, 1812.

An Extract of the Life of the Late Rev. Mr. David Brainerd. Edited by John Wesley. Penryn: W. Cock, 1815.

An Extract of the Life of the Late Rev. Mr. David Brainerd. Edited by John Wesley. London: J. Kershaw, 1825.

Extracts from the Journal of David Brainerd. Edited by William. R. Newell. Toronto: Henderson and Co., [1900].

A Faithful Narrative of the Surprising Work of God. Edinburgh: J. Oswald, 1737.

A Faithful Narrative of the Surprising Work of God. Edinburgh: Thomas Lumisden and J. Robertson, 1738.

A Faithful Narrative of the Surprising Work of God. London: C. Whittingham, [1800].

A Faithful Narrative of the Surprising Work of God. Halifax [Yorkshire]: Holden and Dowson, 1808.

A Faithful Narrative of the Surprising Work of God. Bungay: J. M. Morris, 1823.

**A Faithful Narrative of the Surprizing Work of God.* London: John Oswald, 1737.

A Faithful Narrative of the Surprizing Work of God. 2nd ed. London: John Oswald, 1738.

Freedom of Will. London: Hamilton, Adams, and Co., 1860.

The Following Extracts Were Taken from the Life of David Brainerd. Malton: R. Smithson, 1823

Geloofwaardig Historisch Bericht, van 't Heerlyke Werk Godts. Amsterdam: Hendrik van Bos, 1740. [*Faithful Narrative* (Dutch).]

Geloofwaardig Historisch Bericht, van 't Heerlyke Werk Godts. 2nd ed. Amsterdam: Hendrik van Bos, 1742. [*Faithful Narrative* (Dutch).]

Geschiedenis van het Werk der Verlossing. Utrecht: Abraham van Paddenburg, 1776. [*History of Redemption* (Dutch).]

Glaubwüridge Nachricht von dem herrlichen Werck Gottes. Magdeburg: Christoph Leberecht, 1738. [*Faithful Narrative* (German).]

Glaubwüridge Nachricht von dem herrlichen Werck Gottes. Magdeburg and Leipzig: Christoph Seidels Wittwe, 1738. [*Faithful Narrative* (German).]

God at Work? Edited by Gary Benfold. London: Grace Publications, 1995.

God's Passion for His Glory. Leicester: Inter-Varsity Press, 1998.

The Great Christian Doctrine of Original Sin Defended. London: G. Keith, 1766.

The Great Christian Doctrine of Original Sin Defended. London: J. Johnson and Co., 1766.

The Great Christian Doctrine of Original Sin Defended. Dublin: Robert Johnston, 1768.

The Great Christian Doctrine of Original Sin Defended. Glasgow: Robert Urie, 1768.

The Great Christian Doctrine of Original Sin Defended. Glasgow: James Meuros, 1772.

The Great Christian Doctrine of Original Sin Defended. 4th ed. London: J. Murgatroyd, 1789.

The Great Christian Doctrine of Original Sin Defended. Edinburgh: Murray and Cochrane, 1798.

The Great Christian Doctrine of Original Sin Defended. Glasgow: John Wylie and Co., 1819.

The Great Christian Doctrine of Original Sin Defended. Edinburgh: Peter Brown, 1837.

Hanes Gwaith y Prynedigaeth. Bala: Robert Saunderson, 1829. [*History of Redemption* (Welsh).]

Histoire de l'Œuvre de la Rédemption. Toulouse: Société des Livres Religieux, 1854. [*History of Redemption* (French).]

Historiesch Verhaal, van het Godvruchtig Leven en den Zaligen Doodt, van den Eerwaarden Heer David Brainerd. Utrecht: Jan Jacob van Poolsum, 1756. [*Life of Brainerd* (Dutch).]

History of Redemption. London: T. Pitcher, 1788.

History of Redemption. London: C. Dilly, 1791.

The History of Redemption. London: Religious Tract Society, 1831. (Reprinted 1835, 1837, 1838, 1841, [1850].)

History of Redemption, on a Plan Entirely Original. London: Jones and Co., 1835.

History of Redemption, on a Plan Entirely Original. London: George Virtue, [1850].

*A History of the Work of Redemption. Edinburgh: W. Gray, 1774.

A History of the Work of Redemption. Edinburgh: M. Gray, 1788.

A History of the Work of Redemption. 4th ed. Edinburgh: M. Gray, 1793.

A History of the Work of Redemption. 2nd ed. Edinburgh: Alexander Jardine, 1799.

A History of the Work of Redemption. Edinburgh: John Walker, 1808.

A History of the Work of Redemption. London: W. Baynes, 1808.

A History of the Work of Redemption. London: Baynes, Williams and Son, 1812.

A History of the Work of Redemption. Edinburgh: John Ogle, 1816.

A History of the Work of Redemption. Edinburgh: John Boyd, 1828.

A History of the Work of Redemption. Edinburgh: Stirling and Kennedy, 1832.

A History of the Work of Redemption. Edinburgh: Thomas Nelson, 1839.

A History of the Work of Redemption. Edinburgh: Thomas Nelson, 1844.

An Humble Attempt to Promote Explicit Agreement and Visible Union of God's People in Extraordinary Prayer. Northampton [England]: T. Dicey and Co., 1789.

An Humble Attempt to Promote Explicit Agreement and Visible Union of God's People, in Extraordinary Prayer. London: James Nisbet, 1831.

An Humble Attempt to Promote Explicit Agreement and Visible Union of God's People, in Extraordinary Prayer. London: Unwin Brothers, 1902.

An Humble Inquiry into the Rules of the Word of God, Concerning the Qualifications Requisite to a Complete Standing and Full Communion in the Visible Christian Church. Edinburgh: William Coke, 1790.

An Humble Inquiry into the Rules of the Word of God, Concerning the Qualifications Requisite to a Complete Standing and Full Communion in the Visible Christian Church. Edinburgh: Hugh Inglis, 1790.

Indian-Missionären David Brainerds Lefwerne. Stockholm: P. P. Elde and Co., 1862. [*Life of Brainerd* (Swedish).]

An Inquiry into the Modern Prevailing Notions of that Freedom of Will. Edinburgh: Peter Brown, 1837.

An Inquiry into the Modern Prevailing Notions of that Freedom of Will. London: Thomas Nelson, 1845.

An Inquiry into the Modern Prevailing Notions of that Freedom of Will. Liverpool: Edward Howell, 1855.

An Inquiry into the Modern Prevailing Notions of that Freedom of Will. London: Hamilton, Adams, and Co., 1855.

An Inquiry into the Modern Prevailing Notions of that Freedom of Will. London: Ward and Lock, [1855].

An Inquiry into the Modern Prevailing Notions Respecting that Freedom of Will. London: James Duncan, 1831.

An Inquiry into the Modern Prevailing Notions Respecting that Freedom of Will. Bristol: Thoemmes Press, 1993.

Jonathan Edwards on Knowing Christ. [London]: Banner of Truth Trust, 1990. (Reprinted 1993, 1995, 1997.)

Jonathan Edwards on Revival. [London]: Banner of Truth Trust, 1984. (Reprinted 1987, 1991, 1994, 1995, 1997.)

The Justice of God in the Damnation of Sinners. Edited by C. De Coetlogon. London: J. Buckland, 1774.

The Justice of God in the Damnation of Sinners. Edited by C. De Coetlogon. London: J. Mathews, 1788.

Kitab ta'rikh al-fida'. Beirut: American Mission Press, 1868. OCLC 43639625. [*History of Redemption* (Arabic).]

Das Leben des Indianermissionars David Brainerd. Zürich: Franz Hanke, 1851. [*Life of Brainerd* (German).]

De Leer der Erfzonde Verdeedigd. Amsterdam: Martinus de Bruyn, 1790. [*Original Sin* (Dutch).]

De Leer der Erfzonde Verdeedigd. Amsterdam: Martinus de Bruyn, 1792. [*Original Sin* (Dutch).]

Leerreedenen over Verscheide Gewigtige Onderwerpen. Utrecht: Willem van Yzerworst, 1791. [*Sermons on Various Important Subjects* (Dutch).]

Het Leeven van den Weleerwaarden en zeer Geleerden Herr Jonathan Edwards. Utrecht: Willem van Yzerworst, 1791. [*Life of Edwards* (Dutch).]

The Life and Character of the Late Reverend, Learned, and Pious Mr. Jonathan Edwards. London: C. Dilly, 1785.

The Life and Character of the Late Reverend, Learned, and Pious Mr. Jonathan Edwards. 2nd ed. Glasgow: James Duncan, 1785.

The Life and Character of the Late Reverend, Learned, and Pious Mr. Jonathan Edwards. Edinburgh: Alexander Jardine, 1799.

The Life and Experience of the Rev. Jonathan Edwards. Bristol: Bristol Religious Tract Society, [1780].

Life and Journal of the Rev. David Brainerd. Edinburgh: H. S. Baynes, 1826.

The Life of David Brainerd. Edited by John Styles. London: Williams and Smith, 1808.

The Life of David Brainerd. Edited by John Styles. 2nd ed. London: F. Westley, 1820.

The Life of David Brainerd. Edinburgh: Johnstone and Hunter, 1851.

The Life of David Brainerd. Edinburgh: Johnstone and Hunter, 1853.

The Life of David Brainerd. London: T. Nelson and Sons, 1858.

The Life of the Rev. David Brainerd. London: Burton and Smith, 1818.

The Life of the Rev. David Brainerd. Edinburgh: H. S. Baynes and Co., 1824.

Life of the Rev. David Brainerd. Edited by James Montgomery. Glasgow: William Collins, 1829.

The Life of the Rev. David Brainerd. Edited by Josiah Pratt. London: R. B. Seeley, 1834.

The Life of the Rev. David Brainerd. Edited by Josiah Pratt. London: Seeley, Burnside, and Seeley, 1835.

The Life of the Rev. David Brainerd. London: Religious Tract Society, [1835].

The Life of the Rev. David Brainerd. London: Seeley, Jackson, and Halliday, 1836.

Life of the Rev. Jonathan Edwards. London: Religious Tract Society, [1835].

Life, Remains, and Letters of David Brainerd. Aberdeen: George and Robert King, 1845.

Life, Remains, and Letters of David Brainerd. London: William Tegg and Co., 1848.

Mawʻizah fi ghadab Allah. Beirut: n.p., 1849. OCLC 23485971. [*Sinners in the Hands of an Angry God* (Arabic).]

The Millennium. Gisborne [New Zealand]: Westminster Standard, [1960].

***Miscellaneous Observations on Important Theological Subjects.* Edinburgh: M. Gray, 1793.

The Modern Prevailing Notions Respecting that Freedom of Will. Liverpool: Edward Howell, 1877.

A Narrative of the Late Work of God. Edited by John Wesley. Bristol: Felix Farley, [1744].

A Narrative of the Late Work of God. Edited by John Wesley. 2nd ed. London: Henry Cock, 1755.

A Narrative of the Late Work of God. Edited by John Wesley. 3rd ed. London: G. Whitfield, 1798.

A Narrative of the Revival of Religion in New England. Glasgow: William Collins, 1829.

Nol-La-Woon Hoe-Shim Iya-Kee. Seoul: Christian Literature Crusade, 1997. [*Faithful Narrative* (Korean).]

Une Oeuvre du Saint-Esprit: Ses Vrais Signes. Chalon-sur-Saône: Europresse, 1996. [*Distinguishing Marks* (French).]

Peacaich ann an Lamhaibh Dhe 'n a Fheirg. Glasgow: Duncan Macvean. 1848. [*Sinners in the Hands of an Angry God* (Gaelic).]

Peacaich ann an Lamhaibh Dhe 'na Fheirg. Edinburgh: Maclachlan and Stewart, 1863. [*Sinners in the Hands of an Angry God* (Gaelic).] (Reprinted 1876, 1889.)

Pecadores en Manos de un Dios Airado. Léon: University of Léon, 2000. [*Sinners in the Hands of an Angry God* (Spanish).]

The Posthumous Works of President Edwards, in Two Volumes. Edinburgh: Ogle and Murray, 1875.

***Practical Sermons, Never Before Published*. Edinburgh: M. Gray, 1788.

The Punishment of the Wicked Eternal. Bristol: L. E. Chillcott, 1864.

Quelques Réflexions sur la Vie du Missionnaire Brainerd. Lausanne: Marc Ducloux, 1838. [*Life of Brainerd*: selections (French).]

The Religious Affections. Edinburgh: Banner of Truth Trust, 1986. (Reprinted 1991, 1994, 1997.)

***Remarks on Important Theological Controversies*. Edinburgh: J. Galbraith, 1796.

**Remarks on the Essays*. Edinburgh: [s.n.], 1758.

Remarks on the Essays. 3rd ed. London: J. Johnson, 1768.

Revivals of Religion. Edited by John Wesley. London: John Mason, 1842.

Segni Caratteristici di un'Opera dello Spirito di Deo (1741). Rome: Sentieri Antichi, 1998. [*Distinguishing Marks* (Italian).]

Selections from the Unpublished Writings. Edited by Alexander B. Grosart. Edinburgh: Ballantyne and Co., 1865.

Select Sermons of President Edwards. London: Religious Tract Society, 1834. (Reprinted 1839.)

The Select Works of Jonathan Edwards. 3 vols. Edited by Iain H. Murray. [London]: Banner of Truth Trust, 1958–1961.

***Sermons on Various Important Subjects*. Edinburgh: M. Gray, 1785.

Sermons on Various Important Subjects. London: Printed for the Booksellers, 1795.

Sinners in the Hands of an Angry God. Edinburgh: T. Lumisden and J. Robertson, 1745.

Sinners in the Hands of an Angry God. London: Religious Tract Society, [1830].
Some Thoughts Concerning the Present Revival. Edinburgh: T. Lumisden and J. Robertson, 1743.
Spiritual Pride, Its Deceitful Nature and Evil Fruits. Edited by E. H. Bermondey. London: Ward and Co., [1853].
Die Sünder in den Händen eines zornigen Gottes. Langenthal: Pflug-Verlag, [1960]. [*Sinners in the Hands of an Angry God* (German).]
Thoughts Concerning the Present Revival. Edited by John Wesley. London: W. Strahan, 1745.
Thoughts Concerning the Present Revival. Edited by John Wesley. London: G. Whitfield, 1798.
Traethawd ar y Dyben I ba un y Creodd Duw y Byd. Caernarfon: H. Humphreys, [1907]. [*End of Creation* (Welsh).]
Traethawd ar y Serchiadau Crefyddol. Caernarfon: W. Potter and Co., 1833. [*Religious Affections* (Welsh).]
A Treatise Concerning Religious Affections. London: T. Field, 1762.
A Treatise Concerning Religious Affections. Edinburgh: E. and C. Dilly, 1772.
A Treatise Concerning Religious Affections. Edinburgh: W. Laing, 1789.
A Treatise Concerning Religious Affections. London: Printed for the Booksellers, 1796.
A Treatise Concerning Religious Affections. Edinburgh: J. Ogle, 1810.
A Treatise Concerning Religious Affections. Edinburgh: J. Ogle, 1812.
A Treatise Concerning Religious Affections. Edinburgh: J. Ogle, 1812. [Another edition.]
A Treatise Concerning Religious Affections. Edinburgh: T. Clark, 1822.
A Treatise Concerning Religious Affections. Glasgow: W. Falconer, 1822.
A Treatise Concerning Religious Affections. Glasgow: Chalmers and Collins, 1825.
A Treatise Concerning Religious Affections. London: L. B. Seeley and Son, 1827.
A Treatise Concerning Religious Affections. 2nd ed. Glasgow: William Collins, 1831.
A Treatise Concerning Religious Affections. London: Religious Tract Society, [1840].
A Treatise Concerning the Religious Affections. London: Andrew Melrose, 1898.
A Treatise Concerning the Religious Affections. London: Charles H. Kelly, 1902.
Treatise on Grace and Other Posthumously Published Writings. Edited by Paul Helm. Cambridge: James Clarke and Co., 1971.
A Treatise on Religious Affections. London: G. Story, 1801.
A Treatise on Religious Affections. London: Longman, 1817.
***Twenty Sermons, on Various Subjects.* Edinburgh: M. Gray, 1789.
Twenty Sermons, on Various Subjects. Edinburgh: John Fairbairn, 1804.
Two Dissertations. Edinburgh: W. Laing, 1788.
L'Union dans la Prière pour la Propagation de l'Évangile. Paris: H^r. Servier, 1823. [*Humble Attempt* (French).]

United Prayer for the Spread of the Gospel. London: R. Williams, 1814.

Verhandeling over de Godsdienstige Hartstogten. Utrecht: J. J. van Poolsum, 1779. [*Religious Affections* (Dutch).]

Verhandeling over Gods Laatste Einde in de Schepping der Weereld. Amsterdam: Martinus de Bruyn, 1788. [*End of Creation* (Dutch).]

The Works of Jonathan Edwards. 2 vols. Edited by Edward Hickman. London: F. Westley and A. H. Davis, 1834. (Reprinted 1835.)

The Works of Jonathan Edwards. 2 vols. Edited by Edward Hickman. London: William Ball, 1839.

The Works of Jonathan Edwards. 2 vols. Edited by Edward Hickman. London: James Webb, 1839.

The Works of Jonathan Edwards. 2 vols. Edited by Edward Hickman. London: Ball, Arnold, and Co., 1840.

The Works of Jonathan Edwards. 2 vols. Edited by Edward Hickman. London: Henry G. Bohn, 1865. (Reprinted 1871.)

The Works of Jonathan Edwards. 2 vols. Edited by Edward Hickman. London: William Tegg and Co., 1879.

The Works of Jonathan Edwards. 2 vols. Edited by Edward Hickman. [London]: Banner of Truth Trust, 1974. (Reprinted 1976, 1979, 1984, 1987, 1990.)

The Works of Jonathan Edwards. 6 vols. Edinburgh: Robert Ogle and Oliver Boyd, 1847.

**The Works of President Edwards.* 8 vols. Leeds: Edward Baines, 1806–1811.

The Works of President Edwards. 8 vols. London: James Black and Son, 1817.

The Works of President Edwards. 10 vols. Edinburgh: Robert Ogle, 1847.

Ymchwillad Gofalus a Manwl i'r Syniadau Sydd yn Ddiweddar ar Led Ynghylch Rhyddid yr Ewyllys. Caernarfon: H. Humphreys, [1865]. [*Freedom of the Will* (Welsh).]

NOTES

1. The phrase is Robert W. Jenson's, *America's Theologian: A Recommendation of Jonathan Edwards* (New York: Oxford Univ. Press, 1988). The quotation is from *Green Hills of Africa* (New York: Charles Scribner's Sons, 1935), 22. *Huckleberry Finn* was first published in London by Chatto and Windus in 1884, and Frost's *A Boy's Will* by David Nutt in 1913.

2. See the coverleaf to "Natural Philosophy" in *Scientific and Philosophical Writings,* ed. Wallace E. Anderson, *The Works of Jonathan Edwards,* vol. 6 (New Haven: Yale Univ. Press, 1980), 193.

3. Jonathan Edwards, *Discourses on Various Important Subjects, Nearly concerning the Great Affair of the Soul's Eternal Salvation* (Boston: S. Kneeland and T. Green, 1738).

4. Letter of 30 May 1735, Jonathan Edwards, *Letters and Personal Writings,* ed. George S. Claghorn, *The Works of Jonathan Edwards,* vol. 16 (New Haven: Yale Univ.

Press, 1998), 49–58. For the provenance of the text and the correspondence, see Anne Stokely Pratt, *Isaac Watts and His Gifts of Books to Yale College* (New Haven: Yale Univ. Press, 1938), 32–47; and Jonathan Edwards, *The Great Awakening,* ed. C. C. Goen, *The Works of Jonathan Edwards,* vol. 4 (New Haven: Yale Univ. Press, 1972), 32–46. For the fast-day sermon (on Rom. 5:6), see Jonathan Edwards, *Our Weakness, Christ's Strength* in *Sermons and Discourses, 1734–1738,* ed. M. X. Lesser, *The Works of Jonathan Edwards,* vol. 19 (New Haven: Yale Univ. Press, 2001), 377–89; for the sermon on Ps. 46:10, see Jonathan Edwards, *The Sole Consideration that God is God, Sufficient to Still All Objections to his Sovereignty,* in *Practical Sermons* (Edinburgh: M. Gray, 1788), 39–53.

5. Jonathan Edwards, *God Glorified in the Work of Redemption, by the Greatness of Man's Dependance upon Him, in the Whole of It* (Boston: S. Kneeland and T. Green, 1731); Jonathan Edwards, *A Divine and Supernatural Light, Immediately Imparted to the Soul by the Spirit of God, Shown to be Both a Scriptural, and Rational Doctrine* (Boston: S. Kneeland and T. Green, 1734).

6. Letter of 19 May 1737, Edwards, *Works,* 16:67–70. Jonathan Edwards's extract, separately paginated (1–19), follows an another work by Williams—*Directions for Such as are Concerned to Obtain a True Repentance and Conversion unto God*—and bears a running title, "The Late Wonderful Work of God in the County of Hampshire" (Boston: S. Kneeland and T. Green, 1736). For Watts's remark, see Pratt, *Isaac Watts,* 35.

7. In order, (London: John Oswald, 1737), (Edinburgh: "Reprinted for J. Oswald," 1737), and (London: John Oswald, 1738). For an early account of the relationship, see James Orr, "Jonathan Edwards; His Influence in Scotland," *Congregationalist and Christian World* 88 (October 1903): 467–68.

8. Jonathan Edwards's presentation copy is in the Beinecke Rare Book and Manuscript Library, Yale. Apparently, others agreed with Guyse and Watts that "Children's language always loses its striking beauty at second hand," for Phebe Bartlet's account seems never to have been reissued separately; Abigail Hutchinson's was—eight times by the American Tract Society beginning in 1816.

9. In order, (Boston: S. Kneeland, T. Green, and D. Henchman, 1738)—one without and one with the Guyse and Watts preface—and (Boston: S. Kneeland and T. Green, 1738). The recommendation was signed by Joseph Sewall, Thomas Prince, John Webb, and William Cooper; the attestation by William Williams, Ebenezer Devotion, Stephen Williams, Peter Reynolds, Nehemiah Bull, and Samuel Hopkins.

10. *Glaubwüridge Nachricht von dem herrlichen Wercke Gottes* (Magdeburg: Christ. Leberecht, 1738); *Geloofwaardig Historisch Bericht, van 't Heerlyke Werk Godts* (Amsterdam: Hendrik van Bos, 1740); the reprint is identical, except that the words "Tweede Druk." precede "t'Amsterdam." on a separate line in the imprint, and the date 1742 is substituted for 1740. For Steinmetz's role in making Jonathan Edwards available to a

German audience, see Peter W. Kawerau, "Johann Adam Steinmetz als Vermittler zwichen dem deutschen und amerikanischen Pietismus im 18. Jahrhundret," *Zeitschrift für Kirchengeschichte* 70, no. 1–2 (1959):75–88.

11. *The Glasgow-Weekly-History Relating to the Late Progress of the Gospel At Home and Abroad; Being A Collection of Letters, partly reprinted from the London-Weekly-History, and partly printed first here at Glasgow for the Year 1742* (Glasgow: William Duncan. 1743), 21:7–8 and 22:1–3; *The Christian Monthly History* (Edinburgh: n.p., 1745), 3–4:87–114; and *Nadere Geloofwaardige Berichten van het Heerlyke Werk Godts, geopenbaart in de Opwekkinge En Bekeeringe van veele duysenden van Zielen, op veele Plaatsen in Nieuw-Engelandt* (Leeuwarden: R. J. Noordbeek, 1750), 122–23. Jonathan Edwards took great interest in the Dutch revivals; see his correspondence in Edwards, *Works,* 16:197, 376–77, 537–38.

12. *Faithful Narrative* (Bristol: Felix Farley, n.d.); *Distinguishing Marks* (London: W. Strahan, 1744); *Some Thoughts* (London: W. Strahan, 1745); *Life of Brainerd* (Bristol: William Pine, 1768); and *Religious Affections* (London: G. Story, 1801), a text prepared in 1773 but not published until ten years after Wesley's death. In his edition of *Life of Brainerd,* he separates the words of Brainerd from those of Jonathan Edwards by placing the latter's in squared brackets. For his comments, see "To the Reader," p. 3, and "Thoughts upon Necessity," *The Works of the Rev. John Wesley, A.M.* (New York: Carlton and Porter, 1856), 6:206–7; for an examination of the relationship between Wesley and Jonathan Edwards, see Richard E. Brantley, "The Common Ground of Wesley and Edwards," *Harvard Theological Review* 83 (1990): 271–303.

13. *Distinguishing Marks* (London: S. Mason, 1742; Glasgow: R. Smith, 1742) and *Sinners in the Hands of an Angry God* (Edinburgh: T. Lumisden and J. Robertson, 1745). Whitefield's remarks are found on the verso side of the title page of *Distinguishing Marks,* Willison's on five unnumbered pages following.

14. *Religious Affections* (London: T. Field, 1762); *Freedom of the Will* (London: Thomas Field, 1762); *Life of Brainerd* (Edinburgh: John Gray and Gavin Austin, 1765); *Original Sin* (London: J. Johnson, 1766)—three years later it was reprinted in Glasgow, Dublin, and Belfast; *True Virtue* (London: W. Oliver, 1778); *Life of Edwards* (Glasgow: David Niven, 1785); *Eternity of Hell Torments* (London: W. Justins, 1788); *Two Dissertations* (Edinburgh: William Darling, 1788); *End of Creation* (London: H. Trapp, 1788); *Practical Sermons* (Edinburgh: M. Gray, 1788); *Twenty Sermons* (Edinburgh: M. Gray, 1789); *Humble Attempt* (Northampton in Old England: T. Dicey, 1789); *Humble Inquiry* (Edinburgh: William Coke, 1790); *Miscellaneous Observations* (Edinburgh: M. Gray, 1793); and *Remarks on Important Theological Controversies* (Edinburgh: J. Galbraith and Arch. Constable, 1796). The two sermon collections and the last two items were not published elsewhere.

15. *History of Redemption* (Edinburgh: W. Gray, 1774). In addition to *Faithful Narrative* (note 10, above), Dutch translations include: [*Life of Brainerd*] *Historiesch Verhaal, van het Godvruchtig Leven en den Zaligen Doodt, van den Eerwaarden Heer David Brainerd* (Utrecht: Jan Jacob van Poolsum and Abraham van Paddenburg, 1756); [*Freedom of the Will*] *Een Bepaald en Nauwkeurig Onderzoek van de Thans Heerschende Denkbeelden over de Vryheid van den Wil* (Utrecht: Gisbert Timon van Paddenburg, 1774); [*History of Redemption*] *Geschiedenis van het Werk der Verlossing Beheizende de Schetszen van een Zamenstel van Godgeleerdheid* (Utrecht: Abraham van Paddenburg, 1776); [*Religious Affections*] *Verhandeling over de Godsdienstige Hartstogten* (Utrecht: J. J. van Poolsum, 1779; [*End of Creation*] *Verhandeling over Gods Laatste Einde in de Schepping der Weereld* (Amsterdam: Martinus de Bruyn, 1788); [*Original Sin*] *De Leer der Erfzonde Verdeedigd* (Amsterdam: Martinus de Bruyn, 1790); [*Life of Edwards*] *Het Leeven van den Weleerwaarden en zeer Geleerden Herr Jonathan Edwards* (Utrecht: Willem van Yzerworst, 1791); and [*The Wisdom of God, as Displayed in the Way of Salvation by Jesus Christ, Far Superior to the Wisdom of Angels*] *Leerreedenen over Verschiede Gewigtige Onderwerpen, Naagelaaten door den Weleerwarrden en zeer Geleerden Herr* (Utrecht: Willem van Yzerworst, 1791). The last is a sermon on Ephesians 3:10, delivered in March 1733, and first published in *Sermons on Various Important Subjects* (nos. 11–16), the selection appended to Hopkins's *Life of Edwards* (1765). Except for the Dutch translation, it was apparently never published separately.

16. [*Humble Attempt*] *L'Union dans la Prière pour la Propagation de l'Evangile* (Paris: H[r]. Servier, 1823); [*Life of Brainerd*] *Quelques Réflexions sur la Vie du Missionnaire Brainerd* (Lausanne: Marc Ducloux, 1838), *Das Leben des Indianermissionars David Brainerd* (Zürich: Franz Hanke, 1851), and *Indian-Missionären David Brainerds Lefwerne* (Stockholm: P. P. Elde, 1862); [*Sinners in the Hands of an Angry God*] *Peacaich ann an Lamhaibh Dhe 'n a Fheirg* (Glasgow: Duncan Macvean, 1848) and *Maw'izah fi ghadab Allah* (Beirut: n.p., 1849); and [*History of Redemption*] *Histoire de l'Oeuvre de la Rédemption* (Toulouse: Chauvin et Feillès, 1854) and *Kitab ta'rikh al-fida'*, (Beirut: American Mission Press, 1868).

17. Translations issued by the American Tract Society were published in New York probably in the 1840s: [*Life of Brainerd*] *Das Leben von David Brainerd, Missionar unter den Indianern;* [*Personal Narrative*] *Mittheilungen aus dem innern Leben von Jonathan Edwards;* and [History of Redemption] *Hanes Gwaith y Prynedigaeth. . . .* For the Choctaw translation, see *Hatak Yoshuba Uhleha Hut Chihowa Anukhobela Ya Ibbak Foyuka* (Park Hill, Cherokee Nation: Mission Press, 1845).

18. [*Religious Affections*] (selections) *Cyfarwyddiadau ac Annogaethau i Gredinwyr . . . "Draethawd Ar Serchiadau Crefyddol"* (Bala: R. Saunderson, 1809) and (complete) *Traethawd ar y Serchiadau Crefyddol, yn Gynnwysedig Mewn Tair Rhan* (Caernarfon:

W. Potter and Co., 1833); [*History of Redemption*] *Hanes Gwaith y Prynedigaeth* . . . (Bala: Robert Saunderson, 1829); [*Freedom of the Will*] *Ymchwiliad Gofalus a Manwl* . . . (Caernarfon: H. Humphreys, 1865); [*Original Sin*] *Yr Athrawiaeth Fawr Gristionogol o Bechod Gwreiddiol* . . . (Caernarfon: H. Humphreys, n.d.); and [*End of Creation*] *Traethawd ar y Dyben i ba un y Creodd Duw y Byd* (Caernarfon: H. Humphreys, n.d.). A sermon, "The Manner in which the Salvation of the Soul is to be Sought," first published in *Sermons on the Following Subjects* (Hartford: Hudson and Goodwin, 1780), was translated as *Y Dull y Dylid Ymofyn Iechydwriaeth yr Enaid* (Llangollen: H. Jones, 1845).

19. *The Works of President Edwards, in Eight Volumes* (Leeds: Edward Baines, 1806–1811), and *The Works of President Edwards, in Eight Volumes* (Worcester: Isaiah Thomas, 1808–1809).

20. *The Works of President Edwards, in Eight Volumes* (London: James Black and Son, 1817); *The Treatise on Religious Affections* (London: Longman, Hurst, Rees, Orme, and Brown, 1817). The title page of the latter hints at its preface (pp. [iii]–vii): "somewhat abridged, by the removal of the principle tautologies of the original; and by an attempt to render the language throughout more perspicuous and energetic."

21. *The Works of President Edwards . . . in Ten Volumes* (New York: S. Converse, 1829–1830), reprinted (New York: G. and C. and H. Carvill, 1830); *The Works of Jonathan Edwards . . . in Two Volumes* (London: F. Westley and A. H. Davis, 1834), in facsimile (Peabody, Mass.: Hendrickson Publishers, 1998); *The Works of President Edwards, in Four Volumes* (New York: Jonathan Leavitt and John F. Trow, 1843); *Sinners in the Hands of an Angry God* (Phillipsburg, N.J.: P&R Publishing, 1996).

22. Waldo Beach, "The Recovery of Jonathan Edwards. A Review," *Religion in Life* 27 (spring 1958): 286–89. Miller's book was published in New York by William Sloane Associates; the Yale edition was published both in New Haven and London, and continues to be.

23. The first edition of *The Select Works* was published in London—later in Edinburgh and Carlisle, Pennsylvania—and had a memoir by Murray instead of *Distinguishing Marks;* all subsequent issues exchange the texts. In 1990, Banner of Truth reprinted the two-volume Hickman edition containing both *Freedom of the Will* and *Original Sin;* neither text appears as part of *The Select Works*. The reference is to Ola Elizabeth Winslow, *Jonathan Edwards, 1703–1758: A Biography* (New York: Macmillan, 1940). The next three volumes in the Yale series after *Freedom of the Will* alternate between pastoral and polemical, *Religious Affections, Original Sin,* and *The Great Awakening*, which includes *Faithful Narrative, Distinguishing Marks,* and *Some Thoughts;* even so, Edwards's personal writings do not appear until the sixteenth volume, more than forty years later.

24. *The Experience that Counts!* (London: Grace Publications Trust, 1991); *Experiencing God* (London: Marshall Pickering, 1995); *The Wrath of Almighty God* (Morgan, Pa.: Soli Deo Gloria Publications, 1996); *Altogether Lovely* ([Morgan, Pa.]: Soli Deo Gloria Publications, 1997); *God's Passion for Glory* (Wheaton, Ill.: Crossway Books, 1998).

25. *Original Sin* (London: J. Johnson, 1764), xvi.

26. Patrick Campbell MacDougall, "Edwards on Free Will," [Edinburgh] *Presbyterian Review* 1 (September 1831); William Hazlitt, "On Liberty and Necessity," in his *Literary Remains* (London: Saunders and Otley, 1831), 170–228; Hermann F. Uhden, *Geschichte der Congregationalsten in Neu-England bis zu den erweckungen um das Jahr 1740* (Leipzig: L. H. Rosenberg, 1842), 213–38; Leslie Stephen, "Jonathan Edwards," *Fraser's Magazine*, n.s., 8 (November 1872): 529–51; Georges Lyon, "L'Immaterialisme en Amerique—Jonathan Edwards," in his *L'Idealisme en Angleterre au XVIIIe Siecle* (Paris: Ancienne Librarie Germer Bailliere et Cie, 1888), 406–39; John Henry MacCracken, *Jonathan Edwards Idealismus* (Halle: C. A. Kaemmerer, 1899).

27. Jan Ridderbos, *De Theologic van Jonathan Edwards* (The Hague: Johan A. Nederbragt, 1907). See, for example, Erich Vögelin, *Über die Form des Amerikanischen Geistes* (Tabingen: J. C. B. Mohr, 1928), 109–19, and Gustav E. Müller, *Amerikanische Philosophie* (Stuttgart: F. Frommann, 1936), 17–39.

28. Ursula Brumm, "Jonathan Edwards und Ralph Waldo Emerson," in her *Die Religiose Typologie im Amerikanischen Denken* (Leiden: E. J. Brill, 1963), 73–86, passim; Ernst Wolfram Hankamer, *Das Politische Denken von Jonathan Edwards* (Munich: n.p., 1972); Marcella DeNichilo, *Realta e immagine: L'estetica nei sermoni di Jonathan Edwards* (L'Aquila: L. U. Japadre, 1980); Miklós Vetö, *La pensée de Jonathan Edwards: avec une concordance des différentes éditions* (Paris: Éditions du Cerf, 1987); D. Elwyn Edwards, *Jonathan Edwards, 1703–1758: yn cynnwys golwg ar ei ddtlanwad ar fywyd creyfyddol Cymru a Lloeger* (Caernarfon: Darlith Davies, 1989); Caroline Schröder, *Glaubenswahrnehmung und Selbsterkenntnis: Jonathan Edwards's Theologia Experimentalis* (Göttingen: Vanderhoeck und Ruprecht, 1998).

29. See, for example, Jean Béranger, "Interpretation et utilisation de l'Apocalypse par Jonathan Edwards," in *Le Facteur religieux en Amérique du Nord, No. 2: Apocalypse et autres travaux.* (Talence: Maison des Science de l'Homme d'Aquitaine, 1981), 31–47; Rolf Kühn, Review of *La pensée de Jonathan Edwards*, by Miklós Vetö, *Freiburger Zeitschrift für Philosophie und Theologie* 36, nos. 1–2 (1989): 220–23; Miklosne Kretzoi, *Az Amerikai Irodalom Kezdetei (1607–1750)* (Budapest: Akademiai Kiado, 1976), 67–72 passim; Lina Unali, "La vuotezza di se nella Personal Narrative di Jonathan Edwards," in her *Descrizione di se: Studio sulla scrittura autobiografica del '700* (Rome: Lucarini, 1979), 89–97; Katsuzo Kimura, "A Study of Jonathan Edwards's *Personal Narrative*," *Ryukokudaigaku ronshu* 441 (December 1992): 2–14; Sang Hyun Lee, "Kae-Hyuk

Shin-Hak Kwa Cha-Yon-Eh-Dae-Han Yi-Hae: Jonadan Edwas," in *The 21st Century and the Future of Creation* (Seoul: Korean Institute of Christian Cultural Studies, Soong-Sil University, 1995), 199–219; Marta Isabel Barbosa Malone, "Dois homens—duas mensagens," *Minas Gerais, Suplemento Literario* 15 (27 March 1982): 6–7; Maiya M. Koreneva, "New England and American Literature," in *Problemy Stanovleniia Amerikanskoii Literatury,* ed. Iasen N. Zasurskii (Moscow: Nauka, 1981), 22–88; and Jorge Luis Borges, *Introduccion a la Literatura Norte-americana* (Buenos Aires: Editorial Columba, 1967), 11–12.

30. [*Selected Writings*] *Aidehauazi xuan ji* (Xiangang: Jinling shen xue yuan tuo shi bu: Jidu jiao fu qiao chu ban she, 1960; [*Religious Affections* (abridged)] *The Experience That Counts* (Taipei: Grace Publications Trust, 1994); [*Faithful Narrative*] *Nol-La-Woon Hoe-Shim Iya-Kee* (Seoul: Christian Literature Crusade, 1997); [*Distinguishing Marks*] *Une Oeuvre du Saint-Esprit: ses Vrais Signes* (Chalon-sur-Saône: Europresse, 1996), and *Segni Caratteristici di un'Opera dello Spirito di Deo (1741)* (Rome: Sentieri Antichi, 1998); [*Sinners in the Hands of an Angry God*] *Pecadores en Manos de un Dios Airado* (Léon: Universidad de Léon, 2000), and *Die Sünder in den Händen eines zornigen Gottes* (Langenthal, Switzerland: Pflug-Verlag, n.d.)

Contributors

David W. Bebbington is professor of history at the University of Stirling, Scotland. Of his many books on the history of religion and politics in Great Britain, *Evangelicalism in Modern Britain* (1989) has been the most widely used.

Catherine A. Brekus's first book, *Strangers and Pilgrims: Female Preaching in America, 1740–1845* (1998), was awarded the Brewer Prize by the American Society of Church History. She is currently writing a book on Sarah Osborn, and serves as associate professor of the history of Christianity at the Divinity School, University of Chicago.

Ava Chamberlain is associate professor of religion at Wright State University. An expert on the life and work of Jonathan Edwards, she is the editor his *The "Miscellanies," 501–832*.

James D. German is associate professor of history at the State University of New York at Potsdam. A specialist on religion and politics in the Revolutionary period of American history, he is currently writing a book on Benjamin Trumbull.

Charles E. Hambrick-Stowe is director of the Doctor of Ministry program at Pittsburgh Theological Seminary. A leading expert in the field of early American religion, he has most recently published *Charles G. Finney and the Spirit of American Evangelicalism* (1996).

D. Bruce Hindmarsh is the James M. Houston Associate Professor of Spiritual Theology at Regent College, Vancouver, British Columbia. He has written widely on Modern English Christianity. His book *John Newton and the English Evangelical Tradition* appeared in 1996.

Sharon Y. Kim is assistant professor of English at Judson College in Illinois. A recent doctoral graduate of Yale University, her research interests include female religious piety as expressed in nineteenth-century American fiction.

DAVID W. KLING holds a Ph.D. from the University of Chicago. An associate professor of religious studies at the University of Miami in Florida, he is the author of *A Field of Divine Wonders: The New Divinity and Village Revivals in Northwestern Connecticut, 1792–1822*, and *The Bible in History: How the Texts Have Shaped the Times*.

M. X. LESSER is emeritus professor of English at Northeastern University. The author of books and essays in the field of early American literary and religious history, he is most highly acclaimed for his two-volume bibliography of Edwards scholarship, *Jonathan Edwards: A Reference Guide* (1981) and *Jonathan Edwards: An Annotated Bibliography, 1979–1993* (1994).

GEORGE M. MARSDEN is Francis A. McAnaney Professor of History at the University of Notre Dame. One of the world's leading experts in the field of American religious history, he is the author of *Jonathan Edwards: A Life* (2003).

MICHAEL J. MCCLYMOND is the Clarence Louis and Helene Steber Professor of American Religion at St. Louis University. He has published several books and received the Brewer Prize for his first book, *Encounters with God: An Approach to the Theology of Jonathan Edwards* (1998).

CHRISTOPHER W. MITCHELL is director of the Marion E. Wade Center at Wheaton College and is the author of numerous scholarly articles on both the history of Christianity in Great Britain and the life and thought of C. S. Lewis.

STUART PIGGIN is master of Robert Menzies College and a director of the Macquarie Christian Studies Institute at Macquarie University in Australia. He has published books on the training of missionaries, religious revival, and Australian Christianity, including *Evangelical Christianity in Australia* (1996).

AMANDA PORTERFIELD is professor of religion at Florida State University and past president of the American Society of Church History. Her many writings include *Mary Lyon and the Mount Holyoke Missionaries* (1997).

DOUGLAS A. SWEENEY holds a Ph.D. from Vanderbilt University. He is an associate professor and chair of the Department of Church History and the History of Christian Thought at Trinity Evangelical Divinity School in Deerfield, Illinois. Sweeney is the author of *Nathaniel Taylor, New Haven Theology, and the Legacy of Jonathan Edwards*. He is also the editor of *The "Miscellanies" 1153–1360, volume 23 of The Works of Jonathan Edwards*, and an editor of *The Sermons of Jonathan Edwards: A Reader*.

MARK VALERI is the E. T. Thompson Professor of Church History at Union Theological Seminary in Virginia. His best-known book is *Law and Providence in Joseph Bellamy's New England* (1994).

ANDREW F. WALLS is Honorary Professor in the Universities of Edinburgh and Aberdeen and director of the Scottish Institute of Missionary Studies. His most recent book of essays is entitled *The Cross-Cultural Process in Christian History* (2002).

Index

Abbott, Benjamin, 49
Adams, John, 107
adolescent culture, 63
Alcott, Louisa May, 138, 146
American Magazine, The, 91–93
American Tract Society, 300–301
Anglican evangelicals, xviii, 202, 209, 212, 215–16
Appleby, Joyce, 90
Arnauld, Antoine, 18

Ballou, Hosea, 130
Baptist Missionary Society, 210, 252, 273
Baptists, xviii, 190, 202, 210–15, 252, 272–74; English Baptists, 183–84; Free Will Baptists, 130; Particular Baptists, 207–9, 212
Bartlet, Phebe, 48, 54, 268, 299
Bebbington, David, xiv, xviii, 203
Beddome, Benjamin, 208
Beecher, Lyman, 51–54
Beinecke Library (Yale University), 25
Belcher, Jonathan, 12
Bellamy, Joseph, 21, 93–96, 107, 112, 123, 126, 186–87, 190, 208, 214, 225
Bogue, David, 212, 251, 260, 274, 286
Bonar, A. A., 191
Bonar, Horatius, 185, 191
Borges, J. L., 193

Bradstreet, Anne, 158
Brainerd, David, 11–13, 184, 204, 206, 209–11, 253, 261–62, 268, 272, 310–15
Breck, Robert, 11
Brekus, Catherine, xv
Buddhism, 166–70
Bushnell, Horace, 52
Butler, Jon, 122

Calvinist doctrines, 86, 95, 102, 138; of divine providence, 31, 86; of original sin, 40–46, 48, 50–52, 86, 95, 110, 164, 185, 234
Calvinist theology, xvii, 49, 138, 161, 166
Campbell, John McLeod, 189
Carey, William, 186, 207–10, 252, 273, 275–76
Cave, Edmund, 92
Chalmers, Thomas, 185–87, 269, 274, 317
Chamberlain, Ava, xvi, 61, 160
Chandler, Joshua, 103
Channing, William Ellery, 49–50
Chauncy, Charles, 44, 205
Christian History, The, 91–93
Christian Labor Union, 29
Church Missionary Society, 186, 253, 255, 274
Claghorn, George, 3

Clap, Nathaniel, 126
Clark, Elizabeth, 48
Clark, Samuel, 88
Clebsch, William, 165–66
Coetlogon, Charles Edward, 273, 311, 314
Coleridge, Samuel Taylor, 188
College of New Jersey. *See* Princeton University
Conforti, Joseph A., 121, 122, 124, 133, 187
Congregationalists, xviii, xxi, 49–50, 122, 126–33, 190–91, 202, 211, 252, 272, 274
Connecticut Evangelical Magazine, 111
Connecticut Missionary Society, 107, 111, 130
Cotton, John, 160
Cummins, Maria, 146

Daggett, Naphtali, 111
Dawkes, Thomas, 66–67
Dayton, Cornelia Hughes, 72, 74
Dickinson, Jonathan, 12
Dorr, Julia, 147
Dow, Lorenzo, 49
Duff, Alexander, 269
Dwight, Sereno, 3, 11, 18, 40, 54, 61, 301
Dwight, Timothy, 30, 50

Edwards, Jonathan: and America, 30; and Anglican evangelicals, 178, 202; and children, 40; and Congregationalists, 49, 202; and economics, 90; and Edwardsian piety, xvii, 121, 132; and English Baptists, 184, 202; and an ethic of privacy, 74; and the evangelical community, 88; and Locke, 6–7; and marital love, 158; and Methodists, 202; and his millennialism, 12, 177; and missions, 186, 250, 267, 303; and Newton, 6, 7, 22; and politics, 104; and the Presbyterians, 49, 185; and race, 122, 130; and sexual standards, 72; and his social location, 10; and the Welsh Independents, 184
—Works: *Distinguishing Marks*, 179, 204, 223, 229–32, 300, 302, 304, 311, 316; *End of Creation*, 18, 20, 212, 300, 301, 317; *Faithful Narrative*, 63–64, 178–80, 185, 203–8, 223, 228–32, 268, 270, 298–304, 312, 316; *Freedom of the Will*, 18, 32, 101, 111, 178–90, 203, 208–14, 228, 235, 269, 273, 277, 300–302, 310, 312–15, 318; *History of the Work of Redemption*, xv, 16–33, 139, 180–81, 236, 273, 279–82, 313; *Humble Attempt*, xiv, 177, 179, 183–86, 210, 231, 252, 268, 272–73, 280, 284, 300, 313–14, 317; *Life of Brainerd*, xiv, xix, 121, 179, 181, 186, 202, 205–6, 210, 252, 272, 274, 300, 313–16; *Nature of True Virtue*, 18, 32, 88, 101, 141, 158, 161, 182, 203, 311; *Original Sin*, 18–19, 32, 45, 106, 124, 181, 185, 190, 203, 209, 228, 234, 273, 278–79, 300–303, 310, 313–14; *Religious Affections*, 5, 30, 141, 143, 159, 163, 160, 167, 178–86, 190, 204–5, 209–12, 223, 232, 273, 277, 279, 300–301, 304, 311–12, 316–17; *Sinners in the Hands of an Angry God*, 165, 189,

193, 230, 301–4, 315–16; *Some Thoughts Concerning the Present Revival of Religion in New England*, 40, 139, 179, 204–5, 223, 231–32, 268, 316
Edwards, Jonathan Jr., xvi, 85, 94–96, 114, 123, 126, 180, 236; and antislavery, 11
Edwards, Sarah, 6, 41, 121, 162, 168
Edwards, Timothy, 5
Eliot, George, 148
Eliot, John, 270
Ellsworth, Oliver, xvi, 103, 107
English Methodists, xviii, 206
Enlightenment, the, xvi, 7, 13, 17, 21, 41, 48–49, 94, 182
Enlightenment rationalism, 125; ethics of, 88, 91
Erskine, John, 18, 179–85, 188, 195, 210, 222, 228, 232–39, 270, 272–73, 300
Erskine, Thomas, 188–89
evangelical Anglicans, 272
Evangelical Magazine, 212
Evans, Caleb, 183, 208

Fawcett, Joseph, 182
Fichte, J. G., 187
Fiering, Norman, xiv, 7, 43, 205
Finley, Martha, 147
Finney, Charles, 187
Fisher, James, 231
Franklin, Benjamin, 91, 190, 300, 319
Frei, Hans, 33
Fuller, Andrew, 184, 186, 207–8, 272, 276
Fundamentalism, 27

Gay, Peter, 8
Gentleman's Magazine, The, 92
German, James, xvi
Gildrie, Richard, 64
Gill, John, 209–10
Gillespie, Thomas, 222, 231
Gladstone, W. E., 188
Godwin, William, 182
Goen, Charles, 204
Goold, W. H., 236
Gordon, William, 178–79, 211
Gracey, David, 190
Great Awakening, 105, 121, 123, 126–27, 133, 141, 163, 179, 270
Grotius, Hugo, 88
Guyse, John, 178, 204, 298–99

Habermas, Jürgen, 89
Hall, David, 5, 10, 66, 92
Hall, Robert Jr., 207
Hambrick-Stowe, Charles, xvii
Haroutunian, Joseph, 54
Hayden, Roger, 210
Haynes, Lemuel, xvii, 122, 128–32
Hindmarsh, D. Bruce, xviii, 201
Hinduism, xix, 267, 279–86
Hocking, William Ernest, 27
Hodge, Charles, 190
Holmes, Oliver Wendell, 40
Hooker, Thomas, 159
Hopkins, Samuel, xvii, 5, 11, 61, 105, 122, 125–31, 201, 225, 276, 300; and slavery, 123
humanitarianism, xvi, 268
Hume, David, 43, 114, 179, 185
Hutcheson, Francis, 43, 88, 101, 115
Hutchinson, Anne, 73

James, William, xvii, 164, 166
Jones, R. Tudur, 211

Kamensky, Jane, 67, 72
Kelsey, David, 33
Kennedy, John, 189
Kim, Sharon, xvii, 137
Kling, David, 133
Kuyper, Abraham, 191

Le Long, Isaac, 180
Lesser, M. X., xix, 193, 319
Lindbeck, George, 33
Locke, John, 7, 43, 48, 87, 109, 189
London Missionary Society, 212, 214, 251, 253, 260, 273
Lyon, Georges, 194

Machen, J. Gresham, 27
Mackintosh, James, 183
MacLaurin, John, 179, 222, 226–29, 235, 237–39, 271
MacLeod, John, 227
Marsden, George, xv
Martyn, Henry, 192, 253–54, 274–79
Mason, Charles H., 133
Mather, Cotton, 42, 66
Maurice, F. D., 189
Maurice, Matthias, 212
Mayhew, Experience, 43
McClymond, Michael, xv
McCulloch, William, 179, 222, 226, 229–30, 235, 299
McDermott, Gerald, 22, 25, 166, 280
Methodists, 49, 179, 184–85, 192, 202, 211, 215, 250, 274
Mill, John Stuart, 190

Miller, Perry, xii, 3, 6, 33, 86, 302
Milner, Joseph, 213, 215
Minkema, Kenneth, 5
Mitchell, Christopher W., xviii
Modernists, 27
Moravians, 180, 206, 270
Morgan, Edmund, 112
Morris, William Sparkes, 7
Murray, Iain, 3, 192

New Divinity, 86, 94–95, 102, 104, 107, 110–11, 115, 121–32, 139, 147; and American culture, 125; and slavery, 128
New Haven theology, 51
New Lights, 13, 86–87, 92–93
Newton, Isaac, 8, 22–23
Newton, John, 178, 208, 213
Niebuhr, H. Richard, 33
Niebuhr, Richard R., 194
Niles, Nathaniel, 94
Noll, Mark, 32
Norton, Mary Beth, 71

O'Brien, Susan, 222
Old Lights, 6
Orr, James, 186
Osborn, Sarah, xvii, 122–28, 131–32, 134
Owen, John, 212

Park, Edwards A., 187
Parker, Theodore, 49
Parr, Samuel, 182
Particular Baptist Society for Propagating the Gospel among the Heathen, 207
Patrides, C. A., 21

Phelps, Elizabeth Stuart, 137
Pierpont, Sarah. *See* Edwards, Sarah
Piggin, Stuart, xiv, xix, 251, 266
Pomeroy, Elizabeth, 66–70
Porterfield, Amanda, xvii, 148, 154
Presbyterians, 27, 49–52, 179, 186, 190, 252, 298; Old School Presbyterians, 187; Scottish Presbyterians, 185
Prince, Thomas Jr., 6, 91, 93
Prince, Thomas Sr., 93
Princeton University, 5, 12, 16, 19, 32, 34, 101, 107, 187, 225

Ramsay, "Chevalier" Andrew Michael, 25, 28, 281
Rankin, Jeremiah, 54
Rankin, Thomas, 206
Rauschenbusch, Walter, 29
Religious Female Society, 123, 126
Ricci, Matteo, 29
Ridderbos, Jan, 192
Robe, James, 203, 222, 227–28, 231, 270, 299
Ryland, John, 183, 188, 201–2, 207–14, 272–75
Ryland, John Collett, 201, 205, 207, 209–10

Saillant, John, 129
Schafer, Thomas, 3
Scott, Thomas, 213–14, 274
Scottish Missionary Society, 273
Second Great Awakening, 121
Sedgwick, Catharine, 146
Seymour, William J., 133
Shepard, Thomas, 159, 169–70
Sherman, Roger, xvi, 103–4

Simeon, Charles, 274
Smalley, John, 107, 111, 208
Smyth, Newman, 30
Social Gospel, 29
Spring, Gardiner, 52
Spurgeon, C. H., 189
Stein, Stephen, 8
Steinmetz, J. A., 180, 299
Stewart, Dugald, 183
Stiles, Ezra, 123
Stock, Eugene, 253
Stoddard, Colonel John, 11–12, 70
Stoddard, Solomon, 11
Stout, Harry S., 122, 319
Stowe, Harriet Beecher, 53, 137
Strong, Josiah, 31
Sutcliff, John, 207, 252, 272, 274

Taves, Ann, 163
Taylor, Hudson J., 29
Taylor, John, 43–44, 234
Taylor, Nathaniel William, 51–52, 122
Tennent, Gilbert, 126
Theological Magazine, 111, 112
Tillich, Paul, 33
Tillotson, John, 43
Tinda, Moses, 257, 259–60
Tompkins, Jane, 149
Tracy, Patricia, 3, 62
Treadwell, John, 111
Trumbull, Benjamin, 95
Trumbull, James R., 61

Unitarians, 41, 49, 50

Valeri, Mark, xvi, 124, 159
Vermont Missionary Society, 130
Vetö, Miklós, 194

Walls, Andrew, xiv, xviii, 285
Warner, Susan, xvii, 53, 138, 149; *Daisy Plains,* 150; *Melbourne House,* 147; *The Wide, Wide World,* xvii, 138–42, 146–50
Watts, Isaac, 9, 44, 178, 204, 212, 298
Wellwood, Sir Henry Moncrieff, 233
Welsh Independents, 184
Wesley, Charles, 9, 204
Wesley, John, 9, 163, 178–79, 202–6, 250, 256, 270, 299, 311–17
Wheelock, Eleazar, 12
Whitefield, George, 9, 12, 126, 128, 204, 270, 300
Wigger, John, 133

Wilberforce, William, 178
Williams, Edward, 184, 186, 211, 274
Williams, Stephen, 12
Willison, John, 222, 230, 300
Wilson, John, 17, 18, 25
Winslow, Ola, 3, 62
Winthrop, John, 111, 158
Witherspoon, John, 34, 101
Wolff, Christian, 94
Wollstonecraft, Mary, 182
Wuthnow, Robert, 87

Yale University, xx, 17, 32–33, 51, 111, 113, 123, 130, 224–25, 268–69, 319
Young Folks' Bible, 10

UNIVERSITY OF ST. THOMAS LIBRARIES

BX 7260 .E3 J655 2003

Jonathan Edwards at home
 and abroad

**WITHDRAWN
UST**